THE IMPOSITION OF LAW

STUDIES ON LAW AND SOCIAL CONTROL

DONALD BLACK *Series Editor*
Center for Criminal Justice
Harvard Law School
Cambridge, Massachusetts   02138

THE IMPOSITION OF LAW

EDITED BY

SANDRA B. BURMAN

Centre for Socio-Legal Studies
Wolfson College
Oxford, England

BARBARA E. HARRELL-BOND

School of Law
University of Warwick
Coventry, England

ACADEMIC PRESS

A Subsidiary of Harcourt Brace Jovanovich, Publishers

New York   London   Toronto   Sydney   San Francisco

ACADEMIC PRESS, INC.
111 Fifth Avenue, New York, New York 10003

United Kingdom Edition published by
ACADEMIC PRESS, INC. (LONDON) LTD.
24/28 Oval Road, London NW1   7DX

Library of Congress Cataloging in Publication Data
Main entry under title:

The Imposition of law.

    (Studies on law and social control)
    Papers from a conference entitled The social con−
sequences of imposed law, held in April 1978 at the
School of Law, University of Warwick.
    Includes bibliographies and index.
    1. Sociological jurisprudence−−Congresses.
I. Burman, Sandra. II. Harrell−Bond, Barbara E.
III. Series.
K367.I45   340.1'15   79−51671
ISBN 0−12−145450−9

PRINTED IN THE UNITED STATES OF AMERICA

79 80 81 82   9 8 7 6 5 4 3 2 1

CONTENTS

LIST OF CONTRIBUTORS

Numbers in parentheses indicate the pages on which the authors' contributions begin.

RICHARD L. ABEL (167), Law School, University of California, Los Angeles, Los Angeles, California 90024

STEVEN D. ANDERMAN (237), School of Law, University of Warwick, Coventry, England

VILHELM AUBERT (27), Institute of Sociology, University of Oslo, Postboks 1096-Blindern, Oslo 3, Norway

HUGO ADAM BEDAU (45), Department of Philosophy, Tufts University, Medford, Massachusetts 02155

LORAINE BLAXTER (115), Department of Anthropology and Sociology, University of Papua New Guinea, Papua New Guinea

SANDRA B. BURMAN (1), Centre for Socio-Legal Studies, Wolfson College, Oxford, England

PETER FITZPATRICK (115), Department of Law, Darwin College, University of Kent, Canterbury, England

NORMAN FORER (89), School of Social Welfare, University of Kansas Lawrence, Kansas 66044

BARBARA E. HARRELL-BOND (1), School of Law, University of Warwick, Coventry, England

ALUN HOWKINS (273), School of Cultural and Community Studies, University of Sussex, Brighton, England

ROBERT L. KIDDER (289), Department of Sociology, Temple University, Philadelphia, Pennsylvania 19122

SALLY M. A. LLOYD–BOSTOCK (9), Centre for Socio-Legal Studies, Wolfson College, Oxford, England

H. W. O. OKOTH-OGENDO (147), Faculty of Law, University of Nairobi, Nairobi, Kenya

LEOPOLD POSPISIL (127), Department of Anthropology, Yale University, New Haven, Connecticut 06520

G. R. RUBIN (257), Faculty of Social Sciences, Darwin College, University of Kent, Canterbury, England

ANDRÁS SAJÓ (223), Institute of Political and Legal Sciences, Hungarian Academy of Sciences, MTA Àllam-ès Jogtudomańyi Intézet, Budapest, Hungary

FRANCES SVENSSON (69), Department of Political Science, University of Michigan, Ann Arbor, Michigan 48104

JAMES T. THOMSON (201), Department of Government and Law, Lafayette College, Easton, Pennsylvania 18042

PREFACE

The aim of this book is to unmask the procedures whereby law is imposed, to examine the reactions to such impositions, and to specify the effects within particular sociopolitical contexts.

The book draws on the expertise of a number of disciplines. Lawyers, anthropologists, sociologists, political scientists, a psychologist, and a philosopher examine a variety of situations where the law may be categorized as "imposed" in the sense that it does not reflect the values and norms of the majority of the population or of that segment which will be subject to it. The introductory chapters consider motivations for compliance with the law and methods of obtaining it, and the book continues with case studies drawn from Eastern and Western Europe and from many Third World countries. It concludes with a discussion of what theoretical and methodological approaches are best suited to the examination of such situations. The studies cover both contemporary and historical examples and also consider a wide variety of legislation affecting different social institutions.

In seeking to address these problems, we hope that the studies will be relevant to students of a wide range of countries. Their relevance is obvious to studies of the Third World, where legislation is often viewed as a mechanism for bringing about desired change and facilitating industrial/technological development.

Such problems are not, however, confined to the Third World, and the book also considers cases from industrialized states, where governments are frequently faced with the question of how to regulate some institutions within the society or are attempting to bring about some change in values that is opposed by either the majority of the population or by a highly vocal minority.

ACKNOWLEDGMENTS

We are grateful to Carol Argo, Sally Carpenter, Joy Gibson, Lindsay Hunt, Paulette Pridgen-Pond, and Rita Renvoize for all their assistance in the preparation of this manuscript. In the course of preparing it a conference on "The Social Consequences of Imposed Law" was held, and we should like to thank the School of Law, University of Warwick, for providing hospitality. Several individuals at the Warwick School of Law deserve particular mention: Pauline Bishop, who served as conference organizer; Geoffrey Wilson for his interest and sustained support; and the other members of staff and the postgraduate students for their willing assistance. We also wish to thank Colin Campbell, Yash Ghai, Anthony Honoré, Janet Jordan, Robert Kidder, Patrick McAuslan, Adam Podgorecki, Otto Kahn-Freund, William Twining, and Alan Watson for agreeing to chair the sessions at the conference. The conference would not have been possible without the generous funding from the Nuffield Foundation, to whose trustees we wish to express our appreciation. We are also grateful to the Nuffield Foundation for further funding which assisted with the preparation of the manuscript of this book. We should like to thank the Social Science Research Council, which funds both our positions at the School of Law, University of Warwick, and the Centre for Socio-Legal Studies, Wolfson College, Oxford. The approach of this collection is interdisciplinary, as are some of the essays. Moreover, they cover a wide variety of geographical areas, different historical periods, and legal specializations. Each of the papers was therefore read by one or more referees, and we should like to thank them for their time and expertise. Finally, we thank all of our contributors and Peter McIntyre, who prepared the Index.

1

INTRODUCTION

SANDRA B. BURMAN
BARBARA E. HARRELL-BOND

Ever since philosophers began to question the role of law in society, they have been preoccupied with the basic problem of how men can order their social relations and still remain "free." Two broad traditions have emerged in western philosophy over the centuries. One stretches from Greek political theory, through the work of such writers as Savigny, to modern consensus approaches. The other tradition is represented by names such as Machiavelli, Hobbes, and Marx. In more recent times, constitutional lawyers have developed an interest in this problem, and, with the growth of the social sciences, lawyers and philosophers have been joined by scholars from these newer disciplines. Social scientists are bringing new techniques to the study and raising new questions, using the inductive tools of their disciplines rather than the deductive methods of their predecessors.

Our work in different social sciences and law brought us to this problem: we had each conducted research into social situations where an attempt had been made to use alien law as a means of rapidly changing a society, and in each case it had resulted in very obvious limitations on people's freedom. Our discovery that the same questions had aroused our interest led us to think that a broader interdisciplinary approach might shed more light on the issues. Our ini-

1

The Imposition of Law

tial interest focused on whether there was ever any plausible basis for the widespread belief of imperialists that law could be used to change their diverse subjects. However, when we began to consider other social situations, it seemed to us that the colonial cases were only one end of a spectrum, the other end of which might be characterized as societies in which the laws accord with the values of the population and no compulsion is required. Nor did all the extreme cases of attempted imposition necessarily involve the foreign enforcement of legal transplants; indigenous elites or even majorities could be equally coercive within their own societies. Moreover, we came across several cases that raised the fundamental question of whether the concept of imposed law is helpful in understanding the use of law in achieving social goals, or whether it distracts attention from the other processes that occur. We decided that a collection of studies of this problem from a variety of different disciplinary perspectives might prove enlightening.

When we had contacted a number of scholars about this project, it became evident that we would all benefit from an opportunity to have more lengthy discussions, and as a result a conference was held in April 1978 under the title "The Social Consequences of Imposed Law." We were surprised at the interest in the theme of the conference, demonstrated by the fact that over 100 people attended, the majority from abroad, and from a wide range of disciplines. Everyone agreed that communication between the different disciplines was remarkably good, perhaps because practically every conference paper centered on empirical data to which people were able to relate their diverse theoretical perspectives. There were many other papers presented at the conference that we would have liked to include in this book, but they were not available to us for various reasons.

The studies in this book approach the question of the imposition of law from the social science perspective. However, "imposed law" is an elusive concept. One's instinctive reaction to the notion of imposed law is to believe that one can recognize it, especially when one has experienced it. Living in any society, inevitably a person is legally obliged to do things he does not wish to do, some of which may well appear to be unjust. Virtually everyone, therefore, feels at one time or another that the law is being imposed on him to some extent. Moreover, imposed law would appear to include not only law that forces one to act against one's will. As is indicated by Aubert's study of methods of legal influence (Chapter 3), the range of law that can be regarded as imposed is far wider than the obvious examples and can include even law that is formulated to distribute benefits or resources. The reverse side of such law is the rules that exclude certain people from these benefits or resources and that may well appear unjust to the persons excluded. Anyone who has examined the working of existing welfare states will be aware of the problems of eliminating the many anomalies in the rules governing the distribution of benefits. Many citizens, to whom the welfare state guarantees the right to a minimum standard of living, feel that the law has unfairly discriminated against them if the rules result in an illogical but legal refusal of benefits to which their low standard of living should entitle them. As far as they are concerned, their rights have been infringed by an application of the law.

However, although one may believe that one can recognize imposed law from experience, Chapter 2 by Lloyd-Bostock clearly demonstrates how complicated and unreliable a guide is people's sense of being forced to do (or not do) something compared with the evidence of whether they have in fact been co-erced. For example, people may well rationalize a situation to themselves rather than live with the sense of compulsion or inequity. Yet we would hesitate to say that if for some reason people fail to recognize that evidently coercive law is be-ing imposed on them, it is therefore not imposed law. The social scientist therefore needs to define imposed law in some other way—some way that will not depend on people's recognizing that they have been forced to act, or not act, contrary to their wishes. The definition must therefore contain some objective standard of interference by the law in people's freedom. However, the concept of freedom has been subject to many diverse interpretations in different societies and in different eras. We have inherited a number of these interpretations, which still affect our views of how law operates in society and which underlie the various models used by social scientists.

Though grossly oversimplified, one may dichotomize the traditions of western philosophy into the following two strands. The first, found also in non-western cultures, as Svensson illustrates in Chapter 5, centers around the belief that man is a social animal, most fully realizing his potential in a society ordered for the common good and in which there is general consensus on the laws. This is held to constitute true freedom. Concern with the preservation of "multiplex, endur-ing, affective relationships" (Abel, Chapter 10) and with the breakup of the traditional American Indian society (Forer, Chapter 6) is rooted in this tradi-tion, and within it too (though not exclusively) is the belief that laws preventing individual action that interferes with social cohesion are not an imposition on people's freedom, but an aid to it.

The second tradition begins with a view of man as an atomized individual pursuing his own selfish goals, on whom any social control is an imposition. Within this tradition law may be viewed as a necessary evil, mitigated as far as possible through agreement between conflicting interests; or it may be viewed in the Marxist tradition as embodying the will of the ruling elite, which inevitably clashes with the interests of the rest of the society on which it is imposed. There are many theoretical perspectives that incorporate aspects of both these tradi-tions. That both embody insights into man's nature is reflected in the fact that elements of each rest uneasily side by side in much of our thinking and that it is virtually impossible for social scientists discussing imposed law to ignore them.

Ideally, of course, the social sciences should cover only value-free descriptions of facts, but descriptions of facts in this area are especially liable to conceal value judgments. Svensson demonstrates, for example, how the effect of extending the American Bill of Rights to American Indians can be described either as the provision of greater protection for the freedom of each Indian or as an imposition of alien concepts that threaten the survival of Indian identity. Each description may be factually accurate, but it carries within it a philosophy of what constitutes freedom in society. Moreover, it would seem impossible, without invoking value judgments, to investigate interference by the law in people's freedom, since part of the very definition of what is being investigated—freedom— involves a set of philosophical beliefs. It is, of course, possible to define freedom in alternative ways when stipulating what is to be investigated, but since the scope of any investigation must of necessity be limited, hypotheses on how law operates in society and relates to freedom must be adopted to narrow the focus for data collection to relevant material. This may be done explicitly, or may be inherent in the adopted models of society and the role of law in it, but in the final analysis some philosophical perspective is always present. If greater objectivity is our aim, it must rather be sought by subsequent thorough and imaginative testing for data that support alternative hypotheses. But as long as the underlying philosophies are recognized, the diversity of approach and the data they generate should enrich rather than confuse our understanding of the problem.

Within this book, therefore, there has been no attempt to select essays on the basis of an underlying agreement among authors on their view of society. For example, implicit in Chapter 4 by Bedau, on the death penalty in the United States, is the view that the law is not imposed on the majority if its long-term wishes and interests—represented by the general consensus—are catered for by the way the legal provisions are applied. In contrast, Chapter 6 by Forer, on the Potawatomi Indians in America, Chapter 9 by Okoth-Ogendo on land law in Kenya, and Chapter 7 by Fitzpatrick and Blaxter, on official discretionary powers in Papua New Guinea, view state law as exclusively the tool of the ruling class; therefore, for all other members of society law must by definition be imposed law, the result of the conflict between differing interests. As Kidder points out in Chapter 16, however, some authors have adopted a modified view of the role of law in society and have investigated whether law as actually enforced represents the interests of the governed more than the rulers. They examine a range of very different societies but all come to a common general conclusion. Given the exigencies of lawmaking and law enforcement, law in practice represents an ever-changing compromise among the interests of the lawmakers, the enforcers, and the groups on whom it is enforced. Thus Thomson in Chapter 11, for example, shows how the amount of tax actually paid is the result of the balancing of a number of interests at every level of society in rural Niger. Sajó (Chapter 12) shows the policy of collectivization in Hungary undergoing changes as a result of various similar processes, and the chapters by Anderman (Chapter 13), Howkins (Chapter 15), and Rubin (Chapter 14) all show aspects of English legislation being modified in practice at different periods in history. Judging by this evidence, law is not the exclusive result of either consent or conflict in society but is a product of both.

It is at the level of producing hypotheses on the conditions for, and the nature and consequences of, these compromises that the social sciences can play an important role. At the conclusion of the conference, Robert Kidder put forward a framework for studying the process and consequences of conflicts between lawmakers and the governed, a framework which represents, in our view, an advance in theoretical understanding of the role of law in such conflicts.

He begins by suggesting that the social distance between the lawmakers, and the governed, and the layers of intervening organizational complexity, may be used as a measure of how external a legal system is to the community on which it is enforced. The more external the legal system, the more likely it becomes that any case introduced into it or induced by it will take on meanings and requirements not originally relevant to the conflicting parties. Fitzpatrick and Blaxter provide a good illustration of this. When Papua New Guineans applied to the newly constituted licensing authorities for permission to open a mobile food business, they found themselves called upon to meet alien standards of food preservation. Similarly, the more external the legal system, the greater is the tendency for people with less direct involvement in the conflict to find externally grounded reasons for becoming interested in the outcome of the conflict. Thus, among Kidder's examples are industrialists interested in a region's raw materials, who join in a local struggle over property rights. The more external legal actors there are, and the more layers of outside organizational involvement, the more opportunity does a party to the conflict have to acquire allies. However, having allies means that the party must make compromises to satisfy the diverse purposes involved—which necessitates opening up the internal unit to exploitation for external purposes. Therefore, the more external the legal system used, the more vulnerable does the internal system become to disruption, with all the nonlegal consequences that can result. How unexpected these can be is perhaps best illustrated in Chapter 11 by Thompson. He shows how rule manipulation throughout village, district, and national jurisdictions resulted in damage to the ecology. Because of central government enforcement of tax collection, a system of rule manipulation developed at the local level that undermined viable local government. Villagers lost the ability to enforce collective decisions or take collective action—for example, in forest and pasture conservation schemes. It is examples like this that have led Kidder (Chapter 16) to suggest the use of an interactive model in which the degree of externality of the legal system involved serves as a guide to the sources and extent of disruption likely to occur in the disputing community. The investigator should focus on the points at which interaction between the internal and external systems and actors is likely to be taking place. To find these, he should study the role and sources of power of the lawmakers or enforcers at the internal level and different levels of externality involved. Many of these interactions will be played out through the legal system, since this is one of the major ways in which conflicts are handled.

That interaction can take place in a wide variety of situations and ways is demonstrated by the chapters in this book. Within the legal system, institutions, rules and processes interact with each other, and changes in one may well result in changes in others. In Chapter 10, for example, Abel provides an excellent case study on the lines suggested by Kidder of how within the legal system changes in the institutional framework of the courts can result in changes in legal processes—such as increasing criminal prosecutions for administrative offenses—which in turn result in changes in both the practices and attitudes of the court officials and the courts' original civil law clients. Or Pospisil (in Chapter 8) demonstrates how inadvertently changing the structure of the courts among the Kapauku Papuans of New Guinea, by creating village headmen with jurisdiction restricted to the village, led to a change in the traditional principle that judicial authority derived from voluntary support of the sublineage. By replacing this principle with one of territoriality, enforced by colonial authority, the Dutch changed the rules by which disputes were settled; a man's case was then adjudicated by the law of the locality in which he committed a tort or minor crime, not by the law of his lineage or confederacy, as had been the practice earlier. This in turn reacted on the political structure of the Kapaukuans to bring about major changes in it. On the evidence (though not the theory) that Pospisil presents, the changes in Kapaukuan society would appear to have extended to their social relations (or what he terms their social structure) as well, since their political relations were, according to the data he presents, subsequently determined by factors other than descent and economic patronage.

The way in which the legal system reaches far beyond its own apparent sphere of influence to interact constantly with social attitudes, processes, and structures is the major theme of the book, and it is on the mechanics of this process that Kidder's framework enables us to focus with greater precision. In particular, by highlighting how the imposition of law is always a two-way, dynamic process, he has demonstrated that the case studies in this book that focus on the methods by which the governed subvert the law are not studies of exceptional cases. Rather, they are instances of a process present in all cases of legal imposition to a greater or lesser extent, the evidence for which can be sought at specific, predictable points in the social structure. For example, Bedau could have expanded his study of the governors' exercise of their veto power to include further points of political pressure on their decisions. This would have led him to investigate such questions as the extent to which the moratorium on the exercise of the death penalty is related to political pressures from the considerable black vote.

Kidder's model also provides a framework that enables us to recognize cases of legal imposition so extreme that they might have escaped our attention as constituting legal phenomena and been classified as exercises of purely political power. For example, at the conference Aubert pointed out that although he had lived for 5 years under the Nazi occupation of Norway, it had not before occurred to him to regard the German rules as imposed law. Kidder's model would allow such examples to be placed on a continuum of externality, beside such cases as military governments formed by a country's own nationals. The application of similar methods to analyze these instances may not only provide a basis for their elucidation, but also reveal features unnoticed in cases where the position of the lawmaker is less external.

Discovering and analyzing the evidence necessary to apply the model, however, requires all the skills we have available for examining human behavior and social structures. Obviously relevant to the examination of the process are studies by political scientists, anthropologists, and sociologists of both actual cases and, even more important, the points at which interactions can be expected and the forms these can take in different circumstances. The comparison of varied societies is a particularly useful aid in generating hypotheses. In addition, as Lloyd-Bostock demonstrates in Chapter 2, studies are needed by psychologists of the way individuals react in various circumstances and models based on such studies are required for predicting future reactions. It is seductively easy to build elaborate theories of how groups will react without regard to the complexities of human personality that psychological studies are beginning to uncover. Work is also required by lawyers willing to explore the ramifications of the legal system and to look beyond legal explanations when seeking the reasons for changes in rules and processes. Despite the difficulties of interdisciplinary studies, we hope future work in this very important field will draw on all the skills that are available to help obtain a clearer understanding of the process that we have—as it now appears, rather misleadingly—termed the "imposition of law."

2

EXPLAINING COMPLIANCE
WITH IMPOSED LAW

SALLY M.A. LLOYD-BOSTOCK

This chapter examines some traditional ideas about compliance with law that seem to be especially relevant to contrasts between imposed and any other kind of law. In particular, processes of norm internalization have been invoked by lawyers, psychologists, and other social scientists to explain how rules may cease to be experienced as externally imposed, and therefore complied with in the absence of external inducements. Thus, Hoffman (1977:85) writes:

> The legacy of both Sigmund Freud and Emile Durkheim is the agreement among social scientists that most people do not go through life viewing society's moral norms as external, coercively imposed pressures to which they must submit. Though the norms are initially external to the individual and often in conflict with his desires, the norms eventually become part of his internal motive system and guide his behavior even in the absence of external authority.

Applying this specifically to law, Friedman (1977:69) writes:

> The vast bulk of the population is generally law abiding even when there is not the slightest chance that real punishment will pursue the deviant. The explanation for this phenomenon is not complex. People tend to do what they think is morally right. They follow the dictates of conscience, the product of their socialization. . . .

9

The Imposition of Law

Copyright © 1979 by Academic Press, Inc.
All rights of reproduction in any form reserved.
ISBN 0-12-145450-9

The nature and effects of motives acquired through internalization processes will therefore be discussed and set in the context of other sources of motivation to comply or not to comply with law. Existing psychological theory and research on moral internalization and behavior in relation to moral, legal, and other social norms provide an extensive basis for discussion and, in some areas, tenative conclusions.

The preceding quotations suggest that law that conflicts with internalized norms, or seeks to introduce new patterns of behavior, will lack the support of people's internal motives to comply. Motives for compliance would therefore seem to be bound up in the definition of imposed law. Treating imposed law as a special category could be taken to imply that it is law which does some sort of violence to existing systems of beliefs, cultural norms, or established modes of behavior. Compliance with such law presumably results from external sanctions and inducements. Internal rewards and costs are either absent or, so to speak, on the wrong side of the equation. Imposed law is law that does not have certain motives on its side.

This cannot, of course, work as a definition of imposed law unless it also works as an explanation of compliance or noncompliance. It will be argued in this chapter that invoking processes of moral internalization contributes little to the explanation of compliance with law. The distinction between externally imposed law and law that accords with internalized norms is therefore adopted here only in order to focus discussion on what seems to be implied in the use of the term "imposed law."

Using this distinction, externally imposed law would include cases ranging from particular instances of law within an established legal system to the importation of an entire legal system from another culture. It is debatable whether a definition of imposed law should introduce further distinctions between different types of case, but there can be no doubt that explanation of compliance will need to take account of the wider context in which law has been imposed. As chapters in this book illustrate, what are taken as instances of imposed law often occur in conditions of rapid social change, upheaval, and instability. Such conditions may in themselves affect the ways in which, and the extent to which, law is complied with. Instability and change can threaten entire systems of beliefs or values. It is therefore not enough to look only at how a particular legal innovation compares with existing norms. It is necessary also to understand what happens when such systems as a whole are undermined. This will mean looking not only at how particular moral norms may become internalized, but also at why individuals develop and seek to maintain such systems at all.

Before turning to moral internalization processes, I should clarify what I intend to consider as a question of "compliance." Compliance with law is generally taken to mean not engaging in legally proscribed behavior, or refraining from criminal acts. It is in this kind of context that the influence of moral norms has been seen as a possible supplement to legal threat and punishment. However, learned norms influence not only the ways in which people act, but also what are offered and accepted as justifications and excuses for actions and what is seen as just punishment and reward, a fair solution to a dispute, or a fair distribution of resources. Given these wider possible effects of moral internalization, there are wider possibilities for clashes between moral norms and legal rules.

These possibilities extend to the civil as well as the criminal law and include the general distributive principles underlying a legal system. Deutsch (1975), for example, distinguishes three broad types of values which can form the basis of distributive justice—equity, equality, and need—and discusses with reference to social psychology how different kinds of groups will tend to emphasize one over the others. For both Deutsch (1975) and Sampson (1975), the predominance in Western society of equity principles of justice (balancing reward to input) is a reflection of society's economic orientation, with a consequent emphasis on economic role and competitiveness in socialization processes. Conflict can therefore be expected where law based on such values is imposed on a society without this orientation. Furthermore, legal rules govern not only what is legally accountable, but also what constitutes adequate interpretation, justifications, and excuses, and what sanctions, rewards, or solutions may follow. Since the concept of fairness is common in some form to all cultures we know of, one could expect also to find something akin to procedural rules about how agreement is reached on what has happened and what should be done about it. Imposed law might therefore conflict with existing norms at any of a range of stages in such social sequences. It may sometimes seem more natural to talk about using, or invoking, the law rather than complying with it. But law governs many aspects of interpreting events and reaching a decision or solution. Acting in accordance with any legal rule can be seen as compliance.

Confining discussion to "compliance" in its narrow sense would mean overlooking the interdependence between legal rules or moral norms governing actions and those governing decisions about actions. Nader (1975) quotes research in Sardinia which illustrates this interdependence. Cattle theft was regarded by the shepherds as a matter for dispute to be settled amicably between neighbors, but not as a crime. To regard cattle theft as a crime is to regard it as something which should or should not be judged in certain ways or be subject to particular kinds of sanctions. Under state law it became a crime, and implementation of the law met with difficulties. To take another example, the existence of a feud or the fact that the victim was found stealing crops may not constitute a defense to a murder charge under imposed law, but yet be an adequate justification within existing cultural norms. This again involves a general disagreement over what kinds of killing should carry what kinds of consequences.

Conflict may also arise over what might be called questions of fact rather than questions of law. Interpretations, justifications, and excuses are negotiated by pointing to "facts," which in turn may be open to challenge. We know from crosscultural studies that the way in which an individual perceives his social and physical world is at least partly culture-specific. It is probably fanciful to suggest that conflicts of any real legal importance arise out of differences in, say, depth perception or color discrimination. But take for example cases of "witch-killing" in Africa. To people who believe in witches, it is a fact that the person who was killed was a witch. But this cannot be accommodated as a "fact" within a modern Western legal system. It is in this kind of case that one could expect to find imposed law at its most Procrustean or contorted (cf. Seidman 1965).

The possibility of conflict at this fundamental level throws doubt on the adequacy of a definition of imposed law in terms of conflict with internalized norms. The motives acquired through moral internalization are integrated with other kinds of motives arising out of the way in which the individual has come to structure and respond to his social world, and which may also vary from one culture to another. Where psychological research.is carried out within a particular culture, it is possible to proceed (as the law does) on the assumption that certain internal, psychological "costs and payoffs" apply uniformly, but this assumption no longer holds when the responses of members of different cultures to the same legal system are compared. It is clearly inadequate to talk of people's believing in witches or spirits, or perceiving and thinking in certain ways, because there is a rule or norm about it which they have internalized; these aspects of behavior do not seem to be a matter of moral values or concepts of justice at all. Nonetheless, principles according to which the individual organizes his experience have been internalized, and this in turn generates motivation, possibly to comply or not comply with the law. To act otherwise than in accordance with one's beliefs can be extremely threatening for a variety of reasons and therefore psychologically "costly." The process and effects of moral internalization and the development of concepts of justice need to be seen in this context and kept in perspective as one among many possible sources of motivation to comply or not comply with law.

In the following discussion of compliance I therefore include behavior quite generally in relation to rules and norms, and behavior in contexts where rules or norms may apply. This includes overt behavior, cognitive behavior, and affect, or feelings. Possible sources of internal motivation besides moral norms will be considered, as well as external, social, and material factors and the effects of instability and change. In conclusion I shall try to assess (1) the contribution of the internalization of moral norms in explaining compliance with the law, and (2) whether conflict between such norms and the law provides a satisfactory basis for differentiating imposed law from any other kind of law.

MORAL INTERNALIZATION PROCESSES

It is generally recognized that moral internalization is only one among many possible sources of motivation to comply with law. It is rare, however, for distinctions to be made between the effects of norms internalized by different processes, or between their influence on actions and their influence on reasoning and feelings about actions. Psychological research indicates that the nature of internal motives may vary according to how they were acquired and that the relationship between moral reasoning and overt behavior is problematic. The strongest effects of moral internalization may in fact be on how people interpret, feel, reason, and argue about events, rather than on how they act.

Evidence that different kinds of internal motivation result from different kinds of socialization experiences comes largely from research with children. Hoffman (1977) provides a comprehensive review. One finding to emerge clearly from this research is that different techniques of parental disciplining foster different kinds of learning. Frequent use of inductive techniques (where the parents explain why certain behavior is required) is related to a strong sense of guilt in the child, whereas power-assertive techniques (using force or physical or material punishment) are associated with a fear of sanctions.

Hoffman's theoretical explanation of these differences draws on laboratory experiments in learning, memory, information processing, and moral internalization. Moral-internalization experiments have the drawback of drastically telescoping the socialization process, and raise questions of validity in extrapolating from the laboratory to "real life." They do, however, have the advantage of allowing the child's learning to be studied closely under controlled conditions. Hoffman suggests that two different learning processes are involved and that only one of these leads to true internalization, conducive to what might genuinely be called moral behavior. He suggests that the content of the moral message in an inductive discipline encounter may be stored and integrated with previous knowledge about rules and their application, or the effects of behavior on others, and remembered long after the setting in which they occurred or the person from whom they originated is forgotten. In the absence of any recollection of an external source, the child experiences the ideas as his own, arising out of his own disposition. This kind of learning is conducive to behavior that results from, say, respect for another's feelings or the ability to see someone else's point of view.

In contrast, Hoffman describes the results of socialization processes emphasizing threat and punishment as "the general expectation that people often have, without necessarily being aware of it, that their actions are constantly under surveillance. . . . The result . . . is that the individual often behaves in the morally prescribed way even when alone, in order to avoid punishment [Hoffman 1977:123]." These fears and expectations are explicable in terms of a comparatively straightforward conditioned response. Hoffman concludes that this second type of moral learning is probably the more pervasive and accounts for a good deal of "moral" behavior in many societies.

If Hoffman is right, the idea that imposed law can usefully be distinguished from law that accords with internalized moral norms becomes less convincing. Most of what appears to the outsider to be behavior motivated by internalized moral norms remains to the actor in an important sense externally imposed, motivated by a conditioned fear of sanctions or expectation of reward. Extinguishing or outweighing such fears and expectations may be a quite different matter from, for example, altering a person's sense of what it is to harm someone, which has come to form part of the way he perceives himself and his relationships with others.

A third, rather different type of moral internalization is proposed by research that focuses on moral reasoning rather than moral action. Cognitive developmental theories link the development of moral reasoning to stages in more general cognitive development. Progression through the stages is the result of the maturation of cognitive capacities with age, in interaction with social experience. In particular, experience of role playing or role taking and exposure to levels of reasoning beyond his present capacities stimulate and motivate the individual to progress to a "higher" stage, in order to integrate these experiences and resolve cognitive disequilibrium. The major cognitive developmental theorists have been Piaget (1932) and Kohlberg (1969). More recently June Tapp has adapted the ideas of Kohlberg (who in turn owes much to Piaget) to the more specific question of legal rather than moral socialization (Tapp and Levine 1974). She sees the individual's orientation toward legal rules as passing through much the same general sequence of stages, and law itself as part of the individual's social experience, acting as socializer.

For both Tapp and Kohlberg, this sequence passes through three basic levels. At the first "pre-moral" or "pre-conventional" level, right and wrong are taken as universal, inflexible premises. Obedience to rules is seen as a matter of avoiding punishment. At the second stage, of "conventional role conformity," judgments are made with reference to external authority. Moral value resides in conforming to stereotypical good or right roles and maintaining the existing social order. At the "post-conventional" level, or level of self-accepted moral principles, man is seen as self-regulating, guided by his own sense of justice. Rules or laws command obedience only insofar as they function to achieve a rational purpose. They may be dysfunctional, or unjust, and therefore be changed or not complied with. Only a minority of adults appear to reach this third level. The rule orientations predominant at each of these levels have been summarized as "rule obeying," "rule maintaining," and "rule making."

It seems clear that there is a general move with age from concrete to more abstract moral reasoning, and increasing sophistication in the handling of moral principles and arguments. This parallels progression in general cognitive development and is related to mental rather than chronological age. However, the model has been widely criticized, both in detail and on the grounds that the whole concept of "progress toward higher stages" involves value judgments. It has also been criticized on the grounds that the criteria used in the research to determine an individual's level of moral reasoning reflect the moral values of a democratic western society (see, for example, Irvine 1979). This latter criticism in particular throws some doubt on claims for crosscultural validity and on findings that members of non-western societies proceed more slowly and less far through the sequences than do members of advanced western societies. Even

within western societies there are problems in categorizing an individual according to his level of reasoning, as people do not operate consistently at a given
level. For example, research indicates that the closer to home an issue becomes,
the "lower" is the level of moral reasoning likely to be adopted. Thus, a person
scoring at Kohlberg's post-conventional level when presented with moral dilemmas relating to an unknown character may explain his own behavior in terms of
avoiding sanctions (Irvine 1979).

There are, however, two reasons why research on moral internalization of this
type is significant here. Firstly, it highlights the distinction between moral
reasoning and moral behavior. The way in which people reason about moral
dilemmas apparently contributes little to prediction or explanation of their actual
behavior when faced with such a dilemma (Irvine 1979). An "advanced" level
of moral reasoning does not necessarily imply behavior motivated by complex or
lofty moral principles. Secondly, moral development in this sense involves the
development of skills that, like many skills, improve with practice, are shaped by
experience, and relate to the level of other abilities and skills. The individual
may be striving to integrate morally relevant information and may feel a
commitment to moral values he attains in this way. He is also learning what will
work as a moral argument in a particular context, and how to make behavior
explicable and justifiable to himself and others.

Underlying both these considerations is a distinction between the direct effects
of norms on action on the one hand, and using, consciously applying, and arguing about norms on the other. The following discussion of the effects of moral
internalization looks first at direct effects on overt behavior.

MORAL INTERNALIZATION AND OVERT BEHAVIOR

Despite the intuitive appeal of the idea that behavior is guided by the dictates
of conscience, the evidence points to a rather fragile relationship between moral
internalization and overt behavior. The degree to which internalized moral
norms support or undermine the enforcement of law obviously varies widely
from context to context, but the power of such norms to control behavior in this
way seems on the whole unreliable. Several writers have challenged their
assumed importance and quoted considerable evidence to support their views
(see, for example, Milgram 1963; Reiss 1966; Ross and di'Tecco 1975). It is
only necessary to observe what happens when people are aware that they can
break the law with impunity: for example, the widespread looting that took place
in Montreal while police were on strike in 1969. The vulnerability of internalized norms to temptation and situational pressures has also been demonstrated in research on imitation and modeling. Prior socialization is readily
undermined by observing a deviant model going unpunished. Neutralizing a
bad example is probably an important function of punishment under the law.

What is being examined in modeling experiments is compliance or noncompliance with a rule arbitrarily stated by the experimenter, which one may often not want to regard as a question of moral behavior at all. Indeed, the experimenter's instructions may run counter to the subject's moral beliefs, as in Milgram's (1963) famous experiments on obedience, where subjects were required to administer what they thought were exceedingly painful, if not lethal, electric shocks to others. These experiments have become well known for the very surprising degree to which they demonstrated that ordinary, decent people would act with cruelty toward others, and against their own principles, when placed in this context. However, exposure to a model in a Milgram-type experiment who refuses to comply with the experimenter's instructions produces what might be a very similar disinhibiting effect. Others follow suit and disobey (Rosenhan 1969). Whatever the interpretation of this result may be, it is of importance here that responses to instructions or rules can be to such a large extent influenced by the responses of others in the same situation—especially where this allows the individual to do what he wanted to do all along.

Where law seeks to change customary patterns of behavior, response to it may be mediated by the indirect effects of existing norms on the significance of legal sanctions, the perceived legitimacy of authority, and the social costs of violating norms. As Zimring and Hawkins (1977) point out, the severity of legal sanctions is not simply a matter of, for example, the size of a fine, but can be largely a matter of social stigma. Punishment for behavior with no significant moral connotations for the individual and his social group will not carry these social costs. On the other hand, pursuit of legal rights and entitlements may be socially unacceptable. Where behavior with positive moral value is made illegal, or negatively valued behavior legal, noncompliance may in fact be socially rewarding and punishment may bring kudos rather than stigma. Even at more mundane levels of everyday life, people may become determined to act in a particular way because their choice to do so is being threatened—the phenomenon of "psychological reactance." If belief in the legitimacy of a custom is stronger than belief in the legitimacy of the law, sanctions may actually reinforce support for a now outlawed custom. The likelihood of this increases where a legal system is imported from another culture or for other reasons is not accepted as a source of authority to be obeyed out of duty.

This introduces the possibility that law itself might socialize attitudes and create internal motives to comply. If the pronouncements of the law on what is good or bad behavior are respected as legitimate, this should in itself encourage compliance. In addition, making citizens aware of the social impact of certain behavior might be expected to work in the same way as inductive disciplining by parents. If this is so, legal rules could become fully internalized, as described above. However, such evidence as we have about the effectiveness of a moral appeal to support the law provides little indication of success (cf. Andenaes 1977). It is likely that the more usual emphasis in law enforcement on policing and the threat of sanctions, by accentuating the external coercive nature of law, militates against the internalization of legal rules as morally right.

The apparent docility with which the majority of people comply with law and other social norms may often be better described as a matter of habit than of moral conscience. Like habits, learned norms about specific aspects of behavior may serve an important psychological as well as social function. In a stable social environment, patterns of acceptable social behavior can be developed and repeated. Human cognitive capacities are limited, and behaving in ways accepted as normal is an adaptive and economical way of coping in familiar contexts with the need continuously to select courses of behavior. There is, in fact, no need to assume that the norms or values from which specific behavior derives are necessarily internalized at all. Where moral learning results from the punishment and reward of power-assertive discipline techniques, for example, conditioned fear is likely to be attached to the behavior on which punishment has been contingent rather than to violation of a more general moral principle.

Where behavior does appear to be influenced by moral norms, this influence often arises out of the individual's expectations about the behavior and reactions of others. This suggests that social rather than internal moral costs are involved. An individual's set of moral principles can be very flexible and accommodating and selectively called on to justify behavior preferred for other reasons. To look more closely at how this can work, it is necessary to look more generally at reactions to events where norms of justice may apply.

APPLYING NORMS OF JUSTICE

A considerable body of research in social psychology is concerned with reactions to wrongdoing or harm-doing. Since the research is largely American, its relevance to other cultures is rather a matter of speculation. It does, however, allow one to look quite closely at how individuals react to injustice and why. The approach emphasizes the possibility of different interpretations of the same event, with disagreement over what constitutes a just outcome.

Theory in this area often applies a kind of cost–benefit analysis to social relationships. Equity theory, for example, starts from the proposition that individuals seek to maximize their outcomes from social relationships, where outcome equals rewards minus costs. Systems of fair apportionment evolve in a community and become internalized by its members in the ways outlined earlier. Inequity, as defined within the community, is therefore distressing not only to the victim, but also to the wrongdoer and to outsiders to the relationship, and members are motivated to act equitably and to restore equity to relationships they see as inequitable (Walster, Berscheid, and Walster 1973; Austin, Walster, and Utne 1976).

An important distinction is drawn between actual and psychological equity. Actual equity is restored through an actual adjustment to the relationship: the harm-doer may make restitution, the victim may get his own back, or the harm-doer may be punished. Any of these adjusts the relative outcomes of victim and harm-doer, thus restoring equity to their relationship. In contrast, psychological equity is achieved by a distortion of "reality," whereby individuals convince themselves that a relationship is perfectly fair and therefore that no actual adjustment is necessary.

JUSTIFICATION THROUGH DISTORTION

Austin *et al.* (1976) summarize a number of such ways in which inequity may be rationalized. The harm-doer may argue that the victim deserves to be harmed, and indeed, that he (the harm-doer) is the restorer of equity: Sykes and Matza (1957) found, for example, that juvenile delinquents frequently claim that their victims are "bums," or for some reason deserve punishment. Similarly, minimization or denial of the victim's suffering allows the inequity of the relationship to be denied. Walster *et al.* (1973) quote, for example, studies demonstrating that students administering electric shocks in experiments soon came to underestimate their painfulness. Further permutations of biased estimation of inputs and outcomes are possible. These various possibilities are open to the victim and outsiders as well as to the harm-doer. Although a victim might be expected to seek actual equity as a first choice, he may settle for psychological equity if this fails or carries other costs. For example, a confidence trickster's victim may be unwilling to admit he has been taken for a ride, or a battered wife may find justifying her husband's behavior the least costly solution. Austin *et al.* (1976) also produce evidence that outsiders, including judges and juries, may also settle for psychological rather than actual equity.

In addition to producing extensive empirical evidence, from both experimental and "real life" settings, that these various techniques are in fact used, equity theorists have tried to identify the factors determining choice between them. Walster *et al.* (1973) observed that the two main factors that seemed to determine choice between strategies were their adequacy and their costs. Thus if adequate restitution is simply not feasible, psychological equity may be preferred. However, the individual must convince himself or feel distressed in the ways already discussed. Walster *et al.* note two factors that determine how plausible a justification is to the justifier: the extent of distortion needed and the amount of contact he anticipates (in the case of a harm-doer) with the victim or his sympathizers. He must also, however, convince others or risk social sanctions. The extensive evidence that psychological equity will often be preferred to actual equity illustrates how vulnerable are internalized norms of fair or moral behavior when less costly lines of behavior are feasible.

JUSTIFICATION THROUGH INTERPRETATION

Psychological equity as described in equity theory involves distortion of reality, or denying the "facts," but it is also possible to find ways of justifying (or for that matter, accusing) by defining what has happened in a way that makes preferred norms applicable. Schwartz (1975), in discussing the activation of humanitarian norms, illustrates how such norms may be held in a general sense (such as "be kind"), but neutralized or not activated in a particular setting. The individual's definition of the situation must be such as to make them relevant, and their scope must be sufficiently specific to that kind of setting to generate expectations and hence to influence behavior. Where a general norm exists which could be applied but which is not specific in scope, it must be crystallized. The process of crystallization and activation, and the possibility of neutralization, allows for a considerable amount of leeway. For example, Schwartz discusses altruistic helping behavior. In this sort of case a range of specific norms may direct that an individual respond. He may have caused the harm, be the only person around, be medically qualified, and so on. A range of alternative interpretations, and hence potential justifications, is thus available. Having applied a particular norm, an individual may defend his interpretation vigorously, in terms of fairness, moral beliefs, or just rights. However, his motives in applying the norm may lie elsewhere.

As well as providing for alternative definitions of events, Schwartz's distinction between general and crystallized norms raises another possibility. Where a norm is crystallized, as will be the case in more familiar, frequently occurring contexts, the range of alternatives is more limited, and response is more automatic. It may therefore also be the case that the more specific existing norms are, the harder they are to change or overrule. It should be easier to introduce change at a more general level and where new contexts are created. The phenomenon of "code switching," where individuals revert to familiar modes of thinking when they return to their villages, may reflect this. It is also common for a certain amount of deadwood left over from a previous system to survive change. Elements of earlier pagan ritual, for example, survive to this day within Christianity.

COMPETENCE

The general point underlying the preceding discussion has been that moral and other norms very often leave alternatives open to the individual, and hence opportunities to maximize his own material, social, and psychological self-interest. Awareness of social norms, however it may be acquired, allows the individual to estimate the social rewards and costs attached to different courses of behavior. Similarly, awareness of legal rules and the ways they are likely to apply in practice will influence behavior in contexts where they are seen to be relevant. Motives then become closely tied to competence. The individual needs to know what the law is, what the chances of sanctions are and what the sanctions may be, what excuses and justifications will work, and what other costs and benefits may be involved in, say, using the courts. The outcomes that can be achieved depend also on skill in handling the relevant moral and legal concepts and at working the system generally. Tapp sees progress to more advanced levels in her legal socialization model as part of this, and has argued for legal education programs with this goal (Tapp and Levine 1974). These various aspects of competence under a legal system seem to have little to do with moral motives, though one consequence of vested interests in the mystification of law can be that lack of competence is interpreted as a kind of moral backwardness.

Competence takes on special importance where law is imposed. Nader and Yngvesson (1973:884), for example, write that "those who often suffer [from sudden changes in the law] are the preliterate, the illiterate, the common people . . . at least until they learn by various means how to manipulate or use the newly introduced system." Nader (1975) cites examples where courts were avoided because of lack of money, access, and legal expertise—though, as she further points out, these are reasons common to most complex legal systems. Use of a new system is apparently often determined by considerations quite separate from how far it accords with what has come to feel right through established custom. Thus court procedures in Lebanon were used to humiliate opponents and to change alliances and power patterns in the village (Nader 1975). Further motives for pursuing a dispute in one way rather than another may arise from the brand of justice dispensed and the effects of legal or other procedures damaging to existing relationships. As Nader suggests, this variety of possible motives to pursue a conflict, and pursue it in particular ways, almost guarantees that alternative justice systems will be available, even in relatively homogeneous and stable cultures.

THE EFFECTS OF INSTABILITY AND CHANGE

The special importance of competence in determining behavior under imposed law is essentially a product of legal change and instability. There may be other consequences of such conditions that need to be distinguished from the consequences of mismatch between imposed law and existing justice systems or moral beliefs. The cognitive developmental approach provides one possible framework for looking at how individuals cope with such conditions. Orientation toward law and social rules, and the kind of reasoning that will be employed to resolve conflicting demands, may have important implications for the ways in which individuals react to legal change. Lerner's examination of the origins and forms of the justice motive provides another framework. He concentrates on the individual's commitment to concepts of deserving, and suggests conditions under which this may be abandoned or lead to apparently unjust behavior (Lerner 1977).

Lerner's approach is in many ways similar to the social learning group of theories, but he places his central emphasis on what he calls "the justice motive." This, he believes, is necessary to account for the evidence that "at least at the level of verbalization and cultural symbols, the related themes of justice and deserving are uniquely central, powerful and universal in Western civilization [1977:4].'' He links the development of concepts of deserving to stages in a child's maturation, seeing the later stages as the development of a ''personal contract.'' In essence, the individual agrees to do what is prescribed on the assumption that he will get what he deserves. (It is worth noting that a prerequisite of the development of this contract is a sufficiently stable environment.) A contract may, however, be broken by either side. Lerner (1977:11) writes: ''If the child—and later the adult—becomes persuaded that he lives in a world where these procedures or rules of entitlement do not apply then he will give up living by his 'personal contract' and act as if he lives in the jungle with all the attendant psychological consequences (Erikson 1950; Jessor *et al.* 1968).'' Imposed law that undermines the viability of the personal contract may, according to this theory, result in a breakdown, but not a replacement, of existing systems of values. Behavior may be determined not by existing or new norms but by what the individual has to gain in the context, and in the short rather than the long term.

Lerner's theory also offers an explanation of behavior apparently contrary to humanitarian norms without any breakdown of the personal contract. This follows from his emphasis on the individual's need to believe that he lives in a just world, where he and everyone else get their just deserts. At the same time, he is forced to acknowledge that there is widespread injustice in the world. He has, therefore, to limit his reference group and avoid identifying with, or recognizing responsibilities toward, exploited or otherwise suffering groups. Paradoxically, the need to avoid threats to what Lerner terms his ''belief in a just world'' leads to apparently unjust actions. If he goes even some way toward helping the victimized or needy, he must acknowledge injustice in his world and his responsibility to do something about it. He may therefore avoid offering any help at all. Rather than identify with the exploited, he may wholeheartedly identify with the exploiters, *because of*, not in spite of, the strength of his justice motive. A variety of circumstances may make this easier and insulate him from acknowledging injustice: the behavior of others and the acceptability of his behavior to them, the possibility of denying responsibility or of diluting it, and other conditions of the kind already discussed which make justification possible.

Lerner's theory thus suggests that where instability and innovation present an extreme threat to his belief in a just world, the individual may abandon justice concepts altogether. But where possible he will strive to maintain this belief so that behavior apparently motivated by material self-interest is interpretable in terms of his psychological needs. Similarly, apparently meek acceptance of injustice or exploitation by victims is explicable in these terms. Walster and Walster (1975) examine the evidence that the social philosophy, and hence definitions of equity, that a community evolves and comes to accept is determined by its power structure, providing for the evolution of norms that are to the advantage of particular sections of the community at the expense of others, but nonetheless accepted and vigorously defended by the community as a whole. The exploited join in their own exploitation. Lerner's theory suggests that their powerlessness to initiate change may leave them little alternative. Any change will not only have to overcome the inertia of established norms, which will tend to appear natural and right, but will also be difficult to effect without some shift in power or in the interests of the powerful: "Logic is a good ally for the social reformer; power is a better one [Walster and Walster 1975:38]." Meanwhile, the powerless individual with no realistic alternative may come to terms with his fate, seeing it as his just deserts, and thus manage to continue to believe in a just world.

CONCLUSIONS

Moral internalization clearly has some influence on behavior and can probably act as a brake on social change. However, its role should not be oversimplified or exaggerated. This discussion has raised a number of complications and limitations that, I believe, severely restrict the usefulness of invoking such processes to explain compliance with law or to distinguish between types of law. Psychological theory and research by no means provide definitive answers to the questions raised but do suggest some tentative conclusions.

Firstly, it is questionable whether the concept of moral internalization is really helpful in explaining compliance with the law. Moral internalization is a blanket term that can cover a variety of processes with different consequences for behavior. Hoffman (1977), for example, distinguishes three quite different forms of moral internalization: conditioned fear or anxiety, the integration of cognitive awareness of other people's inner states with the human capacity for empathy, and the active processing of morally relevant information. Moreover, "moral internalization" may be a misnomer for much of the learning that creates motives to comply with norms, since the norms remain external to the individual, complied with out of conditioned fear or anxiety or perhaps habit rather than integrated into his personal beliefs about what is morally right. In addition, internal motives that have little directly to do with the content of norms may influence responses to law. Besides general motives, such as the need to maintain cognitive balance or the need to understand and feel in control of events, motives structured by fundamental beliefs, language, and personality, for example, may be of central importance where law is imported from one culture to another or imposed by one group on another.

Secondly, the proposition that internal moral motives in themselves keep citizens law-abiding in the absence of real threat is simply not well supported by the evidence. On the contrary, the power of internalized norms to outweigh other considerations and inhibit anti-social behavior seems to be rather weak, at least in Western society. Compliance with moral norms may often be explained by reference to the heavy social costs and rewards attached to acting in ways seen as moral or immoral by others, rather than to internal motives. Where law is concerned, such considerations as the threat of sanctions, competence, and the effectiveness of court action as a means of gaining power are apparently often more important than correspondence with moral norms. Even the more general proposition that motives relating to moral and legal norms supplement or counteract each other is an oversimplification. The evidence suggests that motives acquired through moral internalization interact with each other and with other motives, skills, and features of the situation in complex ways, with sometimes unexpected results. Moral costs and rewards are reluctant to appear on the wrong side of the equation at all.

This evidence for a rather tenuous relationship between moral motives and action appears difficult to reconcile with the prominence given to concepts of morality, fairness, and deserving in people's explanations and judgments of their own and others' behavior. However, motivation to justify behavior as moral can be distinguished from motivation to act according to moral norms. Justifying one's own and others' actions as fair or morally right can carry a range of psychological, social, and material rewards. Morally motivated actions should not be confused with skill at moral justification.

The conclusions drawn so far have concerned the role of moral internalization in influencing behavior. If they are correct, this still leaves open the possibility of drawing on lack of correspondence between law and existing norms—irrespective of how they relate to behavior—to provide the basis for distinguishing imposed from other kinds of law. Such a distinction, however, seems unlikely to be useful. As has been shown, moral norms can be applied quite flexibly to justify contrary responses to the same situation, so that the relevant norm for comparison with the law may be rather difficult to identify. Moreover, lack of correspondence with moral norms does not, it seems, provide a clear criterion for distinguishing the more extreme cases of imposition. In complex societies, the relationship between moral and legal norms or rules may be no closer than it is when an alien law is imposed on another society, and the behavior of individuals in each case is as striking for its similarities as for its differences. In both situations people obey the law out of fear of sanctions, find its definitions alien and its solutions "unfair," are confused and baffled by it, use it to manipulate and gain power, and often prefer alternative ways of settling their disputes. Differences in explanation of compliance with different laws within the same society are probably as great as differences between societies.

From the individual's point of view, imposed law is probably a matter of degree. In relation both to his desires and to his internalized beliefs, all law is imposed, but some is more imposed than other. The degree to which law is experienced as imposed may lead different factors to predominate in any explanation of compliance. As well as internal motives, the relationship between legal and other, pre-existing norms affects the way in which motives arising from the individual's expectations about the behavior of others interact with the external inducements of positive and negative legal sanctions. In addition, some circumstances may be peculiar to more extreme examples of imposed law. Where a formal state legal system has not previously existed, the nature of law as imposed may be keenly felt rather than accepted as part of life. Perhaps more important are the effects of social upheaval and instability, lack of competence under a strange normative order, and conflict at a fundamental level with cultural beliefs.

REFERENCES

Andenaes, J.
  1977 "The moral or educative influence of criminal law." Pp. 50–59 in J. L. Tapp and F. J. Levine (eds.), *Law, Justice and the Individual in Society*. New York: Holt, Rinehart and Winston.
Austin, W., E. Walster, and M. Utne
  1976 "Equity and the law: the effects of a harmdoer's suffering in the act on liking and assigned punishment." Pp. 163–190 in L. Berkowitz and E. Walster (eds.), *Advances in Experimental Social Psychology*, Vol. 9. New York: Academic Press.
Deutsch, M.
  1975 "Equity, equality and need: What determines which value will be used as the basis of distributive justice?" *Journal of Social Issues* 31: 137–149.
Erikson, E. H.
  1950 *Childhood and Society*. New York: Norton.
Friedman, L. M.
  1977 "The idea of right as a social and legal concept." Pp. 69–74 in J. L. Tapp and F. J. Levine (eds.), *Law, Justice and the Individual in Society*. New York: Holt, Rinehart and Winston.
Hoffman, M.
  1977 "Moral internalization: current theory and research." Pp. 85–133 in L. Berkowitz (ed.), *Advances in Experimental Social Psychology*, Vol. 10. New York: Academic Press.
Irvine, R.
  1979 "Legal socialisation—a critique of a new approach." In D. P. Farrington, K. Hawkins, and S. Lloyd-Bostock (eds.), *Psychology, Law and Legal Process*. London: Macmillan.
Jessor, R., T. D. Graves, R. C. Hanson, and S. L. Jessor
  1968 *Society, Personality and Deviant Behavior: A Study of a Tri-ethnic Community*. New York: Holt, Rinehart and Winston.
Kohlberg, L.
  1969 "Stage and sequence: The cognitive developmental approach to socialisation." In D. Goslin (ed.), *Handbook of Socialisation Theory and Research*. New York: Rand-McNally.
Lerner, M.
  1977 "The justice motive: some hypotheses as to its origins and forms." *Journal of Personality* 45 (1):1–52.
Milgram, S.
  1963 "Behavioral study of obedience." *Journal of Personality and Social Psychology* 67: 371–378.
Nader, L.
  1975 "Forums for justice: A cross-cultural perspective." *Journal of Social Issues 31* (3): 151–169.
Nader, L., and B. Yngvesson
  1973 "On studying the ethnography of law and its consequences." In J. Honigmann (ed.), *Handbook of Social and Cultural Anthropology*. Chicago: Rand McNally.
Piaget, J.
  1932 *The Moral Judgment of the Child*. London: Routledge.
Reiss, A.
  1966 "Social organization and socialisation: variations on a theme about generations."

Mimeographed paper, Dept. of Sociology, University of Michigan (quoted in Hoffman, 1977).

Rosenhan, D.
1969 "Some origins of concern for others." In P. H. Mussen, J. Langer, and M. Covington (eds.), *Trends and Issues in Developmental Psychology*. New York: Holt, Rinehart and Winston.

Ross, M., and D. di'Tecco
1975 "An attributional analysis of moral judgments." *Journal of Social Issues 31*: 92–110.

Sampson, D.
1975 "On justice as equality." *Journal of Social Issues 31* (3): 45–63.

Schwartz, S.
1975 "The justice of need and the activation of humanitarian norms." *Journal of Social Issues 31* (3): 111–135.

Sykes, G., and D. Matza
1957 "Techniques of neutralisation: A theory of delinquency." *American Sociological Review 22*: 664–670.

Seidman, R.
1965 "Witch murder and mens rea: A problem of society under radical social change." *Modern Law Review 28*: 46–61.

Tapp, J. L., and F. J. Levine
1974 "Legal socialization: Strategies for an ethical legality." *Stanford Law Review 27* (1): 1–72.

Walster, E., E. Berscheid, and G. W. Walster
1973 "New direction in equity research." *Journal of Personality and Social Psychology 25*: 151–176.

Walster, E., and G. Walster
1975 "Equity and social justice." *Journal of Social Issues 31* (3): 21–43.

Zimring, F., and G. Hawkins
1977 "The legal threat as an instrument of social change." Pp. 60–68 in J. L. Tapp and F. J. Levine (eds.), *Law, Justice and the Individual in Society*. New York: Holt, Rinehart and Winston.

3

ON METHODS OF LEGAL INFLUENCE

VILHELM AUBERT

According to certain strong traditions in legal theory, all law is imposed law. Law, according to John Austin (1971:133), consists of "commands backed by force." His predecessor, Blackstone (1847:47), emphasized the superiority of coercion and penalties over rewards as a means to govern. And long before their time, Machiavelli (1532/1952:98) had raised the question on behalf of the prince "whether it is better to be loved more than feared, or feared more than loved? The reply is, that one ought to be both feared and loved, but as it is difficult for the two to go together, it is much safer to be feared than loved, if one of the two has to be wanting."

Within this tradition of legal and political theory, law is seen from the point of view of those who govern and enforce the law. However, when Marx and Engels (1972:165–168) challenged the assumption of benevolent, or at least legitimate, authority, they too took the view that law is a coercive system aimed at subjugating the people. At its height law could appear to be above class interest, acting simply as an arbiter between warring social groups. But, on the whole, bourgeois law was a form in which the capitalist class imposed its will upon the working class.

Against these traditions in legal theory we could pose another intellectual cur-

27

The Imposition of Law

rent with roots in Greek political theory. It is the democratic notion that the legitimate execution of power, including the enforcement of laws, depends upon the consent or will of the people. Historically, it has been linked to concepts of natural law, the belief in a law above, and binding upon, those who actually reign. But by as early as the fourteenth century Marsilius of Padua (translated 1967) had already expressed the notion that the sole source of legitimate political power was the will or consent of the people—separate from concepts of natural law with divine origins.

The blend of metaphysical and empirical elements, as well as the ambiguities in the concept of "the people," makes it difficult to establish the precise content of this current in legal and political theory. In a more or less developed form it appears in the theories of social contract, especially in Rousseau's version, in the historical school of Savigny, and in the writings of Spencer and Sumner, Petrazycki, Ehrlich, and Sorokin. In more recent times, traces of this tradition are found within Scandinavian legal realism, when some of its proponents emphasize the correspondence with the legal consciousness *(Rechtsbewusstsein)* as a defining characteristic of law (Friedmann 1967).

In the positivist and Marxist theories all law seems to be presented as imposed. If law cannot be imposed, if necessary against the will of the citizens, it is not law but some other species of normative regulation that lacks the backing of superior force. In the democratic or populistic tradition, however, the situation is reversed. If law is imposed against the will of the people or its legal consciousness and sense of justice, it is not law at all, but power, force, and suppression.

In actual practice the two views of law blend imperceptibly. Legislators in democratic societies, and even in nondemocratic ones, pay heed to the wishes and attitudes of the people, at least as these are expressed in the ballot or other public demonstrations. Those who enforce the law are also, often in very subtle ways, dependent upon a minimum amount of voluntary cooperation on the part of the groups that are the targets of the legal rules in question. On the other hand, it is clear that many laws lack solid backing in popular opinion but are nevertheless enforced with varying degrees of success.

As models, however, the two contrasting views of the law may help to elucidate the meaning of imposition. In terms of this theoretical juxtaposition, imposition has to do with the lack of correspondence between the interests, needs, attitudes, and convictions of a population and the interests and norms embedded in the law that is governing them. This formulation raises a multitude of questions. How do we establish the real, objective interests of a population or of a segment within it? Can we assume that they are adequately expressed in the articulation of a legal consciousness or some other verbal expression of opinion? And what are the interests or values embedded in the law? Is there an unambiguous answer to that, or does the law rather represent a symbolic compromise between legislators and interest groups with conflicting views on the law? And, most serious, could we say that whenever a government imposes its policy upon

a recalcitrant population, without resorting to illegal m
of law?

It would seem that the most important and drasti
have relatively little to do with law. War cannot be co
ing law, although it may result in drastic legal change
or, in the case of a war of liberation, in the liberated
wise, economic penetration into new regions may e
against which they cannot effectively defend their interests when they
with those of the imposers. Imposition takes place, but is it an imposition of law?

In what follows, I shall not attempt to go any further in the analysis of power
phenomena as such, but rather try to elucidate some elements in legal technique,
the means by which the living conditions, the behavior, and the values of people
could be influenced through the conscious use of legislation and law enforcement. I shall first deal with the sanctions and inducements of which modern law
avails itself. Then I shall deal with the logic of legal rules and the messages they
communicate. A final section examines some methodological obstacles to the
study of law as a means of achieving social goals.

SANCTIONS, INDUCEMENTS, AND
RESOURCE DISTRIBUTION

In order to put the following remarks into a more general perspective, I shall,
for this purpose, divide the functions of law into four overlapping categories:
governance, conflict resolution, resource distribution, and symbolic goal setting.
Our concern here is with governance, with the use of law to influence people,
especially to change their behavior or attitudes. But as a result of the demands
upon the law—to varying degrees—to perform simultaneously some or all of the
other three functions, the legislator cannot pursue this goal wholeheartedly. The
legislator who wants the most effective communication with the law's target
group may want to use simple pedagogical language in the written statement of
law but is restrained from doing so by the demands of judges and other lawyers
for technical precision which is necessary for the purpose of litigation and adjudication.

On the other hand, the legislator may seem to want a change of behavior or
attitudes in the population toward some vaguely formulated value. However, the
laxity of enforcement and the absence of adequate provisions to make the law effective may be a symptom that the law serves a symbolic function and is not intended as a means of governance. It may, as Thurman Arnold (1938) pointed
out long ago, rather cover up conflicts and contradictions among the legislators
themselves.

Traditionally, theorists of governance through legal influence have, as mentioned earlier, emphasized coercion, threats, and deterrence. One reason for the
reliance upon penalties and threats must be sought in a principle we may term

onomy of sanctions.'' It was clearly expressed by Machiavelli 1952:97): ''A prince, therefore, must not mind incurring the charge of ▲lty for the purpose of keeping his subjects united and faithful, for, with a very few examples, he will be more merciful than those who, from the excess of tenderness, allow disorders to arise, from whence spring bloodshed and rapine, for those as a rule injure the whole community, while the executions carried out by the prince injure only individuals.''

The principle was repeated by Blackstone and by his nearly contemporary Danish colleague Nørregaard (1784:34), who put it this way: ''It would be impossible for the state to reward all compliance with the law and thus procure, for example, 1000 obedient subjects, instead of punishing one transgressor.'' In recent years the relationship between penalties and rewards has been discussed in a similar vein by the American legal sociologists Schwartz and Orleans (1973:63–97): ''Sanctions are officially imposed punishment aimed at enforcement of legal obligations. They are said to constitute the core, if not the defining characteristic, of the legal order.'' They go on to say: ''Our legal system contains very few instances in which people are explicitly rewarded for compliance, rather than punished for deviance . . . for reasons of economy explicit rewards tend to be employed where only small segments of the population are supposed to be their recipients. . . . Extension of rewards to all who observe the law would be expensive, difficult to administer, and ineffective if the recipients were numerous.''

Originally, the principle of sanction economy was invented in societies where the state commanded relatively limited resources apart from the monopoly of physical coercion. And the technology of punishment was cheap. To execute people by decapitation, hanging, or shooting, or to punish criminals by inflicting bodily injury upon them cost very little. Today, incarceration has replaced bodily injury and the death penalty in most industrialized societies, and prisons are expensive installations. On the other hand, through an effective system of taxation, modern states control a large part of the national product. As Charles Reich (1964:733) put it: ''One of the most important developments in the United States during the past decade has been the emergence of government as a major source of wealth. Government is a gigantic syphon. It draws in revenue and power, and pours forth wealth: money, benefits, services, franchises, and licenses.''

As a consequence of this development, the conditions under which the principle of the economy of sanctions operates have changed a great deal. Severe penalties must be used sparingly. A fine is the major vehicle of sanction economy on the penalty side. Vast numbers of laws are studded with penalty clauses stipulating a fine as the normal sanction. How they are enforced is, by and large, unknown. On the the resource side, discussed by Reich, there arises a question of distinguishing between handouts that are intended to reward meritorious behavior, and money or services that must be seen simply as a mode of distributing the wealth among the citizens.

Before we enter into that question, however, we must have a closer look at one assumption that underlies all reasoning about santions. One assumes that it is possible, or even easy, to distinguish between goods and burdens, between satisfying and frustrating events in the encounter between the citizen and the public authorities. Does this assumption hold generally or in certain areas?

Private law does not have governance as a direct and primary aim. Within the framework of the rules of the game of the market—protecting property rights and fulfilling valid contracts—the actors arrange their own affairs. The law does not make specific demands upon them but serves rather as a means to prevent or settle disputes. Thus, if conflicts arise, the rules of private law may be a resource for one of the parties while incurring a disadvantage for the other party. There are both a winner and a loser in such cases, since the litigation does not add to the value of that which is to be distributed between the litigants. On the contrary, legal suits regularly incur costs for one or both of the parties.

Research has shown that within the criminal law the introduction of therapeutic and pedagogical measures has created an ambiguous situation. It is hard to draw the line between measures that represent resources and measures that represent disadvantages to the offenders. However, it seems that on balance the disadvantages outweigh the advantages and that also the resocializing measures might constitute threats to the offenders, the disclaimer of penal intent notwithstanding.

On the other hand, penalties for breaches of confidentiality by medical doctors, lawyers, or census bureaus are looked upon as resources by the groups that constitute the targets of the penal threats. The penal clause is necessary in support of the credibility of these professionals when they promise their patients, clients, and informants to keep privileged information secret. It may also give public agencies an acceptable reason for keeping secrets that might be more revealing about their own weaknesses than about those of their clientele.

Schelling (1965) has pointed out that as a general principle it is often an advantage for a party to a negotiation to stand under some kind of external threat that makes his future behavior more predictable to the other party. The civil sanctions—invalidity or indemnity charges that might accrue from a breach of promise—are often necessary in order to make promises credible.

Certain important types of rights and duties for the citizens contain simultaneously elements of burdens and of resources. This is true of schooling, of military service, and of hospitalization on psychiatric or related grounds. Pensions to not-so-old people and to those who seem incapable of performing available jobs have been discussed from this point of view. The money received constitutes, no doubt, a resource. But could it not also be seen as an inferior alternative to government-created job opportunities for those who have lost some of their working capacity, but not all of it?

This latter point leads to a consideration of laws and mechanisms of resource distribution as elements in larger systems. Their effects cannot be gauged in isolation but must be determined in relation to other laws and other similar mechanisms. We shall return later to the problems connected with the systemic character of legal means of influence and governance.

Let us turn to the question of resource distribution as a means to reward desirable behavior on the part of the citizens. There are some relatively clear-cut cases where the intent, albeit not the sole intent, of an award is to encourage people to act in a certain way in support of a publicly defined goal. Special subsidies to firms that are established in peripheral regions in Norway are a typical example. The conditions under which such subsidies can be granted, as well as the character of the subsidies, are specified in a separate code. A closely parallel attempt by the Norweigian government to encourage another sector of the economy, dairy farming, through milk subsidies is, however, not regulated by law, but is based upon parliament's general authority to make appropriations over the state budget.

Milk subsidies reach the individual farmer through the general price mechanism, independent of any application on his part or any evaluation of the merits of his farming. This contrasts with the system for subsidizing industrial development in peripheral regions and also with many aspects of the agricultural subsidy system. In fact, a whole plethora of arrangements—through grants, subsidies, loans, licensing—exists to encourage people to behave in certain desired ways. These systems are regulated by law, although they do not fall into the area covered by the principle of *nulla poena sine lege.* On closer inspection, however, one can see how they raise important problems in relation to the rule of law, problems that the milk subsidies do not evoke.

Laws whose major and explicit goal is to specify what and how and to whom to bestow benefits involve issues such as the grounds for and consequences of withholding resources. Charles Reich, (1964) emphasizes this aspect of the functions of the interventionistic modern state. It can use its command of positive resources, its systems of licensing, franchising, etc., as a means of administrative social control without formally violating the rule of law.

To what extent the denial of an advantage or a privilege is a penalty depends upon the motivation of the denial as well as upon whether one could normally expect an application to be granted. To withhold a passport or to invalidate a driver's license on political grounds would clearly be considered a punishment and a rather severe one at that. Expulsion from government service because of professional incompetence would be a somewhat more dubious case. The refusal of a loan from a public bank for the establishment of an industry on the grounds of inadequate planning or the unlikelihood of achieving a viable mode of production and marketing should probably not be regarded as a penalty. However, the unsuccessful applicant might come to look upon the negative response as evidence of the coercive power of the state, if not as a penalty. The perspectives of the granting agencies and the applicants on such decisions are notoriously at variance.

Many types of resource distribution have, clearly, no rewarding intent. Within the field of social insurance and health policy, it is clear that care, treatment, and support of ailing people are not intended to encourage the occurrence of ailments. But then it is assumed that illness and invalidism are unamenable to manipulation by conscious choice. In certain borderline areas, such as alcoholism, pension authorities, in making discretionary decisions against an applicant, have sometimes been suspected of harboring disciplinarian motives or of attempting to deter people from drinking.

The examples of resource distribution as a legal means of inducement have the common characteristic that the application must be granted if the applicant fulfills the criteria specified by the law. Thus, viewed as a reward, many of these bestowals violate the principle of sanction economy. They are, as Schwartz and Orleans (1973) claim, costly. Others, however, are not.

Licensing does not cost the government much beyond the maintenance of agencies to administer the necessary evaluation. What the recipient gains is an immunity to the threat of penalties for unlawfully engaging in those privileged activities, such as driving a car or running a shop. The government uses its authority to inflict penalties as a means of distributing privileges. In other cases it may use this penal authority to protect the licensed from the competition of the unlicensed, through patent rights or professional monopolies.

What we have not yet come across are exemplary rewards: the use of a few high prizes to encourage many to strive toward excellence rather than merely adequate performance. We may have located positive sanctions but not sanctions that form a counterpart to penal sanctions. The latter rely much upon general deterrence and the use of exemplary penalties or, at least, penalties that are known to hit only a small sample of those who qualify.

The negative counterparts to the inducements mentioned above are certain kinds of taxes, fees, and customs. Progressive income taxation does not aim to reduce the motivation to work hard, although it may have that effect upon certain groups of taxpayers. But taxes on the consumption of tobacco and alcohol are intended to some extent to discourage people from excessive smoking and drinking. One interesting aspect of this method of governance is that it penalizes certain behavior without drawing any distinction between lawful and unlawful behavior. Conceivable conflicts with the rule of law are avoided through the use of the general price mechanism in preference to a system of individual licensing and prohibition.

Exemplary rewards are less evident in modern legislation, but they do occur. In Norwegian law one can find some codes authorizing lotteries or other such devices. These encourage people to participate in investments in certain activities, the outcomes of which depend upon a regulated and controlled mechanism of chance. The issuing of premium bonds is a typical instance of the use of an exemplary reward. Many may be induced to save in this form by the hope of becoming a winner or by the attraction of the suspense, but few will actually win the prizes.

Certain kinds of competition arranged by state authorities may fall into the same category, although one does not often find the principles of these competitive arrangements directly authorized in law. Bestowals of medals and honors and also certain kinds of mercy and remission may have exemplary intent and/or effects. In practice, the most important type of competition outside the market is perhaps the system of examinations, authorizations, and promotions in government-dominated areas of activity. Many exert themselves in order to obtain grades or ranks, but few actually achieve them.

I have dealt with the difficulties of using the economy of sanctions in resource distribution in another context (Aubert 1977:1–19). The rule of law demands predictability, and this cannot be obtained under conditions of competition. If the competing parties have a guarantee of a certain result, the competitive element is excluded. Thus, we would expect to find the use of exemplary rewards in areas where the market, with its competitive mechanisms and its specific morality, penetrates into public administration. The labor market within the government services is an example of such a borderline area.

The panorama of sanctions, inducements, and distribution devices outlined above shows that it would be difficult to draw a distinction between legal imposition or governance and other modes of exerting power and influence. One implication of this may be that a transfer of law from one society to another on a major scale can take place today only as part of a more general penetration into economic and political spheres.

VALUES AND NORMS

The great disparities between statutes pertaining to different areas, having different aims, and employing different methods of sanctioning and communicating call for a typology of legal rules. One important dimension can be formulated in terms of the two concepts "value" and "norm." By a value I refer to a goal: the perceived end-product of individual actions or of coordinated social interaction programs. There is a subjective as well as an objective referent to the concept of value. It may refer to the desired object or state of affairs as a reality, something that exists out there or that could be made to exist. But value may also refer to an image in the mind, as in a blueprint: for example, a statute depicting a desirable state of affairs or containing an evaluation. When the term *value* is used here the context will probably make it clear what referent is intended.

By norm I refer to a rule of behavior. The tendency in traditional law is to demarcate the borderline between acceptable and nonacceptable behavior, while often leaving open the question of what would constitute excellent behavior. The law deals with marginal behavior; it sets the minimum standards of conduct. In Lon Fuller's (1964) terms, it is a morality of obligation, not one of aspiration.

The enforcement of the rule of law in the confrontation with crime has been closely linked to a legislative technique, the backbone of which is constituted by a set of precisely formulated prescriptions of unlawful behavior. It is characteristic of norms, in the somewhat restricted interpretation we put upon the term, that they present social and behavioral activities as a map with clear borders marking the distinction between compliance and noncompliance, but with a more or less empty space inside the limits of acceptable behavior. This focuses the attention upon borderline problems, upon ambiguities, uncertainty, and transgressions, often upon rather hypothetical or rare cases of doubt. This has left a deep imprint upon the legal mind.

In spatial terms a map of values would be structured around points of attraction, in-between which would be varying degrees of light and shade indicating the degree to which behavior is conducive to furthering the value. The borderline problems are less prominent. It is, in principle, possible to gauge degrees of excellence, the level of approximation to the ideal, or the probability that a chosen course of action will lead to the stated goal.

Modern law abounds with examples of formulations where a goal is established to further resocialization of criminals or general law obedience, to give youngsters an opportunity to become useful citizens (school legislation), to establish employment opportunities in peripheral regions, or references to fairness and honesty in marketing, etc. These I would subsume under the term *values*. By norms I refer here to those traditional formulations of rules that clearly delimit what is forbidden—defining theft or assault and battery, for example— not to speak of all the procedural norms and rules that stipulate the formal conditions for validity of wills and marriage contracts.

The distinction between values and norms is a relative one in terms of the verbal formulas chosen as well as the deductions that can be made on the basis of the clause in question. In a norm-formulated clause, the implicit value may be quite clear. And certain value clauses may indicate what kinds of behavioral norms are to be derived from them. Not infrequently, however, the distinction presents itself as one between means (norms) and ends (values), and this relationship may be encumbered by considerable uncertainty, leaving a wide area for interpretation and discretionary decisions. This is especially so when the law relies heavily upon value formulations, for example, upon the general clause technique.

The distinction between the two types of legislative technique is related to differences in modes of handling problems and conflicts. What is specifically relevant here is the distinction between the deductive or syllogistic element in legal thinking, which presupposes precise norms, and the scientific approach, which looks upon concrete behavior in terms of its consequences relative to stated goals. The choice between different legislative and conflict-solving techniques has implications for the furtherance of the two, partly contradictory, ideals of efficiency and rule of law.

The rule of law demands a great reliance upon behavioral norms within the area of crime and punishment. This principle has been frayed at the edges and sometimes undermined by utilitarian principles. The meting out of penalty and the choice between different types of reactions are left to a high degree to the discretion of the court, assisted by nonlegal experts, or even transferred to welfare agencies outside the judiciary. The definitions of punishable actions have remained intact, however, if we confine ourselves to the law in books. If we observe the practice of police and prosecution, a different picture emerges. All kinds of extenuating or mitigating circumstances, as well as practical routines, case loads, and so on, determine (to a large extent on a discretionary basis) what charges will be brought or dropped.

The uncertain and somewhat arbitrary, or at least unpredictable, behavior of the prosecuting attorneys and the police follows in part from the need for economy and highly selective enforcement. It is a characteristic of penal laws that they are applied only in a fraction of those situations where they could have been enforced. This is also true with respect to many rules of contractual law. But in public law the legal provisions are, with fewer exceptions, actually applied when the occasion arises—for example, after an application for a benefit, an exception, a license or certificate, a franchise, or a grant or loan.

One reason why the strict principles of the rule of law have been set aside in criminal policy is that a perceptual blurring of the negative and the positive content of sanctions has taken place. Penalties have been substituted by, or been confounded with, resocializing, educational, or therapeutic programs. The new professions that have been made responsible for these programs, as well as their imagined or real benevolence, tend to diminish the emphasis upon the rule of law.

The two types of legal rules and legislative techniques are symptoms of two types of logic: a logic of deduction and a logic of prediction, to put it simply. The logic of deduction has ancient roots in legal thinking and is to a large extent derived from the demands that arise out of disputes where a third party is called upon to make a decision. The logic of prediction is that which we find embedded most firmly in some of the natural sciences, but also more recently in economics, psychology, and sociology. These two types of logic are becoming enmeshed in each other. Law is encroaching more and more on those fields where previously medical men, engineers, economists, and practical men of affairs were left to their own devices and ways of thinking. Science, on the other hand, is permeating law to the extent that the trial judge often acts upon the predictive advice of psychiatrists and similar experts. He may also act, in his own right, as an expert on the social consequences of his application of the law.

The blending of law and science has two types of consequences. When the law relies heavily upon value formulations or expressions of social goals and delegates discretionary power to social policy experts, the decision-making process becomes "delegalized." The rule of law is becoming less firm in the sense that it may become more difficult for the citizen to ascertain precisely what his rights are and how he could go about protecting them if he felt that the experts had mistakenly violated his interests. Rights, although possibly increasing in quantity and quality, are becoming less justiciable.

The other side of the coin is the process of "legalization," whereby previously unregulated transactions and decisions are made subject to law. Decisions that used to be considered part of market transactions or belonging to the domain of a profession are becoming vulnerable to a challenge from the consumer, the client, or the patient on the basis of justiciable rights. A most striking example of this latter tendency is the growth of legal suits against medical doctors on the grounds of some professional failure. Generally speaking, the tendency toward legalization is probably a corollary of the growth of responsibility of the welfare states.

An urgent task of the sociology of law is to contribute to a clarification of the dilemmas involved in this trend. This would also include a closer scrutiny of the fate of the jury system, a problem I have not been able to deal with in this context. Delegalization may be a threat to the rule of law with certain anti-democratic implications. This is one aspect of the debate about the dangers of leaving too much power in the hands of experts, usually experts other than those trained in law. But delegalization may also pose problems when decision making and the provision of a service are left to lay members of a community, acting on the basis of some elective principle or informal consent. I am referring to situations like the one in which housewives with some time to spare could contribute very efficient and inexpensive service to old people, children, and handicapped individuals in their neighborhood on a semiprofessional basis. But what if such systems fail to be established or do not function properly? The system as such may be superior to a bureaucratic system in terms of the total amount and quality of the services provided. However, if something goes wrong it may be difficult to assign responsibility and find a remedy. To deal with situations where something goes wrong has been a major responsibility of the law and of legal personnel, and it also occupies a good deal of politicians' time and energy, Here lies, probably, one of the sources of resistance to decentralization in the decision-making process.

There seems to be an inherent tendency in the welfare states toward legalization, which has been running parallel to the growth of the power of experts. One aspect of this could be that the "morality of obligations," emphasizing compliance with minimum standards, is gaining ground among the experts at the expense of the "morality of excellence." The increasing vulnerability of the medical profession may encourage a tendency to play safe by following technical test routines that may be expensive and time consuming but not necessarily the best way of dealing with the patient's complaints. The profession and the scientific community may reward the daring innovation or other signs of excelling, but the law does not.

THE METHODOLOGY OF STUDYING LEGAL IMPACT

Some 200 years ago legal theory, which was at the time permeated by notions of natural law, branched off in two new directions. On a foundation of natural law Adam Smith established a new science of economics and an ideology of the free market. A little later Jeremy Bentham, while declaring his opposition to the natural law of Blackstone, created a new science of legislation based upon the calculus of utilities, which was in practice closely related to the calculus of utilities underlying economic thinking.

In retrospect, Adam Smith appears as the founding father of modern economics, a branch of learning that has, at least on the surface, undergone a pattern of growth and development similar to that of a natural science. Economics has turned out to be a cumulative branch of learning. It has been cumulative in a chronological sense, showing a certain capacity to preserve, systematize, and learn from past experience. It is also cumulative in the sense that it has provided a basis for large organizations occupied by the gathering and analysis of masses of economic data, in a more or less concerted, albeit not too successful, effort to predict and control.

In his time Bentham seemed, as much as Adam Smith, to be in the process of laying the foundations of a new science of legislation. In retrospect, however, Bentham appears as a lone voice in the desert in his role of spokesman for a sociological study of the impact of legislation, although his general approach had considerable influence upon future legislators.

The social science of legislation has not advanced much since the time of Bentham, although the number of trained lawyers has increased a great deal. The laws have been systematized to a high degree and the internal logic of the legal system has been made more consistent. New bills are carefully prepared with the assistance of legal experts as well as a variety of fact-finding agencies and personnel. But these efforts lack the cumulative impact that can be perceived in the growth of economics. If there is a cumulative tendency, it is embodied in the statutory law itself more than in legal, let alone sociolegal, scholarship.

Deterrence is one of the topics on which Bentham shed considerable light. In recent years studies have been conducted that, as isolated pieces of research, are definitely superior to Bentham's speculations. To these studies the researchers have brought formidable statistical techniques and sophisticated methods of data-gathering. But the general theory of deterrence has not progressed much, if at all, since Bentham. There is little advice to be gained from research on where and how and with what kind of sanctions one might influence people to comply with the law (Andenaes 1975:338–365). And there is even less illumination to be gained on theoretical issues that arise in this area.

Why has this situation arisen, and why is it so different from the picture we have of economics as a science? It cannot be explained simply in terms of the failure of lawyers rooted in the conservatism of the profession to utilize a scientific approach. It must have something to do with the essential differences between the subject matter of the sciences: the market and the law.

The market is a system in a sense in which law is not a system. Changes in certain parts of the market system have calculable repercussions in other parts of the system. All values can be translated into money. In contrast, the law is a system in a vague, logical or quasi-logical sense. It is the task of legal personnel, including legislators, to uphold and develop further this systematic aspect of the law. Some have presented it as a deductive system. But that is claiming too much. Whatever one may say about the degree of consistency in the law, it is a system of words, terms, concepts, and rules. It is not a system of action or behavior. Legal scholarship may deal with a system in the normative sense, but the sociology of law does not. That is one reason for the apparent lack of theoretical structure within the study of law.

The latter point may be illustrated by the fact that a legal system is consistent or inconsistent irrespective of whether the frequency of noncompliant acts is high or low, at least within certain wide limits. Traditional legal scholarship does not deal in terms of frequencies. Whether a type of case occurs once in a decade or many times a day does not matter from the point of view of the lawyer. In the market, frequencies are vital: Every transaction counts as a contribution to the GNP.

When we concern ourselves with the social impact of legislation, we have to deal with frequencies. How many motorists drive in a drunken state under specified conditions with respect to rules, inspections, and sanctions? If such questions can be answered, the answers remain isolated findings without known or even knowable repercussions. The fact that the law against drunken driving is logically consistent with the other parts of the criminal law is no great help. However, one may dimly perceive that if an increased level of noncompliance with the law requires more supervising personnel on the roads or more space in the prisons, this would, in a way reminiscent of the market, have consequences for the opportunity to pursue other legal aims. Controls and sanctions are scarce resources, and there may be regularities in their distribution. They may be translated into taxpayers' money.

One difficulty with this economic approach to the impact of social legislation is that some sanctions, like the death penalty, are cheap in money but very costly in human and political terms. An even more serious difficulty is that there is no common denominator on the effect side. How could one make a comparison between a reduced incidence of drunken driving, resulting in a lower accident rate, and a reduction in shoplifting or tax-evasion, let alone nonpayment of debts. The market necessarily involves quantification, whereas the law does not. The two disciplines speak different languages. The sociologist has barely begun the task of translating the various values involved in lawmaking, law enforcement, and legal impact, and we do not know what his chances of success are.

By picking out deterrence in the criminal law, I have made the situation in the sociolegal area seem more chaotic than it is. One may point to large areas of administrative law where the lawmaker has achieved massive conformity of behavior on the part of the personnel and also among clients of the agency in question. Pensions are being paid out according to the laws, traffic regulations are being more complied with than violated, and so on. There must be a mechanism, or mechanisms, by which people, especially in organizations, are capable of being ordered more or less in accordance with standards set from above. What are these mechanisms?

All I can do here is to make some vague suggestions about the direction I think further analysis should take. Studies of deterrence work with a stimulus-response model, assuming relatively rational behavior analogous to the economic man in the market. This is a one-sided approach of limited research potential. It would be a fallacy to transfer the assumptions underlying the study of the market to the study of behavior within organizations.

Public servants are paid for administering the law pertaining to their fields of authority. Their careers depend to some extent upon the way in which they execute "the will of the lawmaker." To interpret these actions predominantly as behavior on a labor market would, however, be a mistake. Markets and organizations differ with respect to the ideologies that govern them. To be egoistic in the market carries a meaning for the actors very different from being similarly egoistic as a member of an organization, say an employee of a public agency. People are not simply need-satisfying organisms; they seek—and seem to find—meaning in what they do, even in what they have to do. For a member of an organization, *esprit de corps*—solidarity with co-workers and leaders—becomes an important source of meaning and motivation. The material advantages gained by deviating from formal obligations are easily outweighed by the distastefulness of a meaningless job. The charter laws of public bureaucracies are primary sources of meaning for the employees. It is necessary when studying the impact of law to abandon the simple-minded hedonistic image of man which has bedeviled so much research in this era.

This does not mean that public agencies and their clientele automatically obey any legislative enactment or execute the statutes with maximum efficiency. One reason why bureaucracies show a willingness to carry out the requirements of the laws is that these administrative laws owe much of their contents to initiatives from the very agencies whose performance they regulate. They share responsibility with the formal legislators for the laws. The laws are not imposed upon them. However, this sharing of responsibility may not reach the lower rungs of the bureaucratic ladder, thus leaving room for divergent attitudes and conflicts within the organizations charged with the task of executing the laws. Some laws may even be sabotaged if they run counter to the interests or ideologies of the personnel.

Studies of legal impact have tended to focus upon situations where the legal message is supposed to reach its target group without complicated intermediary organizations. Studies of the impact of drunken driving laws are in this respect not representative. Many statutes of great social significance operate, if they function at all, through dense layers of bureaucratic agencies, public as well as private. Tax laws are good examples, filtered as they are through the public taxation offices and furthermore through the firms where the taxpayer is employed and his tax is deducted on payday.

It is an old experience, which also occurs in the area of traditional criminal law, that legal sanctions are often accompanied by other social sanctions, and that the latter in many instances may be the more powerful ones. In administrative law the environment contributes to the sanctioning system, not only as an informal social pressure but as a formal system of control and inducement. The legal and the extra-legal processes are interwoven in complex patterns that are not easily accessible to the observer. Thus, administrative laws unsupported by the proper resources of finance and personnel may remain symbols without real impact.

Legal impact is an ambiguous term. It immediately directs attention toward the connection between legal innovation and social change. This approach seems fitting enough in relation to administrative law in the welfare sector, to banking and credit legislation, and also to what has been termed market law. In the core of the criminal law, in procedural law, and in the traditional civil law (in both civil law and common law systems)—property, torts, and contracts—the question of legal impact presents itself in a somewhat different perspective. It cannot be assumed that the aim of the law in these areas is to effect changes. They must often be interpreted primarily as a means to consolidate or protect, not least to protect the operation of market mechanisms. This is not to deny that modern market legislation aims at regulating market mechanisms.

When legal reforms were introduced under the ideological mantle of economic liberalism and laissez faire, they were regarded as a means of social change. It was felt that if old statutes and ordinances that had restricted trade and the establishment of new enterprises were abolished, a process of social change would ensue. However, the function of the law was considered a passive one: to do away with state interference so that the inherent dynamism in the economy could unfold itself. But from the point of view of social change, those legal reforms of the nineteenth century did not, in principle, differ from some of the modern market legislation. For the latter also presupposes the independent existence of individual motivation as well as social structures and processes that, through the intervention of new legal controls, will lead to desired goals, such as better products for the consumer or more employment opportunities. But whereas legislators in the nineteenth century took a permissive attitude toward strong economic interests and tended to restrain state control, the emphasis in this century has shifted to a more directive approach, where the state plays a more active role through subvention, subsidies, loans, and advice.

The law of contracts has shown a great deal of continuity in Scandinavia as well as in other western European countries. This is also true in corporate law. Changes have been piecemeal and gradual and to a large extent left in the hands of lawyers. A group of relatively conservative professionals has manned the committees charged with preparing bills revising old laws or codifying business customs. Judges with similar ideological leanings have interpreted and enforced the laws while adjusting them to changing social and economic conditions. Thus, one might be led to the conclusion that this is a field of the law characterized more by preservation and stability than by change.

However, within the framework of a relatively stable, although not unchanging, set of legal rules defining and delimiting the freedom of contract, a series of new contractual forms and corporate structures has arisen. In this process the inventiveness of lawyers in private practice has played an important part. Thus, it would be somewhat misleading to maintain that this is an extra-legal development, facilitated by the absence of law rather than by law. It is, on the whole, questionable whether one is justified in making much of the contrast between the legislator's commissions and omissions.

Many of the newer contractual forms and corporate structures could have been prohibited, and some of the innovations have actually been forbidden or placed under restrictions. But how are we to deal with the problems of legal impact when it means tracing the consequences of a lack of legislative initiative? Under what conditions is this a relevant sociological problem? The answer must refer to possible alternative developments presuming activity on the part of the lawmakers and a certain opportunity to estimate the probable consequences of hypothetical enactments. Such speculative work, as it would necessarily be, is called for, particularly if there is a social demand for legal regulation. One might say that the study of failure to initiate new bills becomes more pertinent when the demand is more widespread, the interest groups behind it are stronger, and the sources of the demand are closer to the government.

CONCLUSIONS

In order for laws to have an impact, the message must reach its target, and there must be some inducement to comply with the expectations expressed in it. I have dealt with a few selected aspects of these two connected issues—what sanctions are used and how the message is construed—and have tried to explain why the sociological study of these problems has shown such limited progress. It would have been helpful if I could also have pointed to a way out of this predicament. I can only make a few suggestions:

1. Sociology of law must work closely with theories of organizations, for it is through organizations that modern law primarily becomes effective, if at all.
2. In these studies the ties to the old definition of law as an exclusively coercive order must be broken and much emphasis be laid upon the legislator as a distributor of resources.
3. More emphasis must be put upon law as a part of the total social system, a point derived from the speculation about economics and law as systems. Society is our concern, and among sociologists law has for a long time been a neglected element in the social structure.
4. One must pay more attention to the very meaning of the "impact of law and legislation." Distinctions must be made between change and conservation, between fundamental and more trivial changes, and between the consequences of legislative commissions and omissions.

REFERENCES

Andenaes, J.
    1975   "General prevention revisited: Research and policy implications." *The Journal of Criminal Law and Criminology 66:* 338–365.
Arnold, T.
    1938   *The Symbols of Government.* New Haven: Yale University Press.
Aubert, V.
    1977   "On sanctions," In *European Yearbook in Law and Sociology.* The Hague: Martinus Nijhoff.
Austin, J.
    1971   *The Province of Jurisprudence Determined.* London: Weidenfeld and Nicolson. (First edition 1832.)
Blackstone, W.
    1847   *Commentaries on the Laws of England, I.* London: John Murray. (First edition 1765.)
Engels, F.
    1972   *Der Ursprung der Familie, des Privateigentums und des Staats.* In K. Marx and F. Engels, *Werke. Band 21.* Berlin: Dietz Verlag.
Friedmann, W.
    1967   *Legal Theory* (5th ed.). London: Stevens & Sons.
Fuller, L.
    1964   *The Morality of Law.* New Haven and London: Yale University Press.
Machiavelli, N.
    1952   *The Prince.* New York: New American Library. (First published 1532.)
Marsilius of Padua
    1967   *The Defender of Peace,* translated and with an introduction by Alan Gewirth. New York: Columbia University Press. (Defensor Pacis, 1324.)
Marx, K. and F. Engels
    1972   *Werke. Band 21.* Berlin: Dietz Verlag
Nørregaard, L.
    1974   *Forelæsninger over den Danske og Norske Private Ret* (Lectures on the Danish and Norwegian Civil Law). Copenhagen: A. Loldin.
Reich, C. A.
    1964   "The new property." *The Yale Law Journal 73:* 733.
Schelling, T. C.
    1965   *The Strategy of Conflict.* Cambridge: Harvard University Press.
Schwartz, R. D., and S. Orleans
    1973   "On legal sanctions." In Michael Barkun (ed.), *Law and the Social System.* New York: Lieber-Atherton.

4

THE DEATH PENALTY IN THE UNITED STATES: IMPOSED LAW AND THE ROLE OF MORAL ELITES

HUGO ADAM BEDAU

The conclusion is inescapable, we think, that this rare penalty, inflicted upon the smallest handful of murderers, is no part of the regular criminal-law machinery of . . . any . . . State. It is a freakish aberration, a random extreme act of violence, visibly arbitrary and discriminatory—a penalty reserved for unusual application because, if it were usually used, it would affront universally shared standards of public decency. Such a penalty . . . has no place in a democratic government.[1]

[The Attorneys for NAACP Legal Defense Fund] have set themselves up as the guardians of evolving standards of decency, and they are asking this Court to set itself up as a super legislature.[2]

THE DEATH PENALTY AND IMPOSED LAW: TWO MODELS

Let us begin by considering two examples drawn from the recent history of capital punishment in the United States. Curiously enough, both occurred in Oregon (Bedau 1965, 1979).

[1] Attorneys for the NAACP Legal Defense Fund, brief on behalf of the petitioner, *Aikens* v. *California,* in the Supreme Court of the United States, October Term 1971; reprinted in Mackey (1976:288).

[2] Ronald M. George, Deputy Attorney General of California, during the oral argument before the Supreme Court on 6 January 1972 in *Aikens* v. *California;* quoted in Meltsner (1973:272).

45

1. In the mid-1950s, the governor of Oregon, Robert D. Holmes, announced that henceforth he would commute any death sentence that reached his desk in a clemency proceeding. On conscientious grounds he was completely opposed to capital punishment, and he intended to use his commutation authority in accordance with his convictions. During his one term as chief executive, he did commute all (three) death sentences that came before him; no legal executions occurred in Oregon during his term of office. As he knew, however, there was no public clamor to end executions, nor was there a long history of abolition only recently reversed by a maverick legislature. No commission on criminal law reform in Oregon had called upon the governor to end the death penalty summarily by exercise of his clemency power. Nor could the governor defend his initiative as a reasonable anticipation of imminent repeal of capital statutes by the Oregon legislature or of their invalidation by the Oregon appellate judiciary. Capital indictments may have been infrequent, but so was murder; jury nullification in capital cases was unknown. In short, Governor Holmes's policy of commutation amounted to a virtual edict, and came as close to the imposition of law—in this instance, the abrupt suspension of the constitutionally authorized and duly enacted death penalty, in favor of a substitute punishment of life imprisonment—as is possible in a constitutional democracy.

2. A decade later, in the mid-1960s, the people of Oregon voted to revise the state constitution so as to abolish the death penalty for all crimes and to substitute a punishment of ''life'' imprisonment. This was done, after extensive public discussion in all the media, at a duly constituted referendum and after enactment by the Oregon legislature of the relevant statutes should the referendum pass. Pass it did: it was carried in all but 4 of Oregon's 36 counties; and in the most populous, Multnomah, where the abolition campaign was concentrated, the referendum was endorsed in a ratio of almost 2 to 1. The total vote was an impressive 455,654 to 302,105. The death penalty had been incorporated in the state constitution since 1920, and considerable publicity and discussion preceded the vote. Nor was the issue of abolition debated wholly in the abstract; in the balance were the lives of three persons then under death sentence. Throughout the months prior to the election, no organization or spokesman emerged to defend the death penalty. It is true that the success of the referendum owed more to the skillful management of the abolition campaign by a moral elite (as we might call them) than to any irresistible upsurge of public revulsion at the spectacle of further executions. Nevertheless, unless we are to treat all law duly enacted and enforced as imposed law, the repeal of capital punishment in Oregon in the 1964 referendum qualifies as a clear case at the opposite end of the spectrum.

We have, therefore, in the first instance a model of imposed law and in the second a model of its opposite, what might be called self-imposed, or autonomously accepted, law. We may now formulate the main question to which the rest of this essay is addressed: which of these two models most nearly fits the current status of the death penalty in the United States?

THE DEATH PENALTY AFTER WORLD WAR II

As recently as the end of World War II, executions, death sentences, and capital statutes were commonplace throughout the United States.[3] All but 2 of the 50 competent jurisdictions (48 states, the District of Columbia, and the federal government) had at least one capital statute; several authorized the death penalty for any of a dozen crimes. Some of these were in the form of a mandatory death penalty; most were in the form that left choice of sentence between death or "life" imprisonment to the discretion of the trial court. Death sentences were frequent. Although most were meted out to offenders convicted of murder, in the Southern states as many as 20% each year were for rape. Executions occurred nationally at the rate of 10 per month. Public opinion, insofar as it was measured at all, was in favor of the death penalty by a ratio of two to one. Opposition to the death penalty was scattered and relatively uninformed; active concern was found mainly among the thousand or so members of the American League to Abolish Capital Punishment (founded in 1925).

The death penalty seemed securely fixed in the law. No legislature, state or federal, had abolished the death penalty for murder since Missouri had done so in 1917 (it was reinstated there 2 years later). Bills to abolish the death penalty were not uncommon; occasionally one would be scheduled for a public hearing, but rarely did the leadership allow such bills to be brought to the floor for a vote. Not until 4 decades after 1917 was any legislature to repeal any capital statute anywhere in the United States (Deets, 1948:591; Bennett 1958). In the executive branch, with powers ranging from the decision whether to indict for a capital offense to the decision whether to sign the death warrant, there was no pronounced reluctance to enforce the death penalty. Although commutations of death sentence to "life" imprisonment were not unknown, they were infrequent; probably no more than 5% of death sentences were voided in this way.

In the trial and appellate courts—state and federal—the death penalty was also a fixture. However, all but a few jurisdictions gave the trial courts statutory authority to sentence to "life" imprisonment after conviction of a capital crime, and the courts did so in most cases. The choice between the death penalty and "life" imprisonment was based on a bewildering variety of factors, ranging from sympathy through vengeance to racial or ethnic prejudice. Judges at trial rarely plea-bargained a murder defendant into prison in order to secure his conviction

---

[3] For the sources of data not otherwise indicated in the text in this section, see Bedau (1967), Bowers (1974); Mackey (1976), National Criminal Justice Information and Statistics Service (1977), and Sellin (1952).

or the conviction of his co-defendants. At the appellate court level, death-sentence convictions were occasionally reversed. The grounds for appeal were narrow, and review of state death-sentence convictions in federal courts was difficult to obtain. The constitutionality of capital punishment—despite the express requirements of "equal protection of the law" (Fourteenth Amendment), "due process of law" (Fifth and Fourteenth Amendments), and the prohibition against "cruel and unusual punishments" (Eighth Amendment)—seemed secure. No capital statute and no mode of inflicting the death penalty had ever been declared unconstitutional. No class of offenders, such as juveniles, had ever been declared constitutionally exempt from the application of a death-penalty statute. No death sentence had ever been voided by any appellate court on any ground except that the conviction on which it was based was in error.

The national history of racism powerfully distorted the use of capital punishment. This was nowhere more evident than in the sordid facts about lynching, capital punishment in the streets—the most violent symbol of black helplessness and white brutality. Not until the mid-1950s did the annual rate of lynchings decline to a level where the Bureau of the Census ceased to collect and publish data on them. Until about 1935, they occurred at the rate of more than one per month; 90% of the victims were black (Guzman 1969). As for legal executions in the South, even during the late 1940s, six blacks were put to death for each white. Every empirical study of the death penalty and race in the United States confirmed the judgment of Gunnar Myrdal: "the South makes the widest application of the death penalty and Negro criminals come in for much more than their share of the executions [1944:554]."

All things considered, then, the status of the death penalty 30 years ago in the United States hardly provides us with an instance of imposed law. Death sentences and executions were too frequent and too widely favored; commutation of death sentences and repeal of capital statutes were too rare; the whole issue of capital punishment itself hardly caused a ripple of public controversy.

THE DEATH PENALTY TODAY

Today, after a decade of significant change, the national scene is very different in several respects.[4] Capital statutes, it is true, continue in force in 36 jurisdictions. By the end of 1977, however, virtually none authorized a mandatory death sentence, and for reasons to be explained shortly, it is doubtful whether any death sentence imposed under a mandatory death statute could be carried out. Few crimes, apart from murder, including felony-murder, were subject to the death penalty. Of the 16 abolitionist jurisdictions at the beginning

---

[4] For the sources of data not otherwise indicated in the text in this section, see Bedau (1977); Bedau and Pierce (1976); Bowers (1974); Greenberg (1977); Meltsner (1973); Wolfe (1973).

of 1978, perhaps as many as 9 could be regarded as unlikely to reinstate any capital statutes.

Executions have all but ceased to occur. Except for the aberrant case of Gary Gilmore's death by firing squad in Utah on 17 January 1977, which he could have avoided or at least delayed if he had so desired, more than a decade has passed without any executions in the United States. Executions began their historic decline during World War II; they dropped noticeably again a decade later, especially in the South, where two-thirds of all executions in the United States have taken place since 1930. The greatest decline, amounting to *de facto* abolition, did not occur until a concerted legal campaign was launched to secure review of all death sentences by the federal courts and nullification on constitutional grounds of all capital statutes. This phenomenon, a central event in the entire topic under discussion, will be discussed in greater detail below.

Capital sentencing, however, has by no means come to an end, nor has it even dramatically diminished. At the beginning of 1978, there were over 400 people under death sentence in 17 states. Since the mid-1960s, when the judicially imposed moratorium on executions began, upwards of 1300 death sentences have been handed down by the trial courts in 42 jurisdictions (including Washington, D.C. and the federal government). Since the watershed year of 1972, 90% of the nation's death sentences have issued from 11 jurisdictions, 8 of them in the South. Predictably, sex, followed by race, continues to be the strongest correlate of a death sentence. No more than 1% of those sentenced to death are female, although about 23% of criminal homicides are committed by women. As for race, about 55% of all those sentenced to death are nonwhite, slightly more than the proportion of all criminal homicides committed by nonwhites (Kelley 1977:9).

The most noticeable change in regard to the death penalty in the past generation, therefore, has been the sharp drop in its actual use. All other major indicators—public attitudes, legislative policy, trial jury practices—have remained largely unchanged or have changed much less dramatically. Looked at institutionally and politically, the change that explains the decline in executions is the assault on the death penalty mounted in the federal appellate courts.

Over a period of 5 years, between 1972 and 1977, the Supreme Court of the United States forged a series of major holdings that have modified the status of the death penalty across the nation. In each of these holdings, the Court relied mainly upon the constitutional prohibition of "cruel and unusual punishments" and the constitutional requirement of "equal protection of the laws." *Furman* v. *Georgia* (1972) brought an end to capital punishment as generally practiced, because the Court ruled that trial courts, in exercising arbitrary and discriminatory power to sentence in capital cases, violated the Constitution. During the next 4 years, dozens of state legislatures (though not Congress) reinstituted capital punishment through statutes believed to be consistent with the *Furman* ruling. Some states enacted mandatory death penalties; the others enacted capital statutes with explicit guidelines to control the trial court's choice between a death or a "life" sentence. In *Woodson* v. *North Carolina* (1976), the Supreme Court struck down the mandatory death penalty for murder, and a year later, in *Roberts* v. *Louisiana,* the Court extended its ruling to include the punishment for murder of a police officer. In both rulings the Court argued that the Constitution required "individualizing sentencing determinations" and "consideration of whatever mitigating circumstances may be relevant," which was impossible under statutes mandating the death penalty. In *Coker* v. *Georgia* (1977), the Court struck down the death sentence for rape, even if applied by a jury under statutory guidelines permitting the consideration of mitigating circumstances, on the ground that given the relative gravity of the offense, the severity of the punishment was "excessive" and therefore an unconstitutionally "cruel and unusual punishment."

Although these rulings boosted the campaign to secure judicial abolition of the death penalty, they fell short of a ruling that capital punishment per se was unconstitutional. In *Gregg* v. *Georgia* (1976) and its companion cases, the Supreme Court upheld several different capital statutes, all of which imposed the death penalty for murder under procedures that required the trial courts to weigh mitigating as well as aggravating factors relevant to the determination of sentence. Thus the United States began the final decades of this century with the death penalty still permissible under law in most jurisdictions, still sought by prosecutors and meted out by trial courts, and still given nominal approval by the bulk of society, even though the nation's highest appellate court has invalidated all but a handful of such sentences brought before it since 1967.

THE IMPOSED-LAW HYPOTHESIS

Can the present status of the death penalty in the United States be usefully viewed as an instance of imposed law? Can it be best understood in terms of the model of imposed law proposed earlier? The argument for the affirmative, reduced to its basic elements, is as follows:

1. The national moratorium on executions is entirely owing to the initiatives undertaken during the past decade or so by the self-appointed guardians of civil rights and civil liberties in the United States, notably the NAACP Legal Defense and Educational Fund (LDF) and the American Civil Liberties Union (ACLU). Since the mid-1960s these nongovernmental organizations have devoted a significant fraction of their total resources to the fight for abolition and, in so doing, have contributed funds and talent in unprecedented quantity to this cause. Without their efforts, the status of the death penalty today would not be very different from what it was a generation ago.

2. The initiatives of this moral elite have been effective in altering the status of persons under death sentence and the status of capital statutes because they were addressed directly to a counterpart elite in government itself, the life-appointees of the federal appellate bench, including in particular the nine

members of the Supreme Court. It is these judges, and virtually these judges alone, who have ruled progressively against the death penalty in case after case, secure in their immunity from the political process that, had they been directly vulnerable to it, probably would have expelled them from office for ruling as they did from *Furman* to *Coker*. Their immunity freed them to consider the appeal to moral principles advanced by the LDF attorneys and their allies in a manner that no other branch of government could be expected to match.

3. These moral and judicial elites have had continuing support from the highly educated academic and professional elites (social scientists, physicians, lawyers, humanists) from whom they are drawn. Though not unanimously opposing the death penalty, members of this third elite have put their resources at the disposal of the LDF and the ACLU in a variety of ways, not least of which has been the public interpretation, justification, and rationalization of the abolitionist cause and of the tactics of the LDF and the ACLU to implement it.

4. Most of the multi-issue groups and organizations on record against the death penalty, including even the LDF and the ACLU, know that their rank-and-file members have been slow to join this particular campaign. The lay members of the churches, as well as many clergy, have not supported the increasingly firm policy favoring abolition expressed by their national religious organizations and spokesmen for social justice. Although the National Coalition against the Death Penalty, as of June 1978, lists 48 national organizations as its members, this represents only the smallest fraction of the general public, most of whom profess to favor restoration of the death penalty for murder and other heinous crimes. Whatever clamor there may be from time to time against a particular execution, or against a particular death sentence, opposition to the death penalty as such is not and never has been *vox populi*.

5. The present status of the death penalty in the United States may not fit exactly the model of imposition of law formulated earlier in terms of the situation in Oregon under Governor Holmes in the mid-1950s. Yet the preceding facts do show that the present national status of the death penalty far more closely approaches that extreme of the spectrum than it does the other.

That is the argument in its bluntest and briefest form. How sound is it? The conclusion I shall endeavor to establish requires some modifications—namely, that although it is necessary to acknowledge an indispensable role played by moral elites in bringing the nation so far so quickly toward abolition of the death penalty, it is easy to overestimate their effect and to underestimate the degree of public approval for their efforts and accomplishments. A better, more accurate view of all the facts suggests that the visible and prominent acts of the moral elites opposing the death penalty are the surface phenomena of deeper social forces moving slowly, albeit erratically and far from implacably, in the same direction. Thus, the apparent imposition of the law in this instance by the few upon the many is a misleading oversimplification of what in fact is a complex and fundamentally democratic transformation of the law in a whole society.

THE EVIDENCE

Let us first look more closely at the status of the LDF and its allies as a moral elite. If one group had to be identified as chiefly responsible for the recent progress toward abolition of the death penalty, it would be the LDF. It was this group that brought the original class action suits, stopping all executions in 1967 and raising the series of constitutional challenges that has kept the issue in the federal courts. The LDF continues to plan and finance the national litigational campaign against the death penalty on behalf of its typically indigent clients (Meltsner 1973; Greenberg 1977:421–540, 605–661). Any argument that turns on the decisive role of a moral elite in the death-penalty controversy must evaluate carefully the nature and accomplishments of the LDF.

The LDF is without question the nation's oldest and most prominent public-interest law firm. Its crowning achievement is the victory from a unanimous Supreme Court in 1954 in *Brown* v. *Board of Education,* outlawing legally enforced, racially segregated, public education (Kluger 1976). The former executive director of the LDF, who argued the victory in *Brown,* is now a member of the Supreme Court: Associate Justice Thurgood Marshall. As one of the LDF's former litigating attorneys has said, the LDF office law library in New York is characteristically graced by the "shiny minds from the best law schools . . . so many future professors, senatorial aids, and Supreme Court clerks . . . [Meltsner 1973:111].''

The chief function of the LDF since its founding in 1939 has been the litigation of major civil rights issues. In 1975, it had a budget of $3.6 million, about 10% of which was used to finance the anti-death-penalty campaign (McKay 1977:12). Although the LDF maintains a staff of 24 lawyers, 100 other employees, several interns, and other support staff, and has a docket of 800–900 cases at any given time, only 2 staff attorneys are available to handle the 200 or so capital cases (Greenberg 1975:107, 112). Yet this staff has access to constituencies in every major law school in the nation, as well as 400 cooperating attorneys across the land, most of whom practice in the South. The annual receptions held by the LDF in New York, Boston, and other major cities for its benefactors and supporters include a generous sample from every elite in American society: social, financial, political, academic, intellectual, and professional.

Although the LDF is an elite of sorts, and unquestionably part of the nation's moral elite, it is surely a disinterested one, especially with regard to its opposition to the death penalty. The trustees, staff, and friends of the LDF have little to gain personally from the abolition campaign; neither they nor their families, friends, or associates are likely to suffer from the death penalty or gain directly from its abolition. Those who would gain are predominantly the lumpenproletariat of America: it is the poor, the nonwhite, the uneducated, the unemployed, and the sociopathic who are most likely to commit the crimes that run a risk of capital punishment. This is not gainsaid by the fact that about half of the LDF's trustees, staff, and employees are black (McKay 1977:12). The social-class and ethnic affinity between the LDF and its death-penalty clients is far less than that between those clients and many other groups opposing the death penalty, and the motives that led the LDF to undertake its far-reaching, expensive, and controversial litigation campaign grew out of its general desire to defeat racism on constitutional grounds, rather than any other considerations.

What has been said here about the LDF is, to a greater or lesser extent, equally true of the 48 other organizations that make up the National Coalition against the Death Penalty (NCADP). With a few exceptions, they constitute disinterested moral elites whose opposition to the death penalty grew naturally out of separate prior commitments (prison reform, nonviolent social change, racial reconciliation, pacifism, protection of civil rights and civil liberties). It has been suggested that a nation's moral elite is necessarily part of its "strategic elite" (Keller 1968:26). This may be true of the LDF and its abolitionist allies, but it cannot be claimed that these groups are part of the nation's "power elite" (Mills 1956). The political and economic power at the disposal of these groups is far less than their ability to symbolize a widespread moral unity in opposition to the death penalty. The likelihood that such an elite by itself is capable of imposing its views through the law is not very great. Let us turn next to examine the legal and judicial elites allegedly allied with the moral elite in opposition to the death penalty.

The Bar

Support for an abolitionist position among members of the bar in general is difficult to document. Although several legal organizations belong to the NCADP (for example, the National Bar Association, the National Lawyers Guild, the National Legal Aid and Defender Association), it is also true that two of the few national organizations to favor the death penalty are the National District Attorneys Association and the National Association of Attorneys General. (Two of the others are police organizations.) The American Bar Association has never taken a position against the death penalty. In 1976 the leadership prevented a resolution on abolition from reaching the membership for a vote (Sklar 1976b:17), and in 1978 the House of Delegates, by a vote of 168 to 69, defeated a resolution from its Section on Individual Rights and Responsibilities urging state legislatures to repeal all death-penalty statutes (Oelsner 1977). The nation's most prestigious legal organization, the American Law Institute, completed its influential Model Penal Code project in the 1960s by compromising on the issue of capital punishment. It refused to recommend abolition but did go so far as to say that if the death penalty is to be permitted under law, then it should be imposed only after conviction at a separate trial, at which "aggravating" and "mitigating" circumstances relevant to the choice of sentence are reviewed (American Law Institute 1962:§ 210.6).

The Judiciary

Evidence for a pattern of abolitionist sentiment in appellate courts is hard to trace. Strongly abolitionist rulings by appellate courts in capital cases are very rare. Among the state supreme courts, only two (California and Massachusetts) have handed down rulings to the effect that the death penalty is a cruel and unusual punishment under the *state* constitution (*People* v. *Anderson* 1972; *Commonwealth* v. *O'Neal* 1975). Several other state supreme courts, after review of death-penalty convictions issued under post-*Furman* statutes that were obviously inconsistent with the guidelines implicit in the Supreme Court's rulings in *Gregg* and *Woodson,* have nullified these death sentences on the ground that the new statutes are unconstitutional (Turner 1976; Goldstein 1977). Rulings such as these cannot be taken as evidence of any strong judicial inclination in favor of abolition, however, or as support from the state appellate judiciary for the litigation effort of the LDF and its allies to whittle away every constitutional prop, state and federal, for the death penalty.

In the federal courts, there is no record of attitudes or decisions among the district court judges to suggest that a majority favors abolition. On the contrary, what evidence there is shows how reluctant the lower appellate federal courts have been to cooperate with abolitionist legal strategems (Meltsner 1973:126–148). Among the federal circuit courts, only one has ruled against the constitutionality of any capital statute (*Ralph* v. *Warden* 1970).

In the Supreme Court itself, all but four of the major rulings by the court on death-penalty questions during the past decade have been to evade the issue or uphold the constitutionality of capital punishment.[5] In its rulings in those four cases—*Furman* (1972), *Woodson* (1976), *Coker* (1977), and *Roberts* (1977)—the Court was badly split. Each anti-death-penalty ruling was sustained by the smallest possible majority (5 to 4), and only two justices, William J. Brennan, Jr., and Thurgood Marshall, have declared, beginning with *Furman,* that in their view the death penalty per se is unconstitutional under the Eighth and Fourteenth Amendments. Two others, Chief Justice Warren E. Burger and Associate Justice William Rehnquist, have with equal consistency voted against the unconstitutionality of the death penalty. Of the other five justices currently on the Court, each has voted in at least one case against the constitutionality of the death penalty, and each has indicated his personal moral opposition to a legislative policy of capital punishment. Of the five justices who have left the Supreme Court during the past decade, probably three (Arthur J. Goldberg, Abe Fortas, William O. Douglas) would have translated their personal opposition to the death penalty into a constitutional interpretation against it; it is equally probable that the other two (John Marshall Harlan and Hugo Black) would not.

It is beyond question that during the past generation the Supreme Court has paid an extraordinary amount of attention to death-penalty cases (Prettyman 1961). Yet the issue did not enter the agenda of the Court until 1963, when Justices Goldberg, Douglas, and Brennan voted in dissent of the Court's refusal to grant *certiorari* in a death-penalty conviction of rape, *Rudolph* v. *Alabama.* (Under the rules of the Court, any justice may file a written dissent from any ac-

---

[5] After this chapter was completed, in July 1978, the Supreme Court decided two death-penalty cases, *Lockett* v. *Ohio* and *Bell* v. *Ohio,* in a manner favorable to abolition.

tion of the Court, but this is rarely done; and no case will be heard unless at least four justices agree that the appellant's case may have merit.) It could be argued that over the years the Supreme Court has yielded very little to the pressure from moral elites in favor of abolition, and instead has struggled to discharge its constitutional duty without abusing its own role as an elite, insulated from the political process and ideologically opposed to the apparently prevailing public support of the death penalty. During the 1950s and early 1960s the Court did as little as possible to narrow the scope of the death penalty. In the two chief cases litigated in the hopes of severely limiting the death penalty by appeal to the "equal protection" clause of the Fourteenth Amendment—*Maxwell* v. *Bishop* (1970) and *McGautha* v. *California* (1971)—it ruled by substantial majorities against abolition. *Furman* (1972) was indeed a victory for all those who wished to see the United States abolish all death penalties forever, and was hailed as such. Yet it was to prove a narrow and incomplete victory. Four years later, in *Gregg* v. *Georgia* (1976) and allied cases, the court upheld at least the *prima facie* constitutionality of a wide variety of death-penalty statutes, provided only that they gave some semblance of statutory guidance to the sentencing court (Black 1977). *Gregg* did not reverse *Furman,* but it did provide several blueprints for any legislature determined to enact a capital statute that would pass muster by the Supreme Court. In rationalizing its decision in *Gregg,* the Court made a point of citing several kinds of evidence of popular support for the death penalty in the aftermath of *Furman* as a way of showing that judicial repeal of the death penalty in *Furman* was contrary to the will of the electorate: opinion polls showed that the public supported the death penalty in a ratio of roughly 2 to 1; legislatures in 36 states had re-enacted death-penalty statutes for murder and other crimes; in the one statewide referendum on the issue since *Furman,* the death penalty was supported by a substantial majority; trial juries in states where the death penalty had been reintroduced were regularly meting out death sentences, so that within less than 4 years after *Furman* there were again more than 460 people under death sentence in 30 states (*Gregg* v. *Georgia* 1976:179–182).

Taken together, all this undermines the original hypothesis that the appellate judiciary, and especially the Supreme Court, has exploited its status as a powerful and virtually invulnerable elite to press for abolition of the death penalty despite the manifest popular will allegedly opposed to abolition. Likewise, this implies that the abolitionist ideology of the non-governmental moral elites does not have at its disposal such political power as the bar and the judiciary command.

The Governors

It is useful to supplement the foregoing account by a brief look at the role played by state governors in the struggle over the death penalty. If the most populist branch of government (the legislature) tends to support death penalties for murder and a few other serious crimes, whereas the most elite branch of government (the appellate judiciary) tends, with a few conspicuous exceptions, to permit the practice of capital punishment as a legitimate exercise of legislative prerogative, the executive branch falls somewhere in between—probably nearer the legislatures than the judiciaries. Wholesale commutation of death sentences is rare; it would probably be political suicide anywhere in the United States. The sole example in recent years occurred in 1970 in Arkansas, when Governor Winthrop Rockefeller, defeated for re-election, commuted the death sentences of all 15 men awaiting execution (Meltsner 1973:233–236). The reason usually given for refusal of commutation, however, is not the political one, which needs no acknowledgment. It is rather that, since the mid-1960s, the highest courts have continued to keep the constitutional status of the death penalty under review.

Somewhat more indicative of executive attitudes has been the use of the veto power. Massachusetts may be unique in having had two governors in a row, one from each major political party, veto death-penalty legislation and to have that veto sustained as well (Bedau 1973a). Governors in other states in recent years (Pennsylvania in 1974; Tennessee, California, and Maryland in 1977; New York and New Jersey in 1978) have also vetoed legislation to restore the death penalty, but such acts are of ambiguous significance. All these governors know that the polls show that their electorates strongly support legislative reimposition of the death penalty. They also know that, at least since 1976, the Supreme Court has ruled the death penalty is not necessarily unconstitutional. Yet they know that they can no more offend the moral elites in their states, on whom they rely for support, than they can outrage the majority of the electorate. Hence the gubernatorial veto messages typically stress that the legislature has enacted bills that are inconsistent with the guidelines implicit in recent Supreme Court decisions. The most recent veto message by a governor, Hugh Carey of New York, is a conspicuous exception to this rule because of its forthright embrace of an abolitionist ideology (Weisman 1978). It is likely that as more legislatures enact statutes without obvious constitutional defects, gubernatorial vetoes will be harder to secure. In any case, the infrequency of such vetoes and the grounds on which many of them have been tendered help to reinforce the picture of an abolitionist moral elite that finds the levers of political success continually just beyond its grasp.

Let us now turn to another elite allegedly interlocking with the moral, political and judicial elites—that comprising the intellectuals, academics and the philanthropists who finance their research.

Academics, Intellectuals, and the Foundations

The actual role of academic and professional elites in opposition to the death penalty in the United States is difficult to assess. Even though it is true that some of the most influential members of the relevant scholarly disciplines have publicly opposed the death penalty, many more of their equally distinguished colleagues have been conspicuously silent. The scholarly association most directly concerned with the issue, the American Society of Criminology, has, since its foundation in the 1950s, regularly opened its doors to seminars and panels on research related to the death penalty, without taking a policy position for or against capital punishment. Organizations that have taken a policy position, such as the National Council on Crime and Delinquency (NCCD) in 1963 and the American Correctional Association (ACA) in 1966, are lobbyists on a wide range of issues touching the professional concerns of their members. Neither of these organizations has during the past decade devoted a large part of its resources to an effort to secure abolition of the death penalty, perhaps in part owing to the absence of strong grass-roots support for such efforts. In any case, the NCCD and the ACA are not scholarly or academic organizations any more than are the ACLU and the LDF.

Among the organizations that are, few have undertaken even to put a scholarly discussion of the death penalty on the official agendas of their meetings, and fewer still have gone so far as to discuss whether to oppose it on principle. An exception is the American Orthopsychiatric Association (AOA), which has sponsored panel discussions and workshops on the death penalty, supported abolition editorially in its *Journal* (1975), and lent its weight to popularizing the empirical—behavioral, clinical, social—evidence against capital punishment (Bedau and Pierce 1976). The AOA would not rank near the top of anyone's list of elite scholarly or academic organizations in the United States, however. Far more typical is the posture of the impeccably elitist National Research Council. In 1976 the Council undertook to re-examine the issue of deterrence (Klein, Forst, and Filatov 1978), and concluded that "the available studies provide no useful evidence on the deterrent effect of capital punishment [Blumstein, Cohen, and Nagin 1978:9]." There is no likelihood, however, that the Council will attempt to translate this scientific judgment into a policy position.

Some further evidence of the role of the academic and intellectual elites in the United States in the death-penalty controversy can be found in the series of *amicus curiae* briefs supplied to the Supreme Court during the litigation of the *Furman* case. Twelve such briefs were submitted during 1970–1971, all in support of abolition (Meltsner 1973:254–257). Of these, one was written by nine former governors, four by church groups (including the National Council of Churches), and two by private parties. The remaining five included two groups of civil rights and civil liberties organizations, headed by the NAACP and the ACLU, and the National Legal Aid and Defender Association. Only two—a brief by an *ad hoc* group of psychiatrists and another brief from a group of former wardens and correction officers—could be said to have come from professional groups. In no case was there a brief from any established academic organization, such as the American Sociological Association or the American Psychiatric Association. It is not that such organizations oppose abolition, but that their officers and trustees typically do not regard themselves as having any responsibility to use the organizational resources in a partisan role in public controversies. Part of being an elite organization in the world of scholarship is being free from any responsibility to influence national policy on questions of crime and punishment where the policy is not of direct concern to the profession or academy itself.

In this connection, it is interesting to note by contrast who has spoken out in favor of the death penalty in the United States. Although there is no national coalition to restore the death penalty and carry out death sentences with dispatch, there are several organizations on the political right—Americans for Effective Law Enforcement (Carrington 1978), as well as the Liberty Lobby (1974) and the John Birch Society (1974)—that have taken public positions supporting capital punishment, as well as a few intellectuals and academics who have defended the death penalty against its detractors. Among these latter Professor Ernest van den Haag (1975) and the editor of *The National Review,* William F. Buckley, Jr., are perhaps the best known.

One of the most striking features of the growth of knowledge about capital punishment in the United States since the early 1960s is the relative absence of publicly financed empirical research into disputed areas of fact, and the important role played by private research to fill this void. The first and most impressive of such investigations began in 1965, sponsored by the LDF and supported by grants for this purpose from private sources (Meltsner 1973:76–78, 86–89; McKay 1977:11–12; Wolfgang 1978:25–29). From 1973 onward further studies were undertaken, many of them supported by organizations whose officers were sympathetic to abolition (Bedau 1970). Tax-exempt philanthropic foundations are prohibited by law from engaging in partisan political activities, and no self-respecting social scientist wants to construct his research agenda on the basis of his moral convictions alone. Even so, without the enterprise of social scientists who favor abolition and the support of private foundations, the empirical basis on which the death penalty has been examined during the past decade or so simply would not have existed.

Although there are no polls on the point, it seems likely that a majority of academically trained persons in the United States would favor abolition of the death penalty. A content analysis of all the social science publications pertinent to the death penalty controversy published since 1965 has not been undertaken either, but, at a guess, as many as 9 out of every 10 of them have the effect of casting doubt on the empirical beliefs that undergird rational support of capital punishment.

If we shift our attention to less specialized publications we find much the same situation, even though the nation's most prestigious journal of criticism, *The New York Review,* despite its interest in the status of human rights abroad and civil liberties and prison reform at home, has never published anything directly critical of capital punishment.[6] Older liberal journals, such as *The Progressive* and *The Nation,* have opposed it for decades, though their influence, like their audience, is quite small, in contrast to the millions who daily read the major newpapers. The editorial position of the nation's leading newpapers—*The New*

---

[6] See, however, the essay by Andrei Sakharov (1978), in which he explained his support for the Stockholm Conference against the death penalty convened by Amnesty International in December 1977.

York Times, The Washington Post, The Boston Globe, The Los Angeles Times, The Philadelphia Inquirer, and *The St. Louis Post-Dispatch*—has been unanimously opposed to the death penalty for some time.

Thus the original hypothesis, that the moral elites opposing the death penalty receive sustaining support from the academic and professional elite, is at least in part confirmed by closer examination. This confirmation is sustained, although along a narrower portion of the spectrum, if we consider the degree to which groups concerned to evaluate the entire criminal justice system have favored abolition. The two major national commissions created to study these problems—the President's Commission on Law Enforcement (1967) and the National Commission on Reform of Federal Criminal Laws (1970)—took positions virtually in favor of across-the-board abolition of all death penalties. The President's Commission sidestepped the issue somewhat, implying that the problem of capital punishment was really one for the several states to solve for themselves (President's Commission 1967:143). The National Commission officially recommended abolition of all federal death penalties, but to accommodate its dissenting members, it also proposed that if capital punishment was to be retained, then the American Law Institute proposals for a two-stage trial should be adopted (National Commission 1970a:310–315; 1970b:II, 1347–1376). The only public groups that investigated capital punishment and favored retaining it were occasional special commissions established by some of the states, for example, New Jersey (New Jersey Commission to Study Capital Punishment 1964). Most of these state commissions, such as Pennsylvania (Pennsylvania Governor's Study Commission on Capital Punishment 1973), favored abolition. Among private studies, at least four successive national conferences since 1970 have reviewed the criminal justice system and either recommended abolition of the death penalty or conspicuously ignored it (American Friends Service Committee 1971; Annual Chief Justice Earl Warren Conference on Advocacy 1972; Committee for the Study of Incarceration 1976; Twentieth Century Fund 1976). In addition, the National Coalition against the Death Penalty includes among its constituent organizations more than half a dozen national organizations that work with prisoners, correctional reform, and the like.

The groups represented by the several commissions and conferences cited above form a loosely knit coalition of social activists, correctional professionals (criminologists, penologists), lawyers, and intellectuals. The convergence of their views in opposition to the death penalty is best viewed as the only possible public position serious and informed students of crime and punishment can take on the death-penalty controversy in the United States today. To do otherwise— to defend the death penalty in the United States, urge its retention or expansion, insist that it plays a crucial and indispensable role in social defense, or justify it as a proper retributive response to grave injuries—would be to fly in the face of half a century of empirical research and evolving moral principles. It is hardly any wonder that one commentator, when confronted with the claim that the LDF's litigation campaign from 1967 to 1972 deserved most of the credit for the nation's movement toward abolition, was prompted to object that throughout this period there have been "significant abolitionist forces at work . . . which had nothing to do with anyone's grand 'strategy' [McDonald 1974:15]."

The scope and variety of ideologies and classes that make up the moral elite and its academic-professional supporters in opposition to the death penalty are impressive. Only a small fraction of such groups either have no discernible views on the death penalty or have lent it their support. But as many of these groups tend to merge with the general-public, non-elite organizations and with other interest groups across the whole spectrum of political and social opinion in the nation, the picture of abolitionists as an isolated moral elite becomes blurred. Likewise, the prior hypothesis—that it is the imposition of their view of the law that accounts for the *de facto* abolition of the death penalty—becomes less compelling. Finally, let us turn to the evidence that can be gathered from scrutinizing the attitudes of the general public toward the death penalty.

Public Opinion

The conventional wisdom, based mainly on commercial survey research, is that the American public has moved during the past 15 years from being roughly split on the death-penalty question to being in favor of it by more than two to one. A Harris Survey of 1966 reported that 47% of the public opposed capital punishment, 38% favored it, and 15% had no opinion (Erskine 1970:295). A Gallup Poll of the same year reported nearly the same distributions: 47% against, 42% for, and 11% undecided (Erskine 1970:291). From that high point in support of abolition, the trend has been steadily the other way. The Harris Survey of June 1973 reported that 59% of the public approved of capital punishment, 31% opposed it, and 10% were unsure (Harris 1973). Eighteen months later, the Gallup Poll reported that 63% favored the death penalty and 37% opposed it (Gallup 1974). In April 1976 the Gallup organization again canvassed public opinion on this question, and reported that the percentage favoring the death penalty had grown to 65%, those opposed had declined to 28%, and 7% were unsure (Gallup 1976). The Harris organization reported further losses for abolition in February 1977: now 67% favored the death penalty, only 25% opposed it, and 8% were unsure (Harris 1977).

A careful examination of such surveys, however, shows that they reveal very little about the true state of public opinion. The questions typically fail to distinguish between sentencing persons to death and the execution of such sentences; paradoxical as it may at first seem, most of the data tending to show that the public approves of capital punishment is ambiguous as to whether it shows support for the latter as well as for the former. There is no evidence from any source that the public clamors for death sentences to be carried out. The hundreds not executed owing to the rulings in *Furman* and in *Woodson* prompted no mass demonstrations, public outcry, or other unmistakable evidence of general public support for executions. Public support for the death penalty thus seems to be curiously abstract. Perhaps this is because those who profess to sup-

port it know little or nothing about its history, actual effects, and probable consequences (Vidmar and Ellsworth 1974). As to why the public supports it, researchers are in disagreement. Some believe that an adequately informed public
would in fact oppose it, and there is some evidence in favor of such a conclusion
(Sarat and Vidmar 1976). Others have shown that those who favor the death
penalty may do so because of attitudes that are not easily influenced by the later
acquisition of information about the death penalty (Thomas 1977; Thomas and
Howard 1977). Quite apart from other factors, then, the uncertain structure of
the public attitudes in support of the death penalty makes it difficult to argue
from the premise that only a minority of the public manifestly favors abolition to
the conclusion that the failure to execute lawfully imposed death sentences constitutes an imposition of law by a moral elite and a frustration of popular will.
Finally, a better understanding of two important factual issues casts further
doubt on the validity of the elite hypothesis.

Supply of Executions

Research has shown that the significant decline in executions in the United
States precedes by several decades the decision in the mid-1960s by the LDF to
campaign for the judicial abolition of the death penalty (Bowers 1974:21–29).
This fact suggests that the present *de facto* termination of executions is not due
solely to the role of moral elites, or at least not solely to the work of moral elites
since the mid-1960s. Rather, the moratorium is the historic product of a variety
of other factors that antedate it. These factors—including abolition of mandatory
death sentencing (except for the 4-year post-*Furman* and pre-*Woodson* movement in the other direction), provisions for automatic appeal of trial court death
sentences, along with the much earlier distinction between degrees of murder,
the abolition of public and manifestly cruel methods of execution, the tendency
to restrict the death penalty to the crime of murder, and increasing public
criticism of capital punishment—are all important in explaining the decline of
executions. Even if they were originally set in motion and are now sustained by a
moral elite, since the middle of this century these factors have become generally
accepted features of the criminal justice system which no popular majority would
seriously oppose.

Supply of Death Sentences

The uninterrupted flow of death sentences at the trial court in conjunction
with the failure to execute these sentences does not necessarily imply the power
of a moral elite in favor of abolition and at odds with community sentiment.
Such an inference fails to take into account two factors revealed by empirical
research. First, the law on jury selection in capital cases, which requires that
every potential juror be asked if he has any objection to the death penalty (and if
he does he is disqualified), virtually guarantees that the prosecution has a
"hanging jury" in *every* instance (Jurow 1971; Stricker and Jurow 1974). Supposedly, such juries were declared unconstitutional in *Witherspoon* v. *Illinois*

(1968), but the state trial courts have evaded this reading of the decision, and instead have permitted jurors to serve whose opposition to the death penalty is nominal, abstract, and based on remote contingencies. The result is that defense counsel enters every capital trial knowing that the accused does not stand to be judged by a true cross-section of the general public, but rather by a carefully winnowed segment of the community from which every opponent of the death penalty has been excluded. Even if the public were overwhelmingly opposed to the death penalty, as long as capital statutes exist and as long as scrupled juries are permitted by law, an uninterrupted flow of death sentences is all but guaranteed. Second, in the South, where most death sentences are imposed, the racial impact of capital punishment continues as before. Although it is true that convicted white murderers are sentenced to death and that many convicted black murderers are not, there is a dramatic correlation between race and death sentence as soon as we examine the race of the victim. Unpublished research by Dr. William Bowers of the Center for Applied Social Research at Northeastern University shows that the death penalty in such typically southern states as Florida, Georgia, and Texas is reserved almost exclusively for those (white or black) who kill whites (King 1978).

THE VERDICT

The foregoing argument, reduced to its barest essentials, is as follows. Given the original hypothesis that (a) a moral elite has brought about the abolition of the death penalty in the United States and in doing so has imposed its will through law upon the rest of society, there are at least three major subsidiary theses that must be proved before this hypothesis can be accepted. It must be shown that (b) the abolitionists are a moral elite, (c) this moral elite has really succeeded in making its position the dominant one under law, and (d) this constitutes a case of imposition of law. My counterargument has been that a is an oversimplification because although b is true, both c and d are doubtful and in need of significant qualification. Against c and d, I have argued that the abolitionist moral elite is not a prominent part of the nation's power elite, that decline in executions is a long-term trend, that the moratorium of the past decade—with which all branches of government, state and federal, were willing to cooperate—is owing to a protracted series of test cases on the constitutionality of death-penalty statutes, that the public does not so much want actual executions as it wants the possibility thereof (that is, death-penalty statutes), and that the continuing supply of death sentences owes as much or more to minority community sentiment and subtle racism as to any widespread demand for executions. Finally, as the execution of Luis Monge in 1967 and Gary Gilmore in 1978 showed, there is no way that the abolitionist forces can save a condemned man from his fate if he will not attempt to save himself by seeking judicial review, and if the one person in a position to spare him—the chief executive of the jurisdiction—refuses to intervene. The death penalty has *not* been abolished in the United States—not yet.

AN ALTERNATIVE HYPOTHESIS

Historically, the death penalty is flanked on all sides by virtually unrestrained use of corporal punishments (Foucault 1977; Newman 1978). Hanging, decapitation, burning at the stake, and other modes of inflicting the death penalty were accompanied by torture of suspects, branding and maiming of thieves and other felons, and flogging of miscreants. In the United States, all save capital punishment (by hanging, the electric chair, the gas chamber, or the firing squad) have disappeared from the official repertory of legal methods of punishment. How are we to account for the preservation of the death penalty when all punitive practices associated with it have long since fallen into the trash can of history? Nothing is more striking than the fact, too rarely noticed, that those who defend the death penalty on retributive or utilitarian grounds do not go on, as their professed theories of justification would entitle them, to advocate the reintroduction of other methods of corporal punishment. Why this remarkable moral isolation of the death penalty in the arguments of its advocates? Perhaps what needs explanation is how the death penalty, with so few friends to speak for it in the United States, nevertheless manages to keep its grip on social practice to the extent that it has. Some consideration, necessarily brief and inconclusive here, needs to be given to an alternative hypothesis.

Crudely put, the failure to abolish the death penalty during the 1960s is due more than anything else to the influence of "law-and-order" political rhetoric, beginning with the 1968 presidential campaign, to which the liberal wing of the Democratic Party was vulnerable and which was cynically and effectively exploited by the Republicans and other center and right-wing critics in their efforts to gain and hold public office. The verbal assault on Ramsey Clark, Attorney General during the final years of the Johnson Administration and the only person ever to hold that office and to speak out forcefully against the death penalty (Clark 1970), was a warning of what would happen to anyone who might try to address the American people on this issue. A decade ago, public opinion was about equally divided. The "swing vote"—between 10% and 20%—was moved in the direction of retention by some of the most powerful voices for public education in the land. President Nixon, and later President Ford, used the vantage point of the White House and the solid support of the Department of Justice to defend the death penalty and criticize the Supreme Court from the moment its decision in *Furman* was announced (Bedau 1973b; Sklar 1976a). In the guise of defending the constitutionality of the death penalty, the right of the states to determine their own criminal justice system without interference from the federal judiciary, and the need to combat the rising tide of crimes of personal violence, the death penalty was defended on a national scale in an un-precedented fashion. A perfect example of these forces at work was the California Death Penalty Initiative of 1972 (Wolfe 1973: 409). Thus, the possibility of genuine public education and public acceptance of abolition, a political reality for a brief period in the mid-1960s, floundered along with many other social reforms.

CONCLUSION

Perceptive criminoligists familiar with the American scene now insist that, from the standpoint of crime control, the death penalty is a matter of "marginal significance" whose importance "could hardly be *under*estimated," and whose abolition or retention is "an issue of singular inconsequence [Morris and Hawkins 1977: 79, 81, 82]." Only its symbolic significance, therefore—the fact that it is the paradigm of certain powers of government and social attitudes—can account for the continuing controversy over its status under law in the United States. Perhaps the most that can be said in the end, therefore, is that the LDF, the ACLU, and all those groups and individuals in and out of government in the United States who have supported efforts to end the death penalty have suc-ceeded only in channeling a historic development that is subject to forces they can no more accelerate than others can destroy or retard.

ACKNOWLEDGMENTS

I am grateful to Mark Bedau for the initial discussion, to the Sociology Colloquium at Tufts University and Richard Moran for comments on the version presented at the Warwick Conference, and to Constance Putnam for criticisms of the final version.

REFERENCES

CASES

Aiken v. *California, dismissed as moot,* 406 U.S. 813 (1971).
Bell v. *Ohio,* —U.S.—, 98 S. Ct. 2977 (1978).
Brown v. *Board of Education,* 347 U.S. 483 (1954).
Coker v. *Georgia,* 453 U.S. 584,97 S.Ct. 2861 (1977).
Commonwealth v. *O'Neal,* 367 Mass. 440, 339 N.E. 2d 676 (1975).
Furman v. *Georgia,* 428 U.S. 153 (1972).
Gregg v. *Georgia,* 428 U.S. 153 (1976).
Lockett v. *Ohio,* —U.S.—, 98 S. Ct. 2954 (1978).
Maxwell v. *Bishop,* 398 F. 2d 138 (8th Cir. 1968), *vacated on other grounds* 398 U.S. 262 (1970).
McGautha v. *California,* 402 U.S. 183 (1971).
People v. *Anderson,* 100 Cal. Rptr. 152, 493 P. 2d 880 (Cal. Sup. Ct. 1972).

Ralph v. *Warden,* 438 F. 2d 786 (4th Cir. 1970).
Roberts v. *Louisiana,* 431 U.S. 637 (1977).
Rudolph v. *Alabama,* 375 U.S. 889 (1963).
Witherspoon v. *Illinois,* 391 U.S. 510 (1968).
Woodson v. *North Carolina,* 428 U.S. 280 (1976).

OTHER SOURCES

American Friends Service Committee
    1971   *Struggle for Justice: A Report on Crime and Punishment in America.* New York: Hill and Wang.
American Law Institute
    1962   *Model Penal Code: Proposed Official Draft.* Philadelphia: American Law Institute.
American Orthopsychiatric Association
    1975   "Capital punishment." *American Journal of Orthopsychiatry 45:*580–726.
Annual Chief Justice Earl Warren Conference on Advocacy
    1972   *A Program for Prison Reform.* Cambridge, Mass.: Roscoe Pound-American Trial Lawyers
        Foundation.
Bedau, H. A.
    1965   "Capital punishment in Oregon, 1903–1964." *Oregon Law Review 45:*1–39.
    1967   *The Death Penalty in America: An Anthology* (rev. ed.). Chicago: Aldine Publishing Co.
    1970   "Social science research in the aftermath of *Furman* v. *Georgia:* Creating new knowledge
        about capital punishment in the United States." Pp. 75–86 in M. Riedel and D. Chap-
        pell (eds.), *Issues in Criminal Justice.* New York: Praeger.
    1973a "Furman's wake in the land of bean and cod." *The Prison Journal 53:*4–18.
    1973b "The Nixon administration and the deterrent effect of the death penalty." *Univeristy of*
        *Pittsburgh Law Review 34:*557–566.
    1977   *The Courts, the Constitution, and Capital Punishment.* Lexington, Mass.: Heath.
    1979   "The 1964 Referendum to Abolish Capital Punishment in Oregon: Notes by a
        Participant-Observer." Unpublished ms.
Bedau, H.A., and C.M. Pierce (eds.)
    1976   *Capital Punishment in the United States.* New York: AMS.
Bennet, J. V.
    1958   "A historic move: Delaware abolishes capital punishment." *American Bar Association*
        *Journal 44:*1053–1054.
Black, C. L., Jr.
    1977   "Due process for death: *Jurek* v. *Texas* and companion cases." *Catholic Law Review*
        *26:*1–16.
Blumstein, A., J. Cohen, and D. Nagin (eds.)
    1978   *Deterrence and Incapacitation: Estimating the Effects of Criminal Sanctions on Crime Rates.* Wash-
        ington, D.C.: National Academy of Science.
Bowers, W. J.
    1974   *Executions in America.* Lexington, Mass: Heath.
Carrington, F. G.
    1978   *Neither Cruel nor Unusual.* New Rochelle, N. Y.: Arlington.
Clark, R.
    1970   *Crime in America.* New York: Simon & Schuster.
Committee for the Study of Incarceration
    1976   *Doing Justice.* New York: Hill and Wang.
Deets, L. E.
    1948   "Changes in capital punishment policy since 1939." *Journal of Criminal Law, Criminology*
        *& Police Science 38:*584–594.

Erskine, H.
    1970   "The polls: Capital punishment." *Public Opinion Quarterly 34:*290–307.
Foucault, M.
    1977   *Discipline and Punish: The Birth of the Prison.* New York: Pantheon.
Gallup, G.
    1974   "The Gallup Poll." Release of October.
    1976   "The Gallup Poll." Release of 29 April.
Goldstein, T.
    1977   "State's high court strikes key sections from death penalty." *The New York Times,* 16
            November, p. 1.
Greenberg, J.
    1975   "Someone has to translate rights into realities." *Civil Liberties Review 2:*4:104–128.
    1977   *Cases and Materials on Judicial Process and Social Change: Constitutional Litigation.* St. Paul,
            Minn.: West.
Guzman, J. P.
    1969   "Lynching." Pp. 56–59 in A.D. Grimshaw (ed.), *Racial Violence in the United States.*
            Chicago: Aldine Publishing Co.
Harris, L.
    1966   "The Harris Survey." Release of 3 July.
    1973   "The Harris Survey." Release of 11 June.
    1977   "The Harris Survey." Release of 7 February.
John Birch Society
    1974   "Capital punishment." *Georgia Journal of Corrections 3:*2:32–37.
Jurow, G. L.
    1971   "New data on the effect of a 'death qualified' jury on the guilt determination process."
            *Harvard Law Review 84:*567–611.
Keller S.
    1968   "Elites." *Encyclopedia of Social Science 5:*26–59. New York: Macmillan and Free Press.
Kelley, C. M.
    1977   *Uniform Crime Reports: Crime in the United States, 1976.* Washington, D.C.: Government
            Printing Office.
King, W.
    1978   "Few on 3 death rows are there for killing blacks." *The New York Times,* 6 March, p.
            11.
Klein, L. R., B. Forst, and V. Filatov
    1978   "The deterrent effect of capital punishment: An assessment of the estimates." Pp.
            336–360 in A Blumstein, J. Cohen, and D. Nagin (eds.), *Deterrence and Incapacitation:
            Estimating the Effects of Criminal Sanctions on Crime Rates.* Washington, D.C.: National
            Academy of Science.
Kluger, R.
    1976   *Simple Justice: The History of Brown v. Board of Education and Black America's Struggle for
            Equality.* New York: Knopf.
Liberty Lobby
    1974   "Capital punishment." *Georgia Journal of Corrections 3:*3:29–30.
Mackey, P. E. (ed.)
    1976   *Voices against Death: American Opposition to Capital Punishment.* New York: Burt Franklin.
McDonald, L.
    1974   Book review. *Civil Liberties,* June 1974, p. 15.
McKay, R. B.
    1977   *Nine for Equality Under Law: Civil Rights Litigation.* New York: Ford Foundation.
Meltsner, M.
    1973   *Cruel and Unusual: The Supreme Court and Capital Punishment.* New York: Random House.

Mills, C. W.
    1956 *The Power Elite.* New York: Oxford University Press.
Morris, N., and G. Hawkins
    1977 *Letter to the President on Crime Control.* Chicago: University of Chicago Press.
Myrdal, G.
    1944 *An American Dilemma.* New York: Harper & Row.
National Commission on Reform of Federal Criminal Laws
    1970a *Final Report.* Washington, D.C.: Government Printing Office.
    1970b *Working Papers* (2 vols.). Washington, D.C.: Government Printing Office.
National Criminal Justice Information and Statistics Service
    1977 *Capital Punishment 1976.* Washington, D.C.: Government Printing Office.
New Jersey Commission to Study Capital Punishment
    1964 *Report.* Trenton: State of New Jersey.
Newman, G.
    1978 *The Punishment Response.* Philadelphia: Lippincott.
Oelsner, L.
    1977 "Bar association rejects a proposal to call for end of death penalties." *New York Times,* 15 February, Sec. II, p. 6.
Pennsylvania Governor's Study Commission on Capital Punishment
    1973 *Report.* Commonwealth of Pennsylvania.
President's Commission on Law Enforcement
    1967 *The Challenge of Crime in a Free Society.* Washington, D.C.: Government Printing Office.
Prettyman, E. B., Jr.
    1961 *Death and the Supreme Court.* New York: Harcourt Brace World.
Sakharov, A.
    1978 "The death penalty." *The New York Review,* 9 February, pp. 43–44.
Sarat, A., and N. Vidmar
    1976 "Public opinion, the death penalty and the Eighth Amendment: Testing the Marshall hypothesis." *Wisconsin Law Review* :171–206.
Sellin, T. (ed.)
    1952 "Murder and the penalty of death." *The Annals of the American Academy of Political and Social Science 284*:1–166.
Sklar, Z.
    1976a "Carter v. Ford on the legal issues." *Juris Doctor* (October):47–50.
    1976b "Trial by ennui." *Juris Doctor* (October):16–18.
Stricker, G., and G. L. Jurow
    1974 "The relationship between attitudes towards capital punishment and assignment of the death penalty." *The Journal of Psychiatry and Law* (Winter):415–422.
Thomas, C. W.
    1977 "Eighth Amendment challenges to the death penalty: The relevance of informed public opinion." *Vanderbilt Law Review 30*:1005–1030.
Thomas, C. W., and R. G. Howard
    1977 "Public attitudes toward capital punishment: A comparative analysis." *The Journal of Behavioral Economics 6*:189–216.
Turner, W.
    1976 "High court on coast voids death penalty." *The New York Times,* 8 December, Sec. A, p. 21.
Twentieth Century Fund, Task Force on Criminal Sentencing
    1976 *Fair and Certain Punishment.* New York: McGraw-Hill.
Van den Haag, E.
    1975 *Punishing Criminals.* New York: Basic Books.

Vidmar, N., and P. Ellsworth
    1974 "Public opinion and the death penalty." *Stanford Law Review 26*:1245–1270.
Weisman, S.
    1978 "Carey vetoes the death-penalty bill." *The New York Times,* 12 April, Sec. A, p. 1.
Wolfe, B. H.
    1973 *Pileup on Death Row.* New York: Doubleday.
Wolfgang, M. E.
    1978 "The death penalty: Social philosophy and social science research." *Criminal Law Bulletin 14*:18–33.

5

IMPOSED LAW AND
THE MANIPULATION OF IDENTITY:
THE AMERICAN INDIAN CASE

FRANCES SVENSSON

To view the steady and apparently inexorable expansion of American law into
the lives of American Indians as a process of the restriction of aboriginal rights
for the benefit of the dominant power is too narrow and legalistic a perspective.
Behind the assault on indigenous rights to land, resources, and treaty-
guaranteed compensation, there has been a more fundamental assault on the
most basic right of all—the right to be Indian. This process must be understood
as part of the general phenomenon of reduction of ethnic differences that occurs
when two distince populations confront each other, one of whom has greater
power (physical, political, legal, and economic) than the other. If ethnic identity
in its aboriginal (that is, pre-contact) state can be described as fully extended—so
that members of an ethnic group collectively enjoy the power to determine their
personal identity within ethnically sanctioned boundaries, to express this identity, to shape their political, economic, religious and social forms, and to control
and exploit their land and its resources according to their own needs and principles—then contact with another group competing for control in one or all of
these spheres necessarily involves a power struggle not only over the material
forms and structures of autonomy, but also over the very right to assert
autonomy. The Chinese are not the only nation to have followed up limited suc-

69

cess on the battlefield with an ultimately successful war of attrition and absorption, culminating in the virtual disappearance of nonhomogeneous elements.
The Chinese, of course, have had the advantage of an overwhelming mass and
homogeneity. In societies like that of the United States, where a national identity
is still in the process of creation and where its reinforcement has been the subject
of considerable social and political concern, the general view has been that major
weapons in the social arsenal should be brought to bear on recalcitrant islands of
alien ethnicity in the body politic. Law has been one such weapon in the
forefront of the assault on autonomous identity.

Law is the systematic articulation of the principles of received social theory,
applied to the concrete problems of administration. In America, it develops out
of the complex interaction of legislation, executive directives and policy statements, judicial review and adjudication, interpretation and reinterpretation of
precedent, and the often flawed and idiosyncratic application by government
agents in the field. In spite of this complexity, law can be seen to arise out of and
reflect the priorities and preoccupations, the assumptions and biases of the historical and sociological contexts in which it appears. Because of this, the law
exhibits specific general themes characteristic of specific phases of historical
development. In the case of American Indian law, the following phases may be
identified:

1. *Accommodation*, during which American law (and British) acknowledged the
   equal status and privileges of Indian tribal laws and jurisdictions
   (1607–1817)
2. *Restriction of Indian jurisdiction and power*, during which Indian authority, as
   recognized by American law, contracted to apply only to Indians in Indian
   country and to crimes committed by Indians against other Indians (crimes
   involving or affecting non-Indians came under American jurisdiction)
   (1817–1830s)
3. *Extension of American jurisdiction and power*, during which the American government began to assert authority over the internal affairs of Indian communities and the relations between and among Indians in Indian country
   (1840s–1870s)
4. *Direct American administration*, during which the American government sup-
   planted Indian tribal governments entirely in most cases and ruled through
   Indian agents working for the Bureau of Indian Affairs of the Department
   of the Interior (1880s–1934)
5. *Reorganization, termination, and retrocession*, a confused period during which
   Indian policy veered from the re-creation of tribal government under the
   Indian Reorganization Act to the attempted liquidation of tribes and treaty
   relations embodied in House Concurrent Resolution No. 108 (Termination) and then back to tribal self-determination (1934–1970s)
6. *Movement toward forced merger of Indian communities into American society*, during
   which new termination bills are being introduced into Congress designed

to dissolve entirely the special, treaty-based status of Indian tribes. At the same time a major assault on Indian ownership and control of land and natural resources is being mounted, primarily by a coalition of private interests (late 1970s).

Underlying these phases in the development of Indian law can be seen the pattern of an ever more inclusive and effective imposition of American law on tribal communities. This imposition has been mainly accomplished by eroding the pillars upon which the autonomous Indian communities rested: distinct identities and the land bases, resources, and political powers to sustain these identities. This chapter will focus on four major areas of Indian law that have been critical to the survival of a distinct Indian tribal identity: personal status, tribal status, land rights, and treaty rights. It will examine the evolution of Indian law as it affects these four areas, and show how special status and ethnic identity have gradually been undermined.

It should be noted that, since the earliest period of interaction between Indian tribes and European forces, this legal struggle over Indian identity has been fought out entirely within the confines of American law. This is an important illustration of the fact that the evolution of Indian law reveals as much about the internal contradictions and conflicts in American social theory as it does about the relative power of the two societies, Indian and non-Indian. The imposition of law over Indian communities, and the constriction of their identity, has meant the successive imposition of one dominant interpretation of the meaning of justice, equality, rights, and responsibilities in liberal democratic theory on American society as a whole. This has profound implications for American society. For, as a noted authority on Indian affairs, Felix Cohen,[1] once noted, Indian affairs have been like a miner's canary, warning of the presence of poison gases of discrimination and oppression in American society. By its acquiescence in the manipulation of Indian identity, American society permits the manipulation of its own.

PERSONAL IDENTITY

Who is an Indian? Needless to say, definitions have changed over the years, both inside and outside the Indian communities. In addition, the question must always be understood as contextual; the answer depends on who is asking the question (tribe, government agency, or private interest) and why. Nonetheless, any definition must refer to descent from the aboriginal inhabitants of North and South America who were present before European contact. The idea of

---

[1] Cohen (1942) is the primary compendium of Indian law, prepared under the auspices of the Secretary of the Interior and the United States Solicitor. Cohen was in charge of the compilation of laws and rulings, with the assistance of a large number of other attorneys working in the field.

"Indian" is itself a European import: socially, politically, and culturally Indian identity has traditionally been specific to a particular tribal affiliation. In other words, one could not be in aboriginal times an Indian, but only a Crow or Cheyenne or Creek. The failure of Europeans to distinguish among the different tribal groups in appearance, customs, or political responsibilities gradually led to an emphasis on racial identity as the basis of Indian status, whereas in aboriginal times cultural affiliation was far more important (hence the adoption of culturally malleable Europeans into Indian communities). This shift has had dramatic implications for the Indian tribes. In the first place, it eroded the basic power of the tribal community to determine its own criteria of membership, clearly an essential power if the community is attempting to maintain political autonomy. Second, it imposed the values (and biases) of an alien community on indigenous values and practices. This had two effects: it eroded the integrity and internal consistency of the tribal culture, and it led to divisions within the aboriginal community (in this case, along racial lines). The latter effect was the result of the racial discrimination that has been so pervasive in America throughout its history. The admixture of non-Indian "blood" into the tribes led not, as in ancient times, to a simple increase in the tribal population, but rather to a cleavage within the tribe between the "mixed bloods" and the "full bloods," with the former frequently acting as instruments of the extension of non-Indian authority into the tribe. No longer did those of Indian ancestry share the general social goals and values characteristic of their particular tribes; the mixture of blood gave rise to a mixture of interests. Identity was diluted both individually and collectively.

The United States government stepped in actively to adjudicate the issue of Indian identity when three basic conditions were met: first, the sharp racial, cultural, and social distinctions between Indians and non-Indians became blurred through interaction and acculturation; second, certain statuses, rights, and privileges available to one group or another became valuable enough to become the subject of dispute; and third, the United States possessed the capability of intervening successfully. These three conditions were met for different tribes at different times, but generally speaking not until the second half of the nineteenth century. Under these conditions, the basic function of a definition of Indian identity was to establish a test whereby it could be determined whether or not an individual should be excluded from or included in the scope of legislation dealing with Indians. Both the tribes and the American government have had a direct stake in this; consequently, both have developed criteria of tribal membership and Indian status. The basic assumptions that underlie both their approaches are that individual and communal status can and should be distinguished, and that Indian identity is at some point and in some circumstances alienable. Clearly, an individual of some degree of Indian descent may or may not be an active member of an Indian tribe, and there is some reason from both an Indian and a non-Indian perspective to reserve Indian status for those who remain part of an Indian community, eliminating those who, whatever their "racial" background, have left it. This means that at some point boundary criteria must be established to mark the place at which diminished Indian blood, culture, political affinity, etc. indicate the transition from an Indian to an American identity. This is the point at which Indian identity is alienated.

The tribes have tended, in establishing criteria of membership, to emphasize combinations of racial descent and residence: for example, a member of the Oglala Sioux tribe must be one-quarter Oglala and a resident on the reservation in order to qualify for tribal services and participate in tribal government. Tribal power to determine membership was seriously attenuated during the period of direct administration by the Bureau of Indian Affairs. Characteristic of this phase was the assertion of an ultimate Congressional power:

> The Indian tribes have original power to determine their own membership. Congress has the power, however, to supersede that determination for the administration of tribal property, particularly its distribution among the members of the tribe [*Farrell* v. *United States*, 1901; Cohen 1942:98].

It should be noted that government intervention was largely a response to the tendency of many tribes to attempt to exclude from enjoyment of tribal resources people of marginally Indian blood and affiliations who asserted rights to community property; such people were often most willing to cooperate with the American authorities at the expense of traditional tribal leadership. When the Indian Reorganization Act of 1934 restored certain powers to tribal government, one of the major areas of tribal action was the establishment of membership criteria that were often more stringent than government criteria—up to one-half or even 100% tribal descent, sometimes on specific sides of the family (patrilineal or matrilineal). Much tribal political debate has centered on membership criteria and periodic reviews of tribal enrollment.

The United States government for its own purposes has generally found practical value in a definition of an Indian person that centered on two principles: first, "that some of his ancestors lived in America before its discovery by the white race," and second, "that the individual is considered an 'Indian' by the community in which he lives [Cohen 1942:2]." An opinion of the Attorney General of the United States has stated in addition that: "Half-breed Indians are to be treated as Indians, in all respects, so long as they retain their tribal relations [Cohen 1942:3]." The Indian Reorganization Act criteria, which have become important in connection with the struggle for control of tribal resources in the mid-twentieth century, slightly extend the traditional government criteria by considering as Indian

> all persons of Indian descent who are members of any recognized Indian tribe now under federal jurisdiction, and all persons who are descendents of such members who were, on June 1, 1934, residing within the present boundaries of any Indian reservation, and shall further include all other persons of one-half or more Indian blood [Cohen 1942:85].

With respect to the qualification of Indians for federal benefits and services guaranteed under the treaty relationship, the government has applied a more limiting formula. An individual must meet two out of three criteria: (*a*) membership in a federally recognized tribe; (*b*) at least one-quarter Indian blood; and (*c*) ownership of land held in trust for Indians by the United States government. It should be noted that all these definitions emphasize that it is not enough simply to *be* Indian; one must belong to a *federally recognized* tribe.

The intervention, both formal and informal, of the United States government in the determination of Indian identity and the artificial competition for scarce resources that the policies and practices of Indian administration have engendered have combined to create a situation in which Indian status has become a political issue—sometimes a liability, sometimes an asset. By and large, both the tribes, struggling to meet the needs of their members with scarce resources, and the government, struggling to reduce the costs of Indian administration, have had an interest in controlling and reducing the number of persons with acknowledged Indian status. The effect of this situation, combined with historical circumstances, has been to leave many people with Indian racial background outside recognized Indian communities and therefore outside the body of those who qualify for Indian services. In the case of urban Indians, most of whose migrations were initiated at the behest and through the agency of the Bureau of Indian Affairs, this has created one of the main tensions in current Indian politics, since a high proportion of these people are no longer entitled to Indian services.

The discussion above emphasizes the ways in which Indian communal authority has been eroded in the crucial area of determination of Indian identity and tribal membership. These are areas of personal identity. The United States government has been asserting, in effect, the right to determine the way a person can properly (that is, legally) think about himself, and the way in which an ostensibly self-governing community can define that individual's relationship to it and its relationship to him. This is a major political act. As an imposition on another community, it is also an aggressive act. This pattern of usurping tribal authority gave way to a policy of direct extension of American authority symbolized by citizenship. The Indian Citizenship Act of 1924, which unilaterally made "all non-citizen Indians born within the territorial limits of the United States" citizens (Cohen 1942:82) has been viewed by many tribes (notably the members of the Iroquois League) as a violation of treaty-guaranteed autonomy and therefore as possibly unconstitutional. It is viewed by almost all tribes as an imposition of alien responsibilities and obligations upon a politically impotent people, whether or not its advantages ultimately outweigh its disadvantages.

The Citizenship Act and its intended effect to turn American Indians into Indian-Americans has had its ironic aspects as well. Up to 30 years or more passed in most states before individual Indians were able to exercise such basic rights of citizenship as voting, although they were liable for such services as the military draft. Partly a result of racial prejudice, this barrier was also partly the product of assumptions that personal inadequacy and inferiority were Indian characteristics—assumptions produced by the European legacy of self-satisfaction and ethnocentricity and by the political doctrine of "wardship" derived from the opinions of Chief Justice John Marshall of the United States Supreme Court in the famous Cherokee decisions of the early 1830s. In *Cherokee Nation* v. *Georgia* (1831), Marshall merely suggested that the relationship of the United States to the Indian tribes was like that of a guardian to his wards. However, Marshall, who was sympathetic to Indian claims of a right to internal self-determination, failed to foresee that his analogy would come to have devastating consequences for Indians as the subjects of American power. Wards are ordinarily legally incompetent because of intellectual disability caused by extreme youth, mental illness, retardation, etc. Indian persons came to be perceived as inherently the intellectual equivalents of these other kinds of wards, trapped in a perpetual "minority." Because of this, restrictions on individual Indian powers— such as the right to alienate land and to receive or spend funds—developed, leading to the assertion of distinctly paternal authority by Indian agents over Indian individuals and their personal affairs. In this way too, then, Indian identity has been manipulated by the imposition of alien law. American law and its interpretation have attempted to mold what it means to be Indian, and what it means to be an Indian individual. The assault on personal identity and status has been accompanied by a similar attack on tribal status.

SOVEREIGNTY AND DEPENDENCE

The tribes had aboriginal sovereignty. Their powers of self-determination were unchallenged before European contact. At least north of Mexico, where no political systems of the so-called state type were found, the practice of political conquest and absorption was apparently unknown, and tribal interactions, when hostile, took the form of skirmishes and raids rather than wars in the European sense. The European powers recognized this sovereignty antedating their own appearance, even when they simultaneously asserted their own political preeminence. In explaining the nature of the early intergovernmental relations, the Supreme Court noted: "In the establishment of these relations, the rights of the original inhabitants were, in no instance, entirely disregarded; but were necessarily, to a considerable extent, impaired [*Johnson* v. *McIntosh* 1823; Cohen 1942:292]." This process of impairment was a major theme of Indian policy and Indian law throughout the nineteenth century. As noted in the discussion of the phases of Indian law, the brief period of accommodation was followed by a long period of restriction of Indian jurisdiction, extension of American jurisdiction, and ultimately the disappearance of Indian jurisdiction entirely during the phase of direct American administration.

Since tribal powers of self-government were not derived from the authority of either the British colonial or the American government, they posed a problem

for American law, which reluctantly admitted them to its purview. Treaty relations themselves seemed to reinforce the case for the Indians' right to self-determination, until some political interests (including states like Georgia during the
campaign for removal of the tribes from what were claimed to be state territories) thought of arguing that the treaties, by restricting the scope of Indian
treaty-making to the United States, undermined the Indian case for continuing
sovereignty and rights of self-government. This particular argument was met by
Marshall in the Cherokee cases, when he argued that inequalities of power alone
were not sufficient to extinguish the right of self-determination. In *Worcester* v.
Georgia (1832) Marshall argued that "the settled doctrine of the law of nations is,
that a weaker power does not surrender its independence—its right to self-
government—by associating with a stronger, and taking its protection [*Worcester*
v. *Georgia* 1832; Cohen 1942:123]." Congress, however, continued to assert
ever-increasing powers of imposed rule over the tribes, both on constitutional
grounds and on the basis of powers spelled out in treaties.

Article I, Section 8, of the United States Constitution (the Commerce Clause)
provides for federal (rather than state) authority to handle commerce with
foreign nations and Indian tribes. In addition, the so-called Apportionment
Clause, also in Article I, provides that "Indians not taxed" will not be counted
toward establishing the proper apportionment of representatives to the House of
Representatives of the United States Congress. These two very general and
ambiguous provisions are the slender reeds upon which all Indian policy and
Indian law has been built. The Commerce Clause was first used to reserve for
the federal government an authority over Indian affairs that was frequently
claimed by the states; Indian affairs were a major bone of contention between
the Federalists and the early states-rights advocates, leading to confrontations
between figures like Marshall (a Federalist) and President Andrew Jackson (a
states-rights supporter) over the status and powers of the Cherokee nation and
the state of Georgia. In addition, congressional powers such as the sanctioning of
treaties, and responsibilities such as concern for the national defense and control
of the public domain, which were also spelled out in the Constitution, were used
to reinforce the right to intervene in Indian affairs. Much of this authority was
delegated for administration to the Bureau of Indian Affairs, which was created
in the War Department in 1824 and finally transferred to the Department of the
Interior in 1849. During the period of direct administration of Indian tribes by
the United States government, roughly from the 1880s to 1934, the BIA exercised virtually absolute power over the tribes and their members. Even at other
times, BIA authority has extended to control of tribal funds, power of veto over
tribal decisions and actions, allotment of tribal lands, probate of individual
estates, administration of individual funds and approval of their expenditure,
enrollment of individuals in the tribes, control of tribal police and courts, etc.

These powers were assumed through the dual processes of threat and promise
incorporated in the treaties. Indian treaties have the status in international and
in American law of any other treaties (for example, with France or England):

"That treaties with Indian tribes are of the same dignity as treaties with foreign nations is a view which has been repeatedly confirmed by the federal courts and never successfully challenged [Cohen 1942:33–34]." They supersede laws promulgated by states, and other national laws, unless and until Congress exercises its power to amend or abolish their writ through explicit new laws. These treaties, it should be stressed, were seldom if ever the result of conquest over the tribes, but rather were a pragmatic response by both parties either to stalemate or to the likelihood of continuing conflict too costly to be sustained by either side indefinitely. Thus the treaties provide for the interests of both parties, although it is also clear that the American government had a preponderance of power and was usually able to dictate terms to some extent. The contradictions of the situation appear in the carrot-and-stick approach. In a number of treaties, beginning with the very first between the United States and an Indian tribe (the Delaware Treaty of 1778), the United States offered the possibility of representation in Congress to Indian nations (see also the Hopewell Treaty of 1785 and the Choctaw Treaty of 1830). In addition, as present Indian litigation supports, most treaties guaranteed respect for retained Indian land, rights of tribal self government, and principles of autonomy, as well as acknowledgment of rights to resources. Payment was tendered, albeit not always at appropriate rates, for lands and resources taken by the United States. On the other hand, the treaty process was all too often characterized by fraud, coercion, deceit, and illegality perpetrated by American agents on the tribes. In many cases, the tribes were threatened with terrible retribution if the treaties were not signed. In spite of this, many tribes preferred armed struggle or withdrawal into conditions of danger and impoverishment to signing away their birthrights, and many treaties were signed by so-called paper chiefs appointed or bribed by the United States to act on behalf of their fellows, or by a self-appointed faction (as in the Cherokee and Creek cases).

The outcome, however, was that the treaties came into effect (sometimes without even being ratified by either Indians or Congress, as was the case with the Sioux Treaty of 1868), and Congress was able to use their provisions to reinforce its extension of power over the tribes. Among explicit provisos used to extend this power were those providing for exclusive trade relations with Americans, congressional power to review treaty provisions, and the administrative power to appoint agents, traders, and military units to reservations, to arbitrate, and to remove members of the Indian service. The extent of these powers can be seen in their culmination, the arbitrary and unilateral conclusion of treaty-making legislated by Congress as a rider to an appropriations act in 1871, justified on the grounds that tribes no longer possessed the political or military potency to warrant treaties. After 1871, no new treaties were made, although the old ones remain in effect. Since that time, Indian law has been produced primarily through legislative and judicial action.

Treaty law has always been central to Indian status in the United States because it symbolizes and is the foremost exemplar of the uniqueness of Indian tribes within the American political and legal context. Indians alone of all ethnic and political groups in American society have treaties with their government. The treaties have become crucial to the current Indian political struggle because they are concerned with two areas of Indian law: sovereignty and resource rights. Until roughly the 1840s, the government made little or no attempt to infringe on tribal self-determination, both from disinclination and from lack of leverage over the tribes. Beginning with the serious military and demographic reversals for Indians of the 1830s and 1840s, the government made more and more inroads into tribal self-determination. The term *sovereignty* became a mockery of the status attributed to tribal governments, even after the restoration of the forms of self-determination provided by the Indian Reorganization Act in 1934. The debate over that bill focused on the inherent capability of the tribes to exercise these powers. It was thought better to err on the side of underestimation of tribal capacity: "The law as finally enacted, left to the future many grants of power included in the original bill, for which it was felt that the Indians were not yet ready [Cohen 1942:86]." Among these powers were some critical to the exercise of self-government, such as the right to remove undesirable employees from the reservation, the right to appropriate tribal funds held in the United States Treasury, and the power to take over services being rendered by the Interior Department. Exactly these powers and rights have been at the center of much tribal agitation for meaningful self-government during the last decade. In their absence, the status of tribal governments as well as tribal individuals can only be described as one of wardship and therefore of dependence. Sovereignty and dependence are generally viewed as incompatible and even antithetical principles. From Marshall onward, however, many authorities have argued that they can be bridged by a notion of "limited sovereignty," under which the tribes retain considerable powers of internal self-determination in exchange for the sacrifice of any powers of external autonomy. The retention of internal authority depends on the retention of rights and powers that the Indian Reorganization Act revived, at least ostensibly. Writing shortly after that act went into effect, the noted authority on Indian law, Felix Cohen, stated: "Since 1933 no law has been enacted which took from any tribe, against its will, any of its liberties or any of its possessions [Cohen 1942:86]." Contemporary Indian activists and tribal leaders would argue that his was a premature judgment.

INDIAN COUNTRY

Indian country is both a geographic and a legal concept. Geographically, it refers to those islands of Indian land, now known as reservations, upon which Indian title applies. Legally, it refers to those areas, again reservations, where Indian jurisdiction in civil and criminal matters applies. The thrust of American law has been to reduce steadily both "territories." The reduction of land title was the first order of business from the first moments of contact. Sometimes by conquest, but mostly by contract, the holdings of the Europeans were inexorably increased at Indian expense. The justification for the often ethically questionable accumulation of Indian lands by the invading society was early put forward in a sophisticated form:

> However extravagant the pretension of converting the discovery of an inhabited country into conquest may appear; if the principle has been asserted in the first instance, and afterwards sustained; if a country has been acquired and held under it; if the property of the great mass of the community originates in it, it becomes the law of the land, and cannot be questioned. . . . However this restriction may be opposed to natural right, and to the usages of civilized nations, yet, if it be indispensable to that system under which the country has been settled, and be adapted to the actual condition of the two people, it may, perhaps, be supported by reason, and certainly cannot be rejected by the courts of justice [*Johnson* v. *McIntosh* 1823; Cohen 1942:292].

Under this banner, the vast majority of North America was lost in non-Indian ownership and control. Even within the islands of Indian land retained in the reservation system, assaults were made on Indian ownership.

Land exchanges were always a central focus of the treaty process. Early treaties provided for access to Indian lands by Europeans, then for the transfer of limited portions of land to European ownership. European demands for more and more land led to further "purchases" and "voluntary" transfers, followed by Indian resistance and conflict. As European population pressures and technological capabilities built up to overwhelming advantage over the tribes, the Europeans were able to force ever more concessions of lands. It took the frontier almost 200 years (1607–1800) to move 500 miles inland from the Atlantic, and less than 50 more to go 2500 more miles to the Pacific. In this expansion, Indian country shrank first to the boundaries of the reservations and then even those barriers were breached. One of the strategies adopted by the American government to break up the tribes as communal units was the assignment of individual land allotments to tribal members who were willing to assimilate to an American life-style. This not only created two "classes" of tribal members—individually or collectively propertied—but also ignored traditional tribal beliefs that land and resources could not be "owned" in the European sense, but only used as part of the harmonious relationship between human beings and other phenomena in the natural universe. The government saw the allottees as agents of "civilization" and enacted legislation to protect them from the retribution of other tribal members, as in the 1862 "Act to Protect the Property of Indians Who Have Adopted the Habits of Civilized Life." Tribal members of more traditional bent tended to see these Indians as traitors to the tribes. The fact that many of them were of mixed descent was a major factor in the early development of hostility toward half-breeds among tribal Indians.

Ad hoc distribution of tribal resources proved to be too slow a method of reducing Indian country. In the 1880s, as the Indian wars slowly died out, a major debate on Indian policy took place in Congress. The argument was over whether or not breaking up all communal land holdings of the tribes and individual allotment on a per capita basis would facilitate assimilation of the Indian population into what was then perceived as the American mainstream—the small family farm. In spite of warnings from a few observers that Indians would come to curse those who supported it, the General Allotment, or Dawes, Act of 1871 (24 Stat. 388) was passed. As one commentator noted: "The supreme aim of the friends of the Indian was to substitute white civilization for his tribal culture, and they shrewdly sensed that the difference in the concepts of property was fundamental in the contrast between the two ways of life [Cohen 1942:208]." The General Allotment Act provided for the distribution of all tribally held lands to individual members, according to a formula of 160 acres to each family head, 80 acres to each single person over 18 or orphan under 18, and 40 acres to other single persons under 18. This had the effect of breaking up the community as a corporate structure; it also freed large amounts of land for appropriation by non-Indians. Aside from small amounts of land reserved to the tribes for future distribution, the acreage thus released was rapidly sold off to non-Indians. Further land was alienated from Indian ownership when the new individual owners could not pay the taxes for which they became liable as owners of freehold titles after varied periods of protection from the consequences of ownership. Between 1887 and 1934, when allotment ended as a result of the Indian Reorganization Act, the Indian land base shrank from approximately 150 million acres to 40 million acres of mostly marginal land. President Theodore Roosevelt once described the Allotment Act as "a mighty engine to pulverize the tribal mass." It certainly succeeded in pulverizing the tribal land base.

Indian country had already been restricted to those areas of land generally undesirable to non-Indians; after allotment and the rapid alienation of remaining Indian lands, this restriction increased. As a result, Indian tribes, with inferior land and in the absence of the training and capital investment that might have made even marginal lands productive, sank into a state of poverty, disease, and hopelessness that even the United States government was forced to acknowledge. After the Merriam Report of 1928, which demonstrated that Indians were worse off after 100 years of American administration than they had ever been before, the government reacted. In 1934, as part of the reforms of the Franklin Roosevelt administration, the Indian Reorganization Act was passed. One of its most important provisions was the prohibition on further allotments of land; another was authorization for acquisition of new Indian lands in order to create more viable reservations. The initial effect of this legislation was to halt the erosion of Indian country as a geographic entity. It also in principle provided the basis for future expansion of the tribal land base, although it proved very difficult in practice for tribes to get either money or support for such expansion.

The Indian Reorganization Act also had a significant impact on Indian country as a legal entity. The powers of civil and criminal jurisdiction at stake are essential for any meaningful kind of self-government. Of these, civil jurisdiction has been the lesser bone of contention, if the governmental function itself is excepted. As noted earlier, tribal governments saw their powers progressively usurped, then totally suppressed during the nineteenth century. The Indian Reorganization Act provided for the reorganization and incorporation of tribal governments, mostly on the basis of charters modeled on the American political system and approved in referendums on the reservations. These governments suffered from certain critical limitations—such as the veto power of the Bureau of Indian Affairs over tribal decisions and access to tribal funds. However, they did possess the power to exercise civil jurisdiction on the reservations among tribal members. Tribal courts and tribal police were maintained for this purpose, as well as for the exercise of limited criminal jurisdiction. In fact, the treaties seldom attempted to intervene in civil matters. This fact has been used with some success by the tribes in their struggle to resist incursions by states seeking to expand their own jurisdiction. "Most treaties contain no express provisions on civil jurisdiction and therefore, by implication, confirm the rule that tribal law governs the members of the tribe within the Indian country, to the exclusion of state law [Cohen 1942:45]." Only in the area of civil law can there be said to be a continuing indigenous legal tradition, and it is a very limited one. Some legal authorities have argued that the "Indian tribes have been accorded the widest possible latitude in regulating the domestic relations of their members [Cohen 1942:137]." In fact, this seems to come down to limited regulation of marriage, family relations, alcohol possession and use, etc. Of these, probably only marriage laws retain a significantly "Indian" (traditional) component, and even these have been seriously affected by the Christian missionary effort. In less traditional areas, tribes have the power to exclude nonmembers from the reservation, to determine membership criteria, and to levy taxes. This last has turned out to be a most important power—one that promises to help the tribes not only to build up their revenue base but also to assert political power over the many non-Indians resident on most reservations who have acquired land titles or economic stakes there. Non-Indians now being subjected to these powers are, however, vociferous in calling for the termination of the tribes. Thus one of the few powers of self-determination left to the tribes may precipitate their demise.

Criminal jurisdiction has always been a more serious affair for the United States government. In this sense, Indian country is "country within which Indian laws and customs and federal laws relating to Indians are generally applicable [Cohen 1942:5]." Before 1817, Indian country was technically that country within which the United States criminal jurisdiction did not apply. Indian tribes exercised full jurisdiction over non-Indian as well as Indian malefactors. This was acknowledged in treaties. In fact, Americans had to have passports to travel in Indian country, as the Creek Treaty of 1790 testifies (Article 7, 7 Stat. 35, 37 - 1790). The changing balance of power between the United States and the tribes led to the Act of 3 March 1817, which extended United States jurisdiction to all crimes committed by Indians or whites in Indian country except those involving only Indians (3 Stat. 383). This state of affairs persisted until late in the nineteenth century, when the murder of a prominent

Indian leader who had been cooperating with the United States (Spotted Tail of the Brule Sioux) by another Indian (Crow Dog) could not be prosecuted by the American authorities. In order to clear up the anomaly that Indian criminal jurisdiction seemed to present, Congress passed the Seven Major Crimes Act in 1885 (23 Stat. 362, 385, 18U.S.C.548), which extended United States jurisdiction to crimes of a serious nature—murder, manslaughter, rape, assault with intent to kill, arson, burglary, and larceny—involving exclusively Indians. This list was later extended to 10 major crimes—including robbery, incest, and assault with a deadly weapon. Even after the passage of the Indian Reorganization Act in 1934, the federal government retained these powers. The effect of this was to undermine seriously the significance of Indian status on both the individual and tribal level. Since personal Indian identity depended on tribal affiliation, anything that eroded tribal status and identity affected the individual Indian.

The next major assault on tribal jurisdiction was ruthless. House Concurrent Resolution No. 108, also called "Termination," was introduced in 1953 with the intent of terminating unilaterally all treaty relationships between tribes and the United States. Reservations would be disbanded, property would be divided among tribal members or sold off, and Indians would simply disappear into American society. A number of supporters of this legislation described it as "freeing the Indians" and eliminating "second-class citizenship." Several tribes were terminated—notably the Menominee of Wisconsin and the Klamath of Oregon—but in general the tribes were able to organize and fight the legislation so successfully that by the early 1960s it was in effect a dead letter, and termination as a policy was officially repudiated by President Nixon in his major address on Indian policy in July 1970. Since that time a more gradual approach has been officially adopted, stressing the subcontracting of federal services by the tribes themselves and the retrocession to the tribes of certain powers not effectively exercised by them since the period of direct administration by the Bureau of Indian Affairs—such as control over education and some health services.

At first glance the twentieth century so far seems to have been a period of revitalization of tribal authority, with the Indian Reorganization Act and the retrocession of powers back to the tribes. Termination, in between, seems to be an anomaly. However, closer examination of underlying patterns in the development of Indian law suggests that the thrust of this law remains, as it has always been, a merging of the Indian population into American society. Two major pieces of Indian law substantiate this. The first, and most important, is the so-called Indian Bill of Rights (Title II of the Civil Rights Act of 1968). This Act extends the protection of the United States Constitution, and specifically the Bill of Rights, to Indians living on the reservation and subject to tribal jurisdiction. Congress assumed that such an act was required in order that all citizens might enjoy the privileges and protections of liberal democracy. Most tribal representatives testified against the Act at hearings held on the reservations, however, arguing that the imposition of the constitutional principles on the tribes was a violation of treaty rights, which guaranteed the tribes powers of self-determination. Legislation providing civil and political rights of this type should, in their view, have been the prerogative of the various tribal governments. In addition, it can be argued that the highly individualistic bias of American social theory and of constitutional principles threatens on a very fundamental level the survival of the communal tribal ethos. To view the tribe as some kind of corporation or municipal structure in which members have shares or constituent claims is to distort the very nature of the tribe as a social and political unit. Tribes have been quick to perceive this and have attempted to mitigate the dangers of extensive suits against tribal resources by making tribal members aware of the political nature of such acts.

The Indian Bill of Rights clearly involved the direct imposition of American law on Indian communities and, by making those communities resemble more closely American political institutions, affected the meaning of Indian identity as distinct and autonomous. A recent Supreme Court decision (*Oliphant* 1977) further emphasized the pattern of undermining the autonomy of the tribal unit by establishing that the tribal governments do not have the authority to try non-Indians on the reservations for violations of tribal law. A kind of extra-territoriality has thus been created. Such fundamental laws restrict the sphere within which Indian identity can be expressed, first limiting the scope of relations between Indians and non-Indians and then molding the possible interactions among Indians themselves.

TREATY RIGHTS

The nature of the treaty relationship has been discussed above. In terms of sustaining an autonomous Indian identity, the treaties are important not only because they reinforce the right of tribal self-determination, but also because they specifically guarantee certain rights over land and resources upon which the survival of the tribal communities must depend. Among these are rights to water, minerals, and natural resources such as timber, fish, and game. In view of the controversies surrounding these claims and the extent to which they were or were not spelled out in the treaties, it is important to note that American courts have held that the Indian interpretation should govern:

> In construing any treaty between the United States and an Indian tribe, it must always . . . be borne in mind that the negotiations for the treaty are conducted, on the part of the United States, an enlightened and powerful nation, by representatives skilled in diplomacy, masters of a written language, understanding the modes and forms of creating the various technical estates known to their law, and assisted by an interpreter employed by themselves; that the Indians on the other hand are a weak and dependent people, who have no written language and are wholly unfamiliar with all the forms of legal expression, and whose only knowledge of the terms in which the treaty is framed is that imparted to them by the interpreter employed by the United States; and that the treaty must therefore be construed, not according to the technical meaning of its words to learned lawyers, but in the sense in which they would naturally be understood by the Indians [*Johnson* v. *Meehan*, 1876; Cohen 1942:38].

Put somewhat more explicitly: "A cardinal rule in the interpretation of Indian treaties is that ambiguities are resolved in favour of the Indians [*Winters* v. *United States* 1908; Cohen 1942:37]." The terminology of treaties was often ambiguous, referring, for example, to the retention of hunting and fishing rights "in the usual and accustomed manner" and at "the usual and accustomed places," without further specification or elaboration. In the case of water rights, reference might be made to a priority for tribes in meeting their needs, without specifying whether these were to be present or future needs. These ambiguities became in the twentieth century sources of great controversies, which currently threaten to bring about the final elimination of tribal status and rights.

In extending their own claims against Indian tribes, non-Indian interests (for example, commercial and sports fishermen, land developers, and farmers) argued that the "usual and accustomed manner" provision limited modern Indians to the use of techniques and equipment with which their ancestors were familiar. They also argued that "usual and accustomed places," which could be anywhere, were superseded by the constraints of the reservations. In the case of water rights, so crucial in the relatively arid American West, it was argued that Indian priorities extended no further than the water needed to sustain a traditional life-style, mostly nomadic. Nomads are not heavy water users. Tribes contested these claims through the courts whenever possible, and generally they have been successful in achieving either protection or, more often and less satisfactorily, compensation, in the judicial processes. The Winters decision in 1908, for example, has been definitive in establishing an absolute Indian priority to water use sufficient to ensure a reasonable quality of life, on whatever economic basis the tribe chooses to adopt. This doctrine has been extended to contemporary efforts by tribes to develop irrigated agriculture, recreation facilities, and other projects requiring considerably more water resources than would traditional life-styles. Needless to say, these Indian rights have been challenged by threatened American interests, a challenge which has taken a political turn after the Indian successes in the courts.

Much the same pattern can be seen with regard to fishing rights. The treaties of Point Elliot and Medicine Creek in Washington State promised the coastal Indians the right to "share equally" in the fish resources of Puget Sound, of which the most important is the salmon. In a complicated series of cases, the tribes fought for access to fish outside the confines of their severely reduced reservations, to which they had been limited by the interpretations of the treaties made by local and state authorities. Finally, in the Boldt decision of 1973 (*U.S.* v. *Washington* 1974), the court ruled that "sharing equally" meant that the fish catch should literally be split half and half between the Indians and the non-Indian fishermen, in spite of the fact that Indians make up a fairly small part of the state population (less than 5%).

The response of non-Indian interests to these and other actions—such as the organization of an Indian energy consortium called the Council of Energy Resource Tribes (CERT) in 1976 to secure better prices for and more Indian control over such reservation resources as coal, oil, uranium, natural gas, and molybdenum—was to challenge once again the very idea of special status for Indian tribes. In 1977, new bills calling for the termination of the treaty relationship and the reduction of Indians to the status of other Americans were introduced into Congress. They called for a complete merger of the Indian population into American society. The vehicle for this merger is the destruction of the tribe as such, for an Indian identity critically depends in the eyes of both the tribes and the American government on the existence of the tribe and on tribal affiliation. The imposition of American law and legal conventions upon the tribes over the years can thus be understood as an assault on and manipulation of Indian identity, with the intention of reducing it to the ethnically meaningless status of the hyphenated American.

CONCLUSION

Identity in the sense discussed here has two faces, individual and collective, and two modes of expression, personal and political. Before the arrival of the Europeans, the nature and scope of Indian identity, tied to its tribal context, were subject only to Indian determination. In the absence of systematic pressure toward change or suppression, this kind of identity could be said to be fully extended. It has been argued here that the effect of some 400 years of interaction between Europeans and Indians in North America and some 200 years of the imposition of American law has been the steady compression of Indian identity in both its individual and collective forms through the systematic suppression of both the personal and the political modes of its expression. Indianness has become the subject of semantic debate rather than ethnological discovery to a significant degree. This is substantiated by the study of American Indian law, of which some examples have been offered. Why it has been the case may be established by an examination of the rationales offered, often in the law itself (for instance, the "civilizing mission") and the effects of the policy (for instance, transfer of vast amounts of land and resources from Indians to non-Indians), and by observation of a long-standing concern with the creation of a homogeneous society of "Americans" (as stated by a long series of Commissioners of Indian Affairs in their annual reports).

The idea of "the American" is, of course, an artificial creation in the special sense unique to all societies based on emigrant populations rather than on the evolution of indigenous populations. Other notable examples of such societies include Canada, Australia, Brazil, Argentina and Chile. In the effort to forge a new national identity there is great sensitivity to any and all forces, real or assumed, that seem to threaten that national identity—racial, religious, cultural, political, or whatever. It has long been conventional political wisdom that heterogeneity is inherently threatening to the body politic. Only by examining such assumptions underlying political action can one explain the intense and sustained assault upon Indian identity even after the tribes were subdued militarily.

Because of the relatively rapid shift in the balance of military and technological power in favor of the Europeans, and because of the absence of traditions of formal law and written languages, no autonomous indigeneous legal tradition was able to compete with American law. Thus the debate over retention or elimination of Indian status has been conducted almost entirely within the American legal community—in Congress, in the executive branch, in the courts, in the minds of Indian agents of the Bureau of Indian Affairs designated to implement Indian policy. This debate testifies to the disagreement in American society about goals, values, and appropriate means and priorities. The fact that Indian interests have survived so long after the loss of real power is probably a tribute to some of the strengths of liberal democracy. On the other hand, the debate has proceeded largely without meaningful Indian participation and often despite the objections of organized Indian opinion, which demonstrates how completely Indian survival is dependent on the whims of American interest. The current thrust toward an involuntary merger of Indian people into American society is the culmination of the process of compressing Indian identity. It is ironic that after decades of intensive pressure for assimilation, the fact of the assimilation of many Indians is now used to justify the termination of Indian status even for those who have resisted.

The imposition of an alien legal system on indigenous populations is widely viewed as characteristic of the colonial situation. In this sense, the relations between the tribes and the American government were colonial. In most colonial situations—for example, in Africa, Asia, or South America—the indigenous population heavily outnumbered the colonial one. This fact alone limits the impact of the imposed legal system because of the difficulties of penetrating a large local community and overcoming its inherent resistance, a situation that has generally meant (as the Rhodesians are learning) the eventual end of colonial domination. American Indians, like Australian Aborigines and Maoris, do not have the luxury of outnumbering the invaders. Indians constitute less than 5% of the American population, in spite of having the highest rate of natural increase of that population since early in the century; there were some 760,000 Indians listed as such in the United States census in 1970, and not all of these retain tribal ties or federal status. The compression of identity is reflected in compressed numbers as well.

From the point of view of Indian activists committed to the survival of both the personal and the tribal Indian identity, the issue is whether it is possible to use the law both to stop the erosion of the basis of Indian status (through the successful prosecution of treaty-law cases before the courts) and to ''reinflate'' that status through the expansion of the rights of tribal membership and of personal Indian status. An Indianness that cannot be expressed or asserted against the claims of other identities has no meaningful existence. The pattern of Indian law has been to circumscribe ever more closely the opportunities for expression and the power of assertion of Indian status. Increasingly Indians have perceived that this is the role of the law as it has developed. Beginning with the Indian Claims Act of 1946, which permitted tribes to sue the government for illegalities perpetrated against the tribes during the treaty process, attention in Indian country has focused more and more on the American legal system. The Native American Rights Fund and other largely Indian organizations have been pursuing crucial treaty cases more and more frequently during the 1970s. And there are more and more trained Indian attorneys. In Indian country, law is where the real action is, not in the demonstrations and occupations, which must primarily serve to draw attention and sympathy to Indian causes. American law has been imposed on the Indian tribes for the last 200 years. The issue now is whether that same law can be used by Indians to impose recognition of Indian rights on a sometimes reluctant American society. The issue is also whether an autonomous Indian identity can survive the struggle.

REFERENCES

CASES

Cherokee Nation v. *Georgia*, 5 Pet. 18 (1831).
Farrell v. *United States*, 110 Fed. 942 (C.C.A.8 1901).
Johnson v. *McIntosh*, 8 Wheat. 543 (1823).
Johnson v. *Meehan*, 93 U. S. 188 (1876).
Oliphant v. *Suquamish Indian Tribe et al.*, 98 S. Ct. 1011 (1978).
U. S. v. *Washington*, 394 F. Supp 312 (W. D. Wash. 1974).
Winters v. *United States*, 207 U. S. 564 (1908).
Worcester v. *Georgia*, 6 Pet. 515 (1832).

OTHER SOURCES

Cohen, F.
    1942   *Handbook of Federal Indian Law*. Washington D. C.: United States Government Printing Office (reprinted 1972).
Deloria, V., Jr.
    1971   *Of Utmost Good Faith*. San Francisco: Straight Arrow Press.
Price, M.
    1972   *Law and the American Indian*. Indianapolis: Bobbs-Merrill.

6

THE IMPOSED WARDSHIP OF AMERICAN INDIAN TRIBES: A CASE STUDY OF THE PRAIRIE BAND POTAWATOMI

NORMAN FORER

On the morning of 4 August 1972, the front page of the *Topeka* (Kansas) *Daily Capital* was dominated by a dramatic photo of a group of Potawatomi Indians "storming" the doorway to the Kansas office of the U.S. Government Bureau of Indian Affairs (BIA). Photographed at the height of the scuffle with sheriff's deputies, the Potawatomi young men and women were supported by the presence of tribal elders and the tribal chairman.

The accompanying article alluded to alleged BIA "attempts to subvert . . . self-determined programs" through the freezing of tribal funds. The precipitating issue was a dispute concerning the extent of federal control over lands that the Society of Jesus (Jesuits) sought to transfer to the Potawatomi in support of a tribal community development project. The article noted that this controversy was further complicated by an intratribal dispute which a few days earlier at a general membership meeting had given rise to the recall of four of the seven elected tribal officers and the election of replacements. (The tribal chairman received a vote of confidence.) The article noted that this meeting had not been authorized by the BIA.

The issue of control of tribal lands and programs soon focused on the question of the legitimacy of the controlling body. The BIA claimed that the new tribal

89

The Imposition of Law

Copyright © 1979 by Academic Press, Inc.
All rights of reproduction in any form reserved.
ISBN 0-12-145450-9

government lacked legitimacy since the method of electing the replacement officers had violated procedures stipulated in the tribal constitution.

The chairman readily acknowledged that the ouster and replacement of officers were unconstitutional but justified the action by arguing that the tribal constitution itself was illegitimate because it was an imposition by the BIA. The chairman claimed that the BIA's long history of constitutional reinterpretation and induced factionalism had the effect of imposing pro-BIA officers and policies on the tribe, thereby impeding self-determination.

According to the chairman and his supporters, the BIA itself was illegitimate: it was merely an agency of a state, the United States government, which had in the past violated its treaties with the Potawatomi nation. These violations had resulted in the massive alienation of Potawatomi lands. The new tribal officers were elected "the Indian way" the chairman claimed, that is, by the whole membership of the tribe in the interests of protecting the remaining tribal lands and customs.

The issue of state law versus law of custom was joined. The debate intensified for 2 months, after which the BIA sought to end it by withdrawing recognition of the tribal constitution, thereby suspending the tribal government and placing the administration of tribal affairs directly in the hands of the BIA agency superintendent.[1]

THE IMPOSITION OF LAW

The law of the state, in contrast to the law of custom, institutionalizes the imposition of the interests of a ruling elite over the rest of society. State law serves to legitimize the implementation of social control. State justice, then, can be viewed as the state-authorized administration of coercion in the interests of the elite. The administration of justice is also a form of socialization in that its coerciveness produces a common belief in the desirability of compliance and hence a tendency toward acceptance of those social values that rationalize the law.

In a multiclass society—that is, a society that has produced a state—elitism is an expression of the ability to control property either through direct ownership or through the support of such owning groups. State law is therefore in constant tension with those social relations and individual behavior that militate against the elitist control of property. Certainly this is true in the United States, where the courts have consistently defined property in terms of title rather than in terms of those social relations that produced it or historically occupied it. The

---

[1] Sources for this event, the ensuing BIA–tribal dispute, and the BIA–tribal election dispute of 1971 are drawn from numerous BIA memoranda, BIA–tribal correspondence, trial transcripts and briefs, tribal leadership position statements and press releases, tribal newsletters, meeting notes and tapes, interviews, and author's participant observation. Copies of source documents are in the author's possession.

mass socialization process engineered by the modern state can be viewed more accurately as a resocialization process: an attempt to eliminate traditional and local group identities in deference to individualistic identification with the goals and life-styles of the national elite. State law is therefore designed to obfuscate the real conditions of propertylessness or marginal ownership and to create a general belief in the independent and non-imposed nature of law. This constant resocialization is designed to create and reinforce a general belief that the law somehow is above society and even above the state as an inspired guide to the mediation of differences among men. Such beliefs enhance the mystical notion that the law, having an independent life of its own, has inherent magisterial and truthful qualities and, even when obviously discriminatory, is essentially just. The divine right of kings has, in modern society, been transformed into the divine right of the word of the law.

To the extent that growing industrialization facilitates class mobility and the breakup of traditional mutual support relationships, the concept of impartial law becomes a dominant norm of society. Through such a concept the propertyless aspire to the status of the propertied. This socialization is never complete, however, since subgroups such as (in the United States) blacks, women, homosexuals, marginal workers, or mental patients initially challenge the legitimacy of the state and its law and then reaccept the state's legitimacy as new opportunities for resource redistribution and upward mobility grow out of the challenge. The constant disruption of community life, the displacement of sub-groups, and the creation of new subgroups—processes inherent in industrialization—guarantee the continuation of these challenges. Moreover, socialization by the state is never complete because the primacy of state and property values violates "natural" human requirements for community relationships. Dissatisfaction with this is increasingly expressed in industrial society through various forms of disruptive and antisocial behavior.

The imposition of state law on Indian tribes in the United States is a naked imposition in glaring contrast to the masked imposition of law in American society at large. This is attributable to the unique position of American Indians in the industrially oriented development of United States nationhood. Indian tribes were the only group in the United States whose existence as national entities demanded collective possession of land, land-based subsistence and exchange production, and a mystical view of the world. It was inevitable that the growth of United States nationhood—based on private ownership, commodity production, industrial expansion, and a rationalist view of the world—required the extinction of Indian nationhood. It is little wonder that until the first third of the twentieth century, federal policy was predicated on the assumption of the physical "fading away" of Indian peoples. Failing that, and despite the liberal policy proclamations of subsequent presidential administrations in support of "Indian self-determination," federal policy has been designed to achieve the dispersal, urbanization, and cultural absorption of Indian tribes.

The upsurge of Indian activism in the past decade is testimony not only to the

Indians' refusal to disappear but also to their reassertion of those aspects of nationhood and cultural coherence still possible in modern society. In calling upon non-Indian support for their resistance to the imposition of federal law, leading Indian activists have pointed to the imposed nature of law throughout U.S. society. "You are all Indians" is a common theme of Indian militants addressing non-Indian audiences.

The unfolding of the Potawatomi case not only reveals a process of U.S. legal imposition common to Indian tribes in general, but also illustrates a type of colonial imposition common in Third-World countries. Broadly speaking, this process includes the following elements: the cultural, commercial, and military penetration of native territories; the destabilization of traditional native societies and governments by encouraging factionalism and/or manipulating existing factionalism; the creation of surrogate native governments; the domination of the surrogate governments through a trustee, protectorate, or "sphere-of-influence" relationship; the institutionalization of this relationship through a system of treaties, law courts, and civil service; the resocialization of the native population to acceptance of the authority of these institutions as well as the authority of the colonial and native institutional bureaucrats; the use of combined colonial and native police and military power to suppress overt resistance to this authority; and the rationalization of the total process on grounds of racial superiority, Christian imperative, economic progress, national interest, mutual self-interest, law and order—in a word, on grounds of "civilization." An understanding of any particular instance of imposition on dependent peoples therefore warrants an examination of these phenomena in terms of their interrelationship and historic evolution. The imposition of law is a fundamental part of the process of the domination and domestication of peoples, both within and outside national boundaries. It is the process of history itself.

In examining the historic roots of the Potawatomi case the factors of treaties, wardship, acculturation, imposed factionalism, institutional control, land expropriation, and tribal resistance are so intertwined that a delineation of each separate theme is hardly feasible in a short chapter. These and other related factors will therefore be presented in broad strokes with some juxtaposition of past and contemporary events. A portrait of the process of legal imposition on American Indians will, I hope, emerge.

THE 1972 POTAWATOMI CASE

In 1972, when the Bureau of Indian Affairs (BIA) withdrew recognition of the tribal constitution of the Prairie Band Potawatomi, it justified its actions on the grounds that the tribe was incapable of self-government because of factional disputes within its leadership. Shortly before its action an agent of the BIA drafted a resolution stating that the tribal officers (Business Committee) "can no longer work together . . . for the benefit of the tribe" and requesting that the "Commissioner of Indian Affairs suspend the [tribal] Constitution and conduct all business for the tribe until such time as the Commissioner deems it advisable to conduct a new election of [officers].'' The resolution was hand-delivered to each of the seven members of the Business Committee by the BIA agent. Four of the seven signed. These four, as previously indicated, had been removed from office 2 months earlier by a vote of the general membership in an election deemed illegal and unconstitutional by the BIA. The anti-BIA faction, which included the tribal chairman and a tribal elder who was head of the traditionalist religious organization, had been given a vote of confidence by the membership and had subsequently refused to sign the BIA-promoted resolution. This faction claimed that the ouster had been prompted by the refusal of the four officers to attend Business Committee meetings, thereby depriving the Committee of the quorum necessary to conduct tribal affairs. The anti-BIA faction claimed that the absence of the four had been promoted by the local BIA superintendent. They cited instances of private caucusing between the superintendent and the four and they pointed to the fact that each of the four held paid jobs within the BIA bureaucracy or other federal programs. The anti-BIA faction claimed that one of the four admitted to having been ordered by the superintendent not to attend Business Committee meetings. ''I do what I'm told,'' he was alleged to have said. ''They [the BIA] are the boss.''

Although the BIA had cited the failure of self-government and the loss of programs of benefit to the tribe as the reasons for its intervention, the anti-BIA faction claimed that, on the contrary, it was their very success at independent program development which had prompted the intervention. They cited a history of virtual absence of BIA support for Potawatomi economic development programs and they cited their own recent accomplishments in the development of a broad range of educational, housing, employment, and social service programs on the reservation. The anti-BIA faction had also, through lengthy negotiation and extensively organized Indian and non-Indian community support, received a promise from the Jesuits to deliver by deed to the tribe an abandoned college and 1382 acres of improved farmland. (The anti-BIA faction cited a clandestine meeting between the superintendent and some of the four and their supporters allegedly designed to sabotage the agreement with the Jesuits.) In addition, the anti-BIA leaders had negotiated a grant of a million dollars of surplus U.S. government equipment and supplies in support of existing reservation programs as well as proposed tribe-controlled housing, health, cultural, recreation, educational, and economic development programs at the college. This was hardly a demonstration of the failure of effective self-government, as the BIA had alleged.

A closer look at the situation revealed a conflict between the anti-BIA faction and the BIA over control of the Jesuit properties.[2] The anti-BIA faction sought means of keeping the properties for tribal use in perpetuity, whereas the Bureau

---

[2] Sources for this event and all subsequent events relating to Jesuit–tribal relations are drawn from Jesuit–tribal correspondence, Jesuit–BIA correspondence, BIA–tribal correspondence, Jesuit and tribal position statements and press releases, meeting notes and tapes, interviews, and author's participant observation. Copies of source documents are in the author's possession.

insisted on describing them as "merchantable." The basic issue was between the competing values of traditionalism and commercialism but was complicated by tribal factional intrigues.

The "divide and rule" principle is an invaluable weapon in the hands of those who wish to dispossess people of their land, their labor, their property, and their lives. It even makes the expropriation legitimate, since the apparent willingness of the oppressed group to acquiesce in their downfall can be cited as proof that justice is prevailing. For example, Article 1 of the 1861 Potawatomi Treaty with the United States declares that the Potawatomi "believe it will contribute to the civilization of their people to dispose of a portion of their present reservation in Kansas." The South African government in setting up its black reserves, or "homelands," similarly contends that blacks seek to be removed in their own interest. By creating a faction within the oppressed community that would find it advantageous to invite penetration and control, the imposing power can choose to recognize this faction as the sole representative of the entire oppressed nation and thereby justify its interference.

Factionalism also serves to weaken defensive efforts against penetration by diverting these energies into internal fighting. This in-fighting itself then becomes a rationale for penetration on the grounds that without the "stabilizing" effects of imposed power ("the white man's burden"), "the savages would eat each other up." For example, the United State–Cherokee Treaty of 1846 offers as its rationale the "serious difficulties [that have] for a considerable time past existed between the different portions of the people . . . which it is desirable should be speedily settled . . . so that peace and harmony may be restored among them." Factionalism also serves as an instrument of social control in that members of the favored faction are placed as administrators, judges, and police in the government structure imposed on the oppressed nation. Imposed factional control thereby becomes the means by which law is imposed. Additionally, the imposed faction, as a result of its favored position, becomes a resocialization force for the acceptance of the life-styles and value system of the imposing power. In its ultimate sense, induced factionalism or manipulation of existing internal divisions is designed to achieve a people's complicity in its own cultural, political, and at times physical extinction. (With regard to the latter see the role of the *Judenrat* and the Jewish police in controlling ghetto communities and facilitating transport to the Nazi extermination camps.)

In the Potawatomi case, from the BIA's point of view, an undesirable faction was in control of the tribal machinery—and indeed the BIA was correct in its assessment. The tribal-leadership faction attacked by the BIA and historically labeled by the Bureau as "conservatives" tended toward nativistic religious revivalism and looked to the reservation as the spiritual and political center of tribal life. Their leading opponents, labeled "progressives," tended toward Catholicism, had fewer proscriptions against intermarriage with non-Indians, and were more urban in outlook. The conservatives tended to view the BIA as an unrelenting enemy. (A common conservative slogan was "BIA means Boss

Indians Around.'') The progressives tended to view the Bureau as a necessary though at times unpredictable ally. In 1971, after a decade of progressive control of the tribal government, the conservatives won an overwhelming electoral victory. The Bureau's arbitrary nullification of the election saw the conservatives reconfirmed by an even greater margin in a subsequent election. Their pre-election development of a few modest self-help programs, coupled with their success in winning the right to hunt and fish on the reservation without a state license, had produced a groundswell of popular support and an alliance with some elements among the progressives. This alliance ended a year later over the issue of the Jesuit properties. In any event, the conflict between conservatives and progressives was bitter: a major source of acrimony extending back over a century and a half as a result of the divisive policies of the United States government, the Catholic Church, and the collusion of both with railroad developers, land speculators, and other commercial interests.

The inadequacy of United States law in dealing with such historically conditioned social groupings became apparent in the judicial proceedings that followed the suspension of the Potawatomi constitution. Judicial insistence on dealing with ''facts'' strictly in terms of the here and now, independent of their historic roots, is a form of imposed law. Historical data that are judicially acceptable are simply previous laws that are themselves previous impositions, justified by a coerced acceptance on the part of the oppressed. A history of coerced and manipulated factionalism is too abstract a phenomenon to be considered as acceptable evidence. Thus, sociology tends to be irrelevant to jurisprudence, and the judicial system thereby absolves itself of historic complicity in the events it is currently judging.

In seeking a class-action injunction against the BIA's suspension of the tribal constitution, attorneys for the Potawatomi argued that the BIA violated the rights of free speech and assembly and due process guaranteed to all American citizens by the U.S. Constitution. Attorneys for the United States argued that Indian tribes as wards of the United States ''from the beginning,'' were not protected by the U.S. Constitution and hence the court lacked jurisdiction in the case. They cited the concept of ''sovereign immunity'' in that the United States, as a sovereign power, was immune from suit unless it granted the right to sue. This right had not been granted to Indian tribes. Moreover, the United States viewed the dispute as an intratribal matter in which the BIA had no part other than to solve it administratively, which it was doing at the invitation of one of the factions.

The Potawatomi attorneys argued that the plaintiffs' rights were being limited simply because they were Indians, since the ''special'' wardship status had never been legislated by Congress. Moreover, they argued, the impediment to self-government was created by the BIA itself through its interference in internal tribal affairs.

With case law supporting the government's contentions of the legitimacy of wardship, the suit was dismissed on jurisdictional grounds by the district court.

The appellate court evaded the wardship issue entirely, yet upheld the lower court on jurisdictional grounds, citing the intratribal nature of the dispute. The U.S. Supreme Court declined to hear the case and, as is customary, did so without explanation.

It took 4 years from the date the tribal constitution was suspended for a new tribal government to emerge—this time a government run exclusively by a pro-BIA faction. The Jesuit properties were never transferred to the tribe, and the college campus was subsequently sold to commercial interests.

UNITED STATES-INDIAN RELATIONS

In order to understand the inextricable relationship between social experience and the law affecting not only the Potawatomi but all American Indian tribes, it is necessary to understand the roots of United States policy toward its native peoples—in other words, what the U.S. Attorney meant by "from the beginning." (Government apparently views history in terms of the continuity of its policy rather than in terms of the effect of the policy on its subjects.)

Political concepts of guardian–ward relationships and the guardian's trusteeship over the property of the ward, when applied to national entities, stem from the nature of colonial penetration. Though colonialism obviously benefits the sponsoring country, there are also liabilities. Armed resistance by the native population stimulated by unregulated expropriations and exterminations by colonists requires expensive and risky military support from the home country. Additionally, the lack of regulation not only leads to factional conflict among competing colonists, promoting factional conflict among their sponsors back home, but also runs the risk of promoting conflict among competing colonial powers. Most significantly, however, the lack of regulation can create a political and economic power base that ultimately can challenge, compete with, and even split away from the home country. It was these considerations, in differing degrees, which gave rise to both the Spanish Laws of the Indies in 1542 and the English Royal Proclamation of 1763 as both Crowns sought to regulate penetration into their respective areas of the New World. Both Spanish and English laws recognized Indian title to Indian-occupied lands and required that no such land pass to white ownership without the approval of the Crown, consent of the Indians, and "fair" compensation. Both also acknowledged that Indians should be free of outside interference. The effect of both was to recognize Indian sovereignty (the Spanish explicitly and the English implicitly). The seed of the concept of wardship lay in the concept of the Crown's protection of the sovereignty and property of a presumably less civilized people.

The basic flaw in English policy was that though it extended the authority of the Crown to political relations and, consequently, to land transfer relations with the Indians, it left responsibility for the regulation of trade with each separate colony. This contradiction between a dying feudalism and a nascent capitalism was not to be resolved by subsequent U.S. government Indian policy. Traditionally, the U.S. government has proclaimed itself as the protector of Indian "independence" and property rights against commercial interests (land speculators, railroad builders, traders, farmers, ranchers, fishermen and, more recently, corporate lumber, water use, coal, gas, oil, and mineral extractive interests). However, as it increasingly became the instrument of these private interests, the government itself became the chief instrument of the expropriation and exploitation of Indian resources. The government's public posture of protector, combined with its covert behavior as exploiter, has led to what on the surface appears to be a continual vacillation between liberal reforms for enhancing Indian "self-determination" and the reactionary expunging of Indian culture and property rights. Regardless of intent, it will be subsequently demonstrated that both reformist and reactionary policies produced essentially the same outcome: the separation of Indians from their land. Certainly this outcome is the result of more complex factors than the typical bureaucratic bungling to which some theorists ascribe the inconsistencies and confusion of Indian policy. The attempt by the state of Georgia, under the pressure of commercial interests, to expunge Cherokee Indian treaty rights and incorporate their lands, though it was declared unconstitutional by a liberal United States Supreme Court decision in 1833, did not prevent President Jackson from ignoring the decision and expelling the Indians. This revelatory episode demonstrated the subordination of the American judiciary to acquisitive interests. The façade of "government through impartial law," though it is generally maintained in its application to whites, reveals its true nature when applied to "domestic dependent nations."

The Cherokee case is of additional significance in connection with the argument justifying expropriation as "sanctioned by the natural superiority allowed to the claims of civilized communities over those of savage tribes [United States Congress 1829–1830]." At the time of their expulsion, the Cherokee, striving desperately to prove their right to self-government on the white man's terms, had produced a written language, a translated Bible, a tribal press, and advanced methods of agriculture, as well as legal and educational systems based on white models. They were no more successful in impressing the government than were the Potawatomi 150 years later when they had reached their hasty apex of modern community development programming. In fact, it is safe to assume that such self-determined social development, traditionally encouraged by white liberals, simply invites federal intervention, since Indian success stabilizes tribal life and makes it more resistant to expropriation and removal.

The fiction of a protective United States government has served the white commercial interests well, for it has seduced and still seduces Indians into ignoring even the immediate past in the hope that the current "system" (new treaties until 1871, special social welfare and educational programs, land claims courts, BIA-organized Indian councils and conferences) can be made to work for them.

The factionalism in Indian political life, so strikingly exemplified in the Potawatomi case, boils down to a split between those "conservatives" who remember previous federal practice and those who have "progressed" beyond the lessons of history.

The contradiction between central political control and local economic interests (the English Crown's dilemma), when magnified by the much wider differentiation between local political entities in America, has led to the current confusion of contentious governmental jurisdictions in their relationships with Indian tribes. The Potawatomi, in seeking to develop reservation-based programs, found themselves dealing with tribal government, federally sponsored intertribal councils, local municipal governments, local school districts, county government, state government, and federal government, with intertwining vague and conflicting jurisdictional prerogatives that would induce schizophrenia in a Solomon. It is a testimony to their faith in their own survival that the Potawatomi traditionalist leaders would embark on a patient journey through this maze. Their political encounters were religiously sanctioned, guided by the sacred drum and peyote rites. Indeed, formal religious ceremony preceded each venture. Perhaps there is wisdom in the contention that only mysticism can prevail over bureaucracy.

For the American government, the question of Indian wardship, never legally enacted, appears to emerge inferentially. The Constitutional Convention of 1787 simply gave Congress the power "to regulate commerce . . . with the Indian tribes." It is this slim legal reed, devoid of specified Indian rights and reinforced by Congressional treaty-making powers, that has since provided a major basis of Court opinion in federal–Indian relations. Court justification of federal authority over Indians has on occasion also been derived from "general welfare, national defense and national domain clauses of the Constitution [as well as] the peculiar nature of the relations between the two races independent of [Constitutional] authority [Prucha 1962]." This only serves to emphasize the absence of any consistent basis for Indian law. In practice, federal Indian laws and administrative codes have been little more than legalized endorsements of expediency. It follows that 185 years after enactment of the U.S. Constitution, the U.S. Attorney, supporting the withdrawal of federal recognition of the Potawatomi constitution, should argue:

> Historically, the powers of the Secretary of the Interior and the Commissioner of Indian Affairs and their agents have been far reaching when applied to the Indian Nations. . . . that Congress possesses a paramount power over property of the Indians by reason of its exercise of guardianship over their interests, that such authority may be implied, that plenary authority over the tribal relations of the Indian had been exercised by Congress from the beginning, and the power had always been deemed a political one, not subject to be controlled by the Judicial Department of the government.
>
> The relationships here involved resemble those between a guardian and a ward. The guardian has the duty of taking care of the person as well as managing the property and rights of the ward considered less capable of administering his own affairs [Brief for the Defendant on Motion for Preliminary Injunction at 12, 13, *Potts* v. *Bruce*, 533 F. 2d 527 (10th Cir. 1976)].

It also follows that the Attorney was upheld by the courts. Not to have done so would have been tantamount to providing a legal base for the repossession of the United States by its native people.

In their specious and vague opinions expressed when dismissing the Potawatomi case, the judges apparently either did not understand or willfully evaded the constitutional and historical issues raised by the plaintiffs. A crucial problem that the defense attorneys recognized from the outset was the lack of education judges have with regard to the peculiar nature of Indian law. Law schools generally have few, if any, programs in this specialty. For example, in the Potawatomi case the query raised by the district court judge is perhaps made more incredible by the realization that the Potawatomi are, after all, U.S. citizens:

> The Court: Now since the plaintiffs allege that their rights under the First and Fifth Amendments are being violated, are you saying now that they have no rights under those amendments unless they are expressly granted or recognized by some congressional enactment?
> Mr. Miller (U.S. Attorney): By treaty between the federal government and that Indian tribe, neither of which I believe exists in this case. Yes sir, that is the government's contention [Transcript of Proceedings at 6, *Potts* v. *Bruce,* 533 F. 2d 527 (10th Cir. 1976)].

The Potawatomi traditionalists maintained a fatalistic attitude towards the anticipated opinion of the judges. Experience had taught them that it was not necessary for judges to have a knowledge of history, but merely an instinct for social stability. Obviously, a problem in confronting imposed legal systems is the inability or refusal of its agents to perceive the world from alternative viewpoints.

The public and congressional debate leading to the forced removal of Indian tribes, the Potawatomi among them, from the eastern United States to new "homelands" west of the Mississippi River (Indian Removal Act, 1830,) revealed the essential collusion of reactionary "racist" and liberal "humanitarian" forces. As Sartre indicated in his analysis of the dilemma of the Jews in France: "Between his enemy and his defender, the Jew . . . can do no more than choose the sauce with which he will be devoured [Sartre 1948:58]." The philosophic heirs of the elitist, pro-manufacturing Federalists and their populist, agrarian, decentralist opponents were the different sauces as far as the Indians were concerned. Both were wedded to the sanctity of private property and both were anathema to the "communistic" Indians. Indeed, the great agrarian democrat, President Thomas Jefferson, in a presentation to the Potawatomi in 1802 urged them to cease their nomadic hunting and fishing and "cultivate the earth," "raise herds," and "spin and weave." The United States, said Jefferson, "will with pleasure furnish you with implements for the most necessary acts and with persons who may instruct how to make and use them." Jefferson supported the position of President Washington's administration, which also sought to instill in Indians a "love for exclusive property [Prucha 1962]." Jefferson argued that this educational approach would teach Indians "to do better on less land, [since] increasing numbers [of whites] will be calling for more land." This policy, he said, would achieve "a coincidence of interests [McNickle 1973]." Jefferson supported a gentle, voluntary removal on the ironic grounds that it would be necessary to isolate Indians from the depredations of white society in order that Indians might have time to resocialize themselves (apparently to the same depredations). Thus, cultural assimilation, as a means of separating Indians from their land holdings, was formulated early in United States policy.

The more militant acquisitors, like President Andrew Jackson, held it an "absurdity" to contract treaties, recognize Indian sovereignty, or deal with Indians in any manner other than that appropriate to "savage peoples." Jackson relied on the coercive power of the central government, as did his elitist, pro-manufacturing predecessors. Jackson, however, symbolized democratic militancy and agrarian populism. Thus the traditionally antagonistic manufacturing and agrarian interests found some reconciliation in the expropriation of the Indian.

The United States, early in its political life, supported church missionaries in their task of persuading the Indian to accept private entrepreneurship and resettlement. Four interested parties—commercial, clerical, agricultural, and governmental—initially banded together to decide how federal Indian policy could best be turned to their own advantage. Later, Indian intratribal solidarity had to be fractured in order to create a faction amenable to these interests, and hence a fifth collusive partner. This relationship has remained to the present day, with the government gradually, but by no means completely, removing the resocialization process from the churches to its own educational and welfare institutions.

POTAWATOMI HISTORY

The first major fragmentation of the Potawatomi came as result of the Indian Removal Act (1830), under the terms of which the tribe ceded its lands around the southern Great Lakes. By 1835, the external tribal structure had fallen apart as groups fled to Canada and northern Wisconsin. The main body, some 7000–8000 people, moved west in several waves to reservations in the Iowa Territory and along the Missouri River. Some continued west and ultimately settled in Mexico. Internal divisions were already apparent at the time of removal, partly as a result of the assimilationist influence of Jesuit missionaries. Although the Jesuits set up their first mission school for the Potawatomi as early as 1669, the tribe, with minor exceptions, resisted religious conversion for the next century and a half. Greater assimilationist success was achieved by métis, the offspring of French Catholics who had intermarried with Potawatomi or who otherwise associated with the tribe. They gradually became the dominant brokers of trade and political relations between the Indian and white worlds. As the impact of the Indian Removal Act destabilized the tribe, Jesuit influence grew and the métis became the fifth collusive partner. Ultimately, in the face of traditionalist opposition to new federally imposed treaties, the métis became the Church-imposed tribal representatives for purposes of signing these treaties. In the twentieth century, their physical and philosophic heirs became the hard-core "progressives" in opposition to the "conservatives." In 1972, however, after nearly a century of disengagement from tribal politics, and stimulated by new Church imperatives to advocate social justice for Indians and other minority groups, the Jesuits emerged as strong allies of the Potawatomi traditionalists in opposition to federal domination and accommodation by the progressives.

Until their expulsion from their Great Lakes homeland in the 1830s, the Potawatomi, an aggressive tribe, were generally resistant to external controls. Fighting as allies of the French against the English and with England against the colonists, their warriors, mastering advanced techniques of military organization, were a major force in inter-European and intertribal border warfare. In the decade of the expulsion, influenced by Jesuit promises of protection and mission schools in a new homeland, a distinct Catholic-oriented group, the Mission Band, emerged. The divisions between the predominantly traditionalist faction (Prairie Band) and the Catholic faction were further aggravated by their settlement in separate reservations in the western territories. Under a new treaty in 1846, both factions were removed to a Kansas reservation, ceding 5,000,000 acres in Iowa and Missouri in exchange for 576,000 acres in their new home. The Jesuits, again employing both federal and tribal funds, set up a mission school and an agricultural training program (St. Mary's) in the center of the new reservation. By this time, tribal numbers, depleted by migration, epidemics, and the effects of forced marches, were reduced to some 3200 people, half of whom were now Catholic.

A classic series of moves by the five interested parties saw the further reduction of tribal lands to 77,000 acres in the 1860s. The interests of each party were as follows: white settlers, whose movement into surrounding territories was facilitated by the Kansas–Nebraska Act of 1854, wanted the choice Potawatomi lands. The railroad builders not only sought passage through the reservation but also wanted to acquire tribal lands, which could then be resold to settlers at inflated prices. The resultant capital would underwrite railroad expansion as well as satisfy profiteering urges. The federal government saw increased settlement as a continuation of continental "manifest destiny," further inspired by substantial railroad bribes to a range of congressmen and federal bureaucrats. The Jesuits, noting the influx of white Catholic settlers and railroad workers, saw the need for institutional permanence in a new state that they hoped would become a center of Catholic influence in the expanding country. The métis saw the opportunity for enrichment as land speculators and traders, and their poorer Catholic brethren saw the promise of becoming independent farmers and eventual U.S. citizens.

The strategy for implementing this grand design was as follows: the Jesuits would urge the Indians to sign treaties that would dissolve (sectionize) the communal tribal holdings and convey private title of land parcels to separate Indian families and individuals. The federal government would grant the Jesuits 320 acres to guarantee continued educational and religious services to the tribe. Railroad entrepreneurs would purchase the surplus Potawatomi lands, amounting to two-thirds of the reservation, at a fraction of their market value. In return for Jesuit cooperation, the entrepreneurs would enlarge the mission with a gift of land and would use their influence in Washington to promote other Jesuit institutional interests. The métis and other Catholic Indian leaders would promote the deal to the rest of the tribe. The federal government would give U.S. citizenship in 5 years to those Potawatomi who accepted sectionizing.

This grand design, facilitated by government coercion of the Indians and the bribery of government officials by the railroad interests, proved largely successful. In 1861 this design yielded an official treaty between the United States and the Potawatomi. Subsequent changes in the fortunes of competing railroad entrepreneurs inspired an amended treaty, this one hastily ratified in a secret session of the United States Senate in 1868. This treaty gave the Santa Fe Railroad the option to buy the surplus tribal lands at one half the price authorized in the 1861 treaty. Samuel C. Pomeroy, the president of the Santa Fe Company, had, as a senator from Kansas, been a key figure in the earlier treaty. The Jesuits also benefited from the amended treaty through additional land acquisition. Tribal consent to the amended treaty was given by a single signatory—a métis land speculator whose participation had been initiated by the Church.

As a result of the amended treaty, the Santa Fe purchased some 340,000 acres of the Potawatomi reservation at $1 per acre. The railroad quickly resold approximately half of this land to white settlers at an average of $4.40 per acre. The balance was sold for $1 per acre to supportive government bureaucrats, politicians, financiers, and railroad directors.

The Mission Band Potawatomi, accepting land allotments as a result of the 1861 Treaty, soon saw themselves swindled by their own métis leaders and other traders. By 1866 virtually all were rendered homeless paupers, not fit for their promised U.S. citizenship, and most moved south to a new Indian territory. Ironically, their group earned for themselves the official federal designation of Citizens Band Potawatomi.

The Prairie Band, stubbornly resisting land allotments, was removed to a corner of the dismantled reservation and continued to hold land communally for a while. By the end of the decade its numbers had diminished to about 450 persons. The diminished area (77,000 acres) became their new reservation and remains so today.

The Jesuits, although failing ultimately to make Kansas a center of Catholic influence, did emerge in time with clear title to some 2300 acres around St. Mary's Mission. With the dispersal of the Catholic Citizen Band and the rejection of Catholicism by the traditionalist Prairie Band, the Jesuits in 1869 turned St. Mary's into a school serving the growing white population. St. Mary's College subsequently became a Jesuit seminary. The college ceased operation in 1969.

The dispersal and decimation of the Potawatomi was symptomatic of the general fate of Indians as a people. At the time of the Prairie Band's final removal, the U.S. Indian population was approaching its lowest point of some 200,000, or about one-fifth the estimated population at the time of Columbus's discovery some 400 years earlier.

The elimination of effective physical resistance thereby eliminated that 350-year-old political necessity for recognition of Indian sovereignty. In 1871, Congress passed a resolution declaring, "Hereafter, no Indian nation or tribe within the territory of the United States shall be acknowledged or recognized as an independent tribe or power with whom the United States may contract by treaty [Appropriation Act, 1871]." Although this resolution did not nullify the legal concept of Indian sovereignty inherent in existing treaties, in practice it provided a firm basis for subjecting Indian tribes to the legislative imposition of the federal government. This imposition removed all impediments to the implementation of Indian wardship and permitted unquestioned use of earlier federal statutes suppressing Indian religion, language, and dissent.

The mandated sectionizing of Indian land, a method advocated as far back as colonial times and achieved in the Potawatomi situation and other earlier treaties, became institutionalized (though not completely implemented) for all tribes in 1887 through the passage of the Dawes Allotment Act. As with the 1830 Indian Removal Act, the Dawes Act was advocated by a coalition of railroaders, land speculators, bankers, and "Christian humanitarians," the latter still advancing the old arguments of Indian self-development. The traditional Potawatomi aggressiveness, transformed by the Prairie Band remnant into a mixture of antifederal contentiousness and passive resistance, led their BIA agent to report at the turn of the century:

> There exists among them an extremely obstinate and unprogressive element that clings to their inherent idea of romantic barbarism. They still persistently refuse to recognize their allotment of land or the right of the Government to make such disposition of their lands contrary to their wishes. Happily their numbers are comparatively few and even they are not beyond the power of example and persuasion [Sandhaus and Verbanic 1973].

Persuasion consisted of withholding federal payments due to the Prairie Band and giving double allotments of their land to whites, Indians from other tribes, and the agent's relatives. Fearing the total loss of their reservation, the Prairie Band finally accepted allotments and became "private entrepreneurs." With the loss of communal property came the inevitable vitiation of traditional communal government.

Despite some occasional successes as subsistence farmers, the allottees were bankrupted in the economic depression of the 1930s. By 1978, approximately

80% of the reservation had passed into white ownership. The Indian-owned balance, small checkerboard blocks of 20–80 acres, is leased to white farmers through the BIA (a practice established by the local BIA in 1875). Some 550 dispersed acres are communally owned, largely through repurchases by recent tribal governments. At the time of the 1887 Dawes Act, U.S. Indian communal holdings comprised some 140 million acres. As private entrepreneurs the Indians saw approximately 90 million acres pass to white ownership during the following 45 years.

The hard core of Prairie Band traditionalists reacted to every subsequent federally imposed law and program with the same resistant style they offered the Dawes Act. They deemed insulting a 1924 enactment making all Indians United States citizens, and were one of a small percentage of tribes that did not elect to accept the provisions of the Indian Reorganization Act (IRA) of 1934. The Act, still viewed favorably by most historians as a radical change in Indian policy of the Roosevelt New Deal humanitarianism, had as its stated goal "the revitalization of Indian life [U.S. Department of the Interior 1938]." The continuing upturn in Indian population in the 3 decades prior to the Act made a policy based on the anticipated extinction of the Indian no longer feasible. Some 90,000 landless Indians only added to the social instability occasioned by the mass of wandering unemployed of the Great Depression. Typical of all reforms in periods of major economic crisis, the Act served to organize the potentially volatile poor under the aegis of the government. Specifically, the Act halted the land allotment policy, eliminated direct suppression of Indian culture, appropriated funds for land purchases, advanced credit for subsistence agriculture, and, most significantly, permitted and encouraged the organization of tribal government on the white Western model.

For traditionalist groups like the Prairie Band, whose decisions were made through informal consensus under the guidance of tribal elders, a written constitution and majority voting procedures could only produce further divisiveness. The BIA promotion of new leaders whose assimilationist tendencies made them suitable for such functions as dealing with the federal bureaucracy, managing tribal funds, and employing white professionals, would further intensify internal divisions. The Indian Reorganization Act thereby became the instrument for the creation of a new generation of "progressives." In addition, since it made the Department of the Interior (the parent body of the BIA) the final arbiter of all tribal governmental decisions, the wardship status became fully institutionalized.

The growth of federal administrative bureaucracy inherent in a regulated relationship that provided no local autonomy inevitably produced the situation in which Indians are now the most overregulated people in the United States. The maze of red tape, contradictory edicts, and successive layers of decision-makers render ineffective even those "revitalization" programs that were honestly intended. Modest successes in tribal program development depend on the establishment of personal relations between progressive leaders and particular

BIA bureaucrats, thereby making the entire tribe increasingly dependent on the BIA. A simple shift in BIA personnel frequently kills the most laboriously engineered tribal strategy for shepherding a program through the bureaucracy. With success depending on personal relations rather than clear-cut policy, the BIA can and usually does frustrate the actions of a tribal leadership it distrusts. This was clearly shown by the freezing of Potawatomi tribal funds (mentioned earlier) and the suspension of their surplus equipment grant at the height of their reservation development program. Additionally, a commitment made under pressure by one bureaucrat can simply be nullified by another on the grounds that the former lacked jurisdiction. For example, when the Potawatomi traditionalists "invaded" the Kansas BIA offices (described at the opening of this chapter), they left peacefully as a result of a telephoned commitment by the BIA regional office that BIA representatives from the Washington central office would quickly come to the reservation to adjudicate the tribe's grievances. When the officials arrived, they claimed that they lacked not only adjudicating authority but also investigative authority. Their meeting with the tribe lasted 45 minutes. Under the threat of a renewed occupation of the BIA office by the traditionalists and militant Indian allies coming from outside Kansas, the Commissioner of Indian Affairs agreed to a meeting with Potawatomi traditionalist representatives in his office in Washington. The Commissioner failed to appear and was represented by a subordinate. The subordinate, an Indian, negotiated what the traditionalists considered a satisfactory resolution of their grievances. Several weeks later, the traditionalist leadership received a telephone call from the BIA central office, this time from bureaucrats with whom they had had no previous contact. The leaders were told that the Washington agreement had no effect on the grounds that though the commissioner's representative had negotiating authority, he lacked the authority to consummate agreements.

This instability within the BIA also creates instability among the progressives. Programmatic commitments made to the electorate are wholly unreliable. The frequency with which tribal leaders are repudiated is legendary in contemporary Indian politics. The current massive impoverishment and debilitation of American Indian reservation life proves the failure of the reformist Indian Reorganization Act.

In short, the Indian Reorganization Act "modernized" federal–Indian relations. Instead of cultural suppression, it promoted cultural assimilation. Instead of forced removal from the land, if fostered a reservation poverty that spurred continuing migration and dispersal into the urban slums of now more than 60% of the Indian population. Instead of callous indifference, it promoted a suffocating dependency. Instead of the outright theft of land, which would offend white liberal sensibilities, the Act fostered BIA manipulation of tribal governments to legitimize the opening of reservation lands to outside industrial and commercial exploitation. The "final solution" of the Indian question is now being promulgated under the banner of "revitalization" and self-determination."

With the tribes safely "reorganized" under BIA-dominated governments, the stage was set to expunge the agitating memories of the violation of 371 treaties imposed by past federal power. The process of expunging past grievances is also the process of expunging the sense of historic continuity which is the core of traditionalist strength. In 1946 an Indian claims court was established in which tribes could bring suit for past treaty violations or inadequacies. In exchange for payment at the evaluated price of the land at the time of the treaty, the tribe would sign away forever their claim to lost lands. The debate over the desirability of accepting claims and thereby legitimizing the status quo seriously widened the split between progressives and conservatives.

The inducement of claims money was an effective way of diluting the "racial" content of tribal life. Through the manipulation of tribal rolls or by constitutional changes or reinterpretations made by collusion between local BIA officials and progressive leaders, "instant Indians" would be created. Basing their Indianness on distant lineage rather than cultural affinity or "blood quantum," these newcomers would be used to support the progressives against traditionalist resistance. For example, in 1956 a claims award was made to the Prairie Band. Disbursement of the funds was withheld for 4 years, during which time the BIA created new "Prairie Band Potawatomi." In 1960 the BIA changed past stipulations for Prairie Band tribal membership, eliminating blood quantum and reservation residency requirements, thus undercutting the former preeminence of the traditionalists. Under these new regulations tribal membership jumped from 800 to 2100. The following year progressives and their newly enrolled allies endorsed a new BIA-devised tribal constitution which incorporated the changes in the roll requirements, thus retroactively legitimizing the new "Indians". A similar technique was utilized again in 1976 by the BIA in constructing the latest Prairie Band constitution, resulting from the BIA's withdrawal of recognition of the 1961 constitution. The presence of new claims money was again an important part of the picture.

The wardship relationship therefore makes it possible for the BIA to manipulate claims money and welfare programs as well as create new constitutions, new governments, new "Indians," and, as the Prairie Band saw in 1971, arbitrary new elections for officers to forestall tribal control by anti-BIA traditionalists. In those occasional instances where such delicate measures fail, traditionalist leaders and supporters can be terrorized by local, state, and federal police, tribal police and white and "Indian" vigilantes. This more extreme measure was used in the tragic electoral fiasco on the huge Pine Ridge reservation in South Dakota in the aftermath of the 1973 Wounded Knee insurrection. Even during the many months of nonviolent disagreement with the BIA that preceded the Potawatomi "takeover" of the local agency office, the Potawatomi leadership complained of harassment by federal police. To summarize, the imposition of governmental structure on a subordinated people creates a situation in which the imposer in effect negotiates with himself with regard to the fate of the oppressed group.

If the Indian Reorganization Act was a twentieth-century expression of Jeffersonian liberalism, then Eisenhower's Indian termination policy can also be seen as the twentieth-century expression of the reactionary removal policies of the previous century. The Eisenhower termination policy of 1953 unilaterally abrogated all Indian treaties, severed wardship, eliminated all federal Indian welfare programs, and gave tribal members "full freedom" as individual American citizens. It was not surprising that the historically recalcitrant Prairie Band was soon attacked by the enforcement of this policy. The enforcement of termination on two major and several lesser tribes had disastrous effects as land taxes and encroachment by corporate interests quickly destroyed the economic base minimally required for community life. It is not coincidental that the two major tribes terminated, the Klamath and the Menominee, had vast timber resources and had succeeded in lumber-processing ventures that provided a modest but stable standard of living and a network of self-help social programs (again confirming the observation that tribal independence invites federal destruction). Termination stimulated such intense nationwide Indian resistance that the policy itself was terminated after 4 years. In the intervening period, 1.8 million acres of some of the most productive Indian land had passed to white ownership.

The termination policy is again being sought through the recent introduction of bills in both houses of Congress. At this point in history, the motivation for the bills should leave little to the imagination. Western U.S. Indian reservations currently hold between 25 and 40% of U.S. uranium reserves and about 5% of all oil and natural gas reserves. Those reservations also hold one-third of all western coal. It is estimated that by 1985 47% of all United States coal will come from the west. The history of the BIA-arranged leases to oil and mineral companies at "rock bottom royalties to the tribes" led to the formation in 1975 of the Council of Energy Resource Tribes, a coalition of tribes from 10 western states. The coalition was organized under the leadership of the Navajo, the largest tribe in the United States (population 150,000). Now that the energy crisis is the keystone of U.S. domestic policy, the Navajo tribal chairman observed "that America will not be permitted to march to [energy sufficiency] as it marched to the Pacific—over the backs of this country's native people [Sheils, Copeland, and Beck 1978]."

The coalition was disregarded by the government until the summer of 1977, when its leaders met with representatives of several OPEC countries to discuss strategies for increasing royalties. The following September, termination legislation was introduced in Congress.

The fact that the Indian Reorganization Act required tribal consent, albeit manipulated consent, in no way lessened its imposed nature. For tribes like the Prairie Band that had withheld consent, the BIA proceeded to manage the tribe as if consent had been granted, reasoning that though consent was withheld, the Act was not explicitly rejected. Such "legal logic" suggests that imposed law is not really law at all in any common meaning of the word, but simply an arbitrary exercise of state power, rationalized as law.

For 4 decades the Prairie Band traditionalists fought off repeated BIA attempts to bring the tribe under the Indian Reorganization Act. They had their own governance system developed from the historic pre-eminence of tribal elders. Calling themselves tribal councilors, they made themselves eligible for representation purposes in pursuit of land claims against the government by adopting a slim and vague constitution. The BIA approved the constitution in 1932 since it gave the elected leadership only advisory powers to the BIA and seemed harmless enough. The traditionalists viewed possible land-claims awards as a means of re-establishing an economic underpinning for the continuation of their reservation life-style and as an alternative to federally controlled development programs. Thus they sought, as in the past, to reject in practice their imposed wardship status. To this day, Prairie Band traditionalists refer to themselves as a "treaty tribe," an affirmation of their belief in their unsurrendered sovereign rights. The tribal councilors naturally led the Prairie Band fight against termination.

Ironically, it was the tribal councilors' success in pursuing land claims that in 1961 gave the BIA the leverage to increase tribal rolls, devise a new constitution, and drive the traditionalists from power. In seeking a declaratory judgment and injunction against the new constitution, the distribution of the land-claims awards, and a federal court determination of tribal rolls, the tribal councilors cited their authority as stemming from "tribal custom, tribal law, tribal election, and heredity." The case was dismissed, but that did not prevent the tribal councilors, now operating as a *sub rosa* government, from continuing their protest through letters and petitions to the BIA. Their suit served to delay the distribution of judgment money and further isolated them and their supporters from the rest of the tribe. By 1970, with the advanced age and deaths of key figures among the elders, a younger group was preparing to assume leadership and resume the struggle.

A century and a half of federal assault against the Indian way of life had seriously weakened the political strength of the Prairie Band traditionalists. The destruction of their reservation economy had produced a gradual migration to the small towns and a major city outside the reservation. The reservation now became a symbolic organizing center, its population of no more than 150 rising and falling as the young left and the aged returned. The impact of American consumerist and individualistic culture on traditional spiritual and collectivist values, and especially on the young, gave rise to the psychological ambivalence, petty squabbling, personal opportunism, and suicidal rage of alcoholism and fratricidal conflict that are the classic consequences of colonialist impact. Despite this psychological damage, and in many ways because of it, the movement that arose was far more aggressive than any of the previous traditionalist movements, possessing as it did the militancy born of desperation. Survival for the younger Prairie Band militants was no longer exclusively a question of land: most of the land had already been lost. Survival now lay in resolving, through direct confrontation of all aspects of anti-Indian racism, the daily agony of a personal identity crisis. The ancient fatalism of the older traditionalists had produced a rejectionist strategy. Rather than be humiliated by publicly confronting the manipulativeness of a BIA superintendent or a "progressive" tribal officer, the traditionalists would rise as a body and walk out of a meeting. Infected by the pragmatism of urban contact, the new militants would rather take over a meeting, or a BIA office, or other public property in an attempt to beat the white man at his own game.

The resurgence of the Prairie Band movement by 1970 came during a period of national upheaval—the United States involvement in Vietnam. This unpopular conflict, waged as it was without the legally required declaration of war by Congress, had in the eyes of its opponents delegitimated the U.S. government, revealing its class and coercive nature. This view had great appeal for many non-Indian subgroups who felt oppressed by the domestic imposition of federal power. Although the national Indian community remained essentially out of the public anti-war debate, the issue was not lost on anti-government Indian activists, who had no difficulty in identifying with the dark-skinned Vietnamese. The anti-war movement provided for the Indian activists, and through them the Indian people, a sympathetic ear and potential alliances with a major anti-federal, anti-racist popular movement.

Out of the tempest of the period, the militant American Indian Movement (AIM) emerged in 1968 from the urban ghettos and spread rapidly to the isolated reservations. Its leaders, speaking in a mixture of slum argot and a poetic hortatory style evocative of the past, combined contemporary social analysis with an appeal to traditional warrior bravery and traditionalist religious and cultural resurgence. AIM cadres not only proceeded to occupy various federally-owned sites to dramatize treaty violations, but also organized urban and small-town demonstrations to protest against incidents of anti-Indian racism. As in all new movements, the ideology of its leadership went through a process of reformulation and clarification and was at times perceived differently by grass-roots adherents. Nonetheless, the general thrust of AIM, as articulated by its leadership, was clear:

The contemporary problems of all Indian individuals and tribes had been conditioned by the historic process of United States expansion and anti-Indian racism. Indians should transcend tribal parochialism and intratribal factionalism. They should, wherever feasible, reject federal Indian policies and should seek to re-establish treaty rights, tribal sovereignty, and self-determined economies in a coordinated drive that would encourage the return of the exiles and a regeneration of traditional culture. The various tribes would have to confront federal power and defeat it in order to separate from it. In short, AIM sought to re-establish in a contemporary context the Indian community of the pre-colonial period.

AIM's activism shocked the nation, dispelling the stereotype of Indian passivity. Most significantly, AIM's boldness was the window through which the majority of the American public rediscovered its native population as social fact rather than myth. In contrast to the situation in which many mainline whites were troubled by the defiance of their own children, the AIM upstarts were frequently embraced by their elders, who saw in the movement an ally for the re-establishment of traditional authority. Rebuke came initially from within the myriad Indian organizations that were tied to federal programs. However, as the movement gathered momentum and elicited serious responses from the government (a success the mainliners had rarely achieved), AIM had a polarizing effect within these organizations and their constituent communities.

It was from among the children of the Prairie Band traditionalists that the impetus came for the organization of AIM chapters among various groups of Kansas Indians. This resurgence, by 1970, saw the regrouping of the remnants and elderly supporters of the old tribal councilors, now refreshed and supported by younger activists, some of whom assumed public leadership roles. Calling themselves the Tribal Action Committee, they were, as previously indicated, successful in recapturing in 1971 the constitutional tribal government they had lost 10 years earlier.

With no claims money immediately at stake, most of the BIA-created "white" Prairie Band and many progressives had little motivation for participating in tribal politics. Indeed, some progressives joined forces with their old traditionalist enemies in the mistaken hope that this new militancy might somehow produce new land-claims money. The traditionalists, with some misgivings, were willing to accept their errant brethren, as befitted proper traditionalist behavior.

The BIA's arbitrary cancellation of the 1971 election results (discussed on p. 95) was immediately countered by an attempt for injunctive relief through the federal court. Although the suit, predictably, was dismissed on jurisdictional grounds, the arbitrary nature of federal wardship was made strikingly clear to a newly activated Indian constituency. Organized protests, including public demonstrations and picketing, phenomena previously alien to traditionalist elders, saw AIM members, non-Potawatomi Indians, and some white supporters rallying to the defense of the Prairie Band. A subsequent election was held by the BIA off the reservation in a federal armory, and there were a number of other efforts by the BIA to discourage tribal participation. Despite this, the traditionalists were reconfirmed by an overwhelming majority of the voters who had participated in much greater numbers than in any election of the previous decade. The subsequent conflict with the BIA over the Jesuit properties produced a broadening of public rallies and protest demonstrations. For a while, the Prairie Band situation was a focal point of the national militant Indian movement and became a symbolic issue of an AIM-organized nationwide march that sought redress of many Indian grievances. The march led to a confrontation with BIA officials at the central BIA offices in Washington, D.C. In November 1972 a breakdown in negotiations led to the occupation and ransacking of the offices. Out of the wreckage the question of Indian sovereignty emerged as a national issue, albeit one still dimly understood by the non-Indian community.

THE POTAWATOMI AND INDIAN SOVEREIGNTY
AS A MODERN NATIONAL ISSUE

Youthful Prairie Band members were active in this march and were equally active the following year as participants in the armed insurrection at Wounded Knee on the Oglala Sioux reservation in South Dakota. There, as was typical, the issues involved the federal imposition of an allegedly corrupt pro-BIA tribal government that was reportedly in collusion with a variety of white commercial interests for the purpose of exploiting reservation lands. Several Prairie Band elders joined their children at Wounded Knee. The Prairie Band youth who went off to fight received the blessing of their elders at a ceremony on the Kansas reservation.

In March 1973 the Prairie Band traditionalist leadership organized a caravan of some 80 Kansas Indians for the purpose of reinforcing the Wounded Knee redoubt. Their appeal for support from the non-Indian community had yielded a truckload of food, clothing, and medical supplies. Trailed by carloads of federal and state police, the caravan was diverted to the South Dakota Rosebud reservation, sections of which were being used as an AIM staging area for the relief of Wounded Knee. Similar caravans were arriving from various parts of the country and a support force of several hundred militants was in the process of being organized. (A small number of white supporters, mostly Kansas members of Vietnam Veterans against the War, were also present.) A discussion between the Potawatomi leaders and several AIM leaders soon revealed a dilemma in activist strategy stemming from the nature of Indian wardship. The Potawatomi suit, based on the denial of U.S. constitutional rights and testing the legality of wardship, was at this time awaiting adjudication in the federal courts. The politics of seeking tribal control of the Jesuit lands had not only led the Potawatomi to seek the protection of the federal courts but had also produced alliances with non-Indian supporters and a relationship with non-Indian private and public institutional funding sources. It was logical, then, that the Potawatomi saw a crucial direction for Indian militancy in the building of a national Indian-led coalition against wardship and for the establishment of full U.S. constitutional rights for Indian tribes (without surrendering the rights and federal supports stipulated in past treaties). This approach, they argued, would free Indian tribal governments and property from federal control. A string of sovereign Indian states within the borders of the United States could not, they said, be established without armed revolt against federal military power. Such an approach would alienate potential non-Indian political support and, given the level of Indian military strength, was, to say the least, impractical. The achievement of Indian self-determination, as the Potawatomi leaders saw it, was therefore unavoidably tied to the question of their civil rights as U.S. citizens.

AIM leaders rejected this emphasis, arguing that it would be futile, as one leader stated, "to enter the oppressor's Congress and Courts to defeat the oppressor.'' They saw a separatist approach, that is, the upholding of Indian treaty rights and full tribal sovereignty, as the only acceptable solution. It was apparent to proponents of both positions that though the concurrent pursuits of full civil rights and sovereignty rights were ideologically contradictory, both approaches were in fact part of the overall thrust of the new Indian militancy. Moreover, ideological consistency was at the moment irrelevant to the expression of outraged resistance to federal power that the Wounded Knee insurrection represented. The Potawatomi leadership had come to South Dakota not only to support the Wounded Knee activists but also to propose the following strategy: maintain the armed defense of Wounded Knee as a symbol of determination, but utilize the gathering Indian support to organize demonstrations in major cities to publicize the civil rights and wardship issues and build non-Indian political support. In the light of the need for unity, the proposal was never advanced. Soon, numbers of the Kansas Indians infiltrated the Wounded Knee perimeter to join its defenders. Some of the Potawatomi subsequently returned home to organize a coalition of Indians and non-Indians in an unprecedented civil rights march through the streets of a major Kansas city.

The apparent philosophic contradiction of simultaneous demands for Indian sovereignty and U.S. constitutional rights, of an appeal for federal intervention while attacking federal authority, stems from the contradictory nature of imposed law. Imposed law forces its subjects to seek their ''rights'' within the constraints of an alien and hostile legal system without the option of relief from that system. It therefore begs the question to accuse the Potawatomi of inconsistency for their use of federal institutions in their attempt to free themselves from federal control, or to accuse AIM of opportunism for demanding BIA intervention for relief from a corrupt and illegal tribal government and then militarily occupying a section of the reservation in the name of Indian sovereignty because of the BIA's refusal to intervene. The oppressed have no choice but to deal with the legal system that oppresses them. The fact that the oppressed also seek to devise their own legal system that is philosophically antithetical to the imposed system is a consequence of oppression rather than the oft-noted ''instability'' of the oppressed. The social requirement for philosophically consistent responses to an imposed system of inconsistencies stems from the ruling elite's attempt to obfuscate the imposed nature of law. Certainly, the ''value'' of consistency was not lost on the Potawatomi when they noted that though the BIA refused to remove the corrupt and unpopular Pine Ridge tribal government on the grounds that such action would infringe on ''Indian self-determination,'' the Bureau had no such qualms when it came to removing a popular and democratic Potawatomi government. The ''solution'' for dealing with the negative social consequences of imposed law is for the imposee to achieve the power to become the imposer. That such a method fails to solve the problem philosophically does not prevent it from being the way of the world.

The Wounded Knee insurrection saw the use of substantial federal armed power, including armored personnel carriers and self-propelled guns. Ultimately, there was a negotiated settlement, although there were some deaths through exchanges of fire. In the aftermath, the severe repression of Sioux dissidents and national AIM leaders and members overflowed in administrative harassment of some Prairie Band activists as well as attempted federal co-optation of their Kansas constituency. An attempt by the BIA to devise a new tribal constitution and bring the Prairie Band formally under the Indian Reorganization Act was beaten back. By 1975, as a result of 5 years of intense anti-federal conflict, the emergence of ideological and interpersonal factionalism among the young militants, and the BIA's withholding disbursement of some 5 million dollars of new land-claims money, resistance crumbled. A pro-BIA faction was elected to leadership under a new IRA tribal constitution. Having seen tribal government captured by the traditionalists through the old constitution, the BIA was not about to allow a repeat performance. The new constitution gave extraordinary powers to the new tribal leadership and put up many impediments to grass-roots participation and possible future control. To reinforce these actions some new "Prairie Band Indians" were again discovered and enrolled as tribal members.

For the next 3 years the traditionalists pondered the meaning of their tumultuous venture into public politics. Attendance at religious services grew. With the introduction in Congress of new termination legislation in 1977, and the organization of a national Indian protest march that passed through the Potawatomi reservation in the spring of 1978, the traditionalists have once again emerged. Again, some new, youthful leaders have been sanctioned by the elders. Again, local Prairie Band issues will be joined with the perceived aspirations of native American people.

REFERENCES

CASES

Potts v. *Bruce* 533 F. 2d 527 (10th Cir. 1976).

OTHER SOURCES

Burnette, R., and J. Koster
    1974   *The Road to Wounded Knee.* New York: Bantam Books.
Clifton, J. A.
    1977   *The Prairie People: Continuity and Change in Potawatomi Indian Culture 1665–1965.* Lawrence: The Regents Press of Kansas.
Connelly, W. E.
    1915–1918   "The Prairie Band of Potawatomi Indians." *Collections.* Vol. 14. Topeka, Kan.: Kansas State Historical Society.
Deloria, V., Jr.
    1970   *Custer Died For Your Sins.* New York: Avon Books.
Fulop-Miller, R.
    1963   *The Jesuits: A History of the Society of Jesus.* New York: Capricorn Books.
Gates, P. W.
    1954   *Fifty Million Acres: Conflicts over Kansas Land Policy, 1854–1867.* Ithaca, N.Y.: Cornell University Press.

McNickle, D.

    1973 *Native American Tribalism: Indian Survivals and Renewals.* London: Oxford University Press.

Prucha, F. P.

    1962 *American Indian Policy in the Formative Years: The Indian Trade and Intercourse Acts, 1790–1834.* Lincoln: University of Nebraska Press.

Sandhaus, R. and W. Verbanic

    1973 *Emergence: A Grass-roots Account of American Indian Activism* (collected materials for a documentary film). Kansas City, Kan.: Sandhaus–Verbanic Productions.

Sartre, J. P.

    1948 *Anti-Semite and Jew.* New York: Schocken Books.

Sheils, M., J. Copeland, and M. Beck

    1978 "Resources: The rich Indians," *Newsweek* (March 20): 61–64.

Taylor, T. W.

    1972 *The States and Their Indian Citizens.* Washington D.C.: United States Department of the Interior Bureau of Indian Affairs.

United States Congress

    1829–1830 *House Reports.* 21st Congress, 1st Session, No. 227. Serial set No. 200, Vol. 2. Washington, D.C.: U.S. Government Printing Office.

    1871 *U.S. Statutes at Large.* Vol. 16, p. 566. 41st Congress, Session 3, Chapter 120. Washington, D.C.: U.S. Government Printing Office.

United States Department of the Interior, Bureau of Indian Affairs

    1938 *Report of the Commission of Indian Affairs,* p. 210. Washington, D.C.: U.S. Government Printing Office.

7

IMPOSED LAW IN THE CONTAINMENT OF PAPUA NEW GUINEA ECONOMIC VENTURES

PETER FITZPATRICK
LORAINE BLAXTER

In this chapter we would like to present some results of our research on the effects of imposed law on economic ventures in Papua New Guinea. We try to show that such law suppresses or restrains these ventures and we suggest an explanation for this.

It is first necessary to outline the context of our research. With the advent of independence, which occurred in stages from 1972 to 1975, the Papua New Guinea government continually stressed the need to increase the participation of Papua New Guineans in economic life. This was of course not an unusual policy for a Third-World government, but the setting in which the policy was to operate was somewhat unusual in that Australian colonial rule had severely restricted Papua New Guinean economic activity, especially in the so-called modern sector. Australia, until recently, generated little economic activity within the colony and confined itself to protecting the limited economic activity of its settlers against competition from Papua New Guineans. Recently, however, it attempted to alter this situation by means of a program of "accelerated development." In this program the emphasis lay on economic growth, mainly through greater Australian and foreign investment. The benefits of such growth would, according to the development terminology of the day, trickle

The Imposition of Law

down to the mass of Papua New Guineans. This new investment was allowed in all fields except for restrictions on cash-cropping, but as Papua New Guineans were at an enormous competitive disadvantage, they remained excluded except as employees from almost all economic activities in the modern sector—cash-cropping being the only significant exception. Thus, when the post-colonial government sought to increase Papua New Guinean participation in the economy, it had little to build on by way of available skills, technologies, and capital.

One dramatic solution to this problem was to promote development that used the types of skills and technologies already available and that needed little capital. Hence the government adopted a policy of encouraging the growth of what became known as the informal sector. The informal sector comprises small-scale service, craft, market, and bazaar-type activities. It is distinguished from the formal sector by characteristics such as ease of entry, small capital invest-ment, use of indigenous resources and of skills acquired outside the formal school system, reliance on personal relationships for organization, and lack of protection by government or even harassment by it (Fitzpatrick and Blaxter 1975). The idea of an informal-sector approach came from the report on employ-ment in Kenya for the International Labour Office (ILO 1972). The report saw the informal sector as "the source of a new strategy of development [ILO 1972:505]." It was concerned to get away from the "residual model" of this sec-tor: that is, a model "based on the presumption that the informal sector is a reservoir of unemployment and marginally productive activity into which those who cannot obtain paid jobs in the formal sector sink, barely making ends meet by begging, hawking or embarking on petty crime [p. 506]." Instead, this sector was considered in the report to be "often economically efficient, productive and creative," a sector of "growth," "viability," and "dynamism [pp. 51, 505]." The report placed great emphasis on legal restrictions as a major obstacle to the expansion of the informal sector and inveighed particularly against trade licens-ing (ILO 1972:119, 226, 228, 326, 504). In line with this emphasis, the Prime Minister of Papua New Guinea asked us to do a survey of laws that could inhibit the development of the informal sector. Having done this, we also drew up a program for the repeal or modification of these laws, which was approved by the cabinet. The implementation of the program was at first taken up with con-siderable enthusiasm by the Law Reform Commission and the National Plan-ning Office, but has since been hindered by a succession of difficulties.

We have not been able to study the nature and sources of these difficulties, but we mention them because the inability of these influential bodies to implement the program suggests why law suppresses or restrains Papua New Guinean ven-tures. The explanation is that dominant class elements are served by these restrictive laws and that these elements have a decisive influence on state action. The elements—not always compatible ones—are the foreign bourgeoisie and an emergent national bourgeoisie. The representation of class interests at the level of state action raises great empirical and theoretical problems (Hirst 1977). All we are trying to show in this chapter is that the ways in which law restricts Papua New Guinean economic activity lend weight to this explanation. So the chapter is a description and, it is hoped, a persuasive illustration of a thesis. As an illustration it is narrower than it could be because we have, for brevity's sake, chosen to discuss only one aspect of our work, but probably the most significant one—licensing. We hope by the use of this example to throw light on licensing as a method of legal imposition.

In studying the imposition of law, however, it is not sufficient to look only at these dominant class elements. The people upon whom law is imposed have to be subjected to it, and in this respect the law cannot be viewed as something merely imposed from the outside: "It is possible," Talleyrand said, "to do many things with a bayonet, but one cannot sit on one [Nwafor 1975:44]." There must be some operative acceptance of the law by those on whom it is imposed.

The ethos of constraint is perceived and in a sense accepted by the people. There are many examples in Papua New Guinea's colonial history of licensing and other laws creating such an inhibiting environment that any economic innovation is perceived as illegal (for example, McCarthy 1963:81; Sankoff 1969:72). A young official told us:

> I had come from Bangkok. I used to get a good meal on the canal there for about 5 cents. When I came back I told my uncles, "Instead of taking raw fish to the market, take it in canoes and cook it on the canoes and sell it for meals in town." Their response was that they would get into some kind of trouble [with the law].

Another example we discovered concerned two men wishing to set up small stores in an urban resettlement area. They were discouraged after finding out some of the numerous legal requirements they had to satisfy to achieve their aim. A development worker asked them to carry on so as to provide test cases, but they declined, saying, "We are only villagers." It appears from these examples, then, to borrow Paulo Freire's terms (1970:31; 1972:11), that the wide-ranging prescriptions have been sufficiently internalized by people for them to know that innovation will usually be regarded as illegal.

GENERAL PERSPECTIVES ON LICENSING

There are now some two dozen economic activities subject to licensing in Papua New Guinea, and some of these are described in general terms, such as "mobile trading." The licensing of mobile traders is controlled by local government councils. In one large urban center this licensing process has been captured by the council's finance committee, which is in turn controlled by the major (and foreign) business interests in that city. As a result, any applications for mobile trading licenses have been refused because the finance committee considers that mobile traders—particularly small-scale peddlers—can unfairly undercut the trade of businessmen operating from fixed premises.

In the country's largest city a direct refusal to grant licenses is considered illegal, but the outcome is the same. Four women from a nearby village wanted to sell meals in the city from a mobile bar. Before a mobile trader's license could be granted, it was necessary to satisfy several eligibility conditions established by the city council, one of which required for the sale of meals "potable water from a reservoir tank of at least ten (10) gallons capacity which shall be fitted within the body of the vehicle [so in this oblique way a "vehicle" is required] with an approved pumping apparatus." This as well as other conditions would have involved the women in expenditure well beyond their plans and means, so a governmental lending agency was approached for financial backing. To meet the conditions for payment, the enterprise had to be conducted in a highly organized way and to ensure this a government extension agency for "business development" became closely involved in the enterprise, imposing its own requirements. These complex eligibility conditions and requirements did not fit the skills and resources of the women, and, almost certainly as a result, the enterprise failed.

These various restrictions or restrictive conditions are backed by an official hostility to small-scale mobile trading. A senior health inspector (who was particularly influential because he trained almost all the health inspectors operating in the country) in extolling some new restrictive laws said that they "will keep people [street sellers] off the streets where they are a great problem, difficult to check on, leave rubbish and have no toilets" (cf. Douglas 1970).

From these examples two types of licensing can be distinguished. There is directly restrictive licensing, where obtaining a license depends on some sort of official discretion and where the explicit aim of the powers that be is to restrict the number of licenses granted. Then there is what can be called standards licensing, where getting the license depends on meeting certain conditions, and the explicit or ostensible aim is not to restrict the number of licenses. The two types are not always distinct. Restrictive licensing is often accompanied by the imposition of conditions of the standards variety, and in the case of standards licensing the conditions to be met sometimes involve considerable official discretion in their application. In addition, standards licensing is in some instances used illegally in a directly restrictive fashion, as was shown by the example of the city council that restricted the issue of mobile traders licenses. Apart from that factor it may be asked how standards licensing differs in empirical effect from legally prescriptive standards generally. The key difference is that for a license, one must, usually periodically, approach an official and obtain approval for one's legitimate existence in a particular role. In this way licensing is a distinct mechanism for enforcing and maintaining standards. More particularly, obtaining any license entails becoming involved in the official process, and, to be successful, the prospective licensee may be obliged to create and sustain a self-definition that officials consider appropriate. For example, licensing provides a focus for what we call a "cluster effect." Contact with an official to get a license enables a check to be made not only on standards or requirements attached to the license but also on compliance with all standards or requirements considered relevant. These points will be illustrated later. We simply suggest here that, even apart from its directly restrictive aspect, licensing either lays down or serves as a focal point for conditions of eligibility that pitch the development process well beyond generally available skills, technologies, and resources—both material and psychological.

Official explanations, of course, differ considerably from our interpretation of licensing laws. Often these explanations emphasize the maintenance of standards and the protection of public revenue, and less altruistic motivation is strongly denied. Although in this chapter we do question official explanations, we are not concerned with motivation and the sincerity with which such explanations are propounded by officials. All we say is that restrictive licensing can be objectively assessed in the terms we have suggested. It is difficult to confirm this kind of assertion quantitatively for the whole range of licensing measures. We examined only seven of them in detail, but we found that five of these came into the category we outlined earlier. These seven were not chosen specifically to prove our point, but possibly some bias arises in our selection. However, we did examine all licensing measures generally, and our examination indicated that the great majority could be interpreted in the way we have suggested.

We will now describe and partly analyze the ways in which licenses are restricted and controlled. We look first and mainly at direct restrictions, where officials have explicit power to restrict the issue of licenses. Next we look at standards licensing, where eligibility conditions often form what we call a "cluster effect" around the licensing process. Finally we look at the ethos of the public bureaucracy: the dominating influence of the official and the control-oriented attitudes that officials bring to bear on the operation of the licensing process.

DIRECT LICENSING

The most comprehensive and, perhaps, potentially the most significant piece of directly restrictive licensing is a business-licensing law that has not yet been in operation. It covers most retail and mobile trading and numerous other more narrowly defined areas. This law aims to protect Papua New Guinean businessmen from the perils of—as the promoting officials put it—overcompetition, to ensure that they obtain "reasonable profits," and to create "efficiency." Officials consider small village stores (which some of them describe as "lavatory stores") to be most inefficient. No thought seems to have been given to what are reasonable profits and to how they can be ascertained in any or all cases. The long history of the making of this law provides an indication of where official priorities lie when there is a conflict between promoting national businessmen and protecting significant foreign investors. When the law was be-ing prepared, the Australian government expressed concern that the proposed administering authorities (local government councils) could, in granting licenses, prefer nationals over the few large foreign investors that dominate the country's retail and wholesale trade. The then colonial administration, in response, explained that an appeal procedure was to be provided in the proposed law to counter such an eventuality; the appeal could, in terms of the law, be argued on the grounds that the granting of a license was in the national interest.

A law that is more generally concerned with the protection of the foreign in-vestor is that providing for the licensing of the retail sale of liquor. The current law and policy date from 1963, when the prohibition on the consumption of li-quor by Papua New Guineans was lifted. In both its letter and its application the law promotes large-scale drinking facilities. Somewhat laughably—to those ac-quainted with Australian bars—this matter of scale was seen as a civilizing in-fluence: it was thought that blacks would learn "proper" drinking habits from white drinking companions. It was also thought that with large bars different ethnic groups would come together and that this would promote racial harmony of some kind. The opposite has generally been the case: intergroup violence in bars is commonplace and whites have deserted public bars for private clubs. Despite the most compelling social reasons and the supporting recommendations of a government-appointed commission of inquiry, the situation remains basic-ally unreformed and the policy continues. For example, a large foreign investor was recently granted a site for a bar on one of the capital's busiest intersections, yet shortly before that a license had been refused for a proposed small Papua New Guinean tavern on another site because the density of traffice nearby was said to involve a risk of accidents. The granting of a license for the former establishment was officially justified in terms of attracting foreign investors into the accommodation business; a license to run a mass drinking facility near ac-commodation is presented as an inducement to the investor. (Incidentally, if the inducement is necessary, then it follows that Papua New Guinean drinkers, who are usually quite impoverished, must support rich tourists.) To follow this argu-ment through, it is officially asserted that involving Papua New Guineans in small-scale liquor selling would detract from the inducement to foreign investors.

The licensing law relating to road "passenger motor transport" is also de-signed to protect foreign-owned bus operations from the incursion of passenger trucks owned by nationals. This is officially justified in terms of the need for effi-ciency in urban passenger transport. However, foreign bus operators are not very large-scale investors, and this protective function is fading in significance as nationals become more effective and aggressive in taking over the passenger road transport industry, mainly in the use of the passenger trucks. Such trucks are, however, subject to licensing not just to restrict their number in comparison with the number of buses, but also, as the licensing board has put it, "to provide adequate returns for the operators," who are taken to be "operators owning one or two vehicles." But the great majority of trucks are owned by communities.

The trucks are not just objects of economic investment; they are also objects of consumption, and to restrict their operation on these grounds is to deny communities the right to provide their own transport. An instance concerning this licensing system does give cause to doubt the official ability to determine the extent to which licenses should be restricted to secure these adequate returns or, as officially put in relation to the business-licensing law, to secure reasonable profits. The licensing board recently determined that a certain number of trucks would be needed for the capital city area, and licenses were issued accordingly. Soon after this decision, a survey revealed that there were more unlicensed trucks than licensed ones, and the same board hastily issued more licenses to legitimize the situation. (At this point the police put a low priority on prosecuting unlicensed passenger vehicles.)

The control of passenger trucks is also justified in terms of ensuring "a higher degree of stability and service . . . in the industry," as the licensing board has put it. The business-licensing law is officially justified in quite similar terms. This sort of justification was neatly tested in the case of the licensing of buyers of coffee beans from growers. Here the relevant licensing board did not have legal power to restrict the issue of licenses, but it did so nonetheless. This was justified because, in the words of the government representative on the board, "a free-for-all in licensing would create chaos." Although the board considered that licensing should be used "to ensure buyers' profitability," licensing was mainly used to protect foreign interests in the coffee industry. The great majority of licenses were issued to foreign coffee processors who farmed out many of these licenses to the actual coffee buyers, who were usually nationals. In this way, and sometimes in conjunction with tied loans, the buyers were bound to the particular processor who held the licenses. "Chaos" was eliminated in the interests of foreign processors. The obligations of buyers toward processors helped minimize the risk involved in fulfilling forward contracts entered into by processors and exporters. This system was abolished in 1974, and, apart from some minor and temporary problems, coffee buying appears to remain as free from chaos as it ever was.

This directly restrictive type of licensing process, serving as it does particular interests, can be strongly influenced by those interests. For example, the foreign interests dominating the coffee industry effectively controlled the licensing board just mentioned. It took the persistent and bitterly contested efforts of a strong nationalist minister in the government to overcome the board's objections to the abolition of the licensing system (the board was, in law, accountable to that minister). Control of licensing processes by emerging national businessmen is less in evidence; we are here dealing with basically unsettled and embryonic phenomena where it is hard to discern general patterns. However, the licensing of passenger trucks has had since 1968 to settle down, and associations of license-holding businessmen have been formed. These associations do not appear to be very well organized but they can be particularly powerful because the licensing board tends to defer to them mainly through their representation on district advisory committees set up with the encouragement of the board to advise it on the granting of licenses. The government agency concerned with business extension services encourages and supports these associations by helping in their formation and organization and by championing their cause at meetings of the advisory committees. All this is considered perfectly correct and proper: as one member put it at a meeting of an association in discussing a fare increase: "We are not to help the people. We are to do our best for the Truckers' Association." At a meeting of several local government councils about the issue of licenses, one of the most senior officers in business extension advised that "[passenger truck] operators should come together to set up an association to control everything."

Several licensing powers have been given to local government authorities. These bodies seem to be particularly susceptible to external pressure, as the example of mobile trading at the beginning of the chapter illustrates. Also, as we show later, numerous local government councils have used a licensing rule to outlaw street trading altogether. Apart from this, it is probably true that the licensing powers of the local authorities have not so far been significant enough to warrant much effort in gaining control of them. This situation could well change with the introduction of the general business-licensing law described earlier, under which provincial government bodies will be the licensing authorities.

STANDARDS LICENSING

Standards licensing, with its restrictive conditions, is often a feature of directly restrictive licensing as well. For example, in licensing coffee buyers the board concerned used to insist that a licensed buyer have a storage shed conforming to a standard that would preclude all but a few nationals from holding licenses. The department concerned with "business development" has insisted on a high fee for a license under the general business-licensing law in order, as a senior official put it, "to discourage subeconomic operations." The board that licenses passenger trucks advocates that licenses be limited to trucks over a certain size. It justifies this policy on the grounds of economies of scale.

Even in "pure" standards licensing prohibitively high fees are levied for a secondhand dealer's license and a mobile trader's license. We found a self-taught plumber who was refused a license because he could not answer arcane questions about plumbing in skyscrapers. We found the perhaps unthinking labeling described earlier requiring a mobile trader to have a "vehicle." Similar examples arose in the case of a restaurant license and a license to sell meat: to obtain these licenses the proprietors' premises had to conform to certain standards—so if the prospective licensee did not provide meals or meat from "premises" he did not get a license to do these things.

A more detailed example can be found in corporate law, which says, basically, that a group of more than 20 cannot operate a business unless it is registered as a corporation—unless, in the terms of this chapter, it is licensed. This form of licensing involves conditions and procedures that can be met and mastered only with the help of a highly paid specialist. This is a potent source of discrimination against Papua New Guinean group organizations. This situation has been justified by officials solely in terms of the maintenance of standards—mainly standards relevant to the protection of investors in corporations—and these standards were quite explicitly expressed by officials in terms of so-called modernizing goals that could not be compromised. Those few Papua New Guinea groups who have recently been able to apply for registration as a company have found that the attempt to fit certain aspects of Papua New Guinean group organization into this system has led officials to insist on the maintenance of standards in pedantic and often legally erroneous ways.

We will finish this section with some illustrations of the cluster effect—the propensity we suggest for official standards and requirements to cluster around the licensing process, since obtaining a license assuredly involves contact with officials. We described earlier how the requirements of governmental lending and extension agencies could cluster around obtaining a mobile trader's license. Similarly, an application for such a license would spring the local government council's health inspector into operation to check on compliance with the (onerous) pure-food laws. The relevant licensing board requires an applicant for a passenger truck license first to be approved by the government extension agency dealing with business development to ensure he or she is a "high-caliber operator." This board then approaches the police for "character checks" and it will often seek the approval of the local government council in the area where the applicant resides; in this we have examples of councils recommending against applicants whom they have classified by rather dubious criteria as "squatters" or as not "good businessmen."

As we mentioned earlier, officials usually disagree with our definition of the functions of standards licensing; they would rather justify this sort of licensing in terms of the maintenance of standards and the protection of revenue. It is impossible to dispute conclusively arguments about the maintenance of standards since there is an inescapable evaluative element involved. But the arguments can get suspiciously fanciful: for example, prohibiting or restricting street sellers is often justified on the grounds of preventing obstructions, yet in most Papua New Guinean urban conditions, this excuse can only be considered absurd. Rationalization in terms of the protection of revenue is frequent. This justification is used by very many local government councils who require small-scale street sellers to be licensed unless they operate in the council's market area, where a fee is payable, and then the councils refuse to issue any licenses to street sellers. One official boasted that in a large urban area he cleared the streets of a thriving street trade that his tolerant predecessor had allowed to grow up, and this, he asserted, was done to protect market revenue: but it is difficult to see how the amount of market revenue theoretically lost cannot be collected from license fees, especially as much small-scale selling is itinerant and incompatible with being confined to the small market area.

THE ETHOS OF THE PUBLIC BUREAUCRACY

We found official objections to the changing of standards and to the abolition of directly restrictive licensing almost invariably centered on the need for official control—the alternative being seen as chaos. We noted earlier the health inspector's objection to street sellers as being "difficult to check on" and we noted how various forms of licensing were officially seen as necessary for "stability" and "efficiency" and to prevent "chaos." In response to reform measures radically modifying restrictive standards, a senior official said that this would be the "end of everything."

Although it is not officially perceived as such, this apparent need to check on, or control, can be patently—and purposively—counterproductive. The official constraints on obtaining the license for the food bar that we mentioned almost certainly led to its failure because the constraints were so inappropriate for and alien to the people running the enterprise. Fitzpatrick (1975) has analyzed the registration of cooperatives in Papua New Guinea in basically these terms. Briefly, after the Second World War there was an upsurge of informal group economic activity, sometimes with undertones of political self-determination. To contain this, the colonial administration borrowed the cooperative form from British colonial regimes. Registration as a cooperative entailed accepting and becoming closely involved with the requirements of a government extension agency for cooperatives. These requirements were officially aimed at securing the conventional economic success of cooperatives, and to this end extension officials became closely and dominatingly involved in running them. This alienated the directors and members of the cooperatives and so, in the longer term, led to their failure in a great many instances. These failures and the failures typified by the food bar are characteristically explained by officials in terms of a lack of motivation on the people's part, this lack being seen as an inherent defect.

A specific aspect of this trend is the top-heavy influence brought to bear in the making and application of licensing laws. A few examples will help make the point. A comparatively insignificant but quite staggering example concerns the formulation of the law for the licensing of second-hand dealers. Here the police successfully insisted on a very high license fee to restrict access to licenses simply because they wanted to cut down the number of outlets for a particular type of second-hand goods—stolen cars. Whether a liquor license will be granted in relation to a particular site is, in most cases, decided by the chairman of the licensing body in conjunction with the government's lands department before the public hearing takes place that is meant to provide evidence for determining the issue. A new law for the registration (or licensing) of "business groups" as corporations passed through the cabinet on the basis of official confirmation that it accorded with and implemented a decision previously made by the cabinet, when in fact it differed radically from that decision. Many more examples could be cited, but the general point to be made is that this control orientation imports a measure of contempt for the people who have to be controlled and sometimes for their political representatives.

The general orientation of control and restriction is not, we have tried to show, merely negative. The conditions on which licenses can be granted effectively define who is to benefit from the process. Perhaps in some cases no discrimination is intended, or the conditions imposed are genuinely felt to be beneficial—it simply happens that almost everyone fails to meet the conditions. These conditions are an integral part of the control orientation of the bureaucratic mechanism. This control—at least the sort of control we have described and analyzed—is neither very positive nor, in terms of its officially ascribed functions, very effective. It is nothing like the earlier visions of the virtues of planning, of powerful but concerned and progressive Third World public administrations—and certainly it is nothing like "social engineering" or "modernization" through law. Officials do not really control reasonable profit levels or secure stability with direct licensing, and most standards licensing can be enforced only in urban areas and then often only patchily. Official goals implicit in the assertion of the inviolability of standards are clearly unattainable. Control goes only as far as holding down initiative, as Balandier puts it in the context of the "colonial situation" (1970:29); control ensures that any innovatory move is captured and then shaped or suppressed through contact and entanglement with the public bureaucracy, which acts in support of dominant class elements.

REFERENCES

Balandier, G.
    1970   The Sociology of Black Africa: Social Dynamics in Central Africa. New York: Praeger.
Douglas, M.
    1970   Purity and Danger: an Analysis of Concepts of Pollution and Taboo. Harmondsworth, England: Penguin.
Fitzpatrick, P.
    1975   "A new law for co-operatives." Annals of Public and Co-operative Economy 46:277-287
Fitzpatrick, P., and L. Blaxter
    1975   "Colonialism and the informal sector." Australian and New Zealand Journal of Sociology 11:42-45
Freire, P.
    1970   Pedagogy of the Oppressed. New York: Seabury Press.
    1972   Cultural Action for Freedom. Harmondsworth: Penguin.
Hirst, P.
    1977   "Economic classes and politics." Pp. 125-154 in Alan Hunt (ed.), Class and Class Structure. London: Lawrence and Wishart.
International Labour Office
    1972   Employment, Incomes and Equality: A Strategy for Increasing Productive Employment in Kenya. Geneva: International Labour Office.
McCarthy, J. K.
    1963   Patrol into Yesterday. Melbourne: Cheshire.

Nwafor, A.
    1975   "History and the intelligence of the disinherited." *The Review of Radical Political Economy* 7:43–54.
Sankoff, G.
    1969   *"Wok Bisnis* and Namasu: a perspective from the village." Pp. 61–81 in I. J. Fairbairn (ed.), *Namasu: New Guinea's Largest Indigenous-owned Company.* Port Moresby: New Guinea Research Unit.

8

LEGALLY INDUCED CULTURE CHANGE
IN NEW GUINEA

LEOPOLD POSPISIL

If one does not believe that culture is superorganic in the sense that the individual has little influence upon its content and structure, if one does not subscribe to the doctrine of social determinism but allows the individual to play a creative role along with the more abstract social forces of his cultural environment, then culture change at the level of the individual has to be conceived as a learning process. True, there are those few who initiate the changes, but there remains the rest of the society who, by adopting these changes, transforms the innovations into culture change. Thus the learning process forms the dynamic basis of any alteration of culture. Miller and Dollard (1964) describe this process as a change in the individual's opinion by which a new response becomes dominant over the previously accepted one. This learning process, the authors hold, must be fostered by encouraging the desired response with rewards, and extinguishing the previous and now undesired response by withholding rewards or inflicting punishment. Thus only those responses that are continuously rewarded are learned, and those that are not are slowly extinguished. Indeed, the extinction may be accelerated by punishment, the antithesis of reward. In the authors' words, "the stronger drive, and hence greater escape-reward, which may be secured through relatively strong punishments produces a more rapid and per-

The Imposition of Law

manent abandonment of a response than do the weaker and more diffused rewards presumably involved in extinction [Miller and Dollard 1964:41].'' Since law uses rewards and punishments as its sanction and because it applies to the whole of society and its subgroups, law can be very effective—indeed, the major instrument for effecting culture change.

Law as a major agent of social change has been long recognized by such sociologists as Durkheim and Weber. Their theories usually concern law that is imposed internally, that is, established by the authorities of the indigenous population on the basis of accepted social and cultural values. In a situation of acculturation, especially colonial acculturation, the law that produces the culture change is imposed by the authorities of the dominant, intrusive culture, often against the will of the indigenous population. Since it lacks popular support, and people comply with it only because they fear punishment will be administered by the colonial officials, most if not all of this type of law must be regarded as authoritarian, as opposed to customary law (Pospisil 1971:193–209). This chapter describes the effects of authoritarian law upon the Kapauku Papuans of New Guinea, a people whose aboriginal legal system I had the privilege to study in 1954–1955 before colonization, and whose culture change, induced mainly through the imposition of foreign law, I was able to observe from its inception in 1956 until my last research in 1975.

I shall concentrate upon only two areas in which the foreign law produced major changes. It will be shown that, first, acculturation primarily affects the regulation of what I have called societal structure, that is laws dealing with the essential aspects of the society's subgroups and their mutual relationships—precepts that in our traditional terminology would be regarded as part of constitutional law. Second, the imposed colonial law, with its fundamentally different values, will be shown to clash head-on with the values of the native culture, producing major political problems and changes in what we may call the laws of procedure, although this chapter does not explicitly deal with the latter. In contrast, it will be seen that laws dealing with the social structure (regulating the individual's ego-centered relationships with his fellow tribesmen—for example, laws of contract, marriage, inheritance, and property, all of which are laws of substance) are left virtually untouched.

IMPOSED LAW AND THE RESULTING CHANGE IN SOCIETAL STRUCTURE

THE CONCEPTS OF SOCIAL AND SOCIETAL STRUCTURE

In order to analyze properly the effects of imposed colonial laws upon a native culture, one has to understand a dichotomy in the social organization that bears directly upon our problem and its interpretation. In my previous publications, I found it necessary to make a distinction between social structure and societal structure. I applied the term *social structure* to the analysis of ego's relations with the rest of the members of his society. In other words, this concept refers to the structure of ego's social relations and applies to those instances in which ego is the common point of reference, and in which all the relationships, as well as categories and aggregates of people, are defined and described relatively (in relation to ego) and are not treated as absolute units within the matrix of the society. In contrast, the term *societal structure* is applied to the analysis of the nature and relationships of the society's segments (subgroups). This concept refers to discrete groups, described absolutely without any dependence upon the functioning of a single individual (ego) as a point of reference (Pospisil 1961, 1963a, 1963b).

ACCULTURATION VERSUS URBANIZATION

In the past 20 years I have conducted two long-term studies of the processes of economic and sociopolitical changes, one among the tribal Kapauku Papuans of New Guinea, and another among the Tirolean peasants of Obernberg. These two inquiries into social change have dealt with two different processes, usually labeled in the anthropological literature as *acculturation* (in the case of the Kapauku) and *urbanization* (in the case of the Tirolean peasants). The two processes are usually defined in terms of the situation in which they occur. Acculturation is usually thought of as a process whereby a society undergoes significant cultural change because of prolonged contact with another society of a different culture and language. Urbanization is traditionally viewed as a process by which a rural population, usually consisting of peasants, undergoes a significant subcultural change because of the influence of the urban subculture of a neighboring city. There is usually only a dialect difference between the speech of the urban and rural populations. Whereas in acculturation we are dealing with two different, originally unrelated societies, in urbanization the process is effected by the interaction of two structurally united subsocieties—the urban and rural segments of an organically unified larger society.

My two research endeavors indicate that there is more than a contextual distinction between the two processes. Indeed, my data show that there is a basic structural difference between acculturation and urbanization—an intrinsic rather than an extrinsic contrast. Whereas urbanization affects primarily the structure of the basic interpersonal relations that are ego-centered (belonging to the sphere of social structure), acculturation during the first 2 decades of the Kapauku exposure to the West and Indonesia affected primarily their societal structure. It altered the relations as well as the nature of Kapauku social groups such as political confederacies, lineages, sublineages, and villages.

Urbanization in the Tirol affected the cultural ordering of ego's relations with other members of his society, while leaving unaltered the composition and function of the Tirolean families, association, and communities. It changed the patterns of ego's friendship and political networks while it did not alter the structure and function of the Obernberg community and its subgroups. In contrast, acculturation to the Kapauku has involved the disintegration of their society and its segments (groups). Some of the subdivisions of the traditional society have disappeared altogether; others have become ephemeral or almost nominal, having lost most of their important functions. New groupings have been dogmatically imposed upon the people by their colonial masters, and other group formations have arisen spontaneously in reaction to pressure from the outside.

The forces behind these changes in the two societies were radically different. In the Tirolean urbanization the alterations of ego's relationships occurred without formalized pressure from outside (for example, from the city), resulting not from decree but usually voluntarily through a change of values induced by economic forces. The acculturation of the Kapauku resulted from pressure exerted through political changes and was usually dictated by the foreign colonial power. Though Kapauku social structure (kinship, friendship, and partnership) has been left almost intact, their societal structure has been altered ruthlessly by the new political superstructure of the colonial state. The mechanism by which these profound acculturation changes were accomplished was the imposition of a highly formalized foreign legal system concerned mainly with what has been called public law (*ius publicum*), and within it what we may call constitutional and criminal law.

TRADITIONAL SOCIETAL STRUCTURE OF THE KAPAUKU

The Kapauku Papuans, a linguisitic group of approximately 45,000 people, are horticulturists living in the western part of the central highlands of West New Guinea (Irian Jaya); they subsist on the cultivation of sweet potatoes and the breeding of pigs. Patrilineal descent and partilocal polygynous families are the main characteristics of their societal structure. About 15 households, each of whose members live in one main house, form a village. The male villagers and their children belong to the same patrilineage.

Members of two or more patrilineages, which might belong to the same or different sibs, used to unite into political confederacy. These unions were reasonably stable and had varying numbers of lineages and members. They constituted the most inclusive politically organized groups within the Kapauku tribe. In the southern half of the Kamu Valley, a typical confederacy consisted of two, three, or four lineages of different sibs, whose members (about 600 in number) inhabited three to nine villages. This political union was a confederacy in the sense that any of its constituent lineages was politically and legally semi-independent and did not have to participate in the confederacy's wars if its headman regarded the war as unjustified. While headmen, called *tonowi*, administered law and order within this group, a confederacy's relations beyond its territorial boundaries were confined to political negotiations and wars.

The confederacy's headman, who had to possess the four Kapauku qualities of leadership (health, wealth, generosity, and eloquence), was usually a middle-aged man, brave in war and skilled in magic. Invariably, he was also the leader of the largest constituent lineage, within which, if it was further subdivided, he was the headman of the most powerful sublineage. Furthermore, within the sublineage he was usually the head of its largest constituent household. Thus the statuses of the Kapauku traditional headman were cumulative: achievement of a higher status in a more inclusive group depended on his being headman of the strongest constituent subgroup. In settling internal disputes the headman of the confederacy functioned as a sort of chief justice for the whole political unit. His word was also decisive in interconfederational affairs, including disputes of his constituents with outsiders and problems of war and peace. Every subgroup of the confederacy (lineage, sublineage, and household) had a leader of its own with the same personal qualifications required of the confederacy headman. Because the headmen of the various subgroups held differing ideas of proper behavior and justice, each subgroup had its own legal system, which varied to some extent from corresponding systems in other groups.

CHANGES IN SOCIETAL STRUCTURE RESULTING FROM THE IMPOSITION OF COLONIAL LAW

Whenever a colonial power moves into new territory it inevitably effects immediate and profound changes in the native political structure. "Pacification," the word used for establishing colonial control over a territory, usually means not only eliminating native warfare and enforcing intra- as well as intertribal peace, but also taking away the people's independence and limiting or completely abrogating the powers of the native political leadership. By establishing itself as a government over a formerly politically fragmented area, it converts external conflicts, such as wars, self-redress, and diplomatic negotiations, into internal disputes that are dealt with and adjudicated peacefully by the courts of the new administration.

IMPOSITION OF COLONIAL OR STATE SUPERSTRUCTURE

In the process of pacification, the colonial or state government establishes a new territorial legal level that has not existed before, with all its courts and police machinery to enforce the decisions of the colonial judges. Furthermore, it almost always takes from the native chiefs or headmen their jurisdiction over grave criminal offenses, thus no longer allowing them to impose the sanctions of death or maiming. As a result, their political functions are either severely curtailed or completely obliterated and replaced by a new "native" system of controls subordinated to the colonial government. Thus the *pax coloniae* imposes a new legal system that is directed at, and often enforces profound modifications in, the power structure of the society and its subgroups. In other words, the colonial legal system is primarily concerned with public law of the constitutional type, which affects and alters the aboriginal societal structure.

The Kamu Valley, pacified by the Dutch colonial government in 1956 after my first long study (1954–1955), was no exception to the rule. The elimination of native warfare, which was endemic in this region, deprived the Kapauku political confederacies of one of their major functions—common defense. Inter-confederational disputes, formerly solved either by diplomatic negotiations or war, began to be referred in 1956 to the court of the Dutch civil administration at Moanemani in the Kamu Valley; serious criminal offenses were brought to the attention of the district officer at Enarotali and, later, at Waghete in the Tigi Lake region. All the more serious cases that involved contestants from formerly different confederacies were referred to the court of the Dutch administrator at Moanemani. Now that murder and other crimes of physical violence had been to a large extent at least temporarily eliminated through fear of the colonial officers and their constabulary, the bulk of Kapauku litigation concerned itself with con-tracts and property disputes, for example, bride-price payments, loans, and sales of pigs.

The colonial administrator was often called upon to adjudicate a great variety of civil cases, and one would think that in the sphere of civil law the colonial courts would have exercised an influence similar to that wielded in the spheres of constitutional and criminal law. Such was not the case. In civil matters as well as in criminal cases not involving homicide, the administrator at Moanemani availed himself of traditional Kapauku law by making decisions based upon the aboriginal principles of social control. How did the Dutch officer in his new role as dispenser of civil justice discover what the tribal law was? While visiting his court I was astounded to see my book *Kapauku Papuans and Their Law* (1958) being used by the administration officer as a legal *codex*—as the "authorized version" of the Kapauku law. Although I was amused, this was certainly not the reaction of all the Kapauku. As a matter of fact, my book was very unpopu-lar with some of them for an obvious reason. My work dealt only with the legal system of the Ijaaj-Pigome confederacy of the southern part of the Kamu Valley, which differed from every other confederacy's legal system. By applying the Ijaaj-Pigome legal system to the whole of the Kapauku society, the Dutch Offi-cer had invested the system with a status it had never previously held. The only amused people were my Ijaaj-Pigome friends, who joked about it or even poked fun at the other Kapauku. One of them, tongue in cheek, even mockingly threatened the others: "If you fellows don't behave we shall make our American big man write another and even tougher book." In an effort to undo the injus-tice, I explained the problem to the officer. He was surprised and admitted that he thought the opposition to his ruling was due to the stubborn nature of some of the litigants. So from then on my book served only as a reference or a guide-line to the judge rather than as a *codex* that was to be rigorously enforced.

The Dutch administration, then, established a new legal system that was imposed upon the aboriginal jurisdictional hierarchy of family, household, sublineage, lineage, and confederacy at a higher and much more inclusive level than traditional Kapauku law had been. It eliminated interconfederational wars and political negotiations and brought peace to the entire region, allowing the capitalistic-minded Kapauku entrepreneurs to trade over long distances without fear of being killed. Nevertheless, as we shall see, the colonial peace was a mixed blessing rather than an unqualified asset.

When the Indonesians succeeded the Dutch, the Kamu Valley was assigned its own Indonesian district officer, who resides in Moanemani. However, in other districts in the Kapauku territory there has been a more radical change: in Waghete of the Tigi Lake region and in Enarotali on Lake Paniai, native Kapauku themselves have been appointed as district officers. Moreover, the Kapauku districts, such as those of the Kamu Valley, Enarotali, and Tigi, have been incorporated into a more inclusive region called Paniai, presided over by an Indonesian resident officer (*bupati*) with headquarters at the newly built and fast-growing city of Nabire on the coast of Geelvink Bay. Nowadays, all serious legal cases are transferred to a judge at Nabire, where there is a jail for confining offenders against Indonesian *adat* (customary) law. Only capital offenses are referred to the court in Jakarta.

CHANGES IN THE NATURE OF POLITICAL AND LEGAL AUTHORITY

The establishment of colonial rule, with its economic influence and the imposition of a new public legal system, had a devastating effect upon the traditional Kapauku political leadership. The aboriginal political system was based upon a native egalitarian philosophy in which conformity with norms of conduct was achieved by inducement rather than compulsion. The Kapauku did punish offenders for crimes and torts, but offenders were never forced to conform. Individual freedom was highly valued and was never taken from anyone, not even from a criminal. Such institutions as jails, house arrest, war captivity, serfdom, and slavery were unheard of. Because wealth was one of the highest goals of the individual, persuasion very often took an economic form: fines and withdrawal of extension of credit were frequently used as political and legal inducements.

Leadership in the household coincided with ownership of the house; the authorities in polygynous and nuclear families were defined on the basis of kinship and marital bonds, for example father, husband. However, such formal criteria of authority were absent in other types of Kapauku groups. In all these there was only one type of authority, whom the natives called the *tonowi* (the rich man). Since he was an informal authority, he can be called a headman. The Kapauku headman's status was defined by two sets of criteria of a different order. First, the personal and social criteria determined the headman's qualifications as an individual leader. Second, societal criteria established his status in society according to his position in the particular subgroups of the society.

Whereas the first criterion determined an individual as a leader, the second designated his rank in the hierarchy of the *tonowi*.

The most important of the personal and social criteria for Kapauku leadership was wealth. A *tonowi* had a great amount of cowrie-shell money, extensive credit, several wives, at least 20 pigs, a reasonably large home, and many cultivated fields. His wealth carried with it the highest prestige and was the main measure of his status. Most *tonowi* achieved their position by their own endeavors; only here and there might a generous inheritance accomplish the same result, but only if it was bestowed upon a capable man. An incompetent young heir might soon lose the property he inherited from his father.

The hoarding of wealth did not in itself carry prestige; it was the distribution of wealth and the extension of credit that counted. Wealthy creditors not only became leaders but were also regarded as moral individuals. Although wealth was certainly an important qualification for becoming a leader, not all wealthy men had followers and could hand down decisions of social consequence. Only some of them achieved this status. People might follow the decisions of a wealthy man either because they were his debtors and were afraid of being asked to repay, or out of gratitude for past financial aid, or because they expected some future financial favor. To comply with the requests and decisions of the wealthy man meant economic security. Since wealth depended on successful pig breeding as well as upon the man's health and age, the political powers and leadership within a Kapauku lineage, sublineage, or confederacy could change rapidly. New individuals succeeded to leadership only to lose it years later to more successful and generous pig breeders.

Eloquence was the final criterion of the Kapauku *tonowi*. Ijaaj Timaaj-jokainaago of Botukebo, although a very rich, generous, and honest man, was not a leader of his lineage because he was afraid to speak at a gathering. He was pushed aside by a man who was less rich and was regarded as less "moral," but who was an excellent public speaker. To summarize, a Kapauku leader had to be wealthy, generous, and eloquent. Bravery in war and shamanistic skills, although they enhanced his prestige, were not required of a *tonowi*.

Obedience to the decisions of a *tonowi* by his followers was motivated by the type of relationship that existed between them. For example, kinsmen supported and followed their rich relative because kinship created an emotional bond and imposed certain duties, although expectations of future favors were probably the most important considerations. Even individuals from neighboring confederations might yield to the wishes of a *tonowi* in case his help was needed in future.

Debtors formed another dependable category among the *tonowi*'s adherents. Fear of being asked to repay loans, coupled with appreciation for the credit allowed, made them stout supporters. They could always be relied on in war or in a legal suit. They were vitally interested in their creditor's life and well-being because they could only lose by his death: debts and credits were inherited and, since cordial and personal relations were not necessarily shared by the heirs, the repayment of inherited credit was often demanded on the death of the *tonowi*.

A very special group of the *tonowi*'s partisans were his "boys," or adopted young men. They were not only dependable and faithful, but they were always at hand. They came to live with the rich man to secure his protection, to share his food, to learn how to transact business, and finally to be granted a substantial loan for buying a wife. In return they offered their labor in his gardens and around the house, their support in legal and other disputes, and their lives in case of war. They formed a bodyguard for the *tonowi* and their physical presence alone ensured respect for their leader. The *tonowi* functioned as an adjudicator in disputes among his followers.

The personal criteria mentioned earlier were the basis for achieving political and legal authority among the Kapauku. However, they did not identify the rank of the authority within the hierarchy of the Kapauku headmen. A comparison of the amount of wealth of two authorities, for example, failed to indicate which one of them was the leader of a more inclusive group and thus superior in rank to the other. To determine the headman's rank, societal criteria had to be considered.

A headman's societal status (as opposed to his status as a headman) was defined by his position in the subgroups of the society and by their mutual relations. The societal status designated his rank in the hierarchy of the various types of headmen; it determined the amount of his power, the scope of his jurisdiction, and the type of law he was supposed to administer. The following generalizations can be made about the principles that determined the societal status of a *tonowi*. First, every functioning subgroup had a leader. Second, his status depended on the inclusiveness of the group of his followers. The headman of a confederacy was thus superior to the headman of a sublineage. Third, achievement of a higher status as headman of a more inclusive group depended on the simultaneous possession of a lower political status as headman in one of the constituent subgroups. Thus political statuses were cumulative. The *tonowi* of a political confederacy retained his position as *tonowi* of his lineage and sublineage, and as head of his household and family. His followers, power, and the type of law he administered differed in every instance. Fourth, the most populous of the subgroups that together formed a group on the higher level of inclusiveness provided the authority for this higher group, as evidenced by the leader of the Ijaaj-Pigome confederacy who came from its strongest constituent subgroup—the Ijaaj-Gepouja lineage. Because his own sublineage was stronger than that of the headman of the Ijaaj-Enona sublineage, he became the headman of the lineage, despite the fact that his village of Aigii was smaller than that of his rival. Within his sublineage the headman of the confederacy resided in the largest village (Aigii) and possessed the largest household in it. Fifth, in certain groups several headmen may have shared the position of *tonowi*. In the case of multiple headmanship, all headmen shared the jurisdiction equally. However, only the wealthiest represented the unit in disputes with outsiders.

The aboriginal system of legal authority and headmanship clashed head-on with the new administrative policies and legal regulations of the Dutch and later

Indonesian governments. In their political function the Kapauku *tonowi* were deprived of their former involvement with peace and alliance negotiations, and they ceased to be regarded as free heads of autonomous units or as headmen of the independent political confederacies. They became subjects of the Dutch government and, later, Indonesian citizens subordinated to the colossal state machinery that operated in faraway Jakarta. In their legal authority the *tonowi* fared no better. All capital and serious crimes were officially exempted from their jurisdiction and delegated to district officers or to judges residing in the foreign (to the Kapauku) territory of Nabire or even in the distant capital of Indonesia. In the functions they retained, such as adjudication of civil cases and what we would call minor crimes and misdemeanors, they were neither hindered nor supported by the state government—they were simply ignored.

However, the last real blow to the *tonowi* was dealt unwittingly by the Dutch administration in a nonpolitical field. No matter what the effect of the pacification and the civil administration might have been, it could not account for the spectacular loss of power and influence of most of the native headmen. Actually, at the beginning the Dutch administration had shown a deep interest in preserving the old system of political leadership. The reason for this loss of power puzzled me when I was there in 1959, and I could not explain it to the Dutch administration. Not until I reviewed the amount of outstanding debts and credits in 1959 and 1962, and compared them with those recorded during the unacculturated period of 1954–1955, did I learn the real reason for the collapse of the *tonowi*'s power. We have seen that before colonization the Kapauku followed the decisions of a local headman largely because of their indebtedness to him or because they felt grateful for past loans and expected future favors. The comparison revealed that in 1962 the outstanding debts owed by the Kapauku to their headmen were only 31.5% (equivalent to 11,915 pounds of pork) of what they had been in 1955 (equivalent to 37,710 pounds of pork). It was obvious that the lessening of the headmen's power and, ultimately, the complete collapse of their leadership, resulted from this marked decrease of indebtedness of the common native to his leader. The young men, who formerly had to borrow heavily from the headman to pay the bride-price, no longer had to depend on the *tonowi* after the advent of the white man. They found paid work at Moanemani, where the administration was building an airstrip. This single act of constructing an airport had the unexpected effect upon the native Kapauku culture of completely undermining its political and legal authority.

The new law of the Dutch and later that of the Indonesian state also affected the decision-making activity officially left to the *tonowi*. All old interconfederational disputes, formerly settled either by diplomatic negotiation between the headmen of the confederacies involved or through armed conflict, were now brought by the natives themselves to the court of the Dutch official or, later, to the Indonesian district officer at Moanemani. As my case material shows, the agenda of the "court" at Moanemani became crowded with interconfederational marriage disputes concerning bride-price payments and with conflicts over ownership of or payment for pigs, the two most important types of transaction in the Kapauku economy. In contrast, marital troubles were very often arbitrated, or sometimes interfered with, by the missionaries. In one instance a missionary was almost killed by an enraged father of the bride (my old friend Jikiiwiijaaj tried to decapitate him with his machete). The only interconfederation disputes that were not brought to the attention of the "civilized" authorities at the outset of colonial power were those concerning payment of debts incurred because of past wars, which were regarded as illegal by the new rulers and were therefore settled secretively by the local *tonowi*.

CHANGE IN SOCIETAL STRUCTURE:
DISAPPEARANCE OF CONFEDERACIES

The elimination of native warfare and the delegation of cases of serious crime to the Dutch or Indonesian officials deprived the Kapauku confederacies of one of their major functions. Political ties that had formerly bound Kapauku lineages closely into confederacies began to loosen, and the lineages and their constituent villages became more independent. The authority of many leaders of the former confederacies and of lineages and sublineages declined, but not all headmen suffered political eclipse. In some instances, the influence of a few leaders of the former political confederacies began to spread beyond the old and steadily vanishing political boundaries. This was a direct challenge to the administration of the colonial power. Because of the degree of acculturation of the various groups, new alliances were formed and new antagonisms originated. Thus, while the old type of confederacy leadership declined beyond recognition even as early as 1959, leaders of the newly formed broader alliances assumed unprecedented influence over a much larger area. This change was initiated unwittingly by Jupikaapaibo, an enterprising headman of Mauwa (close to Moanemani, the seat of the new administration) and a member of the Goo sib. He seized upon the new opportunities and befriended the Dutch administrator to such a degree that the latter made him an intermediary between himself and the Kapauku. After this appointment, the old types of confederacies collapsed, and their constituent lineages began to regroup themselves into two large conglomerates. One was led by Jupikaapaibo, the other by Jokagaibo of the Ijaaj sib, who was already a very wealthy man and since 1960 had been leader of the fading Ijaaj-Pigome confederacy. Jokagaibo derived additional prestige from friendship with me, the only other "secular" white man in the valley. As a result, in 1962 the Kamu Valley was divided roughly into two politically opposed segments. One, having in its center the villages of Mauwa and Moanemani, comprised roughly the western and northwestern part of the valley. The other, which united several formerly hostile political confederacies, comprised the eastern and southern parts of the valley, including the lineages of the former Ijaaj-Pigome confederacy, and their former archenemies, the Waine-Tibaakoto confederacy. Similarly, all over the Kamu Valley former traditional enemies were united into the two new alliances, which divided the valley into two politically hostile camps. This division, however, never resulted in open violence, and conflicts were confined to the courts, where the two camps always supported their constituents. Thus Jokagaibo wielded legal and political authority in a new group much larger than his former confederacy. In his new role Jokagaibo not only adjudicated disputes among his followers but also defended their interests at the court of Moanemani as an informal spokesman and adviser, especially when the opponent in the dispute belonged to Jupikaapaibo's camp.

With the advent of the Indonesian administration, the political situation in the Kamu Valley changed outwardly and formally only slightly—to the extent that the valley was assigned its own district officer. However, the Indonesians initiated an important change in the informal native political structure. After a bloody uprising, in which the Kapauku of the Kamu Valley fought united against their new rulers, whom they considered their oppressors, the political moiety system of the Kamu disintegrated again. In its place the whole Kamu Valley was united and now stands in opposition to the Tigi Lake region, which supported the Indonesians. Thus for the first time in Kapauku history a whole region has been informally united politically—this time on a territorial rather than a descent basis. A few of the formerly important headmen have emerged as an informal body of political leaders of the valley. They are often called upon to deal with the formal Indonesian administration and represent the "Kapauku point of view," and among themselves they settle civil legal cases as well as criminal cases that do not involve murder, serious bodily injury, grand theft, or insurrection against the state. It should be noted that, structurally and functionally speaking, this recent Kapauku informal leadership is of a new kind. No more are these leaders the large moneylenders whose constituency is linked to them through the fetters of extended credit; no more are political loyalties determined by gratitude for past financial favors or expectation of future economic assistance. The new leaders are purely political individuals who have risen to their present positions because of their opposition to the Dutch and Indonesian governments.

CHANGE IN SOCIETAL STRUCTURE:
VILLAGE REPLACES LINEAGE

Before colonization, the village had no political functions among the Kapauku societal segments. If one understands the nature of the old Kapauku village and that of the sublineage, the reason becomes obvious. The territory of the Kapauku sublineage constituted a true home for the natives. There they could and did own garden land in any part, and they were free also to build their houses in any locality in this territory. Clusters of their homes formed semi-permanent villages. When the land around such a settlement had been exhausted, the people, often individually, moved their homes to other localities. New villages sprang up in former forests and marshes, and old residential localities reverted to bush. Thus on the sublineage or non-subdivided lineage territory there were often several communities, their location and number changing with time. The enduring grouping was the sublineage, not the village. The political and judicial functions were vested in this descent-oriented group. A village was endowed temporarily with a purely economic role and was politically integrated into the more inclusive sublineage. A sublineage whose members resided in several villages was likely to have several headmen. If these happened to live in different villages, they tended to be identified with the place of their residence, and thus they resembled, but only superficially, village headmen. Actually their jurisdiction covered the whole sublineage territory: they could hear and decide cases of dispute in any village of their sublineage, irrespective of their residence. In order to avoid conflict with fellow sublineage headmen with the same jurisdiction in the territory, a judge of a conflict was simply the headman who first participated in hearing testimony and arguments.

Before the pacification of the area by the Dutch authorities, the villages, although they existed, did not constitute politically organized groups. With the coming of the Dutch administration, the officials, often ignorant of the native political structure and influenced by their past colonial experience in Indonesia, regarded the local *tonowi* as *kapala kampoeng* (village chiefs) and assigned to them jurisdiction within the local villages. Indeed, for the sake of convenience and efficiency they often gave them the official title of *kapala* (although this was not usually authorized by the Dutch government). Thus, the idea of village chieftainship slowly emerged. Because the Dutch preferred to deal with *kapalas* than with the headmen of poorly understood descent units, a new legal level of village authority was created. As the administration gained importance through economic influence and police enforcement of its law, the formal village leaders gained strength and prestige, thus securing the political position of the village in the new colonial hierarchy of legal levels.

With the rise of the village chief the *tonowi*'s influence, as well as the political role of the old lineage system, diminished. In this way the colonial government, through imposition of new public law, changed the societal structure of the Kapauku society, and it also introduced two principles into the native judicial system that were originally alien to it. First, through elevating the village to the most important administrative unit, in which the *kapala kampoeng* kept the peace and solved local legal conflicts, they introduced territoriality as the principle of jurisdiction. A man's case was adjudicated by the law of that locality in which he committed a tort or a minor crime, irrespective of his lineage or confederacy affiliation. Second, by introducing the *kapala* system into the native power structure, they created a new type of authority, deriving the *kapala*'s tenure not from the voluntary support and informal recognition of his people but from a formal appointment of the colonial authority. There was a formal office of chief created in each village, an office that had to be filled. As was not the case with the *tonowi*, the *kapala*'s amount of power, his jurisdiction, and the means of implementing his verdicts were legalistically determined with great precision. Furthermore, his tenure was not informally ended, marked by a simple disregard of his decisions by his former followers, but was concluded by official fiat which bore no relation to the popularity of the man.

Gradually, what was once an informal political structure, marked by constantly shifting power and change, became petrified and formalized into the *kapala kampoeng* village chieftainship. It is interesting to note that a similar process of change from informal headman to formal village or band chief occurred among the Nunamiut Eskimo of Alaska under western influence. There the informal *umealik*, similar to the *tonowi*, was superseded by the *atanek*, a local chief resembling in most respects the Indonesian *kapala*.

THE CLASH OF IMPOSED LAW WITH TRADITIONAL VALUES

Not only the traditional societal structure of the Kapauku and their conception of informal authority collided with the western and Indonesian legal systems. Principles that permeated both of these bodies of law were much more profound and disruptive and were diametrically opposed to deep-seated values of Kapauku society.

THE PROBLEM OF PUNISHMENT

Both of the imposed systems are based on principles of subordination of the individual to the state, a political institution represented by and embodied in the state bureacracy, judiciary, and police. Their sanctions are primarily punitive in nature, imprisonment being the most frequent punishment, even for minor offenses. Ideally, prison is supposed to function as a corrective or rehabilitative measure. But subordination to the state and putting offenders behind bars clashed with basic Kapauku values placed upon personal freedom and individual integrity. The Kapauku believe that a man deprived of independence of action and liberty is doomed; his soul will eventually leave him, and he will die. To understand the gravity of imprisonment to a Kapauku we must have some understanding of his philosophy of life and his value system. To him the essence of life is liberty—personal freedom from coercion and physical restraint.

Traditional Kapauku philosophy maintains that man has a dual nature, spiritual in the form of his soul, and material in the form of his body. The question then arises: "Who am I?" Ego is certainly not the body, because the Kapauku ardently argue that one can live even after losing a large part of it, such as limbs. Neither can ego be *ani ipuwe enija* (the soul)—because the Kapauku actually prays to his own soul and thus dissociates it from ego. When ego is neither the body nor the soul, then it is obvious that to a Kapauku "I" means consciousness; it means the thinking process that the Kapauku conceive to be the cooperative effort of the body and the soul. Consequently, for the

Kapauku, as for some European philosophers, to think means to be—*cogito ergo sum*. Thus, strictly speaking, "I" exists only when I am awake. Dreams and visions are experiences of the soul alone, while "I" ceases temporarily to exist. In accordance with this idea, the Kapauku language translates the English verb *to live* as *umii-tou*, which reflects very accurately the notions discussed here. Whereas *umii* means "to sleep," referring to the separate existence of the soul, *tou* means "to stay in place," referring to the material existence of the body. To live, *umii-tou*, suggests to the Kapauku the free cooperation of body and soul. My body stays in place (*tou*), my soul dreams when I sleep (*umii*), and I live (*umii-tou*).

Should the cooperation of the body and the soul be impeded, ego would either cease temporarily to function (as in a dream or vision), or would be obliterated altogether should the cooperation cease permanently (as in death). Cooperation of the soul with the body is certainly obstructed, according to the Kapauku, when the soul cannot freely determine the actions of the body. Interference with the cooperation of the body and soul thus constitutes an impediment to life itself and is consequently always regarded as dangerous and often as fatal. It occurs when a person is in a coma and cannot direct his body. It also occurs if a man is forced against his will to behave in a specific way—as for example, in forced labor—or if he is prevented from moving freely by being tied or confined to a house or territory. In Kapauku society, therefore, there are no prisoners of war, jails, serfdom, slavery, or enforced behavior. Kapauku do not force their children to do things. Punishment is always a reprimand for past wrong behavior, never a means to coerce a behavior.

Freedom of movement and of premeditated action is a basic condition for life. Consequently, in Kapauku society, one cannot expect to find *enforcement* of laws or of an authority's decisions; *inducement* would be a more suitable term as the means for social control. Punishment works as an inducement for better behavior in the future but not as an enforcement of immediate behavior. Thus one is independent in the sense that all actions should follow one's own decisions rather than somebody else's. The latter would be regarded as a cessation of the vital cooperation of soul and body, equivalent perhaps to a slow but unavoidable death. It is not surprising, then, that the Kapauku inflicted physical (corporal) punishment such as beating, wounding with an arrow, or execution, very sparingly; and they never deprived a convicted wrongdoer of his freedom. In their repertory of effective punishments, psychological sanctions such as shaming and public reprimand, together with such economic sanctions as payment of damages, played the dominant role.

Unaware of this basic philosophy of the Kapauku, the Dutch administration imposed upon them not only Dutch law but also its favored method of punishment—imprisonment. The introduction of such an unheard-of punishment was a deep shock to these freedom-loving people. "The worst thing that can happen to a Kapauku is to be put into the white man's jail in Enarotali. We do not like to have even our enemies put there and we hate the police for this practice," said a man from the Tigi Lake area. And he continued, "Jail is the worst thing. The man's vital substance deteriorates and the man dies. We used to kill only very bad people, but now one may get into prison simply for stealing or even fighting in a war. One dies if shot by an arrow, but in jail one has to suffer before death. One has to stay in one place and has to work when one does not like it. Jail is really the worst thing. Human beings should not act like that. It is most immoral." These statements express the profound rejection of the "civilized" punitive system by the Kapauku. The Kapauku belief in the destructive nature of imprisonment was self-fulfilling. Because prisoners believed they would lose their health, they did indeed pine away, so that the perplexed administration officers had to reduce jail sentences to bare minimums in order not to jeopardize the captives' lives. This, of course, did not diminish the resentment of the populace, although the administrators meant well. They thought that the native practices of beating up an offender, wounding him with an arrow, or executing him were far harsher punishments than serving a relatively brief jail sentence while working in a "civilized" community. Indeed, they reasoned that the individual could learn important skills in prison. The Kapauku thought otherwise. They preferred the violence of war to the limitation of their freedom. Since I was aware of the Kapauku's resentment of the white man's way of punishing offenders against their law, I predicted an early uprising and recommended that fines and damages should be substituted for imprisonment, and that the jail should be ceremonially abolished. These recommendations were rejected, and the Kapauku revolted within a year (1956). After bloody fighting they were defeated and "pacified," at least temporarily. Their second uprising and battle for freedom, at that time directed against the Indonesian authorities, occurred more than 10 years later. The outcome this time was not a defeat but a compromise for the Kamu Valley. Indonesia has kept the region under the political control of their district officer, while the police force, composed of uniformed Kapauku, keeps peace and order in the valley. Since jail has not yet been abolished, even this settlement should not be regarded as final.

THE PROBLEM OF FORCED LABOR

In addition to the trouble with the jail system, the Dutch administrators faced the problem of building public roads. The Dutch administration decided to provide the natives with road-building tools and equipment, and even pay them a reasonable amount of money which they could spend in the government store. In the beginning there seems to have been some enthusiasm among the Kapauku, but this dwindled very fast. Finally, the officials had trouble getting men to work even for higher wages. The reasons were obvious: the administrators violated several basic values of the Kapauku.

The Dutch road was to be public (in public ownership) and the work was intended to be carried out as a common effort, in teams supervised by the Dutch engineers. Nothing could have been stranger to the Kapauku than this arrangement. Kapauku of both sexes prefer to toil alone. They dislike sharing responsibility and they abhor limitation of their freedom to work slowly or quickly and to spend a certain amount of time on a job in one day. They are always suspicious that a co-worker will exploit them and derive undeserved prestige from work to which he did not contribute enough effort. Also a Kapauku likes to see his task clearly defined so that he can say for example, "I have to cut the trees as far as the neighbor's fence." To work with somebody else on the same plot means that one's task is not so well defined as it might be, which is undesirable. For this reason, co-wives worked on separate sections in the same garden. If an individual wanted to help a co-wife or a friend, for example, she (he) would subdivide the total work and then finish a well-defined portion of it.

Aboriginal labor contracts always stipulated the amount of work to be done for a certain amount of pay and were never concerned about the time spent on it. Consequently, Europeans who hired Kapauku on the basis of a daily or hourly rate made a serious mistake. They deprived the native of initiative and the pleasure derived from work and planning, and turned him into a slow, unreliable worker. "If I am paid by time, the longer the work lasts the better for me," said one of my informants, reflecting upon the white man's system of payment.

Moreover, common ownership of anything seems absurd to the Kapauku. In their society everything, including land, houses, boats, and tracts of virgin forests, is owned individually. "That is yours and here is my property and everyone knows what belongs to him" is a common statement in the defense of private individual ownership. "If we were both owners we would quarrel too much, we would steal from each other in order to obtain most from the field. My children and wives would probably go hungry—oh, it would be bad." Thus the idea of a public road was utterly nonsensical to the Kapauku.

Exasperated by broken promises and the lack of labor, the official in charge of the road building sent out police to round up recalcitrant workers from the various communities. Bobii Ipouga of Tadauto, for example, was bound and taken by police to their outpost in spite of the fact that his community had already sent 12 people to work on the road in the past. Later, 3 additional men, with hands bound, were sent off to the public project. The Debei Valley people sent a delegation requesting me to intervene with the Dutch on their behalf. I therefore wrote in protest against the forced labor to the district officer. He, ignorant of what his subordinates were doing, stopped the enforced recruitment of labor, but he wondered how to get on with the construction. I volunteered to conduct an experiment. Explaining to the natives the advantages of roads in the Kamu Valley and documenting my claims with pictures from *Life* magazine, I persuaded them to build their own road—and entirely without payment! The Kapauku planned and built the new road by themselves. It connected several villages and even traversed a treacherous swamp. The success was not due to my lecture. The Kapauku regarded the road as theirs. They had employed a very different system in its construction and maintenance. Instead of being a communally owned facility, the new road, like their main drainage ditch, was owned individually: each segment that traversed somebody's property was owned, worked upon, and cared for by the owner of the land. The road was thus communal only in the sense that everyone could use it. When I returned in 1962 the Kapauku road in the Kamu Valley was still as good as new, whereas most of the government roads had suffered from neglect in spite of the fact that the caretakers were paid. The moral here is that industrial countries should never impose on developing nations and tribal peoples their management ideas and legal regulations. No matter how well meant, ideas that are basically foreign and antithetical to the dominant principles of the native culture are usually counter-productive.

CONCLUSION

The analysis of the effect on Kapauku acculturation caused by the imposition of Dutch and Indonesian law shows that the resulting process of actual change has been selective—it has not affected the whole culture equally. By differentiating conceptually between social and societal structures, I could show that it was the societal structure that underwent profound modification, that the legal effort of the Dutch colonists and, later, the Indonesian state, concentrated upon what we may call public law, or constitutional law, by altering profoundly the segmentary structure of the aboriginal Kapauku society. Its political confederacies have disappeared, its lineages and sublineages have lost their important functions and *raison d'être,* and its traditional alliances and political cliques have been dispersed. New groups with new functions have come into being. The village, formerly simply a locality where sublineage or lineage members co-resided, became the political and administrative unit. This new type of village cannot be compared with the old dispersed settlements that had no legal, political, religious, or ceremonial functions.

Whereas the former political groupings and unions were based on descent and free association (in the case of a confederacy of lineages), the new village, district, and regional system operates on the basis of residence. The former aboriginal type of jurisdiction was based on the personality principle of law—for example, the status and descent affiliations of a man determined the system of jurisdiction—but the new legal system employs the territoriality principle in questions of law.

The administrative and judicial authorities presiding over the new territorial units are also quite different from the former native leader, the *tonowi.* The *tonowi* was an informal headman; his assumption and tenure of the status of leadership depended upon his personal skills and the free recognition of his followers. The new colonial and state officers and the *kapala kampoeng,* the village chief, are formal authorities, appointed by their superiors rather than determined by their popularity among their constituents. Whereas the *tonowi's* amount of power and scope of jurisdiction varied with his own desires and ability, the *kapala*'s rights and duties are determined by inflexible rules. Thus the former fluid, ever-changing political structure has been replaced by rigidity, and the variation of power and jurisdiction among the individual headmen has given way to a monotonous, formally determined uniformity. Moreover, the sanctions employed by the new colonial and state authorities (imprisonment and the policy of communal and sometimes forced labor) offend the basic value the Kapauku placed upon individual freedom and integrity.

When I compare induced acculturation of the Kapauku with the urbanization of the Tirolean peasants, it sheds a new light on the two processes, which have often not been distinguished or, if differentiated, then only on the basis of the type of situation in which they occurred: acculteration has hitherto been seen as the result of contact between a tribal culture and another civilization, whereas urbanization is usually regarded simply as the effect of contact between city dwellers and peasants. The comparison of the data on the Kapauku tribesmen and those of the Tirolean peasants, however, shows that the two processes differ more profoundly, namely in their structural effects. Whereas the first primarily produces changes in the nature and relationship of the society's segments (societal structure), the second affects the structuring of the ego-centered relations (social structure). Whereas the legally acculturated Kapauku are still Kapauku as individuals, in spite of the fact that their traditional society is gone, the urbanized peasants of Obernberg in the Tirol are a new breed with new interpersonal attitudes and ego-centered relations, although their Obernberg society persists with little change in the organization and nature of its subgroups.

REFERENCES

Linton, R.
    1945   *The Cultural Background of Personality*. New York: Appleton-Century-Crofts.
Lowie, R.
    1947   *Primitive Society*. New York: Liveright.
Miller, N. E., and J. Dollard
    1964   *Social Learning and Imitation*. New Haven: Yale University Press.
Pospisil, L.
    1958   *Kapauku Papuans and Their Law*. Yale University Publications in Anthropology No. 54. New Haven: Department of Anthropology, Yale University.
    1961   "Structural Change and Primitive Law: Consequences of a Papuan Legal Case and Cultural Contact." Paper presented at the Annual Meeting of the American Anthropological Association, Philadelphia.
    1963a *Kapauku Papuan Economy*. Yale University Publications in Anthropology No. 67. New Haven: Department of Anthropology, Yale University.
    1963b *The Kapauku Papuans of West New Guinea*. New York: Holt, Rinehart and Winston.
    1971   *Anthropology of Law*. New York: Harper & Row.

9

THE IMPOSITION OF PROPERTY LAW IN KENYA

H.W.O. OKOTH-OGENDO

THE CONCEPT OF LEGAL IMPOSITION

This chapter is an attempt to explain the historical processes by which English property law was and continues to be imposed upon indigenous society in Kenya, and to analyze the nature and impact of that law on the structure, content, and efficacy of indigenous social and political institutions. But before this is done, it might be useful to attempt a definition of the phenomenon of "legal imposition" and to explain why the imposition of law is such a rampant practice in the Third World, particularly in Africa. This is important because, in the context of post-colonial societies, the use of that phrase might imply concern merely with the normative and institutional legacies of colonialism. The phenomenon of imposition, in my view, is much wider. It encompasses any situation where fundamental change is contemplated in society through the medium of laws or legal institutions whose content is clearly contrary to the perceived and accepted normative order of those whose behavior it seeks to regulate or change. Imposition thus implies, first, an attempt to induce fundamental change; second, the application of norms that are external to society; and third, an absence of democratic consensus from that society. Although a situation of this kind often

The Imposition of Law

involves the use of foreign models, this is not essential. The model can be internal. Thus critics of "villagization" in Tanzania might regard its legal framework as an imposition, even though the model is substantially drawn from the practice of *ujamaa*[1] in African society (Nyerere 1968:337).

An explanation of why legal imposition is a rampant practice in Africa and how it occurs must be both epistemological and ideological in nature. From an epistemological point of view the process of imposition may be seen as an essentially intellectual exercise. Twining has explained this in terms of the psychological urge to reproduce one's own kind (1966:115). This can be put in much simpler terms—namely, that in concrete lawmaking situations, draftsmen, legislators, and administrators always resort to models that have been transmitted to them through the educational process. This is exemplified by the fact that although there are some signs of increasing radical rhetoric within university and governmental institutions in Africa, the technical vocabulary and concepts used by African scholars to extract and communicate empirical data, and the actual content of legislation being churned out of many African legislatures remain largely conservative. Indeed, because the basic training of most teachers, students, and policymakers in Africa remains Anglo-American and European, western concepts, ideas, and models will, it appears, continue to dominate the legislative processes of African countries for a long time.

The process of legal imposition is also ideological in the sense that it is a function of the type of political economic system the state elites identify with. This explanation can be taken at two levels: the macro and the micro. At the macrolevel continuous imposition of law can be seen as an expression of dependency relations between the Third-World (the periphery) and industralized nations (the metropolitan centers). In other words, the impetus for imposition of law can be seen at this level as being generated from without rather than arising from within. Elsewhere we have discussed some of the intellectual and political economic factors that make this sort of dependency possible (Okoth-Ogendo 1975:37). It is sufficient to say that this is the classic explanation for the persistence of neo-colonial institutions in most Third World countries.

At the micro-level the imposition of law in Africa can be seen as an overt act of commitment by policymakers to particular values. These values (or norms) require the development of an institutional framework within which they can be expressed. It becomes logical for policymakers to commit themselves to imposing this required framework either through direct transplants from societies with similar ideologies or, as is more usual in post-colonial states, by making incremental adjustments to the existing structures to bring them gradually into line with similar institutions in the ex-metropole. The result of such impositions—whether the change is radical or gradual—is to restructure the flow of na-

---

[1] *Ujamaa* is a Swahili word which means "familyhood." The concept is used in Tanzania to refer to the principles governing collective living and management of resources by villages in the rural areas.

tional resources in a manner that increases the inequality of the distribution of benefits in the society. In the process, the elite (who include these policymakers) adopt a system of values that justifies their favorable position. They are, understandably, committed to the survival of this system.

THE PROCESS OF LEGAL IMPOSITION IN KENYA

An historical account of the processes through which English property law was imposed on indigenous society in Kenya under colonialism and a brief description of contemporary practice clearly demonstrate the centrality of epistemological and ideological factors in those processes. The history may be described in three phases.

THE FIRST PHASE (1897–1915)

The early phase was an extremely intriguing one, if only because the first colonial policymakers and administrators did not start by imposing a new code of property law on nineteenth-century Kenyan society. Although the 1882 Indian Transfer of Property Act (TPA)[2] had been extended to the new imperial possession in the late 1890s, and a set of Land Regulations (LR)[3] had also been promulgated, these as yet had no relevance to Africans and were of only marginal practical significance to the small body of Asians and Europeans that owed allegiance to the British Crown. They were irrelevant to Africans for two main reasons. First, there was no basis in imperial law for the extension of these statutes to persons not yet considered British subjects. As early as 1833 the law officers of the British Crown had argued that "protectorates," of which Kenya was then one, were nonetheless foreign countries and as such their residents could not be considered British subjects.[4] Second, as a matter of practice colonial administrators (including the courts) refused to organize African property relations under a system that they regarded as too advanced for "acephalous" societies.

That these two statutes were only marginally useful to Asians and Europeans resulted from the fact that both fell short of institutionalizing the kind of property structure under which these communities understood and expected to organize production.[5] The LR provided only for a system of occupation licenses, whereas the TPA was concerned largely with procedural aspects of transferring property rights and the substantive rights and obligations of transferors and

[2] Text contained in Vol. XI., Group 8, *Laws of Kenya.*

[3] Text contained in *British Parliamentary Papers,* Vol. C–8683, Dec. 1897, Africa No. 7:63 ff.

[4] In an opinion to the Crown on the status of the Ionian Islands.

[5] Francis Hall, an early settler, denounced the Land Regulations as the most idiotic land law that ever was seen!

transferees. Thus the nature of tenure and in particular the precise quantum of rights an individual could acquire over land in Kenya during this phase remained rather uncertain. A great deal of that uncertainty had to do with a series of unresolved jurisprudential and policy issues concerning the effect of protectorate status on control and use of land, and the extent to which indigenous property institutions could be used as a basis for imperial exploitation in the same way as had been the case in the penetration of West Africa. These issues were, first, that as late as 1897 the imperial political view was still that declaration of protectorate status conferred no rights to deal with land; second, that indigenous social institutions were not considered sufficiently developed to enable European settlers to acquire permanent land rights by private arrangements with Africans; and third, that there was as yet no clear indication of the value of the new acquisition to the imperial economy. In other words, two preliminary tasks were considered necessary before London could permit institutional change during this phase, namely, a re-evaluation of imperial legal theory and a persuasive demonstration of the viability of the new possessions.

These were fulfilled in three main ways. First, the law officers of the Crown handed down an opinion in 1899 that imperial law recognized only "protectorates with a settled form of government," which, they argued, Kenya did not have.[6] Second, it was argued, with the support of available anthropological "data," that it was fallacious to assume that Africans had any proprietary institutions, or such institutions as could form a basis for the production of those raw materials that the imperial economy needed.[7] Third, and more decisively perhaps, it was strongly argued that not only did the colony possess limitless potential for the production of raw materials such as cotton, rubber, and sisal fiber, which the British textile industries badly needed (Wolff 1974), but the production of these raw materials was possible only under a system of tenure that would give to the producers maximum freedom of control.[8]

The significance of the debates in this first phase is the fact that although the pressures for the imposition of English proprietary institutions of Kenyan society were clearly shaped by the type of production system the imperial government and the settlers wanted to promote, the actual manner in which solutions were arrived at was political and ideological in form. It is clear from various pronouncements that early colonial administrators were arguing for the only property system they understood, as were anthropologists, whose data and conclusions were the result of little more than attempts to examine African land relations from the conceptual categories of western property theory. Thus the stage was set for the imposition of alien laws and institutions that were to have

---

[6] Contained in Foreign Office Memorandum No. 7356.

[7] Anthropological fallacies on the nature of African land tenure institutions (or the "absence" of them) abounds in the literature. See, for example, the discussion in Okoth-Ogendo 1975.

[8] This derives from the view in capitalist political economy that individual ownership *per se* will generate industry and enterprise.

fundamental consequences for land relations in African society (Obed 1970; Okoth-Ogendo 1975).

The first of these laws was the East African (Lands) Order-in-Council, which was promulgated in 1901 to give effect to the opinion of the law officers cited above by vesting all land in the protectorate in the commissioner, in trust for Her Majesty. The second was the Crown Lands Ordinance of 1902, promulgated by the commissioner under the 1901 Order-in-Council, under which he gave himself the power to make outright grants of land or leases for 99 years for the purposes of European settlement. What these statutes[9] did was to create a framework that made it possible for colonial administrators to make many important decisions about the destiny of the indigenous peoples within the colony. For example, the 1902 Ordinance enabled the resident commissioners (later governors) to convert the prevailing (anthropological) view that Africans did not own land into an important juridical tool, for they were now able to operate on the essentially feudal assumption that effective political control over people living in a defined territory *per se* implied ownership of the physical *solum*. [10] The political sovereign was then considered able to confer upon and guarantee valid title in favor of whomever it wished. This view was carried to extremes when in 1915 a third statute, a new Crown Lands Ordinance, declared *inter alia* that "Crown lands"

> shall mean all public lands in the protectorate which are for the time being subject to the control of His Majesty by virtue of any treaty, convention, or agreement, or by virtue of His Majesty's protectorate . . . and shall include all lands occupied by the native tribes of the protectorate and all lands reserved for the use of the members of any native tribe [SS. 5, 54, and 56 of Ordinance No. 12/1915].

The 1915 Ordinance was a significant victory for protectorate administrators in several ways. First, the desire for a property system tailored to the free enterprise system of economy had been achieved. This was done by giving the commissioner the power to grant 999-year leases at nominal rents to European settlers.[11] Second, the last impediment to freedom of settlement had been removed by converting Africans to what the courts described as "tenants at will" of the Crown.[12] Third, the Ordinance gave the governor power to create reserves for the use and occupation of Africans: a mechanism that was seen not merely as an administrative necessity but also as a means of guaranteeing security for the settlers. An important effect of these statutes was that from the perspective of colonial legal theory indigenous proprietary systems were not only being phased out,

[9] S.R.O. 661 and Ordinance No. 21/1902, respectively.

[10] On how this assumption was used to partition Uganda see Pratt, and Low 1960.

[11] As the Colonial Office remained adamant on the question of freeholds, the protectorate authorities and the settlers settled for perpetual leases.

[12] See *Isaka Wainaina and Another* v. *Murito wa Indagara and Others, and the Attorney-General* (1922–1923) *Kenya Law Reports*, 102.

but were also being replaced by a normative order that was both *qualitatively* and *quantitatively* alien to indigenous social organization. Because Africans could not acquire rights under this new order, the juridical status of their production systems within the colonial legal system was rendered uncertain and extremely anomalous.

THE SECOND PHASE (1915–1939)

That uncertainty and anomaly led to frustration and unrest in the African areas. As a result a new phase of legislative development occurred between 1915 and 1939, the primary objective of which was to impose an institutional framework that, it was hoped, would stabilize African property relations without conceding any of the gains that the settlers had already made. The main thrust of these developments was the elevation of the juridical status of areas settled by Africans, first by gazetting them in 1926 (Government Notice 354/1926), second by bringing them under a statutory system of administration in 1930,[13] and third by taking them out of the juridical claws of settlement altogether in 1938.[14]

The gazetting involved a declaration of some 24 "reserves" within which Africans could reside. These were drawn on ethnic lines and were located in areas that were either unsuitable for European settlement or had not yet been cultivated. The 1930 Ordinance advanced the juridical position of these reserves no further than laying down the terms upon which the Crown held "native lands." Such land remained Crown land in law and was therefore subject to expropriation at any time. The Ordinance set up a board consisting almost entirely of colonial administrators and settlers to manage and control the reserves and in particular to advise the governor on the exercise of his power to lease land within the reserves to non-natives.[15] In practice the board's function went beyond this to include the maintenance of public order and the facilitation of recruitment and supervision of labor.

Developments up to 1930, however, did not really solve the problem of insecurity within the reserves. This led an important land commission,[16] set up in 1930, to conclude that these reserves, together with any land to which Africans might be "entitled" should be excised from "Crown" lands altogether and be vested in a trust board to hold and administer them for the benefit of the people resident therein. Legislation along these lines was passed in 1938 and was subsequently guaranteed by a Kenya (Native Areas) Order-in-Council in 1939. The 1938 legislation provided that

[13] Through the Native Lands Trust Ordinance No. 9/1930.

[14] Through the Native Lands Trust Ordinance No. 28/1938.

[15] Provision was made in S.3 of the Ordinance for an African member. There is no record that any was appointed.

[16] The Kenya Land Commission (chaired by Morris Carter). The Report is contained in Cmnd. 4556/1934.

in respect of the occupation, use, control, inheritance, succession and disposal of any native land, every tribe, group, family and individual shall have all the rights which they enjoy or may enjoy by virtue of existing native customary law or any subsequent modifications thereof . . . [S.68].

Although this legislation was hailed as a milestone in the protection of African land rights, the structure it created was not only alien but also paternalistic, for it was still based on the principle that Africans were incapable of holding land directly. They could do so only through a trusteeship until such time as their concept of property had developed to something equivalent to ownership as understood in western property systems. Thus the radical (original) title to "native lands" could not be vested in the natives themselves.

The general structure of imposed law and legal institutions as of 1939 therefore consisted of the following elements: the territorial basis of land law was now firmly grounded in the theory that radical title to land was vested in the imperial sovereign through his representatives in the colony. This was the case not only with "Crown land," but also with land reserved for occupation and use by indigenous (African) people. Within this juridical framework, immigrant communities, mainly Europeans and Indians, could acquire rights equivalent to English freeholds and leases, whereas Africans, *inter se,* continued to be governed by customary law. However, the 1938 legislation, which provided for the application of customary law, made it clear that no power of disposition could be exercised under that law (S.68).

THE THIRD PHASE (1939–1963)

It can be said that, from a structural point of view, the 1939 Order-in-Council completed the process of imposition of English property laws and institutions which had begun in 1897. Indeed, this structural arrangement remains to this day. Thus legislative developments after 1939 were simply responses to problems arising from the continuous but irregular and unsystematic interaction between the African and European sectors of the economy and political developments within the African areas. At the prompting of agronomists, administrators began to appreciate for the first time that the economic condition in the reserves was an important factor in the continued unrest in the African areas (Okoth-Ogendo 1976). For example, years of neglect by agricultural and social development officers assigned to these areas, coupled with a rapid reduction in the availability of cultivable land, had led to a stagnation in the development of the technology of land use. By the mid-1940s population pressure was already acute in several parts of the country, especially in central and western Kenya (Van Zwanenberg 1972).

Initial attempts to deal with this situation were largely administrative. At first it was thought that population growth was the problem and therefore a solution could be found in the reserves. When this failed, administrators thought that the problem was inferior land and inadequate technology and that therefore soil reconditioning, strip-terracing, and destocking could improve things (Okoth-Ogendo 1976:152).[17] Finally, however, agronomists came up with a diagnosis that had tremendous consequences for property relations and the organization of production within the reserves. They argued that the basic problem was neither overpopulation nor the need for improved technology but the system of African land tenure itself. Certain inherent characteristics of the indigenous land system, they claimed, were obstacles to agricultural development. These characteristics were, first, the communal nature of control—the cause of much uncertainty in decision making; second, the diffuseness of rights of use, which often led to incessant disputes; and third, the system's inheritance rules, which often led to fragmentation of holdings and sub-economic land units within very short periods. If these could be removed, the argument continued, a green revolution would occur in the African areas. The solution they offered was that the African tenure system should be overhauled and replaced by a tenure system similar to that obtaining in the settlers' areas. This was to be done through a three-tier process involving the adjudication of claims, the consolidation of fragmented holdings, and the registration of adjudicated claims in a state-maintained register.

Administrators feared that such a drastic program of tenure reform would generate political problems far in excess of the benefits that the agronomists predicted. This hesitancy gave way, however, to practical considerations when in 1952 African political unrest exploded into a full-scale revolt by the Mau Mau, precisely on the issue of land scarcity and economic stagnation in the African areas (Roseberg and Nottingham 1966). The Mau Mau revolt completely changed the *raison d'etre* of the reforms that agronomists had proposed. Land policy became essentially a political tool: a means of creating a contented peasantry that would be secure in the ownership of its land and willing to defend it against so-called "political mavericks hankering for the redistribution of land [see discussion in Sorrenson 1967]." Swynnerton (1954), then Deputy Director of Agriculture, devised a plan in which his main argument was that redistribution of land was not a precondition of the green revolution in the African areas. What was needed, he argued, was to convert land in these areas into individually owned units under the freehold system and then intensify farming within them. The role of the state in this process would be similar to that in settler areas, namely to provide the infrastructure, technical advice, and credit.

The ideological function of Swynnerton's proposals was evident. In a historical context they were an example of political expedience and as such simply one more attempt to provide for the political and economic security of the settlers. In order to implement them, however, it was necessary, first, to adjust the existing structure of agricultural administration to the realities of the political situation and, second, to apprise African peasants of the peculiar attributes of individual tenure. The former task was carried out in 1955 through a comprehen-

---

[17] See Sessional Paper No. 8/1945, "Land Utilization and Settlement in Kenya."

sive agricultural ordinance (No. 8 of 1955) which consolidated all the land management and development legislation that had been in operation in the African and European areas during the past half century. The Ordinance did not, however, provide for a unitary structure of agricultural administration. On the presumption that African agricultural practices had not reached a level of development justifying the applications of institutions similar to those of the European sector, the Ordinance created separate institutions for the administration of both sectors.

Adjustments to individual tenure took several forms. A working party on African land tenure was set up in 1957 to report, among other things, on a suitable version of the freehold system for the African areas.[18] The party's report led to the promulgation of a Native Lands Registration Ordinance (No. 27 of 1959) which, while providing for the grant of a fee simple title, did not affect inheritance and succession rules. These were thought too sensitive to be restructured and hence better left to customary law. A Land Control (Native Lands) Ordinance (No. 28 of 1959) was also passed for the purpose of "protecting" Africans from the possible consequences of injudicious exercise of their powers under the new tenure reform; some Africans unused to individual ownership might render themselves landless within a very short period. In addition to these measures, a program of public education was mounted in many parts of the country (intensified after the end of the Mau Mau revolt) in an attempt to sell the idea of land reform to the people. This included experimental consolidation schemes in places like Nyanza where opposition to the Swynnerton proposals had been most vigorous.

The implication of tenure reform is that it represented a form of progressive transfer from one normative order to another. Before land was adjudicated, consolidated, and registered, it remained part of the reserves and was therefore still held under a trust administered in accordance with the Native Lands Trust Ordinance of 1938.[19] Once these processes had been accomplished, it ceased to be so held and became individual property. The nature and content of rights vested in such an individual were now evaluated in the context of imposed English law. This was the position in 1963 when a new and comprehensive substantive land law and registration statute was passed. The Registered Land Act (Cap. 300, *Laws of Kenya*) had several aims. First, it was meant to rationalize the situation in the African areas by streamlining and expanding the scope of the 1959 statutes. This was done by importing the substantive land law of England as of 1926.[20] Second, the Act was meant to provide a unitary system for land ownership and registration throughout the country. Thus land owners, mainly immigrant com-

---

[18] The Working Party was asked *inter alia* to investigate whether a modified form of the freehold system could be devised specifically for the African areas.

[19] See S.63 (now S.69 of the Trust Land Act, Cap. 288 *Laws of Kenya*).

[20] Following the comprehensive changes in English real property law as a result of the Law of Property Act, 1925 (15 & 16 Geo.5,c.20).

munities, could now transfer their properties from the regime of the Indian Transfer of Property Act to the new Act.

Thus by 1963 the imposition of English property law had been successfully incorporated into the official normative structure. Although the domain of customary law had not been completely superseded, the policy now was progressively to phase out indigenous practices through the administration of the Registered Land Act. The intention was (and remains) to ensure that the Registered Land Act would eventually be the only substantive property law for all land in Kenya.

THE CONSEQUENCES OF LEGAL IMPOSITION

It is argued above that the imposition of English property law on indigenous society in Kenya during the colonial period was not a haphazard process. It had an epistemological basis in western property jurisprudence and was clearly ideological in function. For the European settlers, an English model of property relations was fundamental to security and the viability of laissez-faire capitalism, a system of production relations that has been consolidated by the post-colonial state. The extension of this proprietary model to African land relations has assumed a much greater significance, for in this context imposition cannot be seen simply as an exercise in the transformation of the technical description of title or of the structure of agriculture *per se*. It must be seen as part of an attempt to restructure society as a whole. Let us examine some aspects of the impact of these new institutions and norms on the indigenous social order.

THE INSTITUTIONAL CONSEQUENCES OF IMPOSITION

There is evidence from research into African land relations which indicates a direct correspondence between gradations of social status and access to land (Gluckman 1969). Therefore, in describing indigenous tenure systems, a distinction must be drawn between access to land, which was open to everybody on account of membership of a lineage or some wider segment of society, and control of land use, which was vested only in the political authority of that segment. But neither right of access nor the power of control was to be equated with the ownership of the physical *solus* under this arrangement. The right of access, on the one hand, remained a multiple phenomenon that varied in nature and content with the kind of land-use activity in which the individual or the community was involved. Control, on the other hand, was normally exercised by the common elder of the lineage or a representative chosen on the basis of genealogy. Such an elder allocated cultivation rights and controlled the type and extent of land use. Where land use required more expansive access rights—as, for example, in grazing—allocation and control would normally be exercised by a council of common elders—for instance, the *Mbari* elders among the Gikuyu, the *Jodong Gweng'* of the Joluo, and the *Kokwet* elders of the Nandi. This hierarchy also operated as an appellate system for the processing of all disputes, whether these involved land or not.

The imposition of English property law and institutions had important consequences for the stability of the situation described above. The introduction of reserves administered by a board of trustees dominated by colonial officers, in particular, had the most drastic impact on African proprietary institutions and norms. In the first instance the boundaries of the reserves were such that they excluded not only non-African communities but other African communities as well. That is, after 1939 non-Africans were not permitted to obtain permanent land rights in any part of the reserves, and no African was permitted to reside in any reserve other than that to which his ethnic group was specifically assigned. Thus the idea of the territorial fixity of ethnic jurisdiction became an attribute of land tenure and land relations among African communities in Kenya. The main impact of these inflexible rules is that they disturbed the equilibrium between patterns of land use and availability of land by making it impossible to acquire permanent rights of access elsewhere. Read in the light of the fact that, despite a steady rise in population growth, the technology of production remained constant throughout the colonial period, this disequilibrium also explains why land deterioration was so endemic in the African areas, particularly in the late 1930s and throughout the 1940s. Indigenous production systems could no longer absorb the effects of changing man–land ratios, either through expansion of ethnic territory or through intensive agriculture.

In the second instance, the reserve system, compounded by population growth, exacerbated competition for scarce land resources within and among lineages, clans, and even families. This led to increased litigation, particularly in those areas where land shortages were most acute. This was the case, for example, in western and central Kenya. Indigenous tenure practices adapted to this situation, first, by evolving new techniques for the identification and adjudication of disputes with greater accuracy and without much damage to group solidarity, and, second, by adjusting the control structure of agricultural land use in such a way as to enable family heads rather than clan elders to exercise greater sovereignty over cultivated land. This, however, was done in such a manner as not to disrupt rights of public grazing across family, clan, and lineage boundaries. Thus, although the actual amount of land reserved for public grazing continued to diminish as more and more of it was brought under cultivation, as soon as the harvest was gathered these areas reverted to public grazing until the next season.

In areas such as central Kenya and Kisii, where permanent cash crops had been established, however, there was little room for this kind of overlap. Not only was multiple land use even on a rotational basis difficult in these areas, but official government policy in regard to the development of these crops in the African areas was clearly against communal control. Consequently, the effect of bringing land under cultivation was to create a situation of family control very much analogous to individual ownership.

These developments weakened indigenous authority in several ways. First, they undercut its structural base by eliminating the control functions of the elders in matters of land use. By the same token, the lineage system ceased to be of much relevance to land *use* even though the actual acquisition of access rights continued to be influenced by it. These changes paved the way for the emergence of exclusive land units based either on the family or on individual rights. This in turn contributed directly to land fragmentation and further litigation over ancestral lands. Second, the economic base of indigenous authority was undermined, allowing the introduction of new land-use patterns, the most significant of which was the development of permanent cash crops on exclusive holdings. Thus it was no longer possible within the context of indigenous institutions to regulate economic activity, even in the area of food production.[21]

Indeed, throughout the colony administrative officers reported a rapid breakdown of social institutions. The fear was that if allowed to spread unchecked this might be the source of political problems in the future. For example, the very highly developed *Githaka* system of landholding among the Gikuyu was said to be giving way to nucleated institutions of land control (Humphrey, Lambert, and Wynn Harris, 1945; Kenyatta 1953). Similar developments were reported among the Abaluhya peoples (Humphrey 1947). All these were areas where labor demands of the colonial economy had had their most destructive impact and where therefore the productive forces upon which these institutions were founded were most severely disrupted.

It seems reasonable to conclude, therefore, that although lineage and clan structures as such had not disappeared, nor their relevance to the definition and supervision of the fulfillment of purely sociocultural obligations been eliminated, the role of elders in land-use administration had been substantially weakened and in some cases superseded by more nucleated forms. The extent of institutional change varied from one part of the country to another. For example, disruption was least evident among the pastoral nomads of northern Kenya and greatest among the highland agriculturalists. The point to stress is that these changes so altered the stability of the indigenous social order that its institutions could no longer be used as a basis for the joint management of economic activity within the reserves.[22]

THE NORMATIVE CONSEQUENCES OF IMPOSITION

The imposition of English property law and institutions also weakened the stability of the indigenous society. In analyzing this effect, however, a distinction

---

[21] In an unpublished work done at the Institute of Development Studies, University of Sussex by Dr. A.O. Pala, it is reported that there were periodic shortages and severe famines in 1907–1908, 1918–1919, 1929, 1934, and 1942.

[22] In a recent study of the sugar industry in Nyanza we found that failure to take these changes into account has partly contributed to the disintegration of "block" sugar farms in the Chemilil area. These blocks were planned on the assumption that clan elders still had authority over land use. See Okoth-Ogendo 1977.

ought to be made between the general impact of colonialism on the indigenous normative order and the specific consequences of the imposition resulting from the tenure reform program already mentioned. Most of the normative consequences stemming from the former were essentially chain reactions from the institutional changes discussed in the previous section, whereas in the latter case the consequences were more specific. Indeed, the effects of tenure reform are likely to be felt for a long time to come.

The Normative Impact of Colonialism

As a system of production relations qualitatively different from indigenous forms, colonialism was, *ipso facto,* expected to alter the normative content of indigenous proprietary institutions. The main instruments of insurgency in this regard were the colonial courts and the "native" administration personnel. Even though throughout the colonial period the substantive law of the reserves remained whatever customary law was applicable to the area in which any land was situated, colonial courts were not slow to inject key notions of English property law into the former system. The courts were quite clear that the legal system gave them the freedom to temper customary law with English standards of justice. As one colonial judge in a suit involving the enforcement of an unsatisfied judgment in customary law said:

> I have no doubt whatever that the only standard of justice and morality which a British court in Africa can apply is its own British standard. Otherwise we should find ourselves in certain circumstances having to condone such things as the institution of slavery [*Gwao bin Kilimo* v. *Kisunda bin Ifuti* (1938) 1 *Tanganyika Law Reports* (Reprint) 403 per Wilson J.].

In the area of property law this freedom was used extensively to mold the evolution of customary law toward a regime that would lead to the concentration of all attributes of ownership of land in the hands of fewer and fewer individuals. Thus the courts injected into customary law such radical concepts as prescription, limitation, and even the power of outright disposition.[23] The first two of these concepts, which relate to the acquisition of rights over land by virtue of long and undisturbed possession, remain a storm center in African property jurisprudence even to this day (Katto 1965).

The role of administrators in the transformation of substantive law was especially evident after 1930, when the Native Tribunal Ordinance (No. 39 of 1930) formalized on a dualistic basis the form of justice that had existed in practice in the African areas since 1897. This arrangement enabled administrators to align the development of customary law not only with their own values but also with the political imperatives of the colonial state (Ghai and McAuslan 1970).

---

[23] The Court of Review Reports are replete with decisions of this kind. The Court of Review (now defunct) was the highest appellate court in matters of African law.

The method most often used was the issuance of "clarifications" and "directives" on matters of customary law to native tribunals, the funtion being to ensure uniformity in the development of customary law. Later, the District Law Panels set up in 1948 were invested with the responsibility of "guiding the development of customary laws and making recommendations for changes therein." Commenting on the work of the panels in Central Province, Morris and Read have observed that they sometimes played a key role "in transforming customary law in a fundamental manner, filling a vital gap in political machinery left by the removal of what traditional organs of legislative action had once existed [1972:205]."

These subtle but deliberate changes were quite consistent with the so-called "civilizing" mission of colonialism. As a juridical fact, this mission was installed in the colonial legal process through the doctrine of repugnancy, which declared that indigenous law was applicable only insofar as it was "not repugnant to justice and morality or inconsistent with any written law."[24]

The Normative Impact of Tenure Reform

Thus, by the time comprehensive tenure reform began in earnest in the mid-1950s, a situation had been reached in the African areas in which not only were indigenous proprietary structures already weakened by the colonial system, but substantial infiltration of English property concepts had in fact occurred in the customary laws of many African communities. This was sometimes used by administrators to silence critics of tenure reform, the argument being that the reform was simply an attempt to implement what the Africans themselves had already come to accept. The actual position was, and still is, that the content of indigenous property law remained rather fluid and was beset by many internal conflicts. As land resources continued to decrease, traditional attachment to the land often grew stronger, even though in most cases the social process could not adequately handle disputes arising from competing claims. Tenure reform was, therefore, a very radical departure from indigenous property relations, despite the fundamental changes described above. In any case, after independence in 1963, reform of African tenure had become a government priority and therefore whether or not a particular society had adopted individual tenure was no longer a relevant consideration.[25] Since I have examined elsewhere the contribution of tenure reform to agricultural production (Okoth-Ogendo 1978), I shall concentrate here on its impact on the social and political organization of the peasantry.

If we are to appreciate fully some of the social conflicts that have arisen as a result of tenure reform, it is necessary to state the judicial view about the legal effect of registration. There are two interpretations of the effect of registration.

---

[24] The "repugnancy" clause, which was first enacted in the Native Court Regulations, No. 15/1897, remains part of Kenya law; see S.3, The Judicature Act. No. 16/1967.

[25] This emerges clearly from the 1963–1966, 1966–1970, 1970–1974, and 1974–1978 Development Plans.

The majority view is that registration under the Registered Land Act confers upon the registered proprietor all the attributes of ownership, free from all extraneous obligations not noted in the register. There is a long line of cases dating from 1964 in which the majority of members of the High Court have argued that registration extinguishes all customary claims other than those arising from succession and inheritance.[26] These latter claims, as noted above, continue to be governed by rules of customary law. A minority[27] of the members of the High Court Bench, however, now argue that there is nothing in the law to prevent registered proprietors from being held trustees of those who would be entitled to interests under customary law. Their view is that trusteeship of land "is inherent" in customary law—a duty that registration *per se* should not be allowed to extinguish. They also point out that unless the courts take this stance, many injustices are likely to be perpetrated through the medium of the law.

There is much to commend this minority view. A survey of peasant attitudes toward the land and their perception of what registration means indicates that the majority of the High Court Bench is clearly out of touch with the realities of the socioeconomic environment in which peasant communities operate. The majority of the peasants in Kenya have not fully accepted the final and divestitive effects of registration. Apart from the fact that registration has expanded economic opportunities for some of them in certain parts of the country—for example, by making loans and better extension advice more accessible—most peasants still believe that the land is a collective or family asset and therefore to be used with due consideration for the needs of future generations. Therefore, subdivision according to customary rules of succession continues unabated despite statutory restrictions on the maximum number of people who can legally own such land (Cap. 3000, SS. 101 (4)). Therefore, in practice, registration has simply increased the use of land without radically altering the heterogeneous character of tenure. In short, as far as most peasants are concerned, land rights remain divisible rather than absolute assets, and should be shared among all members of the family.

A study of family or lineage members occupying land registered in the names of other relatives is particularly illuminating. In a survey[28] conducted in 1974–1975 in Kisii and South Nyanza districts over 95% of a sample of 100 nonregistered occupiers of land in each area justified their presence on the land by saying that registration could not, in their view, alter the fact that the land

---

[26] This is based on a very positivistic interpretation of SS.27,28, and 30 of the Registered Land Act (Cap.300). See *Thuku Mbuthia* v. *Kaburu Kimondo* (1964), Court of Review Reports, No. 17; *Selah Obiero* v. *Orego Opiyo* (1972), E.A. 227; *Esiroyo* v. *Esiroyo* (1973), E.A. 388.

[27] See, for example, *Mwangi Muguthu* v. *Maina Muguthu* (1971), Kenya High Court Digest No. 16; *Mungora Wamathai* v. *Muroti Mugweru,* High Court of Kenya at Nyeri, Civil Case No. 56/1972; and *Samwell Thata Mishek and Others* v. *Priscilla Wambui and Anor,* High Court of Kenya at Nairobi, Civil Case No. 1400/1973.

[28] These investigations were carried out as part of a much wider study on the political economy of land law in Kenya. Results are reported in Okoth-Ogendo 1978.

belonged to the lineage or family of which they were members. They pointed out, for example, that since the registered proprietors themselves had received the land more often by inheritance or family partition than by sale or gift, such proprietors had no moral right to exclude other members of the family from it. When confronted with the majority view of the High Court stated above—namely, that under the new law, the registered proprietor could evict them with impunity—28% of the sample in Kisii and 87% in South Nyanza retorted that such a course of action was inconceivable. The rest of the sample responded as follows: 55% in Kisii and 5% in South Nyanza said they would demand their share; 15% in Kisii and 8% in South Nyanza said they would go to court or move; 2% in Kisii and no one in South Nyanza said they would purchase land elsewhere.

The differences in response between the Kisii and South Nyanza samples need some explanation. A probable explanation for the difference is that since the Kisii district has had a much longer experience of tenure reform (since about 1963), the possibility of eviction by registered proprietors was not as hypothetical to the Gusii as it certainly was to the Luo, whose experience of effective tenure reform dated only from the 1970s. The second response among the Gusii follows from the first. Indeed, demands of this kind, as I note below, have been one of the causes of homicides in Kenya. Of the rest, it is noteworthy that so few respondents said they would purchase land elsewhere—especially since the questionnaire permitted multiple responses. The explanation may well be that most peasants would not have enough money to buy land at current prices in Kenya.[29]

The peasant view of registration has been accepted by Land Control Boards in most districts in Kenya. The theory of control of land transactions in the peasant sector, as stated earlier, was to prevent peasants from rendering themselves landless through injudicious exercise of their powers under the new tenure system. This remains the same, although since the enactment of a new Land Control Act in 1967 (No. 34 of 1967—now Cap. 302, *Laws of Kenya),* the rationale for control has become political and economic rather than social. Although usually very few peasants apply for consent to charge, sell, lease, or otherwise dispose of their land, almost without exception Land Control Boards in the rural areas regard family approval as a prerequisite for the granting of consent to transfer. There were numerous cases in which Land Control Boards in Kisii and South Nyanza would instruct applicants to bring their wives and brothers or, as happened in one case, their application would be refused

> because the father of the seller presented himself before the Board rejecting sub-division and sale of the land in question. Also it was learnt that though the father of the seller was not registered, he was staying on the same piece of land [Minutes of the Rongo Land Control Board 1974].

[29] In a recent survey a Parliamentary Select Committee reported that land in Kwale, which was being sold at Kshs. 600 an acre during adjudication in 1972, was in 1978 being sold at a price in excess of Kshs. 60,000. Although these estimates refer to prime beach land, land prices in other parts of the country have risen astronomically. See *Report of the Parliamentary Select Committee on the Issue of Land Ownership along the Ten-mile Coastal Strip of Kenya,* 1978.

The peasant's attachment to the land is rooted in something more rational than just the trappings of culture and tradition. As long as the land remains the basic source of livelihood for the peasantry, it will continue to be regarded as a family investment. Any attempt to change that conception in isolation from the total peasant political economy is bound to fail, and may also lead to a great deal of social disruption. For example, it is becoming increasingly evident that a large percentage of homicide cases in western Kenya, Embu and Meru districts, are often traceable to disputes over registered land.[30] The explanation is simple. Indigenous social institutions can no longer contain such disputes, and the subordinate courts, because of the doctrine of precedent, invariably follow the majority High Court view given earlier.

Peasant attitudes, however, are likely to change. Indeed, the Kisii data indicate that resistance to the normative framework of the Registered Land Act is unlikely to be permanent. In those areas where tenure reform has also led to substantial changes in the structure of land distribution, the disintegration of these attitudes is likely to be extremely rapid. A brief description of the impact of tenure reform on land distribution in the peasant sector will suffice to illustrate this point.

Until 1968, tenure reform statutes[31] defined only two categories of rights, both premised on the assumption that the power of control in indigenous tenure was equivalent to ownership under English property law. These categories were cultivation and residential occupation rights. They did not apply in those parts of the country where no permanent settlements existed. Thus, in pastoral areas it was not uncommon before 1968 for a few enterprising individuals to lay claims to vast tracts of land on the pretext that their ancestors had once camped there, or that they had intended to live and farm there. A new statute in 1968 (No. 35 of 1968; now Cap. 284, *Laws of Kenya*) dealt with this particular problem by introducing a third category of general territorial rights held by identifiable "groups"—anything from a "tribe" to a nuclear family. Although group tenure was introduced primarily to avert the mass expropriation of land in pastoral areas noted above, the mechanism itself could be and has been used by small-scale agricultural communities as well.

The most significant effect of trying to slot land rights into these categories was that it altered the structure of access to land in the family economy by vesting ownership rights in adult male heads of households without at the same time giving adequate protection to the *de facto* or potential rights of women and children. It is striking in this respect that outside parts of Central Province and the matrilineal descent groups of the Coast Province, women accounted for less than 5% of the total registered proprietors, and children under 18 for even less.

---

[30] Justice E. Cotran, presently a resident High Court judge in western Kenya, suggested in a personal communication to me that as many as 98% of all homicides he has encountered during the 2 years he has been there have their origins in land disputes.

[31] The Land Consolidation Act (Cap.283,*Laws of Kenya*) and the Registered Land Act (Cap.300, *Laws of Kenya*).

Apart from a lack of clarity within the reform mechanism itself, the manner in which reform was conducted also had an important impact on the structure of land distribution in the rural sector. The process of consolidation, for example, did this by creating a clandestine land market in which parcels of fragmented land that could not be physically exchanged were simply sold to other people within the adjudication area. Because land prices were often very low, many people had been able to expand their rural holdings. The data indicate, first, that most sellers tended to be poor; second, that the poor were willing to sell to raise money for social and civil obligations such as taxes, school fees, or subsistence; and third, that the buyers were almost invariably well-to-do neighbors who were able to command the necessary funds from government employment, business enterprises, or salaried relatives and friends (Okoth-Ogendo 1976). Since Land Control Boards had jurisdiction over registered areas only, this market remained unregulated and at times rather volatile.

Experience from Central Province suggests that, coupled with organic developments within the socioeconomic fabric of peasant organization, changes in the structure of land distribution might have several consequences. First, they might accelerate the numbers of the landless. In particular, the position of heirs would become extremely precarious if registered proprietors have a power of expropriation, since, contrary to the practice in English law, the rights of heirs under customary law do not accrue at death. They are transgenerational—that is, they extend beyond any single generation (cf. succession rights). Consequently, the former accrue by reason of physical existence *per se*. This situation has important implications for urbanization. Second, changes in land distribution might weaken the family as the basic unit of production. This follows from the view that an economy that depends so heavily on female labor cannot really afford to weaken the proprietary status of women over land. Customary property law, as noted, avoided this by separating access rights from control and subjecting control to the economic tasks required by reason of the former. The economic role of women in indigenous society, it must be emphasized, depended largely on the protection of their access rights to land.

Beyond these ramifications, it must be remembered that, in a land-based economy, the pattern of land distribution is always an important indicator of political power. In the context of the rural economy in Kenya, this relation is not obvious by any means. It is to be found in the fact that those who were accumulating land in the rural areas were predominantly state *obligees*. Many of them were ''progressive'' farmers, civil service personnel, and, to the extent that the benefits of the Africanization of business enterprises had trickled down to the rural areas, owners of shops, hotels, and catering establishments in rural centers. As an economic class this group had strong links with the political class in the urban centers in terms of patronage and influence. Consequently, there is a level at which they can be seen essentially as the rural end of petty capitalist production and political control that now characterizes Kenya's political economy. In other words, the evolution of new patterns of land distribution also points to the narrowing of the basis of political control in the rural areas in favor of a rural landholding class corresponding somewhat to the oligarchy that now controls the formal sector of the economy. Thus the basis of accountability of power is also changing from indigenous to state norms and principles.

CONCLUSION

This chapter has attempted an assessment of the impact of the imposition of English property law on some of the sociopolitical processes of indigenous society in Kenya. It has been shown that the first reactions to this imposition generated disruptive conflict throughout the society. A model of normative and institutional organization that is alien to a particular community cannot be used as an effective tool for positive and comprehensive change in that community, even though elites may gain from it. A current study of the impact of tenure reform on public-resource allocation and decision making by farmers tends to confirm this. There are the usual problems of communication, internalization, and conflict management which make it impossible to predict the consequences of such imposition. Indeed, the lack of accurate information on the precise content of the new proprietary system greatly affected peasants' reactions to it.

With very few exceptions, law-making and administrative elites in Africa are more convinced than perhaps colonialists ever were that alien models (mainly western in origin) can operate as a basis for the integration of national legal systems and the maintenance of stability in society. However, an important issue arises from this discussion of land reform in Kenya which scholars and legislators in Africa need to resolve if disruptive conflicts of the kind highlighted in this chapter are to be avoided or at least controlled. The issue is not simply that colonialism led to the imposition of alien laws and institutions upon the indigenous order and disrupted it. It is that throughout Africa, and indeed most of the Third World, there still exists a plurality of subsystems that represent not merely different historical processes but also fundamental conflicts over values. Whatever the ideological content or structural characteristics, legislators must face this reality in their attempts to impose a new national legal system.

REFERENCES

CASES

Esiroyo v. *Esiroyo* (1973), E.A. 388.

Gwao bin Kilimo v. *Kisunda bin Ifuti* (1938) 1 *Tanganyika Law Reports* (Reprint) 403 per Wilson J.

Isaka Wainaina and Another v. *Murito wa Indagara and Others, and the Attorney-General* (1922–1923) Kenya Law Reports, 102.

Mungora Wamathai v. *Muroti Mugweru*, High Court of Kenya at Nyeri, Civil Case No. 56/1972.

Mwangi Muguthu v. *Maina Muguthu* (1971), Kenya High Court Digest No. 16.

Samwell Thata Mishek and Others v. *Priscilla Wambui and Anor,* High Court of Kenya at Nairobi, Civil Case No. 1400/1973.

Selah Obiero v. *Orego Opiyo* (1972), E.A. 227.

Thuku Mbuthia v. *Kaburu Kimondo* (1964), Court of Review Reports, No. 17.

OTHER SOURCES

Ghai, Y. P., and J. P. W. B. McAuslan
  1970   *Public Law and Political Change in Kenya.* London and Nairobi: Oxford University Press.
Gluckman, M.
  1969   *Ideas in Barotse Jurisprudence.* Manchester, England: Manchester University Press.
Katto, L. L.
  1965   "Has customary law in English speaking Africa recognised long possession as a basis of title?" *East African Law Journal 1 (3)* 243.
Humphrey, N.
  1947   *The Luguru and the Land.* Nairobi: Kenya Government.
Humphrey, N., H.E. Lambert, and P. Wynn Harris
  1945   *The Kikuyu Lands.* Nairobi: Kenya Government.
Kenyatta, J.
  1953   *Facing Mount Kenya: The Tribal Life of the Gikuyu.* London: Secker and Warburg.
Morris H. F., and J. S. Read
  1972   *Indirect Rule and the Search for Justice.* Oxford: Clarendon Press.
Nyerere, J. K.
  1968   *Freedom and Socialism.* Nairobi: Oxford University Press.
Obed, H. A.
  1970   "Anglo-American Studies of Tribal Law, Concepts and Methods." LLM Thesis, Queen's College, Belfast.
Okoth-Ogendo, H. W. O.
  1975   "Property theory and land use analysis," *Journal of Eastern Africa Research and Development* 5, (1) 37.
  1976   "African land tenure reform." In J. Heyer, J. Maitha, and W. Senga, *Agricultural Development in Kenya: An Economic Assessment.* Nairobi: Oxford University Press.
  1977   "Problems of Land Tenure and Land Use in the Nyanza Sugar-Belt." Unpublished report to the Ministry of Co-operative Development and the Friedrich Ebert Stiftung Foundation.
  1978   "The Political Economy of Land Law: An Essay in the Legal Organisation of Underdevelopment." JSD thesis, Yale University Law School.
Pratt, R. C., and D. A. Low
  1960   *Buganda and British Overrule.* London: Oxford University Press.
Roseburg, C. G., and J. Nottingham
  1966   *The Myth of Mau Mau.* New York: Praeger.
Sorrensen, M. P. K.
  1967   *Land Reform in Kikuyu Country.* Nairobi: Oxford University Press.
Swynnerton, R. J. M.
  1954   *A Plan to Intensify African Agriculture.* Nairobi: Kenya Government.
Twining, W.
  1966   "Legal education within East Africa," *East African Law Today.* British Institute of International and Comparative Law. Commonwealth Law Series, No. 5, 1966, pp. 115-151.
Van Zwanenberg, R. M.
  1972   *Agricultural History of Kenya to 1939.* Nairobi: East African Publishing House.
Wolff, R. D.
  1974   *The Economics of Colonialism: Britain and Kenya 1870-1930.* New Haven: Yale University Press.

10

WESTERN COURTS IN NON-WESTERN SETTINGS: PATTERNS OF COURT USE IN COLONIAL AND NEO-COLONIAL AFRICA[1]

RICHARD L. ABEL

Within the sociology of law the genre known as impact studies, or studies of law in action, has been extremely popular. We have learned again and again that there are limits to effective legal action, that there is a gap between the law in the books and the law in action; we have been offered concepts of implementation, compliance, efficacy, and penetration. Gradually, as the theoretical underpinning of these studies has become more sophisticated, we have recognized that the ''gap'' is not one problem but many. Laws, whether judicial or statutory, no matter how clearly and carefully drafted, do not have an unambiguous purpose or meaning. Therefore, we cannot lay reality alongside the law and see whether or not the two match (to paraphrase a once-popular mode of judicial review) but instead must choose the relationships between law and society we wish to understand. We have also come to see those relationships as far more complex, involv-

[1] The original fieldwork was supported by a Foreign Area Fellowship, and subsequent research by the Yale Law School Program in Law and Modernization. A fuller statement of the theoretical structure of this analysis appears as: ''Theories of litigation in society: 'Modern' dispute institutions in 'tribal' society and 'tribal' dispute institutions in 'modern' society as alternative legal forms.'' In E. Blankenburg, E. Klausa, and H. Rottleuthner (eds.), *Alternative Rechtsformen und Alternativen zum Recht, Jahrbuch für Rechtssoziologie und Rechtstheorie, Band VI*. Opladen: Westdeutscher Verlag, 1979.

167

ing interaction within the legal system (among rules, processes, and institutions) and within society (among culture, social processes, and social structures) as well as between the elements of each of those systems.

This chapter is a study of the imposition of law in the broader sense just discussed. The "law" imposed is not a substantive rule but a legal institution or category of institutions—western courts. This shift in emphasis from substantive rules to institutions is one of the distinctive contributions of a sociological viewpoint, which sees rules, institutions, and processes as equally significant parts of a larger whole. Although the imposition occurred wherever non-western societies were subjected to colonial domination, this chapter is concerned only with Africa, and largely with Anglophonic, sub-Saharan Africa (excluding southern Africa). The imposition did not occur at a single point in time. It began at the onset of colonial rule (whose first, and for a long time only, justification was the maintenance of law and order), was elaborated throughout the colonial period as new judicial institutions were introduced and existing ones modified, and has been perpetuated, even intensified, by the elite regimes that have sought modernization and development following political independence. The consequences I will explore differ from those of the usual impact study in two ways. First, I am not asking whether these new institutions attained their "purpose" but am rather looking for their inadvertent, unintended, unforeseen, or latent consequences. Indeed, it is doubtful whether the imposition of western courts in Africa was motivated by conscious purpose other than the desire of colonial rulers to assert their belief in the superiority of metropolitan institutions. Second, my research has not yet reached the stage where I can speak with confidence of "social" consequences; instead, I will discuss changes in the *use* made of these institutions. Obviously, such changes in the pattern of litigation will, in turn, have consequences for society, a subject for future investigators.

My starting point in this analysis will be the perspective of the litigant, who, until recently, has been relatively neglected by the sociology of law. The reasons for this oversight are several. The original attack on the monopoly of legal dogmatism was launched by the legal realists, whose stated goal was a more accurate, more "realistic" representation of the law. To this end, they sought to augment the static content of legal doctrine with descriptions of the behavior of legal decision makers, primarily judges. Their lead was followed by sociologists, who studied the behavior of other official actors: administrators, prosecutors, and police. Reinforcing this concentration upon officials was the appellate court bias—what Jerome Frank (1949) criticized as "the upper court myth." In appellate courts the litigant is passive, often absent, his place taken by his legal representative; thus the lawyer, who is still an "officer of the court," became a focus of study. A further reason for the relative invisibility of the litigant is the tendency of sociologists and political scientists to concentrate on the criminal process in preference to civil litigation; indeed, there is a recognized discipline, criminology, that studies the former, but no comparable body of scholarship devoted to the latter. In criminal prosecutions the accused is generally viewed as a mere subject, upon whom the process acts, and until recently the victim has not even had any legal standing in the proceedings.

Unlike sociology, the anthropology of law has always accorded the litigant a significant role. For one thing, in the societies anthropologists study, third parties in disputes tend to be less dominant because they lack the coercive powers of the western judge. The role of the litigant in presenting evidence, advancing arguments, marshaling witnesses, and mobilizing political support thus emerges more clearly. Anthropologists have also stressed the capacity of the disputant to choose among a number of alternative responses, and have made that choice of forum a central theoretical issue. Finally, the societies studied by anthropologists generally lack official actors who might obscure our view of the litigant—there are neither police, nor prosecutors, nor professional lawyers—and civil litigation, in which victim and accused play prominent and equal roles, predominates over criminal prosecution.

This litigant's perspective throws new light on the interaction between legal institutions and society. The disputant's choice of a forum immediately affects both his adversary and himself, for each forum will have its own substantive and procedural rules, which influence the outcome of the dispute and the subsequent relations of the parties to each other and to the society. Disputant choice will also affect the dispute institutions, for the cumulation of these choices will determine the number of cases a forum hears, the characteristics and relationships of the parties who appear before it, the subject matter of the disputes it handles, the participation of intermediaries (such as lawyers), and the involvement of the general public with, and its attitude toward, the institution. Finally, the consequences for both the parties and the dispute institutions will have long-term, large-scale significance for the society, influencing the structure of social relations, the relationship between public and institution, and the structure of these, and ultimately other, institutions in the society.

MODELS OF LITIGATION IN SOCIETY

In order to understand the consequences of imposing a dispute institution upon a society, it may be useful to begin by sketching the interaction between society and dispute institution when the latter is *not* imposed, when it grows more or less gradually from within the society. I will do so by contrasting consciously exaggerated ideal–typical images of tribal and western societies. There is an extensive literature comparing dispute institutions in these social settings, and although it contains little explicit discussion of patterns of litigation, it does allow us to extrapolate some notions about litigant behavior. The end product is a theoretical construct of harmonious interaction and mutual reinforcement among the three elements: social structure, dispute institution, and litigant behavior.

DISPUTING IN TRIBAL SOCIETY

Social Structure

Relationships between people are multiplex (that is, functionally undifferentiated), affective, and enduring. Conflict is therefore frequent, intense, and remembered. Almost all interaction is between persons bound by such relationships; strangers rarely meet, and their meetings are not governed by norms. Relationships are *relatively* egalitarian because technology limits the economic surplus that can be amassed, but social and political rank are likely to be significant. Because membership in social groupings overlaps, conflict between those groups is moderated by divided loyalties and cross-cutting ties. Contract is an adjunct of status: contracting parties either are bound by a pre-existing status relationship, or create a fictitious relationship, or elaborate the contractual link until it resembles a status. Rights in and transfers of real property are also an outgrowth of status and therefore ultimately controlled by groups, not individuals. In most instances the status relationship precedes, and is a prerequisite for, the property right. Because the society is technologically undeveloped, serious injuries rarely occur negligently. Marriage legitimates fixed and enduring rights to children; because it intimately involves the families of both spouses, these families are vitally concerned in its celebration, continuance and, failing that, its dissolution.

Dispute Institutions

These institutions lack coercive powers and must therefore secure the consent of all parties, although they may exert considerable social pressure to obtain it. They are relatively unspecialized, undifferentiated, and nonbureaucratic. Disputants are active full participants in the hearing. The institutions are highly accessible to disputants and welcome their disputes. They provide a prompt hearing and an immediate moral evaluation, one that typically finds fault and merit on both sides. But they are often vague about the remedy, urging behavioral reform rather than the transfer of specific goods. Such judgments are carried out slowly and partially, not because the institution is inefficient but because the rights and obligations it declares are being incorporated into an ongoing relationship. No judgment is final. The norms employed by the institution are particularistic, flexible, vague, inconsistent, familiar, and supported by widespread consensus.

Dispute Patterns

Disputes tend to be polycentric, to involve multiple issues, and to have considerable historical depth. Disputants are bound by a continuing relationship which is the source of the dispute, the reason for airing it, and the incentive for accepting an outcome. Disputants are proactive: they bring the dispute to a hearing, advocate aggressively, and are responsible for executing any judgment. There is a high level of disputing. Conflict readily surfaces, and since disputes are polycentric and parties may explore any issue, numerous other grievances are unearthed. As a result, a high proportion of normative violations is publicly corrected, although the sanctions imposed are generally mild. Wrongs are the most frequent subject of dispute, partly because conflict over contract, property, and family obligations tends to occur among intimates and therefore to be handled privately, unless one party wishes to terminate the relationship. These wrongs are almost entirely intentional because unintentional wrongs tend to be forgiven if trivial and, if serious (uncommon in an undeveloped technology), to be interpreted as intentional through beliefs in sorcery or witchcraft. Remedies for wrongs are civil. No specialized functionaries represent the state, but victims are capable of seeking redress and are motivated to do so; furthermore, their interests must remain paramount if the relationship between victim and offender is to be preserved. Social control operates through special deterrence—convincing each wrongdoer not to repeat his error—rather than through general deterrence, making an example of one wrongdoer in order to influence the behavior of others.

LITIGATION IN MODERN SOCIETY

If the above generalizations greatly oversimplify the heterogeneity of tribal societies, we lack even such crude stereotypes for characterizing the social structure, judicial institutions, and litigation patterns of modern societies. There are at least two competing models. The first, which dominates contemporary western sociology, is composed of two elements: an exaggerated contrast with tribal society and an idealization of modern society—a composite of Max Weber and the ideology of liberal legalism (Trubek 1972). But recently there has been a revival of interest in critiques of the rule of law in capitalist states, often influenced by Marxism. Although we do not yet have a fully articulated critical theory of law, it is possible to piece together what that might look like, if only by inverting elements of the rule of law. I shall juxtapose the two models below.

Social Structure

Liberal Legalism. The society is composed of atomized individuals instrumentally pursuing single, narrowly defined, selfish goals. Their interaction is transitory, lacking either past or future, and affectively neutral. Conflict is endemic but simple, superficial, and readily forgotten. Interaction among strangers is the paradigm for legal regulation, which does not intrude into enduring relationships. All actors in the society are formally (that is legally) equal. Each individual voluntarily belongs to a number of varied, special-purpose groups. Because his loyalties are divided, intergroup conflict is moderated: such pluralism is the foundation of the liberal state. Contracts are freely executed by individual strangers. Real property is a commodity, held by individuals and freely exchanged between strangers solely on the basis of economic advantage. With the development of technology and the displacement of interaction among intimates by interaction among strangers, serious wrongs are more frequently caused by negligence than by intent. Family relationships are formed and dissolved at will by individuals who are progressively isolated from extended kin. Relationships between adults are narrowly instrumental and less enduring; children are no longer allocated to adults by tradition but rather on the basis of utilitarian considerations.

Critique. The society is composed of large, corporate entities linked by enduring multiplex relationships constructed in part from affective ties among the elite. Conflict between those entities, or between an entity and an individual, is endemic, complicated, intense, and unforgettable. Because the conflict cannot be expressed openly, it is repressed and displaced. Interaction among strangers diminishes as individuals are increasingly encapsulated within corporate entities. Universalistic rules applicable to all such interactions are progressively displaced by bureaucratic regulations governing the relationship of the individual to the entity. Corporate entities that interact quickly become intimates. Formal (that is, legal) equality is rendered meaningless by gross inequities of wealth, power, and status, both between individuals and between individuals and corporate entities; these inequities are relatively immutable and cumulative. The individual belongs to a corporate entity by ascription rather than choice; he is increasingly likely to belong primarily, or even exclusively, to one; because his loyalties are now united, conflict between such entities is total and unremitting. Most contracts occur between individuals and corporate entities and must conform to boilerplate drafted by the latter. Contractual relationships are progressively elaborated to encompass other social behavior, endowed with affect, and rendered relatively enduring. Both real and personal property decline in importance, and individual titleholders are rigidly regulated in their use and disposition. The significant property rights are exercised by bureaucrats in government and in large, corporate entities; in neither situation are those bureaucrats effectively controlled by their constituencies (citizens, shareholders, union members) through the ostensibly democratic processes. No-fault compensation displaces the adjudication of fault as the response to injuries.

Courts

Liberal Legalism. Courts have unlimited power to coerce compliance with their orders and can therefore disregard the wishes of the parties. They are functionally specialized (internally, if not as a whole), differentiated, and bureaucratic. They hear only legal disputes, narrowly conceived. Litigants are relatively passive, deferring to professional representatives (lawyers) and professional parties (such as prosecutors and insurance companies). The court is highly, but equally, inaccessible to litigants. Yet case overload is chronic because the numbers of official courts and judges are relatively small, with the result that there are long delays in obtaining a hearing. Decisions, generally ordering the transfer of money, are enforced promptly, thoroughly, and with finality. The norms employed are universalistic, rigid, clear, and consistent; though they purport to be restatements of accepted moral principles, formalization renders them esoteric. These norms are employed to evaluate the individual's past conduct.

Critique. Courts obtain the power to coerce individuals at the cost of their capacity to persuade. But the power of the court is dwarfed by that of large corporate entities, whose compliance must be induced. Disputes between related individuals, or between a large corporate entity and its members, are increasingly handled by therapeutic institutions that are unspecialized, undifferentiated, and nonbureaucratic. These institutions deal with the whole individual, disguising control under the euphemism of treatment. Disputes between large corporate entities are also withdrawn from the courts and handled as political matters. Finally, though it is very difficult for an individual to voice a grievance against a corporate entity of which he is not a member, such entities are energetically proactive in asserting claims against nonmember individuals. Because corporate entities are professional parties and are represented by lawyer employees, they find the courts highly accessible; indeed, courts welcome them as litigants because their claims can be processed routinely. Such entities can also make tactical use of the endless delays caused by case overload. The result is differential access, leading to use of the court by corporate entities against nonmember individuals, but not by any other permutation of these two categories. These structural and procedural biases have normative concomitants. Legal rules express the interests of one class at the expense of another, not a consensus of shared principles. Furthermore, they are not sufficiently clear or consistent to determine the outcome of cases, which are influenced more by political and economic considerations. Indeed, most disputes are not adjudicated at all but handled informally according to particularistic, vague, unstated notions.

Litigation Patterns

Liberal Legalism. Litigation tends to be bicentric, to involve few, narrowly defined issues, and to have little historical depth; cases that do not meet these criteria are not litigated. Litigants either are strangers or are willing (even eager) to become strangers; persons wishing to preserve their relationship will not litigate, and the court will in any case decline to hear them. On the other hand, legal institutions intended to preserve relationships (such as conciliation courts) will either be shunned or will disrupt the relationship despite their ostensible purpose.

Because individuals are relatively passive toward the court, responsibility for initiating and conducting hearings, and for enforcing the remedy, devolves upon official actors, such as prosecutors or the enforcement staff of administrative agencies. Interpersonal litigation declines, conflict is repressed or displaced, the dispute institution grows less accessible to individuals, and both the parties who can litigate and the issues they can raise are severely limited. As a result, only a

small proportion of all deviant acts is redressed. As interaction between intimates is displaced by the conjunction of strangers, intentional wrongs decline; as
technology develops, negligent wrongs increase. Although the court is a poor
institution to adjudicate intentional wrongs between intimates (because its intervention destroys their relationship), it is an excellent mechanism for redressing
negligent injuries inflicted upon strangers, who want only monetary compensation. One consequence is that some intentional wrongs between intimates are
translated into negligent wrongs between strangers (through insurance or doc-
trines like *respondeat superior*), and many of those that cannot be transformed are
left without redress.

Criminal prosecution supplants civil litigation for many of the same reasons:
litigants are passive and state officials correspondingly more active; this relationship of dependency is increased by the inaccessibility of the court; offender and
victim are often strangers, so that the latter has little stake in seeing that the
former is punished; in addition, victimless crimes become an ever larger proportion of all crimes as the state regulatory apparatus expands. Because a relatively
small, and constantly declining, proportion of normative violations is prosecuted, the court must rely on general rather than special deterrence—*in terrorem*
sanctions inflicted upon a few offenders and justified by the fear this is said to
inspire in the rest of society.

Contract is the kind of relationship the court *is* designed to handle; consequently, relationships are framed in contractual form and contract disputes
increase. Because real property is treated as a commodity about which contracts
can freely be made, property litigation also rises. And the same dynamic
characterizes family relationships: the court is used to terminate them (divorce)
and to adjust rights and obligations between parties who were previously, or
have just been made, strangers to each other (adoption, custody, visitation, support, and neglect).

Critique. Bicentric litigation is displaced by unicentric administrative proceedings: there is an applicant but often no adversary and thus *no* contested
issue; the applicant simply adduces the facts that fit clearly predefined
categories, as though he were filling out a form. The court ceases to adjudicate
and becomes an administrative bureaucracy, rubber-stamping outcomes decided
elsewhere. To the passivity of most litigants is now added the passivity of
bureaucratic inertia. This vacuum is filled by large corporate entities, who use
the courts as a mechanism for high-volume, routine processing of claims against
individuals: creditors obtaining default judgments against debtors, landlords
executing *ex parte* evictions of tenants, prosecutors eliciting guilty pleas from
unrepresented or nominally represented defendants. The other permutations of
conflict among individuals and corporate entites are extruded from the courts.
Individual claims against corporate entities are handled either by two-party
negotiation (consumer–seller, injured–insurer, citizen–government) or by
administrative agencies (injured employee–employer, tenant–landlord). Inter-

personal conflict is resolved by the parties themselves (spouses, parents and children, co-workers) or mediated by third parties, whether governmental (police) or private (therapists). Conflict between corporate entities is adjusted by two-party negotiation (sweetheart union contracts, oligopolistic market division and price fixing) or mediated or arbitrated by third parties (labor disputes, breach of contract between businessmen, negotiated pleas in the prosecution of white-collar crime).

THE CONSEQUENCES OF IMPOSING INSTITUTIONAL FORMS: LITIGATING IN TRIBAL SOCIETIES AND DISPUTING IN MODERN SOCIETIES

The three models I have constructed share a characteristic common to much anthropological and sociological theory: they are functionally integrated, composed of harmonious relationships that maintain social stasis within a limited amount of self-correcting fluctuation. But the purpose of developing these models was to examine the possiblities of disharmony. We can see these more clearly if we juxtapose the variables of social structure and institutional form by means of a four-square box (see Figure 10.1).

Institutional Form

		Tribal	Modern
Social Structure	Tribal	1. Tribal society	2. Colonialism and neo-colonialism
	Modern	3. Reformist, utopian, and revolutionary society	4. Modern society

Figure 10.1 Institutional form compared with social structure.

The first and fourth squares have already been described. The third includes the very diverse attempts to introduce tribal, informal, noncoercive, unofficial dispute institutions into modern society: conservative initiatives to preserve a tribal society that is being transformed by the impact of the modern world, as in India, Malawi, Rhodesia, or the Bantustans of South Africa; movements to reform the legal systems of late capitalism by introducing juvenile, family, small claims, and (more recently) neighborhood courts; attempts to withdraw from the world, such as utopian or intentional communities in western nations, or the Israeli kibbutz; and efforts to change the world through ''popular'' judicial institutions in Russian, China, Chile, Cuba, Tanzania, Sri Lanka, Burma, and elsewhere. Although this chapter will not be concerned with those phenomena, I believe that the theoretical structure and empirical data it presents help to illuminate them, and that a full understanding of the social consequences of imposed law requires simultaneous consideration of the second and third squares.

WESTERN COURTS IN NON-WESTERN SETTINGS

INSTITUTIONAL CHANGE

The starting point for exploring the consequences of imposing western legal institutions upon non-western settings is a determination of whether such an imposition has actually occurred and if so when, where, and to what extent. A comparison of the models of tribal dispute institutions and western courts reveals that they differ along numerous dimensions, which I have elsewhere enumerated at length and grouped under the concepts of functional specialization, differentiation, and bureaucratization (Abel 1973). Given the impossibility of measuring change in each of these dimensions, I shall select two, chosen for their theoretical salience and the availability of quantitative data: jurisdictional population and geographic jurisdiction. Certainly one of the defining characteristics of tribal dispute institutions is the relatively small jurisdiction each serves, a concomitant of several factors: lack of coercive power (informal pressures operate only among acquaintances, and are most effective among intimates), and the undeveloped technology of tribal societies (limiting communication and transportation). The contrast with western courts is dramatic: at the appellate apex these serve millions of people spread over millions of square miles; even western trial courts serve large populations and areas. Jurisdictional size is unavoidably associated with judicial power, differentiation, and bureaucracy. The larger the jurisdiction the more scope there is for specialization and the greater the pressure to specialize as a result of increases in caseload and the accompanying demands for efficiency. The size of the jurisdiction is itself a measure of the differentiation of the court from society, and increases other dimensions of differentiation. And the size of the jurisdiction, together with the caseload pressures it brings, leads to greater bureaucratization.

It is notoriously difficult to generate comparable data on changes in jurisdictional size over time: figures are spotty and not easily assembled, different places are measured in different ways at different times, population statistics are inaccurate, and there is room for disagreement about the definition of a dispute institution. Nevertheless, the changes are sufficiently large and unidirectional to justify generalization even if they contain substantial errors. Table 10.1 presents the available data on the geographic jurisdiction of Kenya primary courts at two points in time. These courts had been adapted from indigenous, traditional councils of elders in accordance with the principles of indirect rule embodied in the Native Tribunals Ordinance of 1930. 1944 saw the beginning of a process of reorganization that progressively assimilated those bodies to western notions of a court, through changes in structure and process. The Magistrates' Courts Act of 1967 effectively completed that transformation, and was fully implemented by 1969.

These figures must be interpreted with caution. First, they represent an average geographic jurisdiction within each district, obtained by dividing the

TABLE 10.1
Geographic Jurisdiction of Kenya Primary Courts by District, 1944 and 1969 [a]

	Area in km²[b]	Number of courts (1930s)	Number of courts (1944)	Area per court in km²[b] (1944)	Number of courts (1969)	Area per court in km²[b] (1969)
Mombasa	182.25		2	90.00	1	182.25
Nairobi	510.75		1	510.75	1	510.75
Nakuru	5,472.00		3	1,824.75	3	1,824.75
Trans Nzoia	2,720.25		1	2,720.25	1	2,720.25
Kiambu	1,642.50		4	409.50	5	328.50
Fort Hall	1,579.50		5	315.00	4	393.75
Uasin Gishu	3,683.25		1	3,683.25	2	1,840.50
Kitui	26,316.00		6	4,385.25	2	13,158.00
Machakos	13,027.50		8	1,629.00	7	1,860.75
Embu	3,606.75		5	722.75	3	1,194.75
Meru	8,466.75		6	1,410.75	5	1,694.25
Malindi-Kilifi	10,786.50		5	2,157.75	3	3,595.50
North Nyanza	6,075.00	25	8	760.50	14	434.25
Nyeri	1,338.75		5	267.75	5	267.75
Central Nyanza	4,086.00	19	9	454.50	6	686.25
Kericho	4,799.25	17	4	1,199.25	3	1,599.75
Nandi	1,606.50		7	299.50	2	803.25
Taita	13,272.75	5	3	4,423.50	2	6,637.50
Kwale	7,170.75		6	1,172.25	2	3,586.50
Elgeyo-Marakwet	2,270.25		2	1,134.00	1	2,270.25
South Nyanza	6,655.50	33	8	832.50	9	740.25
West Suk	4,410.00		1	4,410.00	1	4,410.00
Lamu-Tana River	26,948.25		8	3,305.25	4	6,610.50
Masai	40,448.25		10	4,045.50	4	10,111.50
Baringo	8,867.25		3	2,947.50	1	8,867.25

[a] The data for this table, and all others that deal with Kenya, were obtained from the following: Kenya, Native Affairs Department (1925–1947); Kenya, African Affairs Department (1948–1957); Kenya, Judicial Department (1955–1970); Bushe Commission (1934); Phillips (1945); Barnett (1965); Saltman (1971); Muslim (1976); as well as unpublished monthly reports by the African Courts to the African Courts Officer for the year 1966, filed in the High Court Registry at Nairobi.

[b] Original sources in square miles.

area of the district by the number of courts. Second, improvements in transportation networks during a quarter century of very rapid socioeconomic change may have altered the meaning of these distances. Nevertheless, with some exceptions, the area served by each court increases, often by a factor of two or three.

But a more sensitive measure of the relationship of court to society may be the number of people the court serves. Table 10.2 presents the average jurisdictional population by district for Kenya courts in 1943 and 1969. Again these numbers must be qualified: in both 1969 and 1943 some of these courts had several judges or panels of judges, so that a better index would have been the population per

TABLE 10.2
Jurisdictional Population of Kenya Primary Courts by District, 1943 and 1969 [a]

District	Population (1943)	Number of courts (1943)	Population per court (1943)	Population (1969)	Number of courts (1969)	Population per court (1969)
North Nyanza	402,396	8	50,999	1,328,298	14	94,800
Central Nyanza	409,260	9	47,696	783,831	6	130,639
South Nyanza	367,225	8	45,903	663,173	9	73,686
Nyeri	164,243	5	32,849	360,845	5	72,169
Fort Hall	195,843	5	39,169	445,310	4	111,328
Kaimbu	128,439	4	32,110	475,576	5	95,115
Embu	155,240	5	31,048	395,900	3	131,967
Meru	180,000	6	30,000	569,506	5	113,901
Machakos	250,000	8	31,250	707,214	7	101,031
Kitui	200,000	6	33,333	354,953	2	177,476
Nandi	44,000	7	6,286	209,068	2	104,534
Kericho	100,000	4	25,000	479,135	3	159,712
Baringo	35,000	3	11,667	161,741	1	161,741
Elgeyo-Marakwet	45,000	2	22,500	159,265	1	159,265
West Suk	22,000	1	22,000	82,458	1	82,458
Kilifi-Malindi	130,000	5	26,000	307,568	3	102,784
Kwale	66,000	6	11,000	205,602	2	102,801
Tana River	17,000	8	2,125	50,696	4	12,674
Taita	53,000	3	17,667	110,742	2	55,371
Masai	45,000	10	4,500	211,112	4	52,778
Samburu	26,000	3	8,667	69,519	1	69,519
Nairobi	60,000	1	60,000	509,286	1	509,286
Mombasa	55,438[b]	2	27,719	247,073	1	247,073

[a] Population data in this and other tables concerning Kenya may be found in the following: East Africa High Commission, Statistical Department (1950); Morgan, Manfred, and Schaffer (1966); Kenya, Ministry of Finance and Economic Planning (1971).

[b] 1948 population.

panel or judge. Still, the change is uniform: *every* district experiences an increase in jurisdictional population. And the magnitude is considerable, ranging from just under 100% to more than 1600%. These changes are the composite effect of several factors: rapid population growth; major demographic movements, from more crowded to less crowded agricultural areas, and especially from country to city; and "rationalizations" of the court structure, in which less active courts were consolidated or closed.

Kenya may be an extreme case within Africa, and in the Third World generally. It has embraced the ideology of "modernization" with unqualified enthusiasm, and has become the locus of activity for many multinational corporations. Data on other African countries are incomplete and far less reliable but still instructive (see Table 10.3).

TABLE 10.3
Jurisdictional Population of Primary Courts for Selected African Countries[a]

Year	Country[b]	Population per court
1929	Northern Nigeria	21,118
1930s	Barotseland	16,000
1930	Kenya	10,300
1931	Tanzania (Moshi Dist.)	7,000
	Nigeria (excl. Lagos)	22,200
1935	Uganda	4,500
1937	Northern Nigeria	20,400
1943	Ghana	5,000
1948	Nigeria	12,031
	Northern Nigeria	20,681
	Western Nigeria	6,271
	Eastern Nigeria	9,115
	Lagos	10,600
1950	Kenya	43,800
	Ghana	13,891
1951	Tanzania	9,300
1954	Eastern Nigeria	18,000
1958	Eastern Nigeria	24,460
	Western Nigeria	13,590
1959	Rhodesia[c]	52,500
1960	Tanzania	9,000
1962	Kenya	66,000
1964	Botswana	3,400
1969	Kenya	124,000
	Zambia	11,200
1970	Ethiopia	20,000
	Uganda	19,000
	Tanzania	15,600
1972	Kenya	133,000

[a] Sources: Aplin (1931:A6); Kenya, Legislative Council (1951:col. 177; 1962:col. 592); Korsah Commission (1951:9-10); Brooke Commission (1952:13, 28; 1953:Appendix); Afrika Institut, Leiden, and Royal Tropical Institute, Amsterdam (1955:196-197); Haydon (1960:72); Robinson Commission (1961:4); Keay and Richardson (1966:77-78, 90, 98); Spalding, Hoover, and Piper (1969:284-285); Russell (1971:8); Roberts (1972:107);Singh (1972:2); DuBow (1973:22).

[b] These are nationwide averages unless some other unit is specified. Here, and through this chapter, the contemporary names of African nations are used rather than those appropriate to the period being described.

[c] This figure pertains to the Native Commissioners' Courts staffed by Europeans.

This comparison reveals that many other countries also experienced significant growth in jurisdictional population over roughly the same period. Ghana, Nigeria, Tanzania, and Uganda each had something of the order of 5000 persons per court in the early colonial period (when some indigenous institutions had been recognized but had not yet changed significantly), and this figure increased to between 10,000 and 20,000 people as the court system was "rationalized." But some countries followed different patterns: Northern Nigeria, with its large population and complex hierarchical, traditional political system had always had courts with large jurisdictions; Botswana had not yet undergone the process of change by 1964; and Zambia had consciously rejected this path on ideological grounds. These countertrends are precisely the kind of variation in institutional structure (one of my variables) that is necessary to permit a test of the hypotheses to be developed.

CHANGE IN LITIGATION PATTERNS

Aggregate Changes

We are now in a position to use the model of law in colonial society to construct propositions about the impact of changes in social structure and dispute institutions upon patterns of litigation.

I start with the expectation that litigation will decline over time because modern courts disvalue litigation, are less attractive to members of tribal societies, and are less accessible to individuals. My data from Kenya strongly support this notion (see Tables 10.4 and 10.5).

TABLE 10.4
Total, Criminal, and Civil Cases Filed in Kenya Primary Courts per Year
1927-1971 (Excluding Tax Cases)[a]

Year	Total cases	Criminal cases	Civil cases
1927	31,937	5,322	26,615
1929	39,176	8,667	30,509
1930	34,977	7,173	27,804
1931	39,675	8,118	31,557
1932	31,328	6,840	24,488
1933	28,580	9,042	19,538
1934	32,550	13,103	19,447
1935	36,543	13,891	22,652
1936	39,167	15,031	24,136
1937	60,883	25,573	35,310
1938	54,835	25,894	28,941
1942	84,223	93,260	44,963
1946	100,000[b]	35,000[b]	65,000[b]
1947	98,921[c]	48,826[c]	50,095[c]
1948	94,633[d]	50,517[d]	44,116[d]

(*continued*)

TABLE 10.4 (cont.)

Year	Total cases	Criminal cases	Civil cases
1949	108,330	62,452	45,878
1950	124,936	69,111	55,825
1959	132,926	89,769	43,157[e]
1960	131,297	NA	NA
1961	144,617	NA	NA
1962	157,333	118,516	38,817
1964	156,280	101,574	54,706
1965	180,459	122,819	57,640
1966	243,139	191,914	51,225
1967	285,735[f]	226,621[f]	59,114[f]
1968	315,555[f]	272,842[f]	42,713[f]
1969	303,218[f]	255,540[f]	47,678[f]
1970	NA	NA	46,837[f]
1971	NA	NA	34,386[f]

[a] Sources: See Table 10.1.

[b] Round numbers.

[c] Central Kavirondo District is missing.

[d] Coast Province is missing.

[e] Decrease between 1950 and 1959 attributable to Mau Mau.

[f] Not strictly comparable because includes resident magistrates.

TABLE 10.5

Criminal and Civil Cases Filed in Kenya Primary Courts per Year per 1000 Population 1931–1971 (Excluding Tax Cases) [a]

Year	Population	Criminal cases	Civil cases	Prosecution rate	Civil litigation rate
1931	4,100,000	8,118	31,557	2.1	7.8
1948	5,252,753[b]	50,517	44,116	10.5	9.1
1959	7,652,000	89,769	43,157	11.7	5.6
1962	8,595,000[b]	118,516	38,817	13.7	4.5
1964	9,104,000	101,574	54,706	11.2	6.0
1965	9,365,000	112,819	57,640	13.2	6.2
1966	9,643,000	191,914	51,225	19.9	5.3
1967	9,948,000	226,621	59,114	22.8	5.9
1968	10,209,000	272,842	42,713	26.7	4.3
1969	10,942,705[b]	255,540	47,678	23.3	4.4
1971	12,000,000	NA	39,386	NA	2.9

[a] Sources: See Table 10.2.

[b] Census years; others are estimates.

Although the absolute number of cases filed increased tenfold over 4 decades, this is largely attributable to the increase in criminal prosecutions by a factor of 25. Civil litigation gradually increased for about 2 decades and then fluctuated widely, but ultimately declined almost to its original level. Furthermore, it is obviously necessary to control for the growth in population—from approximately 4.1 million in 1931 to 10.9 million in 1969. If we construct prosecution and civil litigation rates (cases filed per 1000 population), we see that the civil litigation rate declined by more than a third during the period of most rapid social and institutional change following World War II, whereas the rate of prosecutions more than doubled. Fragmentary data for other African countries show similar patterns, with the exception of Tanzania and Zambia, which, as noted above, deliberately preserved traditional judicial institutions.

The observation of these changes is only the beginning of the inquiry—the phenomenon to be explained, not the explanation. The rapid imposition of western courts upon gradually modernizing societies does appear to lead to a dramatic decline in litigation rates. This decline is accompanied by an equally dramatic increase in the rate of prosecutions. Later I shall explore the possibility that the two are related. But first it is necessary to be more specific about the social and institutional changes that produced the decline.

Social-Structural Explanations

One way to do so is to break down aggregate national rates into rates for smaller units. The transformation of judicial institutions has been relatively (if not entirely) uniform within most African nations, though this is more true of Kenya than of Nigeria. But social change has been far more variable: urban areas have changed very rapidly, rural areas much more slowly. The model of law in colonial society suggests that litigation rates in the latter will decline, whereas those in the former may remain constant or even increase. This is so for several reasons. The tribal social structure persisting in rural areas binds individuals together in multiplex, enduring, affective ties that are difficult and costly to sever. Modern courts characteristically handle disputes by rendering coercive decisions based on narrowly focused issues, and these tend to destroy any relationship between the parties. Individuals living in tribal areas should, according to this model, progressively shun the official courts as those are modernized.

I was able to make a crude test of this proposition by comparing district litigation rates (see Table 10.6). I found that a number of districts with high population densities (between 100 and 300 persons/km²), where I would expect to find frequent interaction and correspondingly frequent disputes, displayed rates of civil litigation that were substantially below the national median. These are rural, traditional, agricultural areas, relatively untouched by interaction with the urban, export-oriented economy. Anthropological accounts all indicate high rates of disputing; evidently, fewer of these disputes are being taken to primary courts today.

TABLE 10.6
Civil Litigation Rates in Kenya (1969) as a Function of Population
Density and Tribal Homogeneity [a]

District	Civil cases per 1000 population	Population per km²	Population density rank	Population of largest tribe as percentage of population	Tribal homogeneity rank
Mombasa	21.6	1555	1	24.0	40
Nairobi	17.9	734	2	37.6	37
Nakuru	8.8	40	23	58.3	33
Trans-Nzoia	8.1	50	20	47.1	36
Murang'a	5.1	176	7	96.0	11
Uasin Gishu	5.0	50	21	32.8	39
Embu	4.7	62	17	87.2	21
Kitui	4.6	11	28	97.3	8
Machakos	4.4	50	22	97.8	5
Kisumu	4.0	192	5	90.5	18
Bungoma	3.9	113	12	83.5	22
Kiambu	3.4	184	6	94.5	15
Meru	3.3	63	16	97.4	7
Nyandarua	3.2	54	19	94.8	14
Kilifi	3.2	24	25	92.0	17
Kirinyaga	3.1	146	9	96.3	10
Kakamega	2.9	220	4	97.9	3
Nyeri	2.9	108	13	97.8	4
Kisii	2.8	304	3	98.0	2
Laikipia	2.4	7	29	57.5	34
Busia	2.4	119	10	65.0	32
Kericho	2.3	97	14	81.3	24
Nandi	2.2	75	15	74.4	26
South Nyanza	2.1	114	11	88.8	19
Taita	2.1	6	31	78.7	25
Samburu	1.5	3	35	74.0	27
Kwale	1.4	25	24	83.0	23
Elgeyo	1.1	57	18	94.0	16
Siaya	1.1	151	8	96.4	9
Baringo	0.8	15	27	73.9	28
Kajiado	0.7	4	32	68.6	29
West Pokot	0.6	16	26	87.9	20
Narok	0.2	7	30	66.5	30
Marsabit	0.2	1	38	34.2	38
Lamu	0.1	4	33	65.8	31
Tana River	0.1	1	39	57.4	35
Garissa	0	1	40	95.7	13
Wajir	0	2	36	97.8	6
Mandera	0	4	34	95.7	12
Turkana	0	2	37	98.8	1

[a] Sources: See Tables 10.1 and 10.2.

But that is only half the proposition. Why should we expect litigation rates to remain constant or increase in the cities? First, these are areas with the highest population densities, and therefore the highest rate of interaction. Second, urban areas are more heterogeneous (see Table 10.6). Heterogeneity signifies differing expectations about appropriate behavior; therefore, interaction is more likely to generate conflict. Heterogeneity also implies that there will be neither traditional institutions nor traditional norms to resolve such conflict. The official courts offer both a normative structure and the coercive power to impose it upon recalcitrant litigants. Third, though this imposition will generally be disruptive of any underlying social relationship, those that bind urban disputants are likely to be fragile, shallow, and instrumental, where the disputants are not complete strangers.

My Kenya data strongly support the hypothesis that litigation rates increase in urban areas characterized by high population density, heterogeneity, large African and non-African populations, rapid urban migration, and significant social and cultural change (measured by percentage of the population in non-agricultural wage employment; see Table 10.7). Eleven of the largest cities in Kenya have by far the highest rates of civil litigation. All are well above the national average and eight are between 2 and almost 10 times that average. All other districts in Kenya are below that average. But since less than 10% of the

TABLE 10.7
Civil Litigation Rates in Kenya (1969) as a Function of Urbanization [a]

Court	Civil litigation rate (1969) (civil cases per 1000 population)	African population (1969) [b]	Percentage increase in African population (1948–1969)	Total population (1969)	Annual percentage increase in total population (1962–1969)	Percentage of population in non-agricultural wage employment (1969) [c]
Thika	40.8	16,531	590	18,387	4.0	37.3
Mombasa	21.6	74,647	135	247,073	4.6	26.8
Nairobi	17.9	163,284	254	509,296	9.6	33.3
Machakos	16.7	5,722	379	6,312	6.4	NA
Kakamega	12.8	5,621	131	6,244	3.5	NA
Kisuma	12.3	24,978	469	32,431	4.7	53.5
Fort Hall	9.8	4,348	314	4,750	-0.2	NA
Nakuru	8.8	42,580	283	47,151	3.1	32.0
Kitale	8.1	10,166	234	11,573	3.1	32.3
Malindi	6.8	7,549	467	10,757	9.2	NA
Eldoret	5.0	15,515	287	18,196	-1.1	63.3
National average	4.4	—	103	—	3.4	3.9

[a] Sources: See Tables 10.1 and 10.2.
[b] Total population excluding European, Asian, and Arab.
[c] Source: Laurenti (n.d.:42,43).

population of Kenya lived in these urban areas in 1969, it is not surprising that the tendency of the rural population to turn away from the official courts as the latter were westernized outweighed the tendency of city dwellers to turn to those courts, and produced a net decline in the civil litigation rate. As urbanization becomes more rapid in future decades, we might expect litigation rates to increase, other things being equal.

Institutional Explanations

Thus far I have sought to explain regional and historical differences in litigation rates in terms of the attractiveness to disputants of the official judicial process embedded in different social structures. For those disputants to whom the court appears to offer at least some benefits, part of the explanation for their choice of a forum may lie in the costs of litigation. These costs are a product of interaction between the structural characteristics of the court and the social structure in which it operates; they may loosely be grouped under the concept of "access."

An obvious starting point is court costs: what the plaintiff must spend before he can file his complaint. In Kenya, during the 40-year period for which I have data, court costs increased less rapidly than cash incomes; the same appears to be true of other African countries and remains true whether the index is the statutory fee schedule, the average fee paid, or the ratio of fee to amount in claim. Yet court costs, which may attract undue attention because they are preserved in official records, are a small proportion of the actual expense of litigation. Indirect costs (transportation, food, and substitute services for litigants, witnesses, and supporters) and opportunity costs (lost wages or entrepreneurial profits) are also significant and likely to grow more rapidly than court costs—the former in rural areas (where distances are large and transportation difficult), the latter in urban areas (where there are both a higher proportion of the population in wage employment and many small businesses).

Nevertheless, all these costs are almost nominal when compared with a factor that is certain to increase in magnitude in the future: the cost of legal representation. Most African countries barred professional counsel from their primary courts until very recently. But today Kenya, Uganda, Ghana, and parts of Nigeria allow lawyers to appear. Because the party who retains counsel thereby obtains an enormous advantage, his opponent is forced to do the same. The growth of the Bar, its diffusion into the smaller cities, rising incomes, and increasing stratification will all contribute to more frequent representation by counsel. Thus, although out-of-pocket costs are not yet a major barrier to primary court litigation, the professionalization and bureaucratization of the judiciary and the proliferation of lawyers are likely to make them a more significant obstacle in the near future.

A disputant may also assess the desirability of litigation in terms of the time he must invest in the process (delay), and the return on that investment (the time the court allots to hearing his case). Such an hypothesis assumes that the disputant wants a prompt, full, unhurried airing of all grievances, an assumption that seems warranted in tribal social settings but may not be justified in the cities. In the absence of direct observation of a large number of hearings, an indirect measure of length is caseload: the more cases filed in a court per year, the less time devoted to each (holding judicial resources constant). Table 10.8 presents changes in the average caseload per court in Kenya, by district, over a 25-year period. The increases are dramatic: manifold in most districts, nearly a

TABLE 10.8
Annual Caseload in Kenya Primary Courts (District Averages) 1942 and 1967 [a]

District	Total cases filed (1942)	Number of courts (1942)	Average caseload (1942)	Total cases filed (1967)	Number of courts (1967)	Average caseload (1967)
Mombasa	1,913	2	956	13,374	1	13,374
Nairobi	3,450	1	3,450	11,571	1	11,571
Nakuru	243	3	81	21,354	3	7,118
Trans Nzoia	606	1	606	3,859	1	3,859
Kiambu	3,228	4	807	11,330	5	2,230
Fort Hall	5,269	5	1,052	11,661	4	2,920
Uasin Gishu	177	1	177	3,663	2	1,832
Kitui	2,911	6	485	4,010	2	2,005
Machakos	5,345	8	691	11,212	7	1,600
Embu	6,207	5	1,241	14,427	3	4,810
Meru	3,986	5	797	15,656	5	3,130
Malindi-Kilifi	2,850	5	570	6,341	3	2,114
North Nyanza	19,033	8	2,379	18,071	14	1,290
Nyeri	4,133	5	827	11,512	5	1,502
Central Nyanza	6,510	9	723	16,509	6	2,750
Kericho	824	4	206	6,244	3	2,081
Nandi	490	7	70	3,811	2	1,906
Taita	1,184	3	395	2,729	2	1,364
Kwale	1,728	6	288	1,376	2	688
Elgeyo-Markawet	542	2	271	883	1	883
South Nyanza and Kisii	11,352	8	1,419	14,073	9	1,564
Baringo	707	3	236	326	1	326
West Suk	489	1	489	525	1	525
Lamu-Tana River	604	8	98	396	4	94
Masai	542	10	54	3,682	4	920

[a] Sources: See Tables 10.1 and 10.2.

hundredfold in one. Yet they do not seem to dampen litigation rates, for the caseload is highest, and has increased most rapidly, in those urban districts that also display increases in litigation rates; and this appears to be true elsewhere in Africa. I shall hazard several reasons for the apparent falsification of my hypothesis, though a satisfactory explanation would require further research: urban disputants may prefer a quick, cursory hearing which translates the interaction or relationship between them into a monetary equivalent; and caseload may be a poor measure of length of hearing both because most of the increase is attributable to the mass processing of administrative offenses by police and prosecutors who are interested only in speed and efficiency, and because these criminal proceedings may not detract greatly from the time available to hear civil cases.

The other variable in this hypothesis—delay—can be measured directly. My Kenya data, taken from 16 courts, are unambiguous: delay is trivial—averaging less than a month from filing to hearing—especially when compared with the delays of several years that are common in courts in western nations; nor did it increase significantly during the 2 decades prior to my research in 1967. Thus temporal considerations do not yet appear to affect forum choice; but again, as delay increases and hearing time decreases to the point where both resemble the dimensions of those variables in western courts, we can expect them to impinge on litigation rates.

The concept of access has meanings that are not purely economic, or at least not readily expressed in monetary terms. Many of these relate to the social or cultural distance between disputant and dispute institutions. I would expect a tribal disputant to be less disposed to approach an institution the more alien it appears to him. A disputant embedded in a modern social structure, however, may prefer the relatively distant modern court: such a litigant is not looking for individualized treatment, understanding, and sympathy from a familiar peer, but for the technical application of formal rules by a professional. Social distance may be desirable, as a symbol of expertise and impartiality.

I have already presented two indexes of social distance—geographic jurisdiction and jurisdictional population (see Tables 10.1–10.3)—and have argued that, as these increase, civil litigation rates decrease in rural areas (tribal social settings) and increase in the cities (modern social settings). Other indexes of social distance display similar correlations: the age of the judge (in Africa, where mature men traditionally litigate before elders, youthfulness in a judge is a mark of differentiation), his education, his income, and whether he comes from the same tribe as the litigants. And the exceptions to this generalization also tend to support the hypothesis: the two countries that have sought to maintain a relatively undifferentiated judiciary—Tanzania and Zambia (at least in the rural courts of the latter)—also continue to have relatively high rates of civil litigation.

A final index of the desirability of the court from the disputant's viewpoint might be the probability of success. The attractiveness of a forum for a disputant will presumably vary with the likelihood of winning and obtaining the relief he seeks. And this variable should be more influential where the costs are high compared with the anticipated benefits—that is, in rural areas where out-of-pocket costs appear larger because of the smaller cash incomes, and where the intangible cost of severing a valuable relationship is greater. Although my data are very fragmentary, they do show a dramatic decline in the probability of success in one court in Kenya, from near certainty in 1948 to less than 50% in some causes of action in 1966; a similar change has been reported for Uganda (Perlman 1970:

68–69), and other Kenya courts display comparable probabilities for 1966. Given these facts and the figures on civil litigation rates, it does appear that rural litigants are increasingly unwilling to take the risk of litigation, especially since they have many alternative dispute processes, whereas urban litigants lack these alternatives and may, in any case, be attracted by the gamble. Additional evidence that calculations of this sort were being made appeared when I compared litigant choice between a civil suit and a private prosecution for the same injury in five primary courts: litigants consistently chose the procedure that offered the most substantial relief at the lowest cost.

Thus institutional variables, grouped under the headings of "access," do interact with social structural variables to influence patterns of litigation. So far, their influence has been relatively insignificant because, although access has diminished as courts have been westernized, the primary courts of Africa, even those of Kenya, do not begin to approach western courts in inaccessibility. Yet all the signs point to decreasing access: rising litigation costs (direct, indirect, and opportunity) as the judiciary is thoroughly professionalized and bureaucratized, and as wage employment increases; the progressive monopolization of representation by professional lawyers; increases in geographic jurisdiction and jurisdictional population as judicial systems are "rationalized" and population continues to grow; a concomitant increase in delay, together with a decline in the time devoted to each case; further differentiation of the judiciary; and a drop in the likelihood of success. In the not-too-distant future access will fall below some significant threshold and use of the courts by individuals for civil litigation will diminish as a result.

CHANGE IN THE CONTENT OF CIVIL LITIGATION

So far I have argued that the transformation of tribal dispute institutions into western courts results in an overall decline in civil litigation rates. But because this overall decline is a composite of an increasing rate in the still small urban enclave dwarfed by a decline in the more populous rural areas, we are forced to recognize that litigation is changing in character as well as amount. My original model suggested a number of hypotheses about changes in the content of civil litigation; I can now try to explore these directly.

According to my model, the content of litigation is the product of two factors, which are at least partly independent: changes in social structure that alter the nature of both disputes and the settlement desired, and changes in the remedies and processes offered by the dispute institution and their costs. I hypothesized that intentional wrongs would be a very frequent subject of disputing in tribal society and highly amenable to the procedures of tribal dispute institutions. In modern society, by contrast, negligent injuries will increase in number and importance and modern courts will provide more satisfactory remedies for them than for intentional wrongs. I tried to determine whether these changes were taking place by comparing cases involving intentional wrongs as a proportion of total civil cases in two populations: among Kenya courts that differed in the extent to which their social environment was tribal or modern, and within other African countries as they experienced social change over time. The results are inconclusive, but intentional wrongs seem to remain a sizable fraction of civil cases, approximately 40%. My tentative interpretation is that the still predominantly tribal social structure continues to give rise to frequent disputes over intentional wrongs, that tribal disputants today are somewhat more willing to endanger their relationships in the process of seeking redress, and that the westernized courts are if anything more attractive to many victims because of their capacity to enforce payment of compensation. A slightly different arrangement of these same variables helps to explain why family disputes tend to show a gradual decline over time: because these relationships are more important than those that bind persons disputing about a wrong, and more likely to be disrupted by coercive adjudication, family disputants tend to withdraw from the courts as those are westernized. African social structure rarely resembles that of contemporary western nations, where family relationships, especially between spouses, have become extremely fragile.

The model of western courts in a gradually westernizing social setting suggests that two other kinds of cases will increase in frequency as litigation over wrongs and family disputes declines. The first is disputes over land, which becomes a scarce and valuable resource as population grows, mineral resources are discovered, and markets for agricultural and industrial products expand. Increasingly, rights to land are exchanged between strangers with the sole purpose of maximizing economic gain. A legalistic court is the ideal forum for asserting such rights; barriers to access, of the kind discussed above, are insignificant in view of the stakes involved. The second category is contracts for the purchase and sale of other commodities, including labor. With the introduction of a money economy, the rise of middlemen, the division of labor, the development of productive technology, the growth of national and international markets, the need for certainty and predictability in economic relationships, the increase in wage employment, etc., contracts proliferate between persons who are not linked by any other relationship. Many of these contracts will be transitory, single-purpose, one-shot occurrences; in others, one party will frequently wish to terminate a relationship that is potentially more enduring. In either instance, only a modern court has the power to compel performance of the contractual obligation or payment of some equivalent in money damages. The fragmentary evidence from many African countries confirms that both land and contract litigation do increase.

All of these developments may be just way stations on the road toward further changes in which negligent injuries supplant intentional wrongs, the termination of family relationships becomes a judicial preoccupation, and the enforcement of contractural rights is monopolized by large corporate entities.

THE GROWTH OF PROSECUTIONS AS AN EXPLANATION FOR
THE DECLINE IN CIVIL LITIGATION

If changes in the composition of civil litigation are difficult to measure, display ambiguous patterns, and permit only tentative and qualified explanations, the models of litigation suggest another set of changes that may be easier to perceive and analyze: the growing dominance of the court by criminal prosecutions. In tribal society the enduring, multiplex, affective relationship between antagonists has several consequences for the dispute process sought. The aggrieved individual has a considerable stake in obtaining redress: it is difficult to ignore a wrong inflicted by an intimate, especially one with whom the victim has frequent contact. At the same time the remedy must not be so harsh that it destroys the relationship. Tribal dispute institutions are adaptive to both these conditions. Because they lack officials who can initiate the dispute process, such institutions can function only where the disputant is proactive in seeking a remedy. And because they lack coercive power, they must obtain the consent of both parties to any solution and therefore cannot impose draconian sanctions. As a result, civil litigation predominates: wrongs are viewed as injuries to individuals. Crimes tend to be limited to witchcraft, recidivist theft, and of course injuries inflicted by persons outside the social group within which disputes are settled.

In the heterogeneous mass society of contemporary western nations, where individuals who interact are connected only by tenuous, narrowly instrumental links, if they are not strangers, the victim has less motivation to exert himself to redress his grievance. Although he may want compensation for his injury, he is likely to seek it from sources other than his assailant and to be relatively uninterested in what happens to the latter. Changes in dispute institutions complement these social structural changes. Police are established and assume part of the task of asserting grievances, which the citizenry progressively abandons. The same institutional changes that make the courts significantly less accessible to the average citizen render them more accessible to the state apparatus, which has now become large, bureaucratic, specialized, professional, and endowed with coercive powers. The colonial state is not only compelled, and equipped, to take over the redress of grievances, it is eager to do so, for the maintenance of public order—the *Pax Britannica*—is its first, and for long its principal, *raison d'être*.

I therefore hypothesized that prosecutions would increase rapidly as the judiciary was westernized, police and prosecutorial staffs were created and expanded, and social structure was gradually changed. I have already shown that this is true for Kenya (see Tables 10.4–10.5). As Table 10.9 demonstrates, it is generally true throughout Africa. Uganda, Ghana, Nigeria, and Tanzania also exhibit dramatic increases in the number of prosecutions, which far outrun population growth. Furthermore, these increases are more pronounced in urban areas, where institutional and social changes are greatest (compare Lagos with the rest of Nigeria, or southern Ghana and Togo with the northern territories of Ghana and northern Togo). Zambia is only apparently an exception: the sharp drop in prosecutions in 1969 actually reflects the transfer of those cases from native and local courts to district magistrates.

Prosecutions, like civil litigation, change not only in number but also in character. In tribal societies, a large proportion of the wrongs committed are redressed in some fashion, but the sanctions are relatively mild. As criminal prosecutions displace tort actions in modern societies, the proportion of wrongs redressed must decline, despite the increase in the absolute number of prosecutions. Professionalization increases the cost of both courts and enforcement staff, which therefore must be reduced in size (relative to population, if not absolutely) and centralized. This new professional enforcement bureaucracy can personally observe only an insignificant fraction of all wrongs; furthermore, it cannot rely on victims to report those wrongs, since the latter will tend to "lump it" rather than petition an inaccessible institution for a remedy that may be denied or be unresponsive to their needs; finally, the bureaucracy can prosecute only a small proportion of the wrongs reported. I hypothesized that the consequence of this decline in the proportion of wrongs redressed would be a shift from special deterrence, in which the penalty is intended to affect the future behavior of the particular offender, to general deterrence, in which the offender is punished as an example to the rest of society. General deterrence requires the imposition of exemplary punishments; there is ample evidence that the severity of punishments increased throughout the colonial era—more rapidly in cities than in the rural areas—and has continued to increase since independence.

The increases in the number of criminal prosecutions, and in the harshness of penalties, are significant quantitative changes in the pattern of litigation. Nevertheless, a criminal prosecution is still initiated in response to a complainant, even if he is subordinated to the professional enforcement staff; it can therefore be seen as a dispute between individuals despite the fact that their relationship is dominated by the interest of the state in general deterrence. But as the state increasingly becomes involved in economic activities (as a regulator in capitalist countries, as a participant in socialist), administrative offenses are created. Prosecutions for violating administrative regulations are a qualitatively different proceeding, for there is no victim other than the state, represented by a proliferating number of administrative agencies. I therefore hypothesized that with social and institutional change, administrative offenses would increase in numbers and come to dwarf prosecutions for violation of the penal code.

The data, though incomplete, are uniform. In Kenya in 1966, for instance, there were 22,875 penal code offenses, or 12% of the 191,914 prosecutions; but the latter figure does not include tax cases, which are the single most numerous category (for example, there were 172,652 tax cases alone in 1962) (Kenya, Legislative Council 1962:col.592); if these were included, the contribution of penal code offenses would be approximately halved, reducing them to about 5% of all criminal cases. Other countries also experienced the growing dominance of victimless administrative offenses, although the content varied: violations of Native Authority rules in Ghana (Korsah Commission 1951:10), unauthorized

TABLE 10.9

Relative Proportions of Civil Litigation and Criminal Prosecutions in African Primary Courts by Country (or Region) and Year [a]

Year	Country or region	Civil cases filed	Criminal prosecutions filed	Civil litigation as a percentage of total cases filed	Criminal prosecution as a percentage of total cases filed
1910	N. Nigeria (Kano)	19,473	1,267	94	6
1923	Uganda [b]	64	11	85	15
1927	Kenya	26,615	5,322	83	17
1929	N. Nigeria	137,002	38,588	78	22
1930	Tanzania [c]	1,307	639	67	33
1931	Nigeria[d]	350,000	150,000	70	30
1936–1940	Botswana	—	—	81	19
1937	N. Nigeria	182,000	60,000	75	25
	S. Nigeria [d]	176,000	85,000	67	33
1938	Zambia	11,332	7,801	59	41
1939	N. Nigeria	143,300	62,131	70	30
1943	Ghana	—	—	c.50	c.50
1945	Tanzania	56,383	50,989	52	48
1948	Kenya	44,116	50,517	47	53
1949	Zambia (Copperbelt)	3,414	3,155	52	48
1949	Nigeria	405,621	168,020	71	29
	N. Nigeria	240,536	85,708	74	26
	W. Nigeria	69,757	34,494	67	33
	E. Nigeria	92,884	44,399	68	32
	Lagos	2,444	3,419	42	58
1950	Ghana (Colony)	—	—	36	64
1945–1958	Ghana [e]	728	1,017	42	58
1950	Uganda [b]	210	233	47	53

Year	Place				
1950–1951	Ghana				
	Colony	29,851	53,164	36	64
	Ashanti	18,351	35,209	34	66
	NT and NT[f]	7,411	13,958	35	65
	S. Togo	2,920	1,938	60	40
1955	Tanzania[g]	1,169	2,059	36	64
1956	Tanzania[g]	2,597	5,241	33	67
1958	Tanzania	2,773	5,516	33	67
1959	Rhodesia	56,800	87,900	39	61
	Native Commissioners' Courts	1,872	24,500	7	93
	African Courts	7,150	0	100	0
1960	Tanzania	51,104	92,852	36	64
1961	Zambia	36,380	59,998	38	62
1966–1970	Botswana	—	—	13	87
1968	Kenya	42,713	272,842	14	86
1969	Tanzania	47,223	182,550	21	79
	Emaoi	—	—	31	69
	Maji ya Chai	—	—	25	75
	W. Meru	—	—	28	72
1969	Zambia	60,769	12,670	84	16
	(Copperbelt)	—	—	51	49

[a] Sources: Aplin (1931:E1); Blackall Committee (1943:23); Korsah Commission (1951:10); Brooke Commission (1952:13, 28, 44–45; 1953: Tables D–G); Sutcliffe (1959); Robinson Commission (1961:13–14); Brokensha (1966:138–140); Fallers (1969:87, 96); Spalding *et al.* (1969:284); Roberts (1972:111–112); DuBow (1973:56–61, 154, 156).

[b] One subcounty court in Busoga.

[c] Mwanza District only.

[d] Excluding Lagos.

[e] One court in Larteh.

[f] Northern Territories and North Togo.

[g] Northern Province.

193

residence in Zambia (Clifford 1960:11), tax default in Uganda (Russell 1971:11). Tanzania is the one exception. Administrative offenses, which had come to outnumber penal code violations by three to one in the late 1950s, dropped rapidly after independence. Prosecutions for contempt of court—a peculiar administrative offense that seeks to promote obedience to legal institutions—declined from nearly 10% of the caseload to nothing. And most of those prosecutions that did involve penal code violations were true disputes, in which a private complainant had chosen (or had been instructed by the court to choose) a private prosecution rather than a civil action, but nonetheless sought, and obtained, compensation (DuBow 1973:51, 56-61, 156, 176–177).

These changes in the manner in which, and the extent to which, the state uses courts to control social, and especially economic, behavior clearly deserve further analysis. But my purpose in this chapter is to explain patterns of civil litigation. There are several ways in which the latter can be influenced by the former. First, criminal prosecution can provide an alternative mechanism for handling an interpersonal dispute. I have suggested above that some disputants in both Kenya and Tanzania are channeled into criminal rather than civil procedures; but the numbers in Kenya are relatively small, and thus such ''remedy shopping'' is insufficient to explain all of the change in civil litigation rates.

However, the growing use of the court by the state may affect civil litigation more significantly in a different fashion: by changing public perceptions of the court. I hypothesized that as the number of criminal prosecutions rose, as more of them involved regulatory offenses, and as the latter grew to outnumber civil cases so that regulatory offenses dominated the time and ultimately the structure and process of the court, potential litigants would cease to see the court as a forum for airing disputes between individuals and come to view it as the instrument of an alien state, part of the apparatus of control. Perceiving it that way, they would avoid it. This proposition requires some elaboration before I attempt to test it. I have used the ratio of civil to criminal cases as the index of ''criminalization'' in the belief that, if the ratio remains high, citizens will not see the court primarily as an agency of control, no matter how large the absolute number of prosecutions may grow. I have concentrated upon the prosecution of administrative offenses for two reasons: such prosecutions vindicate only a state, not a private, interest, and they are more prone to affect the perception of the ordinary citizen who is likely to have violated, and to have friends and relatives who have violated, at least one of the numerous regulations, whereas he is not likely to be a murderer or a thief.

The data on rates of civil litigation and of prosecutions for penal code and administrative offenses strongly support this hypothesis. Civil litigation rates in most African countries rose until the early post-war period. During this time civil cases lost their predominance over criminal prosecutions but did retain a rough equality (see Table 10.9). In the succeeding 20 years, however, criminal prosecutions came to outnumber civil cases, often by four or five to one, and an increasing proportion of these prosecutions (two-thirds to three-quarters) concerned violations of administrative regulations. Although I have data on civil litigation rates for only a few countries, those rates show a general decline since the war.

The picture in Kenya is even clearer (see Tables 10.4–10.5). The civil litigation rate in 1931 is nearly four times the rate of criminal prosecutions. Although both continued to grow, prosecutions grew more rapidly; when they finally outstripped civil cases, the civil litigation rate began to fluctuate and then gradually to decline at a pace that accelerated as the prosecution of administrative offenses came to dominate the courts in the 1960s. Between 1948 and 1971 prosecutions increased by a factor of five, whereas civil cases ended the period slightly below where they began; during that period the prosecution rate more than doubled, whereas the civil litigation rate declined to less than a third. This pattern is repeated in almost all rural districts, whether agricultural or pastoral, more or less westernized; but it does not characterize the cities, where litigants may still want something from the court even though they view it as a symbol of coercion, and where in any case they have few alternatives.

Furthermore, the deviant case of Zambia helps to substantiate the hypothesis (Spalding *et al.* 1969:284–285). In Zambia, criminal prosecutions increased steadily as a proportion of all litigation from the 1930s to the 1960s, outnumbering civil cases as early as 1947; and administrative offenses represented a growing fraction of the category. Civil litigation reached its absolute peak in 1957 (I believe that the rate of civil litigation began to decline even earlier, although I have no adequate population figures). But this decline in civil litigation halted between 1963 and 1965, when the number of criminal prosecutions suddenly started to drop, and reversed dramatically in 1966, when most of the criminal jurisdiction of the native and local courts was transferred to the district magistrates. In 1969 the ratio of civil to criminal cases in Zambia (alone of those countries for which I have data) was greater than one; and the proportion of civil cases (84%) resembled that in many African countries 50 years earlier. And in Zambia, and only in Zambia, the rate of civil litigation (15.2 cases filed per 1000 people per year) reached the level at which it had been found in much of Africa 50 years earlier.

CONCLUSION

I hope this chapter has justified my decision to conceive of the westernization of primary courts in Africa as an instance of the imposition of law, and to view the consequences of that imposition from the litigant's perspective. Legal institutions, whether they are imposed or evolve organically, do not determine behavior; they constrain it, offering new alternatives at the same time that they modify the old. Within these constraints, people choose whether or not to use the westernized courts, and the strategies they will employ if they do litigate. The exercise of these choices has very significant consequences. It determines the law that will be applied and thus influences the outcome of the dispute; in this sense people make law and decide cases. It affects the future relationships of the parties and settings; people embedded in tribal social structures and therefore possessed of alternative forums for airing interpersonal disputes will increasingly shun modernized courts as those are perceived to be instruments of governmental discipline.

Despite huge gaps and flaws in the evidence, I am satisfied that the theory I proposed is basically sound. Social structure and institutional structure do inter- act to produce patterns of litigation. Two major trends in litigation are discern- ible as social and institutional variables are changed. First, tribal social struc- tures and modern courts are incompatible; the introduction of the latter into the former leads to a decline in tribal litigation. This should be a matter of some con- cern, regardless of one's views concerning the relative worth of tribal and modern society. Tribal social relations can be found in all societies, irrespective of their level of technological development or mode of political organization. We are constantly rediscovering multiplex, enduring, affective relationships in economic life, in the extended family, within large institutions, in residential groupings, even between criminals and their victims. Tribal litigation is inte- grative; it preserves and even strengthens those relationships. If courts are modernized, one forum for tribal litigation is removed. Furthermore, the mere availability of modern courts seems to undermine tribal dispute processing elsewhere in the society. Many commentators recently have deplored the absence of tribal modes of dispute processing in contemporary western society (for example, Danzig 1973; Danzig and Lowy 1975; Nader and Singer 1976).

The second trend complements the first. Modern social structures and modern courts are compatible; the rate of modern litigation will rise in modern courts in urban areas, and only there. And modern litigation contributes to the development and maintenance of modern social structures in much the same fashion that tribal litigation integrated tribal society. In its ideal form litigants, who are strangers to each other aside from the focus of the dispute and are equals in resources and competence, assert competing claims in terms of a law that favors neither before an impartial judge who unilaterally pronounces and enforces an all-or-nothing judgment. There have certainly been times and places when actual litigation approximated this ideal type, though it is not clear from my data that litigation in contemporary urban Africa does so, or ever will. But the predictable enforcement of contractual obligations, the predication of tort liability upon fault, the free alienation of, and development of security interests in, property, even the greater freedom to form and dissolve family relation- ships—all can be found in the recent history of western legal systems. And this contribution of litigation to modern society can be valued on grounds that com- mand a broad consensus. Modern litigation is an expression of liberal political and economic theory. The individual litigant, in seeking to maximize his self- interest under clearly defined rules, is seen by classical economics as competing in a free market and thus furthering the most efficient allocation of resources.

Similarly, the modern litigant, in freeing himself from traditional social constraints and asserting his political rights, is achieving maximum self-realization
of his individuality. Thus the introduction of modern courts into modernizing
societies does foster liberal values.

But this chapter, like other recent analyses (for example, Galanter 1974;
Unger 1976), also suggests that these attributes of litigation under liberal
capitalism are short-lived, no more than a brief, transitional way station on the
road toward patterns of litigation that offend against all the values of the rule of
law. Three deviations from the ideal type of modern litigation are already visible
in contemporary Africa. First, there is a decline in the accessibility of the court
to individual litigants, and warning of a much more radical curtailment in the
future, as primary courts are thoroughly professionalized. In modern society,
where much interaction occurs between strangers who are not bound together by
any relationship, individual disputants confronted with an increasingly inaccessible tribunal will simply terminate the relationship—they will "lump it"
(Felstiner 1974). Second, there is growing dominance of the court by criminal
prosecution, and especially by administrative offenses, which renders it less
attractive to potential litigants. Third, adjudication in modern courts, whether
civil or criminal, becomes increasingly superficial—a rubber-stamping of decisions reached elsewhere.

In addition to the accentuation of the trends just described, three other
developments have been reported by students of litigation in western society,
and are clearly incipient in non-western societies as well. Civil litigation is
increasingly dominated by large corporate entities, generally private (Wanner
1974, 1975; Galanter 1975), in much the same way that state prosecutions
dominate the entire court structure. These large entities, "repeat players" in
Galanter's terminology (1974), find that they can use the civil process efficiently
and successfully to extract money from, or compel actions by, individual, one-
shot defendants. Their total dominance of such litigation transforms it from
adjudication into a form of administration. Second, these large entities find that
they can extend their control outside the courtroom, structuring their behavior
and the behavior of those with whom they transact business in such a way as to
ensure a favorable outcome in any future litigation; thus even what appears to be
adjudication is in fact administration, when viewed from a larger perspective.
Finally, the costliness of adjudication, even to large entities, leads to the development of specialized administrative tribunals that handle an increasing proportion
of disputes—and are even more readily dominated by repeat players than are the
courts (Bernstein 1955; but compare Baum 1977).

The displacement of modern litigation by administration, like the displacement of tribal disputing by modern litigation, should also be a source of concern.
Liberal values are subverted. Because litigation no longer takes place between
equals, but rather between large entities and individuals who differ enormously
in strength, we can expect resources to be misallocated and social and political
freedom to be frustrated. And because the courts are shunned, both by indi-

viduals and by institutions, the rule of law, which depends on adjudication, is nullified. The significant rules of behavior are legislated by large entities, not by a democratic government. The model of post-liberal society consists of an oligarchy of corporate entities whose size, organization, and resources give them overwhelming advantages in political, social, and economic life. Individuals relate, if at all, only as co-members of the same entity. Litigation is merely a relatively unimportant mechanism by which those entities exercise control, and is almost totally irrelevant to individuals except as they are controlled by it. This dismal picture suggests that efforts to fiddle with litigation in post-modern society—to restore it to the ideal–typical model of liberal adjudication, for example, by extending legal representation or by creating new adjudicative institutions—are misguided. Rather, the issue is how to regain democratic control over the large entities themselves, which dominate the legal system just as they dominate the rest of society.

REFERENCES

Abel, R. L.
    1973   "A comparative theory of dispute institutions in society." *Law & Society Review 8:* 217–347.
    1979   "Theories of litigation in society: 'Modern' dispute institutions in 'tribal' society and 'tribal' dispute institutions in 'modern' society as alternative legal forms." In E. Blankenburg, E. Klausa, and H. Rottleuthner (eds.), *Alternative Rechtsformen und Alternativen zum Recht, Jahrbuch für Rechtssoziologie und Rechtstheorie, Band IV.* Opladen: Westdeutscher Verlag.
Afrika Institut, Leiden, and the Royal Tropical Institue, Amsterdam.
    1955   *Future of Customary Law in Africa.* Record of a symposium held in Amsterdam. Leiden: Universitaire Pers.
Aplin, H. D.
    1931   *Report on Native Administration in Tanganyika Territory.* Zomba, Nyasaland: Government Printer.
Barnett, T. E.
    1965   "A Report on Local Courts in East Africa." Unpublished.
Baum, L.
    1977   "Judicial specialization, litigant influence, and substantive policy: The Court of Customs and Patent Appeals." *Law & Society Review 11:* 823–850.
Bernstein, M. H.
    1955   *Regulating Business by Independent Commission.* Princeton, N. J.: Princeton University Press.
Blackall Committee (Gold Coast)
    1943   *Report of the Native Tribunals Committe of Enquiry.* Accra: Government Printing Department.
Brokensha, D.
    1966   *Social Change at Larteh, Ghana.* Oxford: Clarendon Press.
Brooke Commission
    1952   *Report of the Native Courts (Northern Provinces) Commission of Inquiry.* Lagos, Nigeria: Government Printer.

1953   *Native Courts Commissions of Inquiry, 1949 to 1952, Appendix and Summe⸱ ⸱ of Conclusions and Recommendations.* Lagos, Nigeria: Government Printer.

Bushe Commission
1934   *Report of the Commission of Inquiry into the Administration of Justice in Kenya, Uganda and the Tanganyika Territory in Criminal Matters, May 1933* (Cmd.4623). London: HMSO.

Clifford, W.
1960   *Criminal Cases in the Urban Native Courts.* Lusaka, Zambia: Ministry of Local Government and Social Welfare.

Danzig, R.
1973   "Toward the creation of a complementary decentralized system of criminal justice." *Stanford Law Review 26*:1.

Danzig, R., and M. J. Lowy
1975   "Everyday disputes and mediation in the United States: A reply to Professor Felstiner." *Law & Society Review 9*:675–694.

DuBow, F. L.
1973   "Justice for People: Law and Politics in the Lower Courts of Tanzania." Doctoral dissertation, Department of Sociology, University of California, Berkeley.

East Africa High Commission, Statistical Department
1950   *African Population of Kenya Colony and Protectorate: Geographical and Tribal Studies.* Nairobi: East African Statistical Department.

Fallers, L. A.
1969   *Law Without Precedent: Legal Ideas in Action in the Courts of Colonial Busoga.* Chicago: University of Chicago Press.

Felstiner, W. L. F.
1974   "Influences of social organization on dispute processing." *Law & Society Review 9*:63–94.

Frank, J.
1949   *Courts on Trial: Myth and Reality in American Justice.* Princeton, N.J.: Princeton University Press.

Galanter, M.
1974   "Why the 'haves' come out ahead: Speculations on the limits of legal change." *Law & Society Review 9*:95–160.
1975   "Afterword. Explaining litigation." *Law & Society Review 9*:347 368.

Haydon, E. S.
1960   *Law and Justice in Buganda.* London: Butterworth.

Keay, E. A., and S. S. Richardson
1966   *The Native and Customary Courts of Nigeria.* London: Sweet & Maxwell.

Kenya, African Affairs Department
1948–1957   *Annual Reports.* Nairobi: Government Printer.

Kenya, Judicial Department
1955–1970   *Annual Reports.* Nairobi: Government Printer.

Kenya, Legislative Council
1951   *Debates.* Nairobi: Government Printer.
1962   *Debates.* Nairobi: Government Printer.

Kenya, Ministry of Finance and Economic Planning, Statistical Division
1971   *Kenya Population Census 1969* (3 vols.). Nairobi: Government Printer.

Kenya, Native Affairs Department
1925–1947   *Annual Reports.* Nairobi: Government Printer.

Korsah Commission (Gold Coast)
1951   *Report of Commission on Native Courts.* Accra: Government Printing Department.

Laurenti, L.
n.d.   "Urbanization trends and prospects." In L. Laurenti and J. Gerhart, *Urbanization in Kenya.* New York: Ford Foundation.

Morgan, W. T. W., N. Manfred, and P. Schaffer
    1966   *Population of Kenya: Density and Distribution: A Geographical Introduction to the Kenya Popula-
            tion Census, 1962.* Nairobi: Oxford University Press. ·
Muslim, A. F.
    1976   "The Administration of Justice in Urban Kenya." Unpublished.
Nader, L., and L. R. Singer
    1976   "Law in the future: What are the choices: Dispute resolution." *California State Bar Jour-
            nal 51*:281.
Perlman, M. L.
    1970   "Law and the status of women in Uganda: A systematic comparison between the Gan-
            da and the Toro." *Tropical Man 2*:60 (Yearbook of the Department of Social Research,
            Royal Tropical Institute, Amsterdam).
Phillips, A.
    1945   *Report on Native Tribunals.* Nairobi: Government Printer.
Roberts, S.
    1972   "The survival of the traditional Tswana courts in the national legal system of
            Botswana." *Journal of African Law 16*:103–129.
Robinson Commission (Southern Rhodesia)
    1961   *Report of the Commission Appointed to Inquire into and Report on Administrative and Judicial Func-
            tions in the Native Affairs and District Courts Departments.* Salisbury: Government Printer.
Russell, P. H.
    1971   "The Administration of Justice in Uganda: Some Problems and Proposals." Unpub-
            lished report to the Attorney General of Uganda.
Saltman, M.
    1971   "A Restatement of Kipsigis Customary Law." Doctoral dissertation, Department of
            Anthropology, Brandeis University.
Singh, C.
    1972   "Structure, Organization, and Personnel of Courts in the Republic of Kenya." Paper
            presented to the Conference on Civil Procedure in Anglophonic Africa, Nairobi,
            November.
Spalding, F. C., E. L. Hoover, and J. C. Piper
    1969   "One nation, One judiciary: The lower courts of Zambia." *Zambia Law Journal 2* (1–2).
Sutcliffe, R. B.
    1959   "A note on the use of local courts in the Northern Province of Tanganyika, with special
            reference to the Masai." Pp. 29–32 in R. Apthorpe (ed.), *From Tribal Rule to Modern
            Government.* Lusaka, Zambia: Rhodes-Livingstone Institute.
Trubek, D. M.
    1972   "Max Weber on law and the rise of capitalism." *Wisconsin Law Review* 1972:720.
Unger, R. M.
    1976   *Law in Modern Society: Toward a Criticism of Social Theory.* New York: Free Press
Wanner C.
    1974   "The public ordering of private relations: Part One: Initiating civil cases in urban trial
            courts." *Law & Society Review 8*:421–440.
    1975   "The public ordering of private relations: Part Two: Winning civil court cases." *Law
            & Society Review 9*:293–306.

11

CAPITATION IN COLONIAL AND POST-COLONIAL NIGER: ANALYSIS OF THE EFFECTS OF AN IMPOSED HEAD-TAX SYSTEM ON RURAL POLITICAL ORGANIZATION

JAMES T. THOMSON

This chapter[1] highlights consequences of a head-tax system imposed by the French colonial regime (1899–1960) in the West African Niger colony and rigorously enforced until 1976 by the civilian regime (1960–1974) and the military regime (1974 to date) which have thus far governed the independent Niger Republic. Ramifications of the tax system for official–commoner[2] relations, ending in destruction of local organizational capacity and consequent environmental degradation, are stressed.

Briefly, the analytic theme asserts that commoners of a rural district in south-central Niger saw the capitation-tax system merely as a tool enabling officials to capture a large part of their annual income. Few commoners found any positive, tangible returns from tax-financed programs. Most therefore considered tax evasion a legitimate way out of an onerous relationship. Moreover, evaders came out ahead in terms of real income, even after bribing traditional tax officials for "exemptions."

---

[1] Research in Niger during 1970–1972, upon which this chapter draws, was funded by the Foreign Area Fellowship Program. That assistance is here gratefully acknowledged.

[2] In referring to rural residents as "commoners," not "citizens," I adopt the terms used by both Hausa-speaking officials and rural residents.

201

The crucial significance of tax evasion, however, lay not in the funds saved but in the dependency relationships created between evaders and exemption-dispensing officials. Social consequences were enormous, as were indirect costs associated with the resulting loss of village collective-action capabilities. Ramifying through the hybrid French administrative-traditional law system, this dependence sapped local ability to set up and run organizations without which public goods indispensable to the maintenance of village environments and economic systems could not be produced. These goods included a stable land-tenure system, effective regulation of livestock movements, maintenance of adequate wood and ground cover, cooperative marketing associations, credit mutuals, and the like. In effect, rural villages in the area were stripped of capacity to handle local problems. Since they had lost, among other things, the ability to manage renewable natural resources, and in the absence of outside programs to provide these goods, the way was paved for increasing environmental degradation and local institutional inertia in the face of this and other pressing problems. The same conditions characterize most Hausa areas of Niger, undermining efforts to develop the rural economy and to improve living conditions for rural dwellers.

The argument is developed in five sections. The first describes evolution of the capitation system from the pre-colonial through the colonial and post-colonial civilian and military regimes, within the changing political–institutional context. Second, public-goods theory as it bears on the problem under discussion—the social consequences of an imposed capitation system—is briefly reviewed. Third, several administrative law cases illustrating tax-system operations are presented, followed, fourth, by an examination of the same in the light of relevant public-goods theory. Fifth, broader social consequences implied by this analysis are elaborated and evaluated.

EVOLUTION OF HEAD-TAX SYSTEM

Inuwa District,[3] the jurisdiction within Mirria County, Niger, where field research for this chapter was done, lies in the core area of the pre-colonial Damagaram Sultanate (Salifou 1970, Dunbar 1970). (See Figure 11.1.) Damagaram was a fairly typical nineteenth-century central Sudanic state, involved in loose vassal relations with the Kanem-Bornu Empire to the east (Barth 1857/1965: III, 73) and deriving its wealth from a combination of local production, imposts levied on the trans-Saharan trade, and slave-raiding forays into emirates of the Sokoto Caliphate to the south.

PRE-COLONIAL TAX SYSTEM

Damagaram rulers, in accordance with then-prevailing African statecraft (Urvoy 1949: 114–120; Smith 1960; Barth 1857/1965), split the sultanate into ter-

[3] A pseudonym, as are all Inuwa personal and place names referred to in the text. County and superior regime official, personal, and place names are the real ones, however.

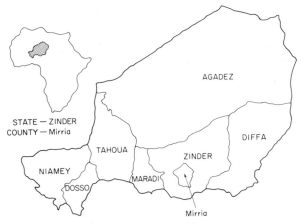

Figure 11.1   The Republic of Niger

ritorial fiefs and allocated them to members of the Damagaram court. Court officials resided in Zinder, the capital, and ran their fiefs through agents posted to
district seats. The latter in turn controlled village headmen in their sectors.
These district-level appointees acted as general administrators, held courts (often
assisted by Muslim law judges—*alkalai*), and collected taxes (Dunbar 1970:
127–133, 156–164).

Under this and subsequent regimes commoners were totally excluded from the
policymaking process. They had no say in decisions setting taxes or allocating
state funds. Like other vital policy issues, these questions were reserved for the
political class, the chiefs (*sarakai*). Commoners could react only after chiefs had
made fiat decisions on tax matters. However, they were not utterly exposed in
dealing with their leaders. A commoner could usually threaten to move
elsewhere, switching allegiance from one chief to another within Damagaram
State. Since the chiefs' status at all levels in a labor-intensive, warfare economy
depended on the number of persons they controlled (Raulin 1965: 119–129;
n.d.:3; Nicholas 1967: 115), the threat carried weight. How much weight varied
with the number of dependents who might leave with a dissident commoner.
Those heading large families enjoyed some advantage in these situations by
comparison with heads of smaller units.

Chiefs thus operated in a partially competitive market and had to moderate
abuses of power to retain the following necessary to assure continued success in
office. This made them on balance more responsive to subjects' needs: exploitation was permissible within limits, but successful chiefs did provide some
minimum of security and protection.

Tax-system organization did not appear to promote this result. Court officials
worried first about meeting obligations to the Damagaram chief and maintaining themselves in appropriate style (Dunbar 1970: 127–128). Since they did not
reside in their fiefs, they had less direct experience of the costs imposed by their
exactions. However, lower-level officials did struggle with the dilemma of

meeting superiors' demands for grain taxes, tribute, and wartime levies, while maintaining acceptable conditions locally to avoid loss of residents and erosion of the tax base. One infers that local officials, particularly village heads, attempted to shield their followers (and themselves) at least partially from their superiors' abusive demands. Under-reporting population figures created a margin of safety by reducing taxes demanded below the theoretical tax liability of the community, and most agents followed this practice.[4]

COLONIAL TAX SYSTEMS

The French made up for European manpower shortages during the early post-conquest period (1899–1921) by using traditional tax institutions in modified form, just as they adapted other pre-colonial government forms to their purposes. They tried to curb the perceived abuses of tax-farming Damagaram officials, and in 1914 even sacked nearly half of the 32 district chiefs (agents) operating in Mirria Subdivision, the core area of the old Damagaram State. But eventually the French gave in and, for want of a cheaper, more efficient system, worked through the traditional bureaucracy of the chiefs. The French colonial commandants controlled the top of the system, but in tax as well as other government activities, their orders were implemented under varying degrees of supervision by the Damagaram authorities and their rural agents.

The major change in Damagaram tax measures introduced by the new military regime—demand for payment in European cash rather than in kind or cowrie shell currency—reflected French West African colonial policy of forcing rural savanna residents into greater involvement in the market economy. Householders could no longer meet their fiscal obligations by merely handing over a portion of their cereal harvests to authorities. Instead, they had to pay in French currency. The restricted size of the monetized economy in Mirria Subdivision forced many residents to seek wage-paying jobs in coastal French and English colonies, particularly Nigeria, Ghana, and the Ivory Coast. This placed a premium on the opportunity to evade taxation, because in most cases cash could be obtained only through forced separation from family and home community.[5] French colonial military draft and corvée labor policies were viewed as equally onerous.[6]

[4] Henri Gaden (1903: 768) indicates that no tax rolls were established by the pre-colonial state, so the Damagaram chief could easily be shortchanged by his subordinates. By the same token, village and district heads could protect their constituents. Dunbar (1970: 156) argues that keen competition for titled offices in the Damagaram bureaucracy probably encouraged candidates for occupied posts to inform the Damagaram chief when incumbents permitted excessive tax evasion in their jurisdictions.

[5] Jean Suret-Canale (1964: 45, 290, 437) discusses the capitation system as generally applied in the French African colonies, and its tendency to promote migration as well as local production of cash crops where possible. Peanuts were introduced to Niger as a cash crop by the colonial regime's fiat decision in 1925. See Thomson (1976:106).

[6] Personal information from the chief of Inuwa District, Mirria County.

In post-World War II reforms, *corvée* labor was suppressed, and the traditional chiefs lost authority to fine and flog parties judged guilty of violations. Chiefs' courts could thus no longer impose settlements, which undercut their prestige in the eyes of commoners. But taxes continued to be collected as before and many chiefs parlayed this into an alternative source of power, as will be seen presently. Chiefs and headmen received a commission of taxes collected, each householder being required to furnish the total funds owed for all individuals and livestock inscribed on his tax card.[7]

POST-COLONIAL TAX SYSTEM

Independence in 1960 changed both institutions and personnel. Nigerien politicians and administrators rapidly replaced most French colonial officials as the operative authorities in the new state. Colonial programs launched to create infrastructures for a more effective transportation system and a more powerful national economy became the focus of more urgent efforts, and health, agricultural, veterinary, cooperative, and primary education services, among others, expanded. But the inherited colonial administrative structure remained largely intact, particularly because establishment of a single-party state in 1959 had throttled political competition before independence.

The general administrative framework approximated that of French public bureaucracy, with administrators (prefects and subprefects) posted to subnational jurisdictions to coordinate efforts of tax collectors, police, and various technical services (listed above) responsible for different aspects of development. However, all these state bureaucrats relied to some extent, often heavily, on cooperation and assistance from traditional authorities at the subcounty level. In Mirria County, such district officials were successors of pre-colonial and colonial chiefs (agents) who represented Damagaram court bureaucrats in rural jurisdictions.

Colonial capitation-tax procedures survived and prospered during the independence era. The regime, intent on collecting taxes as rapidly as possible in rural areas, continued to set commissions to encourage aggressive recovery of amounts owed by villagers. From November, when rates were announced, through January, local headmen earned 7% on all monies collected. Thereafter the rate fell off 2% every 3 months; any money delivered to county officials after July produced no commission at all.

Until mid-December, the Inuwa District chief habitually received taxes at home in his district seat. By late December, however, tax collection dominated all other government activities in the district, and district authorities rode out to encourage or enforce collection in the villages. The generally lucrative and politically rewarding official judicial activities of the district chief took second

---

[7] Individuals were formally liable to the capitation tax from the age of 12 through 60. Both male and female adults were liable.

place to timely payment of district taxes. Development programs suffered serious neglect until at least the bulk of funds had been extracted and turned over to the county government.

In this annual effort, the district chief's retinue of 25 riders—divided fairly evenly into traditional policemen and more prestigious counselors—worked the district village by village. Some five or six officials accompanied the chief. The other riders divided into two-man teams and toured their own sectors in repeated week-long outings, urging village headmen and residents alike to acquit themselves promptly of their fiscal obligations.

Initial visits were usually friendly and low-key. But as the weeks wore on, villages with arrears could expect more pressure from district officials. By February or March, communities who were behind in their payments had to deal with county administrative police (Republican Guards, the successors of the colonial *gardes de cercle*) who traveled armed and extracted as much of the outstanding taxes as possible. Though legally empowered to arrest delinquents and hold them at the county seat until their taxes were paid, guards were forbidden to rough up commoners who could not or would not pay. But floggings occurred annually in Inuwa District. According to one guard who worked Inuwa District during 1971,

> We beat them; if the commoner has something to sell, we beat him to force the sale. Even if he has nothing, we beat him, so others in the village will give him loans. If you take them to Mirria, they think you're not very tough. Us, we just beat them.[8]

Such incidents impressed on district residents the gravity of falling behind in tax payments.

Infrequently guards' behavior provoked a commoner to retaliation. These fights produced more illegal administrative violence, then arrest and short-term detention in Mirria. Guards might be disciplined for embezzling tax funds, but subprefects typically winked at informal floggings.

During most of the period 1960–1974, which included both the high and low points of prosperity in the Inuwa District economy during the preceding half century (1925–1974), commoners viewed taxation as an unmitigated evil. Average per capita income after independence peaked at about $90 (Memento statistique 1969:274).[9] But in rural areas, including the more prosperous peanut-growing region of south-central Niger, per capita income was substantially less. Within south-central Niger, as elsewhere, there were marked urban–rural

---

[8] Oral information from a Mirria County Republican Guard, interviewed while tax-collecting in Inuwa District, 19 February 1971.

[9] During the years 1968–1974, drought ravaged the Nigerien economy, reducing some rural dwellers to starvation levels and reversing the pre-1966 rise in per capita income. After 1974 as the Aïr uranium mines moved into full production, average per capita income rose, but benefits have still not been equally distributed.

disparities.[10] Meanwhile, head taxes rose from 755f CFA[11] in 1956 to 920f CFA in 1963 (Nicholas 1967: 154), and to 1450f CFA in 1972. This amount (about $6 at the 1972 exchange rate) appears minuscule until seen in the context of a maximum national average per capita income of $91. In addition, livestock owners paid head taxes on all animals except barnyard fowls. Nicholas (1967) reports that 95% of rural families devoted more than 10% of the household's collective budget to taxes, whereas 60% spent more than a quarter of the joint budget on taxes. Fiscal obligations claimed more than half the family budget in 3% of cases surveyed (Nicholas 1967: 235). These figures exaggerate slightly the amount of overall budget allocated to taxes because some individual income and expenditure escaped the survey. Nonetheless, they do suggest that taxes were a major budget item for almost all rural Nigerien families in Matamaye County. There were comparable situations elsewhere in Niger. For instance, in 1970–1971, in Maradi County, taxes claimed an estimated 40% of all monies commoners earned through peanut sales (Raynaut 1977: 166).

Imposing head taxes as a function of family size, rather than individual or family unit income or production, made the taxes yet more onerous because they were not related to variations in per capita land holdings. And these variations sharpened after 1960 as the remaining free bush was cleared and cultivated. The system also neglected annual production variations caused by persistent minor droughts—a function of locally erratic rainfall patterns—which plague the West African Sahel even in the best of years. The smallest of these minor droughts can devastate one or two villages within a district; larger ones strike several districts or even several counties. Under these conditions, as is clear to authorities and commoners alike, poor harvests will create hardship for some of the latter in any given year.

Nevertheless, officials collected taxes with consistency and increasing severity until the height of the major drought of the early 1970s. Only then were the hardest-hit districts accorded partial exemptions. Prior to that time, everybody paid, regardless of the success of the harvest. If proceeds from cash-crop sales did not meet the tax bill, various members of the family had either to borrow funds, sell goods, or find salaried work outside the village to raise the indispensable funds.

Thus taxes were a serious problem for most rural Nigeriens right up to the moment of their abolition by the Nigerien military regime in 1977. They were also of concern to officials, since human and livestock head taxes made up 25–30% of annual government income from 1960 to 1975 (Banque centrale 1966: 2–8), and declined as a source of revenue only after 1972, when uranium-sale profits rose.

---

[10] Nicholas (1967: 320–327) presents results of an intensive survey of domestic budgets of 295 family groupings of various size in Matamaye County (Canton de Kantché), which abuts Mirria County

[11] 250f CFA = approximately $1 during the period 1960–1975.

PUBLIC-GOODS THEORY

Over the past 2 decades, political economists have elaborated a theory of public goods which offers a framework for analyzing the problems of imposed capitation taxes in Inuwa District and elsewhere in Niger. Public goods[12] are characterized by *indivisibility*; once produced they are not subject to exclusion. Instead, they are readily available to all within the domain of the good in question, without regard to the individual consumer's participation in production or financing of the good. Thus they differ sharply from private goods, such as cars or cakes, which are divisible into discrete units subject to exclusion. Enjoyment of the latter depends upon the consumer's ability and willingness to pay for them.

National defense is an oft-cited example of a pure public good, because the associated security is not subject to exclusion. A tax-evading Nigerien commoner may give nothing to support the national army, but this in no way impairs his enjoyment of the good. Once a defense unit exists he is presumed, *ceteris paribus*, to enjoy security equal to that enjoyed by any commoner who does pay taxes.

This structure of public goods creates the difficulty faced by large groups trying to provide such goods for themselves on a joint but voluntary basis (Olson 1965). Each potential contributor can see that his enjoyment of the good depends almost totally on what others give, not on the size of his own contribution. His is an infinitesimal fraction of the total needed to finance production of the good. Only if all or most others give, can the good—for example, national defense—be provided. *But if most others do contribute, it will become available to him, regardless of whether he pays.* The failure of any single consumer to help produce the good by giving his fair share will not appreciably reduce the amount supplied.

Some potential consumers will actually give, but free-riders—those who withhold payment, assuming others will make theirs—ensure that funds collected will finance only a suboptimal supply of the good. Many potential consumers see that by refusing to give they can get the public good for nothing and keep the savings to buy private goods for their own exclusive enjoyment (in this example, millet, livestock, shelter, an additional wife, etc.). Eventually, donors conclude they are being exploited by selfish but rational free-riders. Under conditions of voluntary provision, donors can avoid exploitation only by not giving. In the end, inadequate financing may altogether preclude provision of the public good.

Traditionally this difficulty has been overcome by organizing provision of important public goods on a nonvoluntary basis. Governments are set up to resolve the financing problem by taxation. They compel contributions—taxes—through the threat of coercion.

---

[12] Ostrom (1974: 52–68) briefly analyzes public goods in relation to private goods, common property resources, and externalities.

However, as James M. Buchanan (1970: 51–69) asserts, this solution does not remove the temptation to free-ride. At the limit, consistent and efficient surveillance will make evasion too risky. But whenever a potential evader thinks he can get away with it, the incentive is there. In fact, it is heightened if tax collection is efficient enough to guarantee provision of the good at a reasonable level, because the successful evader can then enjoy both public goods, as a free-rider, and private goods as a paying consumer. By contrast, in a situation of voluntary provision a potential free-rider may gain the private, but lose the public, good if others adopt his strategy.

This reasoning is applicable to any tax system (Heidenheimer, Heclo, and Adams 1976: 235–238). It becomes doubly compelling whenever a taxpayer believes his tax burden is unjustly heavy but lacks the legal means of reducing it. The logic of evasion becomes even more attractive when the taxpayer opposes the uses to which tax revenues are put. It is suggested that, in addition to the universal logic of evasion, these two other elements tended to legitimize tax dodging in the eyes of many Inuwa District residents (Thomson 1976: 173–176).

These grievances tended to be mutually reinforcing in the Inuwa District politico-economic context. Residents thought that the high and regressive rates of taxation noted above brought few tangible returns in the form of government-provided goods and services.[13] Law and order, symbolized by the subprefect, usually exhausted the list of state-produced values as far as most district inhabitants were concerned. Even that, as will be seen, was not an unadulterated good. National government agencies dug some public village wells, ran a livestock disease-control program which created a public good by reducing risks of livestock ownership, and undertook some limited agricultural extension work. The last, along with expansion of primary education and adult literacy facilities, arguably generated public goods by improving skill levels, thus increasing area economic potential and longer-term opportunities for all residents. But these and other rural development programs had little real effect on the majority of rural residents. Moreover, those who did receive state-produced benefits often found themselves paying special illegal "fees" to get them.

HEAD-TAX CASES

The analytic framework used in assessing the following cases derives from John R. Commons's concept of institutions (1924/1959: 65–142; Ostrom 1976). He describes all institutions—political, economic, and moral—as *going concerns*, or collective undertakings by groups of individuals. Members organize their

---

[13] I did not systematically survey Inuwa resident's perceptions of the capitation system. However, this statement summarizes opinions expressed both directly during conversations with Inuwa informants and indirectly in accounts of a wide variety of administrative law cases recorded in the district.

behavior by reference to the *working rules* of the going concern. Taken together, these rules constitute an authoritative system of liberties, duties, rights, and exposures which stipulate, respectively, what actions any individual in the concern may, must, can and cannot engage in. That is, officials establish *liberties* by protecting actions from interference by others, *duties* by compelling compliance with others' claims, *rights* by enforcing claims against others, and *exposures* by refusing to enforce claims against others. Working rules are authoritative because the collective power of the going concern may be mobilized if necessary to enforce members' rights and liberties and to see that they fulfill their duties. The rules also define each individual's exposures—that is, the areas where he cannot prevent, by legal suit, damages that other members' actions may inflict on him. Since any institution embodies multiple offices and positions, endowed with different powers and liabilities, various individuals in the going concern inevitably exercise differential capabilities for action.

Using this concept of institutions, one can analyze any village or local community as a going concern. Working rules of the village going concern, as well as changes in them, can be determined by the "trouble case" method of analysis (Llewellyn and Hoebel 1941). It consists of in-depth interviews with informants selected for their knowledge of the history and resolution of trouble cases arising in the interactions of the going concern. When a substantial body of local administrative, land, and family law cases has been recorded, rules can be deduced from them. These rules will define the capabilities and weaknesses of the local and overriding regimes when dealing with specific types of problems as they confront the communities under study.

The following three cases (Thomson 1976: 182–187) reveal fundamental working rules of the pre-1976 head-tax system in Inuwa District. The first brief account reflects the official view of taxpayers' liability under the system. The second and third show how district residents tried, in collusion with officials, to reduce that liability.

CASE 1: VILLAGERS RETAXED TO REPLACE BURNED BILLS

In the Inuwa District village of Taa Bari, 200,000f CFA ($800) in bills collected by the village headman during the 1971–1972 tax campaign went up in smoke when a fire destroyed his hut. Upon decision of the subprefect, the district chief told Taa Bari commoners they would have to contribute another 200,000f CFA to cover the loss. At a village meeting, the headman's relatives pledged a major part, and the remainder was gotten together on subscription from other villagers. Those having unlisted eligible dependents face community pressure in such circumstances to contribute at least the amount of their illicit exemptions.

CASE 2: VILLAGE HEADMAN CHALLENGES "ILLEGAL" TAXATION PROCEDURES, BUT VILLAGERS OVERRULE HIM

In the Inuwa District village of Dajin Kowa resides the licenser, one of the district chief's counselors appointed by Mirria County officials to collect trade license fees in the district. He uses his ability to manipulate the formal rules governing license fees to promote his own political career by enhancing the welfare of his fellow villagers at the expense of overriding regime treasuries. Artisans resident in Dajin Kowa enjoy either reduced assessments or total exemption from the duty to pay fees on their activities (e.g., implement production, leather work, tailoring). The licenser rationalized these tax breaks as political economy measures, encouraging apprentice artisans to expand the scale of their operations and so create a more viable economy and firmer tax base. These instances of collusive tax evasion involve, in the narrow sense, private transactions between commoners and the local official. But they produce positive spillovers for Dajin Kowa people insofar as they do create a comparatively favorable situtaion for tradesmen within the village, facilitating provision of goods and services to residents.

The licenser also met commoner demand for tax relief by exercising his power to determine the taxes collected each rainy season on Dajin Kowa livestock unlisted during the quadrennial census. Mirria County Republican Guards normally inspect each compound throughout the jurisdiction for animals in excess of the householder's listed holdings. In Dajin Kowa, however, the guards permitted the licenser to tax on his own terms, thus giving him carte blanche to manipulate the formal national taxation rates on livestock. He put the question to his fellow villagers each year; they annually agreed that each household should donate 100f CFA to a village fund which was then turned over to the guards.

The Dajin Kowa headman challenged what he termed the unorthodox proceedings by commoners in the summer of 1970, invading the licenser's annual meeting at the village mosque and nearly precipitating a fight with his neighbor, the village Muslim cleric. Villagers separated the two but then agreed as usual to assess themselves at 100f CFA per household. Dajin Kowa residents were generally dissatisfied with the headman's performance in other tax matters—they frequently accused him of misappropriating tax funds for his own use (Thomson 1976: 126-128, 188-189)—and in effect publicly rebuked him for trying to impose more taxes on them regarding unlisted livestock.

CASE 5: PARTY-ADMINISTRATIVE CONFLICT IN ALAGWUM ESCALATES, REVEALING MASSIVE TAX EVASION

In 1964 the Mirria County section of the single national party (PPN-RDA—Parti Progressiste Nigérien-Rassemblement Démocratique Africain) created the first local political committee in Alagwum, an Inuwa District community. The Bugaaje headman of the ethnically mixed village promoted his Hausa assistant as president of the committee.

Isa, another Bugaaje, took the vice-presidency. Within the year, he operated as informal president of Alagwum village Bugaaje, who composed the majority of the local population. This set the stage for a fight over control of the village PPN-RDA committee. To consolidate his support, Isa tried to present himself as a champion of commoner interests by alleging abuses of power by both the Alagwum headman and the Inuwa District chief. He publicly accused the headman of illegally selling stray livestock and splitting the proceeds with his superior, the district chief.

Isa asserts that the two officials sought to discredit him by framing him as a cattle thief. Just before the 1965 harvest, they accused him of selling a stray cow, one of a herd of 10 stolen some months earlier, and pocketing the profit. The other animals had been recovered the previous fall when the thieves tried to sell them through a man who fenced stolen cows in a nearby county.

The district chief had Isa arrested on the charge and sent before the sub-prefect at the county seat (then Zinder). Perjured Quranic oaths by his oppo-nent, the president, and another Alagwum Hausa man convinced the county official that Isa was guilty as charged.[14] He ordered Isa to make restitution to the cattle fence, since the latter had already been forced to pay the original owner for the stolen cow. Isa's fellow villagers reviled him for a thief when he returned to get money for the reimbursement by auctioning family property. Having paid for the cow, Isa was to have been jailed.

The threat of prison and urging by the Zinder PPN–RDA authorities per-suaded him to counter his political opponents by exposing the extensive tax evasion in Alagwum village. This would implicate the district chief as well, since he exercised overriding authority in Alagwum.

Isa named 106 fellow villagers as tax evaders, including two of the head-man's sons. Further inquiry turned up another 30, more than doubling Alagwum tax rolls from 30 to 70 families. Though the subprefect still wanted to jail Isa, the Zinder PPN–RDA secretary-general persuaded him to drop the matter.

Back in Alagwum Isa was soon framed again, accused this time of assaulting a villager who had insulted village PPN–RDA officials. The case again went to the subprefect in Zinder, and was eventually turned over to the PPN–RDA secretary-general for disposition. This time the secretary-general held against Isa and then asked the Alagwum village residents to decide whether Isa should retain office as village PPN–RDA vice-president. The vote went against him because of his "investigatory tendencies."

Defeated, Isa immediately divorced his wife and left town. Eventually he moved his mother as well, because district officials made things difficult for her in his absence.

The following year, when Isa returned to Inuwa to pay his taxes, he learned from the chief that the missing cow had been found. This confirmed his innocence on the original charge, which the chief preferred to keep quiet. Isa agreed on condition that he get his money back, and the Inuwa chief promised to refund the amount personally after it became clear they would have trouble collecting either from the jailed cattle fence or from his brother, who then held the missing cow. But after 2 weeks without satisfaction Isa took his complaint to the subprefect without asking the chief's permission, and convinced the county official that the demand was legitimate. The subprefect contacted his counterpart in the neighboring county and the latter eventually

---

[14] It is almost universally accepted in Mirria County, as elsewhere in Niger, that lying while under oath sworn on the Quran inevitably subjects the perjuror to nasty, supernaturally imposed sanctions. See note 19.

extracted Isa's refund from the cattle fence's brother, closing the case. Isa then moved back to Alagwum.

TAX CASES: ANALYSIS

The first case reveals the cardinal rule of the Nigerien capitation system: taxes always had to be paid. Until their funds were actually banked with the county treasurer, commoners had not "paid" their taxes. The Taa Bari residents in this dispute admittedly turned over 200,000f CFA to their headman, but they still remained payers of last resort when the funds did not arrive. Since the headman and his immediate family were unable to cover the deficit, the subprefect authoritatively prescribed retaxation of the community's commoners. In such situations, and in the more numerous instances of tax embezzlement by local officials, county authorities normally went first to the village headmen directly involved. They or their families were expected to supply the missing funds either by liquidating personal property or by securing loans. But when such remedies failed to cover the deficit, the net was spread wider to include, first, relatives and then fellow villagers.

Commoners' exposure in this regard helps to explain the sort of massive tax evasion documented in Case 3. Tax evasion at the village level depended upon active or tacit collusion among all parties with detailed knowledge of local conditions. Included here were three groups of individuals: village commoners, village officials, and district officials. By informing county officials about illegal tax evasion, anyone from any of these groups could destroy conditions for successful (and profitable) evasion, as vice-president Isa did in the Alagwum political dispute.

Evasion depended on a total conspiracy of silence, maintained by personal interests that dissuaded anyone, but especially commoners, from talking out of turn. These incentives can be briefly described. Village headmen and the district chief each received rebates averaging 5% of the tax due on each taxable adult and unit of livestock. The Inuwa chief's counselors and traditional policemen had no authorization to accept any separate payments whatsoever. Thus, assuming 1972 taxation rate of 1,450f CFA per capita, each adult permitted to evade taxes cost headman and chief approximately 70f CFA each. Multiplying by four—an individual not listed in the quadrennial census would normally be exempt for 4 years—it follows that each evader cost each official about 280f CFA.

The tax evader, on these assumptions, stood to realize gross savings of 5800f CFA during the same period. Thus, commoner and colluding officials bargained over division of the potential net surplus—that is, 5240f CFA, and correspondingly smaller amounts for livestock.

The outcome depended not only on the negotiating skills of the parties, but also on the risks each perceived in the clandestine bribe bargain. These were partly a result of the commoners' (accurate) perception that officials might not honor the arrangement, as in Cases 1 and 3, or that some official might violate it by embezzling funds,[15] thus forcing retaxation. The danger of the deals' being made known to the wrong parties, and the consequences of such an exposure, also slightly affected bargaining, though in practice these risks were minimal. The capitation system, as applied in colonial and independent Niger, taxed individuals as individuals, not as members of a community liable for a global fiscal obligation. Thus no resident had a direct economic incentive to expose those who enjoyed exemptions.[16]

Revelations motivated by spite were also highly unlikely, first, because such conduct would be viewed as anti-social within the community (this attitude was clearly at the heart of Isa's fall from power in Case 3). Second, telltale commoners would have to deal subsequently with embarrassed superiors—the headman, the district chief's riders, and the chief himself. Those who failed to honor the conspiracy of silence could certainly be punished by officials refusing them future tax exemptions, imposing onerous duties, or, occasionally, excluding them from the benefits of development programs. Few villagers thus had any incentive to rat on their fellows.

Local officials had to discount potential gains from exempting villagers against probability and results of exposure. The probability was low. Mirria County officials simply lacked the manpower to execute a census without the aid of district and village authorities. The costs to county administrators of personally verifying a district's tax liability would have been prohibitive. Thus they relied on local administrators in deciding tax eligibility. The district chief, his riders, and village headman could thus engage in tax manipulations with relative security.

Local authorities who colluded with tax evaders might be publicly abused if their conduct came to light, but were almost never fined or dismissed from office for such behavior. In Case 3, neither the Alagwum headman nor the district chief lost his post, despite their complicity in a tax evasion scheme of magnificent proportions.[17]

---

[15] Thomson (1976: 188–192, 318–319) presents several cases of embezzlement and an analysis of how the capitation system pressured local officials into embezzling funds.

[16] Such was clearly not the case, for instance, under the *Ancien Régime* in France. There, tax evasion was a zero-sum game at the local level: evaders merely enhanced the burden of payers (Tocqueville 1856/1955: 125–128).

[17] Faulkingham (1970: 62) suggests that 50% of the taxable adults and livestock in a Madaoua County village 250 miles west of Inuwa District escaped taxation circa 1970. Robert B. Charlick estimates a much lower rate of "slippage," something of the order of 5%, in neighboring Matameye County. Personal communication, Philadelphia, November 1972.

Mirria County officials occasionally tried to counter evasion by arbitrarily increasing the tax liability of many villagers. A major case erupted in 1967–1968 as a result of this strategy. It was finally resolved through investigation by national officials, who authorized a recensus of Inuwa District, among others. The subprefect ultimately responsible for the arbitrary increases was transferred out of the active administration (Thomson 1976:193–197).

Faulkingham (1970: 63) asserts that the Nigerian national government sought to counter tax evasion by constant head-tax increases after 1960.

The chief probably felt compelled to permit at least some tax evasion in his jurisdiction to lighten his own financial burden, because his riders could then live off the land. Certainly the direct benefits given to the riders by the chief did not justify their work output. The major incentive to engage as a rider for the district chief lay in the possibility of profiteering via tax evasion.

Local officials condoning tax evasion also benefited beyond the bribe payments received. First, each additional exemption marginally reduced their workload. Commoners who bore less than their full liability could pay taxes faster because they had less to pay. In years of economic hardship, this was a distinct advantage for riders hard pressed to extract taxes. Second, the local authorities' clandestine tax-relief operations made residence in the jurisdiction markedly more attractive to commoners.

Third, and absolutely critical to control of administrative, legal, political, and economic activity in the district, the village and district officials' determining powers in capitation matters shored up their political authority, which would otherwise have been sharply undercut by colonial policies prohibiting district chiefs from enforcing legal decisions locally by fines and floggings. Since taxes formed such an important part of villagers' annual expenses, and since commoners lacked means to influence the process setting national tax rates, demand for tax relief was high, constant, and intense. Those able to meet that demand disposed of a potent form of patronage, and they knew it. Local authorities used tax exemptions and promises of it to induce quiescent obedience on the part of those they ruled.

In public good terms, the imposed capitation law as implemented in Inuwa District, Mirria County, generated a clandestine going concern to reduce commoners' liabilities to national taxation. Officials of the concern maintained a set of working rules diametrically opposed to those set out in the national tax code. By keeping quiet, colluding villagers and officials could divide among themselves sums illegally withheld from the public treasuries at the county and national level. And private bribe bargains solidifying tax exemptions enabled members of the clandestine going concern to redistribute sizable amounts of tax revenues from overriding regimes to the local level.

Insofar as participants considered activities of overriding regime officials productive of public goods, such as law and order, they received those goods at bargain prices as partial free-riders. Where national regime programs were seen by locals as generating public nuisances, or public bads, they at least cut their losses through tax evasion.

SOCIAL CONSEQUENCES

Tax manipulations in Inuwa District take on importance only in the context of a more general analysis of power and its use in the resolution of public policy problems. Assuming that public problems arise in different sizes and affect geographic domains of varying extent, a cogent argument can be made on efficiency grounds for governments of various sizes, each competent to handle public problems affecting roughly the domain of the jurisdiction in question (Ostrom 1969; Tullock 1969; Ostrom and Ostrom 1977). Assuming further that some problems can best be dealt with at the village level, because they affect villagers most immediately, a case can be made for the importance of maintaining viable village governments, in Inuwa District as well as elsewhere. In their absence, public-policy problems arising at that level often become much more pronounced and pervasive than they might otherwise be, because of inadequate countermeasures from other regimes. Nontreatment often generates serious costs for villagers and may drastically affect their standards of living. Breakdowns in forest- and pasture-conservation schemes during the last several decades throughout the West African Sahelian region, consequent on local inability to control the use of these renewable natural resources, illustrate the point. It is with this general orientation in mind that the consequences of the imposed capitation law in Inuwa District are now examined.

Reforms in the late 1940s stripped district chiefs of their traditional powers to fine and flog commoners convicted or accused of rule violations,[18] and reduced chiefs' judicial prerogatives from those of authoritative decision to mere consensual arbitration. Chiefs who strove to retain prestige and control over commoners found in the Mirria County capitation system an indirect but still quite serviceable sanction to encourage compliance with judicial decisions and administrative commands. Certainly it enabled the Inuwa District chief to keep people in line. Decisions could be appealed to the subprefect or eventually to the justice of the peace, in Zinder, or even higher echelons of the formal judicial or political systems, but to do so without the chief's express consent openly affronted his authority. Commoners normally risked this only if they were assured of protection by a more powerful patron at county or state level. Most thus tended to accept adverse decisions "suggested" by the chief if they could not convince him to permit an appeal.

During the years 1952–1977 head taxes also helped the Inuwa chief concentrate control in his own hands over the district legal process and administrative matters. This power was abused regularly but not flagrantly, so discontent within the district remained manageable. Everybody knew village-level dispute settlements to be unstable because headmen's decisions could be appealed without much risk to the district chief. Indeed, the Inuwa chief made it quite plain that village headmen should not use binding settlement techniques such as the Quranic oath, except in cases concerning accusations of attempted or actual adultery.[19] Other cases, involving land law, family law or administrative law problems, might be settled by an oathing procedure, but the district chief insisted that the oath be administered in his court, where he would have prior opportunity to hear the parties.

---

[18] Thomson (1976: 107) and literature there cited. Gamory-Dubourdeau (1924: 242–243) notes other (illegal) means employed by Mirria County chiefs to dominate their subjects.

[19] In such incidents the accuser—usually the cuckolded husband, but occasionally a close male relative—is honor-bound to threaten mayhem. Some get carried away and actually try to commit it.

Difficulties plagued this conflict-resolution procedure because the administration enjoyed quasi-monopolistic control over the legal process. The district chief (and his retinue) dominated the proceedings. Given implicit threats of future head-tax manipulations, district officials could suppress dissent with relative ease. They represented supreme judicial power in the jurisdiction, and administrative power as well. The post-1965 decline of the PPN–RDA (sole legal political party in Niger from 1958 until its abolition by military decree after the 1974 coup d'état) strengthened the traditional administrators' hold on the jurisdiction by removing the last intrajurisdictional organization capable of challenging the district chief.[20]

Since the Inuwa chief dominated both political and legal recourses in the district, he could twist court actions to his own ends. Though he lacked totally unfettered leeway here, as Case 3 illustrates, he enjoyed relatively pervasive power. Thus, when he had incentives to bend family-law, land-law, or administrative-law rules, he often did (Thomson 1976: 246–250, 331–332). This in turn vitiated rules designed to encourage production of crucial public goods. Inuwa District commoners believed that those who could afford to pay the highest bribe price could tip the balance in close cases, or even obtain a formally illegal decision from the chief. To avoid antagonizing district authorities, losers frequently accepted their losses and withdrew. Regulations meant to uphold pastureland management or promote use of fertile bottom land as truck gardens (Thomson 1976: 254–273) were eroded, as those who won the chief's backing got their way at the expense of rule integrity.

Many Hausa and Kanuri sedentary farmers insisted, for instance, that the Inuwa chief favored herders and stockowners over agriculturists. They asserted that he had to treat herders leniently when they let their animals destroy crops because of the traditional joking relationship (Hausa: *nangi*) existing between the chief's ethnic group, the Kanuri, and that of the bulk of nomadic herders, the Fulbe. But in many Inuwa district villages local people, as well as nomadic herders, often illegally allowed animals to roam untended during the dry season. Inevitably, they broke into fenced gardens and ate or trampled valuable produce. These local livestock owners frequently avoided prescribed penalties for the violations of which they were guilty (Thomson 1976: 269–271).

How does one explain this? Cases indicate that *nangi* did sometimes play a role. But in the long run the chief's financial interest in encouraging an influx of animals to his jurisdiction did more to affect outcomes. Livestock was taxed on a

---

Given the danger of bloodshed, local headmen or Muslim clerics are permitted to administer a Quranic oath. Under oath, the accused either admits his guilt, binds himself to avoid the woman in future, or denies guilt. Since violation of the oath is assumed by all to be automatically punished through supernaturally imposed sanctions (e.g., leprosy or impoverishment), the dispute is terminated. Either the charge was wrong, or it was accurate but future adultery is precluded. A cuckolded husband can demand no further compensation.

[20] In one Inuwa District village a respected Muslim cleric regularly heard land and family-law disputes but always maintained cordial relations with the Inuwa chief; his court clearly played a subordinate role in district legal proceedings.

per-unit basis; each additional unit increased either the size of his rebate or (potentially) the size of the bribe price for an exemption he could demand from owners. Farm produce, on the other hand, was *not* a direct source of tax revenue for district authorities, and thus on balance the chief had an incentive to favor herders.

This pattern of rule manipulation ramified throughout local and supralocal institutions. Villagers were able neither to enforce rule systems within the village jurisdiction nor to have them consistently enforced by officials of the district and overriding regimes. In consequence, local people lost the ability to enforce collective decisions or take collective action, and local government became moribund in the district. Various technical services fought against and lost to exactly the same sorts of rule manipulations (Thomson 1977).[21] Many commoners ended up thinking—rationally—that individual or collective initiatives to produce public goods at the village level were irrational. Thus, if government officials would not do it, it could not be done.

This generalized inability to cope with the regulation problem at the local level, and the profoundly destructive consequences that followed, cannot be overstressed. Continuing desertification throughout the West African Sahel appropriately illustrates the point. Many analysts perceive that human abuses of replenishable natural-resource systems are at least as responsible for the spread of desert-like conditions into the Sahelian zone as are adverse weather conditions (Kellogg and Schneider 1977). Humans have demonstrably caused localized desertification by combinations of overcultivation (Ware 1977: 165–202, esp. 178–181), overgrazing,[22] and deforestation (Eckholm 1976: 101–113; Thomson 1977). Because they lack the organizational means to cope with the regulation problem, local people are left worse off as a result of their own "rational" actions.

CONCLUSION

It has been argued that in Inuwa District, Mirria County, the imposed capitation system created a series of incentives which led commoners to seek tax relief in the form of illegal tax exemptions. Local officials were often able and willing to provide these exemptions and a clandestine going concern arose which allowed colluding commoners and local officials to escape or subvert the formal provisions of the national tax code.

[21] See Thomson (1976: 206–229) for an analysis of the impact of rule manipulations through the Nigerian administrative-law system on rural development, cooperative marketing, and credit mutual programs in Inuwa District, and supporting case data.

[22] Overgrazing appears to be partly a function of the inroads Sahelian farmers have made on the pastoralists' traditional rangeland base, as well as of increases in nomadic human and livestock populations resulting from improved medical care. To make ends meet in the short run, herders often overexploit the remaining grasses (Baker 1976).

Given the structure of legal and administrative institutions in the jurisdiction, an unintended consequence of this strategy was the centralization of arbitrary power in the hands of the district chief and his retinue of officials. They were able to manipulate the rules concerning the provision of a number of other public goods such as land and forest management and related rural-development programs. These manipulations in turn made it impossible for villagers to regulate their own activities. Similar patterns of behavior were apparent in the actions of nationally appointed technical service personnel. Inability to manage critical natural-resource problems reflected village institutional degeneration; ultimately this led to environmental degradation, which, even assuming a long drought-free period, now seriously threatens continued human habitation of the district.

REFERENCES

Baker, R.
    1976   "Innovation technology transfer and nomadic pastoral societies." Pp. 197–185 in M. Glantz (ed.), *The Politics of Natural Disaster: The Case of the Sahel Drought.* New York: Praeger.
Banque centrale des états de l'Afrique de l'ouest
    1966   "L'evolution recente de l'economie nigerienne." *Notes d'information et statistiques 130:* 2–8.
Barth, H.
    1965   *Travels and Discoveries in North and Central Africa.* (3 vols.). London: Frank Cass. (First published in London, 1857.)
Buchanan, J. M.
    1970   "Public goods and public bads." Pp. 51–69 in J. Crecine (ed.), *Financing the metropolis: Public Policy in Urban Economies.* Beverly Hills, Calif.: Sage Publications.
Commons, J. R.
    1959   *Legal Foundations of Capitalism.* Madison: University of Wisconsin Press. (First published in New York, Macmillan, 1924)
Dunbar, R. A.
    1970   "Damagaram (Zinder, Niger), 1812–1906: The History of a Central Sudanic Kingdom." Doctoral dissertation, Department of History, University of California, Los Angeles.
Eckholm, E. P.
    1976   *Losing Ground: Environmental Stress and World Food Prospects.* New York: Norton.
Faulkingham, R. H.
    1970   "Political Support in a Hausa Village." Doctoral dissertation, Department of Anthropology, Michigan State University.
Gaden, H.
    1903   "Notice sur la residence de Zinder." *Revue des troupes coloniales 2:* 606–794.
Gamory-Dubourdeau, Capt.
    1924   "Etude sur la création de cantons de sédentarisation dans le cercle de Zinder, et particulièrement dans la subdivision centrale." *Bulletin du comité d'études historiques et scientifiques de l'Afrique occidentale francaise 7:* 239–258.
Heidenheimer, A. J., H. Heclo, and C. T. Adams
    1976   *Comparative Public Policy: The Politics of Social Choice in Europe and America.* New York: St. Martin's.

Kellogg, W. W., and S. H. Schneider
    1977   "Climate, desertification and human activities." Pp. 141–163 in M. Glantz (ed.), *Deser-*
          tification: Environmental Degradation in and around Arid Lands. Boulder, Colo.: Westview
          Press.
Llewellyn, K. N., and E. A. Hoebel
    1941   *The Cheyenne Way: Conflict and Case Law in Primitive Jurisprudence.* Norman: University of
          Oklahoma Press.
Memento statistique
    1969   *Memento statistique de l'économie africaine/1969.* Paris: Ediafric.
Nicholas, G.
    1967   *Circulation des richesses et participation sociale dans une société Hausa du Niger (Canton de Kantché)*
          (3rd ed.), Bordeaux: Editions de Centre Universitaire de Polycopiage de l'A.G.E.B.
Olson, M.
    1965   *The Logic of Collective Action: Public Goods and the Theory of Groups.* Cambridge, Mass.: Har-
          vard University.
Ostrom, V.
    1969   "Operational federalism: Organization for the provision of public services in the
          American federal system." *Public Choice 6:* 1–17.
    1974   *The Intellectual Crisis in American Public Administration* (rev. ed.). University, Ala.: Univer-
          sity of Alabama Press.
    1976   "John R. Commons's Foundation for Policy Analysis." *Journal of Economic Issues 10:*
          839–857.
Ostrom, V., and E. Ostrom
    1977   "A theory for institutional analysis of common pool problems." Pp. 157–172 in G. Har-
          din and J. Baden (eds.), *Managing the Commons.* San Francisco: W.H. Freeman.
Raulin, H.
    1965   "Travail et régimes fonciers au Niger." *Cahiers de l'institut de science économique appliquée,*
          Série V 9: 119–129.
    n.d.   *Techniques et bases socio-économiques des sociétés rurales nigeriennes. (Etudes nigériennes,* No. 12.)
          Paris: Centre Nationale de la Recherche Scientifique, Niamey, Niger: Institut Fonda-
          mental d'Afrique Noire (c. 1964).
Raynaut, C.
    1977   "Circulation monétaire et évolution des structures socio-économiques chez les Haoussas
          du Niger." *Africa 47:* 160–171.
Salifou, A.
    1970   "Le Damagaram ou sultant de Zinder au XIXe siécle." *Thése pour le doctorat de troisiéme*
          cycle, Faculté des lettres et des sciences humaines, Université de Toulouse.
Smith, M.G.
    1960   *Government in Zazzau, 1800–1950.* London: Oxford University Press.
Suret-Canale, J.
    1964   *Afrique noire; L'ére coloniale, 1900–1945.* Paris: Editions Sociales.
Thomson, J. T.
    1976   "Law, Legal Process and Development at the Local Level in Hausa-Speaking Niger: A
          Trouble Case Analysis of Rural Institutional Inertia." Doctoral dissertation, Depart-
          ment of Political Science, Indiana University.
    1977   "Ecological deterioration: Local-level rule-making and enforcement problems in
          Niger." Pp. 57–79 in M. Glantz (ed.), *Desertification: Environmental Degradation in and*
          around Arid Lands. Boulder, Colo.: Westview Press.
Tocqueville, A. de
    1955   *The Old Regime and the French Revolution.* Garden City, N. Y.: Doubleday. (First published
          1856.)

Tullock, G.
    1969   "Federalism: Problems of scale." *Public Choice 6:* 19–29.
Urvoy, Y.
    1949   *Histoire de l'empire du Bornu.* Paris: Larose.
Ware, H.
    1977   "Desertification and population: Sub-Saharan Africa." Pp. 165–202 in M. Glantz
           (ed.), *Desertification: Environmental Degradation in and around Arid Lands.* Boulder, Colo.:
           Westview Press.

12

COMPULSORY PROSPERITY: SOME EFFECTS OF THE REGULATION OF FARMERS' COOPERATIVES IN HUNGARY

ANDRÁS SAJÓ

"The transplanting of individual rules or of a large part of a legal system is extremely common. [Watson 1974:95]." Imposed law is often a case of involuntary transplant, though in a number of cases the imposed law may originate within the country. We may wish to distinguish between the legislator and the population, depending on who is compelled to accept the transplanted law. In the case of a law forced on a country by a foreign power in occupation or directly extending the application of its municipal laws to the inhabitants of the annexed territory (for example, reception of the French civil code in Belgium or in the Rhenish Confederation) the imposed nature of the law is beyond doubt. This is, strictly speaking, a formal, political imposition of law. According to Marx, however, there is an element of imposition in all national legislation, as legislation is merely the instrument of the ruling classes and legislative acts the means of imposing the will of the ruling class on the ruled. As Marx said, "the law of the stronger, only in different form, still survives even in their constitutional State [1859/1971:193]." It makes an essential difference, however, whether or not the rulers represent a majority of the population and whether or not the rights and interests of the ruled are respected to an acceptable degree.

The Imposition of Law

It is for different reasons that the legal regulation of Hungarian cooperatives[1] is an interesting instance of imposed law. The great majority of the people directly affected by the regulation (that is, those whose duties were established under the various laws—the peasants) were not willing to join a cooperative or to work there. Yet, despite this opposition, it would be erroneous to state that the solution adopted by the cooperative decrees from 1948 to 1959 and since was of necessity contrary to their long-term interests. So to what extent does the Hungarian situation constitute an example of imposed law and, if it was imposed, to what extent was it undesirable?

There are numerous ways of discussing the social and political conditions under which it may be possible to impose law. One obvious possibility is an analysis of which groups within the society accept and which oppose, or would like to oppose, the law either at the outset or later. This, clearly, is a political-science approach,[2] and though some references to this problem are unavoidable, I shall be concentrating on the sociolegal aspects of imposed laws. The cooperative decrees prescribe the organizational framework of the cooperative. This chapter focuses on the problem of the implementation of these norms and on the social conditions and consequences of such implementation. It would, however, be wrong to consider an organizational framework or model in isolation. Two aspects should be added: other legal norms governing the environment of the cooperative, and nonlegal (mostly political) normative influences.

Within the sociolegal analysis special attention will be paid to the following aspects: first, structural problems of the norm[3]; second, the law-implementing mechanisms and the effectiveness of their use by the central authority; and third, law observance and other reactions of the subjects concerned, at both the local and district levels. To analyze the imposed law in the above sociolegal context, a brief sketch of the development of cooperatives in Hungary is given.

---

[1] In this chapter the term *cooperative* is applied to agricultural (farmers') cooperatives. In these organizations members undertake joint farming and share the income in proportion to the work done. The Governmental Decree issued in 1948 on the cooperatives (quoted hereinafter as the Cooperative Decree, 1948) included the compulsory standard statute of the cooperatives. The decree underwent minor changes practically each year. There was a major change in 1959 (law decree No. 9). This was a sign of the growth in importance of the law. Most of the earlier regulations concerning the cooperatives had been ministerial decrees, but in 1959 it was the Presidential Council that passed the law. Since 1967 the laws governing the cooperatives have been passed by parliament.

[2] The political-science approach, though highly attractive, is very dangerous owing to the lack of reliable sources on the actual behavior of the population in the period discussed.

[3] Structural problems of the norm are treated as problems of legality. Jurists generally ask, "Is a piece of legislation in harmony with the bulk of existing norms? Is there any contradiction between the legal texts?" Compare this with the criteria of legality by Fuller (1964:39). For a sociological explanation of the structural problems it is necessary to analyze the processes, agents, and causes of the existing consistencies and/or inconsistencies in the legal system. The sociological approach is a dynamic one, whereas jurists adopt a static one (cf. Carbonnier 1969).

POLICY AND REGULATION OF FARMERS' COOPERATIVES IN HUNGARY

According to the *Statistical Yearbook* of Hungary for 1938, Hungary was a small country with a backward, largely agricultural economy. The agricultural sector, which produced 75% of the nation's exports, faced tremendous difficulties owing to the greatly unequal land distribution and agrarian overpopulation. Out of a total 9,226,323 ha, 2 million ha were taken up by 1558 estates. At the same time, 46% of those working in agriculture were landless and another 24% owned less than 3 hectares—that is, they were in effect below the subsistence level.

Part of Hungary was not yet liberated in 1944 when the political parties of the provisional government, following the suggestions of the Soviet Army Head-quarters, aimed at winning over the Hungarian soldiers, agreed upon a land reform. The distribution of the land took place rapidly, as Hungrian peasants were quite willing to accept regulations of this kind. The main intention of the decree was to distribute the estates over 57.5 ha, beneficiaries being landless agrarian proletarians and, later, smallholders.[4] However, because of the short-age of land compared with the large number of peasants, it was impossible to satisfy the land demands of the agrarian population. Moreover, the plots allocated were not adequate for profitable farming.

In 1948 a fundamental political change took place: the Social Democrats joined the Communist Party and the latter took absolute power. According to the Marxist concept of socialism, means of production, including the land, should be taken into social (common) ownership. However, Engels and Lenin in particular pointed out that for practical political reasons, the confiscation of the landowners' property is a process of varying and even extremely lengthy dura-tion. It is an accepted principle in Marxism–Leninism that this takeover should be realized without violence.

The unprofitability of smallholdings necessitated the introduction of some kind of socialist large-scale farming, but the Communist Party was aware of the dangers of immediate forced collectivization. Such a policy had contributed to the fall of the Hungarian Soviet Republic of 1919, when rejection of the impor-tance of the ownership-centered mentality and interests of the peasantry had robbed the policy of popular support. Large estates had not been distributed but had been turned into cooperatives under central control, and this had sapped support for the Soviet government.

In 1948, however, the main obstacle to large-scale collectivization was the high investment needed for large-scale farming. In the party program issued in June 1948, it was expressly stated that the only way of leading the peasantry to

---

[4] In 1949 25.4% of the land was state property but only 1.1% of this was arable land. The state farms became important only later.

socialism was the cooperative system, but that this was a long process at which individual farmers would have to work. Accordingly, people were taken aback when, hardly a month later, party leader M. Rákosi announced a policy of rapid cooperative development. At the same time he promised a number of restrictive measures against rich peasants (the *kulaks*).

This change in the policy was due to several factors. First, in every Central Eastern European country proletarian dictatorship was now firmly established. Second, the Communist Party leaders, claiming that another war was likely, argued that investment priority must be given to heavy industry and that central control of agriculture was therefore advisable. Third, the "exclusion" of the Yugoslav Party from the socialist community took place only a couple of weeks before Rákosi's statement. In this political atmosphere the acceptance of Stalin's model of socialism as exclusive became imperative. Fourth, the value system of the leading Hungarian Communists had been shaped during their stay in the Soviet Union, and was reinforced by the fact that Soviet support was essential if they were to maintain power in Eastern Europe. Finally, the socialist development of agriculture was only part of a general social-development model. The core of the model was the growth of a strong working class, and for this, industrial development was essential. The existing economic conditions made industrial development possible only if surplus value and labor were redirected (by force, if necessary) from the agricultural sector.

The Hungarian leadership tried to apply the Soviet system[5] in Hungary, not only in using the cooperative framework but also in attempting to bring about the *rapid* development of cooperatives. Unfortunately, Hungary was completely different from the Soviet Union in the 1920s or 1940s. The most important charcteristics of the cooperative *as a formal organization,* described under the Cooperative Decree of 1948, were as follows. First, the cooperative was established as a voluntary organization. The land remained the private property of the members, though farmed collectively, the owners being entitled to an allotment according to the size of their property. After a period of 3 years from the formation of the cooperative, members were entitled to resign. In the most common type of cooperative, members worked together and the income of the cooperative was distributed according to the individual work done (dividends per work unit—that is, the Soviet solution of *trudoden*). Cooperative members elected an executive board.[6] The most important issues of cooperative life, such as land exploitation and the distribution of tasks, were decided by all members. Cooperatives were autonomous, although their originating statute was centrally

---

[5] According to the Cooperative Decree of 1948, there were different types of cooperatives. These were similar to the Soviet and Bulgarian types (the *kolkhoz),* especially the highest level cooperative, the *artel.*

[6] The abbreviation CM (cooperative managers) is applied to the elected members of the executive board and the leading experts employed by the cooperative (bookkeepers, agronomists, etc.).

formulated and modified and they were under central administrative control. This national center acted like other ministries and was a government organ.

As the poor had neither the land, knowledge, nor means of production to farm on their own, it is quite understandable that they were willing not only to enter the cooperative but even to remain there under all circumstances. Their choices and chances of obtaining subsistence were limited: to leave the village and try to find a job in industry, to find work at a state farm if there were any, or to work for the cooperatives. Outside this stratum of peasantry, however, the appeal of the cooperative seemed to be rather limited. The policy aimed to persuade the so-called medium-sized farmers and smallholders (10–25 ha and less than 10 ha, respectively) to join cooperatives and had as its ultimate aim the liquidation of the *kulaks* (25 ha and over), at least in an economic sense. A series of administrative measures was taken against the latter group. These restrictions affected about 70,000 families, and as a consequence many *kulaks* gave up farming. The pressure on the medium-sized farmers was only slightly less. In this situation, many people joined the local cooperatives, and by June 1953 membership had risen to 376,000—that is, 30% of peasant families, as compared with the 90% planned.

There was no proper investment in the cooperatives. Wherever possible new members tried to keep for themselves all the goods and means of production, and a large part of the equipment from small farms could not practically be used in the cooperatives. In addition, there was an even more serious problem: 25% of the members did not work in the cooperative at all and another 15% worked less than 10 working units (the central administration had decreed a requirement of a minimum of 120 working units per member). Given this lack of commitment, the above-mentioned increase in membership calls for an explanation of the methods applied. Agricultural prices were rather low and the resultant lack of interest in farming led to a drop in the productivity of individuals as well as cooperatives. The authorities had somehow to supply the urban population with food, so they extended the obligatory quota system imposed on farmers. Under this system, farmers were obliged to sell a quota of agricultural produce and livestock to the state at extremely low fixed prices (about a quarter of market prices). Failure to do so was considered an offense or even a crime. The cooperatives, too, were bound by the quota, but to a lesser extent, and sanctions were milder. Individual members were in general not liable for it.[7] This made membership of the cooperative more attractive.

However, an alternative response was to abandon farming altogether. Other purely economic measures also lessened the attraction of land ownership: for example, the frequent regulations concerning the size of the area to be

---

[7] According to one of the best historical accounts of collectivization, 462 of a total of 3632 cooperatives were fined in 1952 for failure to meet the compulsory quotas, the great majority thereafter remaining permanently in debt from the payment of the fines (Orbán 1972:125).

cultivated. There were some 400,000 criminal sentences for economic offenses brought against farmers in the first 4 years of collectivization. In 1949 the agrarian population in Hungary amounted to 4.5 million people with 2.1 million breadwinners; 250,000 of these gave up farming and tried to get industrial jobs.

Tensions in agriculture increased seriously up to 1953 and problems were not limited to the villages. Industrial development was slower than planned and could not provide the 650,000 new jobs scheduled, which in practice made impossible the employment of the labor force released or about to be released by collectivization. The constraint might have continued to increase as a response to the internal problems of Hungary had not a new leadership come to power in the summer of 1953. To consolidate the worker–peasant alliance, the new leaders intended to raise agricultural output while at the same time decreasing the industrial growth rate. The policy of compulsory collectivization was given up and the Prime Minister underlined the right of the members to leave the cooperative. From June 1953, 500 cooperatives were dissolved and 110,000 people turned to individual farming within 6 months. In 1955 the Rákosi faction again became predominant and a new campaign for rapid (and, in practice, compulsory) collectivization was started. By June 1956 membership numbers had almost reached those of 1953, but a crisis developed in the first months of 1956 as people refused to work in the newly formed cooperatives.

In the summer of 1956 the party gave up the policy of rapid collectivization. This alteration came too late, however, and the delay was even more harmful in spheres other than agriculture. During the political events in October 1956 the whole political system was shaken. Most villagers remained relatively calm during the critical days; indeed, peasants were glad to re-establish their individual farms. However, not all cooperatives were dismantled: some 120,000 people remained members—in most cases the former landless peasants. The great majority of the surviving cooperatives had been organized before the intensive administrative campaigns.

The agrarian policy of the revolutionary worker–peasant government in practice accepted the status quo in the villages in order to maintain the worker–peasant alliance. The government supported the cooperative movement but without exerting any pressure on individual farmers. The compulsory quota system came to an end. From 1957 to 1958 individual farming prospered, but in 1958 a change in international political life put the cooperatives on the agenda again as the socialist way to socialist agriculture. The party decided to abandon the earlier administrative solution, but this was clearly for political reasons; economic considerations were of secondary importance only. The decree concerning the structure of the cooperative was only slightly changed from that introduced in 1948. As a result of a widespread campaign of persuasion concentrated in certain regions of the country, the membership of cooperatives greatly increased. Three hundred and sixteen thousand families joined the existing cooperatives or formed new ones, and 36% of those new members had owned medium-sized farms. The response of the farmers not yet affected was to wait and see. This withdrawal of labor from private farming led to critical conditions, and collectivization had to be realized even more rapidly. The campaign ended in the first quarter of 1961, by which time 67% of the country's arable land was farmed by the cooperatives. There were 1,200,000 members, and only 6.5% of the population working in agriculture remained in the private sector on an area of 3.3% of the total land.

This spectacular success may be explained in different ways. One explanation is that, after the political events of 1956, peasants realized that resistance was doomed to failure. An alternative explanation is that the ability to resist the strict collectivization diminished as a result of earlier, partly violent, collectivizations. During compulsory collectivization in the early 1950s the political and social structure of the villages—the very organizational source of resistance—vanished, and communal solidarity diminished. This fact has often been neglected in Hungary, as social thinking is centered on the cultural explanations of the phenomena and inclined to emphasize certain inherent mental features, such as the traditionalism of the peasants. It can be proved, however, that the value system of the peasants remained unchanged in the period discussed. In the early period of building socialism, the peasant community was still a "society apart," that is, a relatively closed society with a high degree of autonomy (Mendras, Gervais, Servolin, and Tavernier 1969:43). For Mendras *et al.* (1969:47) the decisive characteristics of a peasant community are the degree of autarchy, central–local power relations, communication outside the immediate environment, and the method of organizing farming (the dependent variable in our case). In the early 1950s, because of the compulsory quota system and central redistribution, the village and the cooperative ceased to be self-supporting. There was no local political autonomy; the role of peasants was defined centrally, as peasants were treated in accordance with the size of land they had possessed before collectivization. The volume of outside communications increased, the central role of the head of the family ended, and the number of directives from the central authorities increased and surpassed the number of communications initiated by the community. The strongest resistance to the system was demonstrated in production, yet even in this field the traditional organizational framework was dissolved. Young people left the family holding, which resulted in loss of manpower. There were no investments and the agricultural machinery used before was destroyed or useless. All this made resistance to collectivization increasingly difficult or impossible. A third possible explanation of the success of the cooperative movement is that political propaganda began to change the opinions of influential farmers of the village—in other words, that change was induced by the opinion leaders. A fourth explanation stresses peer-group pressure—that members of the community began to participate in the propaganda. And yet a fifth explanation rests on the fact that the Communist Party recognized some of the traditional values of the peasantry. Under the law, members' ownership rights were accepted: the restitution of a plot of land in the event that a member gave up his membership was promised.[8] In the first period of the new collectivization—1959—the cooperatives were subsidized. The government could import corn from 1958 to 1962 from western countries. In 1952 that would have been impossible because of the Cold War.

The most likely explanation, however, is that the lasting success achieved has been due to a systemic change. From 1959 to 1965 450,000 people left the villages and found jobs in industry. On the other hand, although with considerable delays, industry slowly acquired the capacity to manufacture the goods required by modern, large-scale farming.

As outlined, however, rapid change did not provide a general solution to the problems of Hungarian agriculture. Peasants accepted the new system partly because it offered them a kind of modus vivendi guaranteeing the so-called household plot, a piece of land not larger than .57 ha, and a limited amount of livestock. In 1961, 52% of the total income of the members derived from household plots; members preferred working on their own to cooperative work. Nevertheless, since 1959, the household plot has been honored in Hungary.

The newly established cooperatives were not very popular. Parents frequently tried to give their most valuable piece of land to their children working in industry. The legislature and the courts responded quickly by ruling that any member of the family joining the cooperative was obliged to offer all the land owned by the household to the cooperative. The peasant family had to decide whose labor force should be sacrificed: it was usually the eldest member of the family who joined the cooperative.

Over a long time the average yield per hectare of the cooperatives remained below the 1959 level. However, the situation was gradually improved by mechanization, the paying of premiums, and better management. The consolidation period lasted from 1961 to 1966, and a considerable rise has been observed since 1966 in the average growth rate of Hungarian agriculture—over 6% in the past decade.

Until 1968 the state administration exercised strict control over the cooperatives and was responsible for the fulfillment of the plans. Although these were not binding on the cooperatives, the local and district authorities were able to convince or to constrain the CM (cooperative managers) to accept most of their suggestions. In 1968 a new concept of economic management was introduced. The system of compulsory plans was abandoned, and now more or less quasi-autonomous enterprises function in a controlled market; this less stringent alternative became available to the cooperatives, too. The main results are interesting. In 1975 Hungarian agriculture produced 23% of the nation's exports, as against 75% in 1938. At the same time the volume of agricultural products was much higher than in 1938, although it decreased as a proportion of na-

---

[8] Ten years later this right was changed to pecuniary compensation. According to the present regulation, the cooperative is entitled to buy the members' land (Act IV, 1967).

tional exports. (Over 25 years the agricultural population had decreased to less than 20% of the national work force.) A similar development in the United States took more than 50 years to achieve, from 1880 (Historical Statistics, U.S. 1960: Series D57, D58). In the mid-1970s the real income of the Hungarian rural population surpassed that of industrial workers and white-collar workers for the first time since 1945. Two facts show the basic importance of the cooperative to the life of its members: the main source of income is no longer from the household plot, and the increase in the average age of cooperative members has come to a halt. In 1967 the average age of members was 46.5 years; in 1974 it was 41.5. These facts suggest that in a way the cooperative movement forced the peasantry into economic prosperity—probably the only possible way to prosperity under the prevailing social system. [9]

DISCUSSION

ADAPTING A LEGAL TRANSPLANT

The 1948 regulations on cooperatives were modeled on Soviet law. We need to answer the sociolegal question of the extent to which the adoption of this new concept into the prevailing Hungarian law led to the difficulties that occurred in the cooperatives. The adaptation of the Soviet legal solution helped to avoid some of the difficulties and inconveniences of elaborating a new regulation and of shaping a new organizational mode. Nevertheless, the inherent inadequacy of the relevant Soviet regulation was aggravated by the different social, economic, political, and cultural system in Hungary. The reception of a law is recognized by jurists to give rise to a particular type of problem—that of the so-called *acculturation juridique,* or resistance by the national legal culture. However, in this case, the lawyers were not interested in the problems of the cooperatives at all, probably because the would-be clients could not afford to pay the fees. The traditional Hungarian legal system, an essentially bourgeois body of rules, was framed to protect the interests of the financially strong.[10] The elaboration of a new socialist law expressing the principles of the proletarian dictatorship became necessary. It was generally accepted among lawyers and lawmakers working on the new socialist system that it had to follow the example of the Soviet system. The socialist transformation was facilitated by the reorganization of public administration and by structural and personnel changes in the judiciary. Hungary was not, however, the Soviet Russia of Stuchka and revolutionary class con-

---

[9] Surveys show that the majority of the members are aware of the advantages of large-scale collective farming, though opinions differ as to most desirable and relative status within the cooperative (Hegedüs 1970; Domé 1972).

[10] A serious hindrance to the development of the smallholding was created, for example, by the credit policy of the banks.

sciousness. In Hungary there was a peculiar bureaucratic machine with rather poorly qualified staff devoted to performing the orders of the government.

The prevailing revolutionary principles vanished as a result of the changes brought about by the authorities. Law implementation was operated in practice according to low-level administrative fiat. It is thus hardly surprising that changes in the wording of the Cooperative Decree and in legal practice were relatively unaffected by the difficulties in production or the attitude of the peasants. These facts served as arguments in the central power struggles only. Local problems also appeared unimportant to the central administration, as the bureaucratic organizations implementing the laws did not report the real problems to the higher authorities. Personnel and conceptual changes at the center, due partly to industrial and macrosocial problems and especially to international development, were the main reasons for the changes in the wording. The real changes were brought about partly by political declarations and partly by the modification of administrative practices (also decided by the central administration) rather than by revision of the legal texts.[11]

LAW-IMPLEMENTING MECHANISMS

In the formative years of the cooperatives the central government apparently had immense power at its disposal. In practice, however, the enforcement mechanism had to substitute for economic forces, and eventually, following changes and great disorganization at the center, the intention of the administrators to implement this policy by force if necessary was discarded. However, the staff of the local councils and local administrative agencies were unable to implement the central agrarian policy; all their shortcomings had to be counterbalanced by extremely detailed, though often wrong, *ad hoc* central norms. A vicious circle of coercion and violence developed as the central authorities insisted on success in collectivization. Given no alternative, the local bureaucrats were obliged, at least at the beginning of the regime, to exercise the coercive powers given under the law. Since this coercion led to many side effects, the pressures from higher quarters increased. The regulations could not be changed by the local administrators, so further coercion was the only available solution. Poor results and bad harvests were attributed to the action of "class enemies" whose "hostile activity" necessitated countermeasures and retaliation. In addition, stringent and even violent enforcement of the rules was taken as proof of administrators' firm devotion to duty. Since local requirements and circumstances could not be properly considered in central planning, the directives became disfunctional. One of the disfunctions was that the bargaining position of the administration vis à vis the cooperatives and other producers was limited.

---

[11] Only the reform in 1967 was brought about essentially through legal enactments, and greater stress had been laid on legal coherence in the laws concerning cooperatives only since 1956.

The role of the courts of justice was only secondary in the history of the cooperatives. An important change took place after 1956. Before that period the main role of the judiciary in the process of collectivization had been to impose penal sanctions. After 1956, the courts helped the consolidation of the cooperatives by civil judgments. Payment of damages by members for failure to fulfill the minimal working unit is an early example—although this judgment was overruled in 1965.

LAW OBSERVANCE BY PEASANTS AND COOPERATIVES

The legal regulations set out to change the conduct of the local peasant population and had the following aims: first, to liquidate *kulaks* (who could not join the cooperatives before 1959); second, to encourage the rest of the peasants to join the cooperatives; and third, to intensify members' activity in the cooperatives. The policy applied seemed to be rather flexible, as differences in the compulsory quotas show. However, the legislature applied a rigid system of social classification to the peasantry, and central plans often changed, sometimes to the benefit of the agrarian proletariat, at other times to the benefit of medium-sized farmers. This inconsistency resulted in a general mistrust of official policy.

Discontent was general among peasants, yet there was no chance of a uniform peasant resistance because of the strong differentiation in ownership. "Displacement may be translated, according to the particular case, by withdrawal, apathy, abandonment of activities, or increased participation [Germani 1965:395]." Hungarian peasants adopted withdrawal, evidenced by restrictive farming, no sowing, etc. Since abandonment of agricultural activity was punishable under the penal code, many peasants drifted into cooperatives in a kind of apathy. In certain strata, such as the poorest peasants and the *kulaks,* there was increased participation in the economy but not in agriculture: they were active in industry.

The early cooperatives were without means and unprepared for the type of cooperative farming expected of them, yet not unprotected from the state collectivization administration. In the early years of collectivization very important bargaining procedures existed for deciding the internal structure of the cooperative, the division of labor, and the division of income, as well as for contacts outside their immediate environment. The bargaining parties have not changed essentially since that time, yet their behavior has changed in accordance with the change in the rules of the game brought about as a consequence of structural transformations. In the early years the center and its administrative machinery tried to control the CM completely. Though most people in the CM acted as agents of the local authorities, the effort to control them and the membership failed. The CM depended on the effective work of the membership. Relying on its own position in the cooperative, it tried to mediate between the cooperative and the authorities. The CM's role vis-à-vis the authorities was to legitimate the form of agricultural exploitation that was found to be acceptable to the members of the cooperative.[12]

The position of the cooperative was consolidated by the lack of professional competence in the early administrative machinery. Local party and state organizations had to run the risk of being blamed if the performance of the cooperative fell short of expectations. As a matter of fact, no cooperative was liquidated for failure to meet its compulsory quota. CM members were treated leniently, too, since they were chosen by the state administration. The cooperatives differed significantly according to the contacts each established with the "higher authorities" and, as a result, the ability of the CM to avoid the strict application of directives unfavorable to the cooperative. As a rule the CM did not discuss directives in public, yet its members spent much time racking their brains for acceptable justifications should they be called upon to account for omissions (Halász and Tóthné 1978:42–43). Under the pre-1959 regulations attempts were made to limit the opportunities for bargaining, but even the regulations themselves were the embodiment of compromises, especially in the case of household plots. This again was taken from Soviet law, itself established as the final outcome of the "historical" bargain that had been made since the late 1920s. The conservation of the rights of ownership to land of the peasants and the payment of land rent was another compromise recognized legally, although there was no clear-cut rule for its enforcement. Such rent was in fact rarely paid, especially where the majority of the members had not formerly held land.

CONCLUSIONS

Stalin used to call the creation of the cooperatives in Russia a revolution from above. As a matter of fact, the introduction of the Cooperative Decree in Hungary encountered a number of obstacles, and although these were almost unconnected with the fact that the law followed a Soviet solution, they were connected with the way in which the cooperatives were introduced. The change was essentially of a "provoked" nature, the aim of the reforms and campaigns being above all to obtain a "demonstration effect" (Germani 1965)—in this case the central administration was striving to make cooperatives (and the whole country) approximate to the example of the Soviet Union as fast as possible. The main reason for the discrepancies between aims and results is to be found in the very fact that a revolution was imposed from above. This was inevitable: as Crozier and Friedberg recently stated, "successful change does not derive from the substitution of the old model with a new one [1977:338]."

The compulsory collectivization of the early 1950s was a political effort to regulate the economic behavior of the Hungarian peasantry. Marx had proved

[12] A considerable number of local bargains of the post-1959 period were also accepted by the central authorities. Since the rules were less harsh, the deviance and rule breaking were also milder.

that the superiority of modern economics consisted in the replacement of noneconomic constraint by economic restraint. The early 1948 political solution had no solid economic or social basis and was of dubious success.[13] However, the destruction of the traditional social structure of the peasantry paved the way to more successful attempts to create cooperatives in a later period when economic conditions were more favorable to large-scale farming.

ACKNOWLEDGMENTS

I am most grateful to V. Peschka, B. E. Harrell-Bond, and Imréné Bárd for their useful comments on earlier versions of the manuscript.

REFERENCES

Carbonnier, J.
    1969   Flexible droit. Paris: Librairie Générale de Droit et Jurisprudence.
Crozier, M., and E. Friedberg
    1977   L'acteur et le système. Paris: Éditions du Seuil.
Domé, G.
    1972   "A közvetlen és képviseleti demokrácia formái és mechanizmusa az ipari és mezogazdasági üzemekben." Unpublished.
Fuller, L. L.
    1964   The Morality of Law. New Haven: Yale University Press.
Germani, G.
    1965   "Social change and intergroup conflict." Pp. 391–408 in I. L. Horowitz (ed.), The New Sociology. New York: Oxford University Press.
Halász, P., and G. L. Tóthné
    1978   Egy termelőszövetkezet harminc éve. Budapest: Kossuth.
Hegedüs, A.
    1970   Változó világ. Budapest: Akademiai.
Historical Statistics, U.S.
    1960   Colonial Times to 1957. Washington D.C.: Government Printing Office.
Marx, K.
    1971   A Contribution to the Critique of Political Economy. London: Lawrence and Wishart. (First published in German in 1859; in English in 1904.)
Mendras, H., M. Gervais, C. Servolin, and Y. Tavernier
    1969   "Le défi pasan." Pp. 17–140 in H. Mendras and Y. Tavernier (eds.), Terre, paysans et politique. Paris: S.É.D.É.I.S.
Orbán, S.
    1972   Két agrárforradalom Magyarországon. Budapest: Akadémiai.
Watson, A.
    1974   Legal Transplants: An Approach to Comparative Law. Edinburgh: Scottish Academic Press.

[13] As a means of sharpening the class struggle the regulation had, of course, important latent effects. This is a neglected though very promising field for investigating the social function of the law.

13

ATTEMPTS TO IMPOSE LEGAL RESTRICTIONS ON TRADE UNIONS IN BRITAIN 1968-1974

STEVEN D. ANDERMAN

The relationship between government and trade unions in Britain has undergone a dramatic change in the post-war period. The level of economic activity and relatively high employment have increased the industrial power of trade unions and work groups, thus enabling them to press for improvements in living standards and treatment and to defend their institutional interests. At the same time, the increased role of the state in "managing" economic development has placed governments of whatever political hue in a position where they view their role as that of keeping demands for improved living standards to levels that do not threaten economic stability.

In the post-war period, succeeding governments have experimented with various methods of reconciling economic goals with the growth of industrial power at workshop level. At first macroeconomic measures were used to curb demand when inflation threatened to worsen the balance of payments, but the adverse effects of stop–go policies and the growth of "stagflation" soon indicated the inherent limitations of macroeconomic measures. During the same period governments also resorted to incomes policies in various forms. Efforts to produce viable and effective incomes policies intensified as the weaknesses of macroeconomic policies became more fully understood. Yet incomes policies

The Imposition of Law

Copyright © 1979 by Academic Press, Inc.
All rights of reproduction in any form reserved.
ISBN 0-12-145450-9

also displayed certain inherent limitations: they could work for a short period of 6 months or a year during a crisis, but if extended for much longer they created social pressures for the restoration of differentials and levels of living. These produced wage explosions which offset the beneficial effects of the periods of income restraint.

It was in the context of this search for more effective means of economic management that succeeding British governments in 1968–1974 turned from the use of policies backed up by specific laws to restrain increases in incomes to more general efforts to use law to limit industrial action in connection with collective bargaining. In 1969, after 3 years of statutory incomes policies, a Labour government introduced a White Paper entitled *In Place of Strife* (Cmnd 3888 1969) and made a vain attempt to enact an Industrial Relations Bill 1970. In the 1971–1974 period the Conservative government succeeded in enacting legislation placing comprehensive legal restrictions upon industrial action. This program of intervention in industrial relations coincided with a shift in its general economic policy toward non-intervention with prices and incomes. As a result, the Industrial Relations Act of 1971 proved to be singularly unsuccessful. In less than 3 years the government that had introduced it had begun to shy away from its use, and in 1974 it was repealed by a newly elected Labour government.

The apparent inability of governments to legislate in this sphere in the face of resistance by the trade-union movement aroused considerable concern. As Robson (1973:119) put it,

> it is no exaggeration to say that the most important domestic issue in British politics is whether the trade unions can ultimately defeat or destroy the policies of *any* government. The outcome of this conflict, which is ultimately based on the confrontation of political authority by industrial power, is by no means clear.

It is the purpose of this chapter to look more closely at these two attempts to impose legal restrictions on industrial action during the period, to consider their more immediate causes, and to examine some of the wider consequences of these failures to impose legislation in the arena of industrial relations. In particular, this chapter examines how strong trade unions were able to limit the power of the state to impose unacceptable versions of restrictive labor legislation, limitations that occurred both at the level of the legislative process and at the level of the application of specific legal sanctions. It is also intended to show how the thwarting of the state's effort to impose restrictive legislation in pursuance of its aims of economic stability and continuous production has led to resort to other means of winning the trade unions' acceptance of governmental policy.

INDUSTRIAL LEGISLATION IN THE 1968–1974 PERIOD

In Britain in the decades prior to the 1960s the law played a comparatively small role in regulating industrial relations. The machinery of British collective bargaining had developed largely autonomously with few direct positive legal supports for the recognition of trade unions by employers. Labor legislation had tended to take two forms: first, the provision of a rudimentary "floor" of statutory employment rights for individual employees regardless of whether they were trade-union members or covered by collective bargaining, a form of legal support that did not directly regulate collective bargaining; second, a "right to strike" defined negatively in the form of legislative immunities from the various criminal and tort liabilities created and applied by the judiciary to the emerging trade unions. From 1906 onward the Trade Disputes Act had created a wide measure of immunity for trade-union officials and strike leaders as long as industrial action was "in contemplation or furtherance of a trade dispute [Kahn-Freund 1977]."

This rather marked non-interventionism of the law could be explained in large measure by the lack of interest of British trade unions in positive legislative supports. Partly as a result of their experience with judicial hostility (Wedderburn 1972; Griffiths 1970:57), partly as a result of their success in obtaining recognition and collective bargaining by their own efforts rather than legislation (Kahn-Freund 1977:68–70), it was a fundamental instinct of trade-union organizations at that stage of their development that they wanted "nothing more of the law than that it should leave them alone [Wedderburn 1971:13]." Yet the narrow scope of legal regulation could also be attributed to the relative satisfaction of upper- and middle-class opinion with the consequences of collective bargaining as regulated by the prevailing economic conditions. The decline of strikes in the 1930s, the collaborative policies of the Trades Union Congress leadership after the general strike and wartime pressures all combined to produce an acceptance of trade unionism and nonregulated collective bargaining (Pelling 1963; Wedderburn 1972:276–277). Non-interventionism rested upon a social balance of power in which the role of the trade unions was essentially a defensive one: preventing undercutting of wages. This comes out clearly in Lord Wright's comments in *Crofter Harris Tweed* v. *Veitch* [1942], that "the right of workmen to strike is an essential element in the principles of collective bargaining" where the "predominant object" of trade-union officials is "to prevent undercutting and unregulated competition."

By the early 1960s, however, the social acceptance of non-interventionism began to break down as the shift in the market power of labor manifested itself in strong workshop bargaining accompanied by unofficial strikes (that is, strikes unauthorized by the trade-union organization) and "unconstitutional" strikes (that is, strikes in breach of industrial-disputes procedures), "wage drift" marked by leapfrogging wage claims and competitive wage bidding by workshop groups, and a growing awareness of restrictive work practices in many sectors (McCarthy and Ellis 1975). The role of official trade unions in these developments was insufficiently understood, but the trade unions were identified in the public mind with interunion or demarcation disputes, certain abuses of union power, and left-wing activism at high levels (McCarthy and Ellis 1975).

During this period the judges, in apparent reaction to these developments, created new torts and resurrected long-unused tort liabilities to justify the use of labor injunctions against the leaders of industrial action.[1] The Labour government partially neutralized this judicial initiative by enacting the Trade Disputes Act 1965. At the same time, however, it responded to the growing concern with industrial conditions by appointing in 1965 a royal commission to examine the development of trade unions and collective bargaining.

The report of the Royal Commission on Trade Unions and Employers Associations, known as the Donovan Commission, in 1968 provided both a diagnosis of the cause of the growth of industrial conflict and a prescription for its cure. It diagnosed the causes of industrial conflict as the decline of the effectiveness of collective bargaining institutions at the national, or industry-wide level, to provide regulation at workshop level, and the demonstrable inadequacies of the institutional machinery of workshop collective bargaining that had emerged in the post-war period. Workshop bargaining, with its autonomy, informality, and fragmentation, the report argued, could be reformed into a more orderly institution only by an extension of official trade-union activity and formal collective agreements and procedures to the workshop level. The Donovan Report recommended an increase in formal written agreements at plant and company level and the revision of the rule books or constitutions of trade unions to include a description of the powers and functions of shop stewards (RCTUEA 1968: par. 38–53).

The Donovan Report stressed that the necessary reforms ought to be effectuated by voluntary means rather than compelled by law. The state should encourage the parties to reform their institutions by the recommendations of a government advisory and investigative institution, the Industrial Relations Commission, rather than by the use of legal sanctions. The report was not opposed to legal sanctions in principle but contained a warning that restrictive law could not play a useful role in industrial relations until the institutions of collective bargaining provided a credible means of resolving disputes. As the commission put it,

> As long as no effective method for the settlement of grievances exists, no one can expect a threat of legal sanctions to restrain men from using the advantages they feel able to derive from sudden action in order to obtain a remedy for grievances which cannot be dealt with in an orderly fashion [RCTUEA 1968: par. 505].

The report persuasively argued that "the most important part in remedying the problem of unofficial strikes and other forms of unofficial action [would] be played by reforming the institutions of which they are a symptom [RCTUEA 1968: par. 454]." Moreover, the commission provided a careful analysis of the practical limitations of enforcing legal sanctions against trade-union and unofficial strikes, either by employees or by the state (par. 477–499).

---

[1] See, for example, *Rookes* v. *Barnard* [1964]; *Stratford Ltd.* v. *Lindley* [1965].

In both respects the Donovan Report advanced an understanding of the way in which industrial sanctions could not work directly to suppress industrial action but required social institutions to reduce industrial conflict to a manageable level. The report, however, lessened the impact of its analysis by holding forth a promise of the possibility that legal sanctions at some point in time might be effective. Thus, the central employers' organization, the Confederation of British Industries, had proposed the imposition of a legal obligation backed by legal sanctions upon trade unions to prevent members from committing unlawful offensive actions and to ensure their return to work. In response, the Donovan Report stated:

> The principal defect of the proposal made to us for forcing the unions to discipline unofficial strikers is that it fails to deal with those causes. It is the method of collective bargaining and the role which unions and work groups play in the bargaining process that has to be reformed in the first instance. . . . If, when this reform has been accomplished, unofficial strikes continue to be a serious problem it will then be time to see what the law can do; but not until then. As things now stand proposals made by the CBI are more likely to lead to internal disruptions in the unions than to a reduction in unofficial strikes. The house of law collapses if it is not built on a solid foundation of fact [RCTUEA 1968: par. 482].

Yet in three important respects the Donovan Report failed fully to explore the solid foundation of fact upon which a house of restrictive labor legislation must be built. First, it did not develop the point that British trade unions might be unwilling, even after reforms, to accept restrictive legislation in a situation where they felt no obligation toward legislative support.

The central trade-union confederation, the Trades Union Congress, had argued in their evidence before the Donovan Commission that they were not beholden to the state for their existence:

> The fact that trade unions in Britain have succeeded through their own efforts in strengthening their organisation and in obtaining recognition, not relying on the assistance of Government through legislaton, is one of the most important factors sustaining their strength and independence. Trade unions have not been given privileges. They have fought for what they have achieved. If they had been granted privileges, if their organisation had been strengthened and sustained by Government action, it might well be logical to argue that trade union function would also be the responsibility of Government; the right to bargain had been granted by Government and Government could take it away. Trade union strength has been developed without the help of any external agency [TUC 1968:142].

The Donovan Report did not deal explicitly with the difficulties or importance of obtaining trade-union support for or acceptance of any restrictive labor legislation. It did not explore the question of whether the trade unions, given their tradition of autonomy, might regard restrictive labor legislation as a threat to their existence as institutions.

Second, the Donovan Report did not deal fully with the point that the reform of internal trade-union authority structures, viewed as a necessary concomitant to a reform by management of collective bargaining structure, might not take place or might be long delayed. The report (par. 96–122) indicated clearly that the structure of trade-union authority in Great Britain did not resemble a hierarchy. What it did not fully explore was the possibility that the autonomy of shop stewards vis à vis the trade-union full-time officials might continue to be a fundamental feature of British trade unions. The report (par. 701) recognized that the limited resources of the trade unions meant that their links with shop stewards would remain fairly tenuous, but it underplayed the importance of the possiblity that shop stewards who had developed work-place bargaining independently of extensive trade-union support might themselves have acquired a tradition of autonomy that might not be susceptible to control by the official trade-union structure.

Third, by holding forth the promise that after a reform of the system legal sanctions might be effective, the Donovan Report failed to give sufficient emphasis to the point that, even with a reform of the institutions of collective bargaining, the only effective mechanism for resolving industrial conflict might continue to be the social machinery rather than the law. It did not press home the point that in a country at the stage of economic, social, and political development that Britain had achieved, legal sanctions might be inherently ineffective as a method of curbing industrial power.

The Donovan Commission had argued (par. 482) that sanctions against trade unions would not be effective under present conditions, because any attempt to require trade unions to discipline unofficial strikers would be more likely to lead to internal disruption in the unions than to a reduction in strikes. The commission (par. 463 and 485) had also pointed to the fact that employers could not on present performance be relied on to enforce legal sanctions against their own employees.[2] It had indicated (par. 495) the inherent weaknesses of the use of direct criminal sanctions against strikes and had portrayed how their enforcement tended to exacerbate rather than suppress industrial conflict.

Yet it did not explain why, even with a reform of institutions, industrial conflicts in Britain might prove not to be susceptible to a legal framework of restrictions on collective industrial action. It did not, for example, develop the point that since industrial conflicts were inherently collective conflicts, the normal physical powers of the state to compel enforcement against individuals or isolated groups of individuals could not be used very readily to bring an end to a strike. It hinted (par. 946) at the fact that the courts were unable to order employees to go back to work or to stay at work because of the limitations on equity jurisdiction to compel involuntary servitude. It did not, however, examine the full implications of the point that in the last resort the refusal to go

---

[2]However, a majority of the commission had also recommended the immediate withdrawal of immunities from unofficial strikers without considering the inconsistency between this recommendation and their findings (par. 894).

to work was a social and political power enjoyed by working citizens in a political democracy (Kahn-Freund and Hepple 1972:7).

The commission accurately assessed the powers of the state to enjoin the leaders of strikes. It also discussed the way in which the state placed pressure on strikers by denying unemployment benefits, supplementary payment, and by delaying tax refunds. It showed how picketing laws could allow other employees to go to work and goods to be delivered to strike-bound premises. It reminded that the state could, under the Emergency Powers Act, use soldiers to do the work of strikers where essential services were threatened. But it did not consider the full implication of the fact that the court system could not directly compel employees to return to work. The royal commission stopped short of developing the proposition that ultimately, therefore, all forms of restrictive labor law—short of police-state measures—directed at forcing large groups of men to return to work, were reduced to a form of persuasion and did not rest upon a foundation of physical compulsion, as did many other areas of law.

To those who wanted to use labor legislation to curb trade-union power, both the analysis and the general prescription for voluntary reform of the Donovan Report were unconvincing. Despite the report's careful analysis of the limitations of legal sanctions in the present circumstances, the notion persisted that the state had reserve powers available to it, even at that point in time, which could be drawn upon to regulate the "activities of mighty subjects [RCTUEA 1968:288]."

This view was based on a rather traditional attitude toward law and the state that would not necessarily have been altered by the rational arguments of a royal commission. Conservative groups influenced by legal advisers had during the late 1950s and the 1960s produced a number of documents advocating a legal solution to the "problems" of British industrial relations (Inns of Court, Conservative & Unionist Society 1958; Conservative Political Centre 1968). Neither politicians nor lawyers were willing to accept that law could not be used to deal effectively with a social problem. It was, therefore, quite clear from the outset that the Conservative Party would not accept the conclusions of the Donovan Report that legal measures should be left to a modest role. Indeed a document advocating the opposite conclusion, *Fair Deal At Work,* was published only 2 or 3 weeks before the commission reported.

The reaction of the Labour government to the Donovan Report, however, was somewhat less predictable. Within a year of the Donovan Report's publication, the Labour government had prepared a White Paper called *In Place of Strife* (Cmnd 3888 1969), containing an attempt to introduce legal restrictions upon industrial action. The legal restrictions proposed by the Labour government in this White Paper were introduced as part of a package deal of measures designed to strengthen the power of trade unions in collective bargaining. Thus the White Paper provided legal support for trade-union recognition and disclosure to them of information, legal rights to trade-union membership, legal protections against unfair dismissals, funds for trade-union development, a narrowing of the disqualification for unemployment benefits, the use of a commission on industrial relations to encourage reform by voluntary means (par. 33), and finally a reassurance that unions would not be expected to have a legal duty to restrain unofficial strikes (par. 96) or be subject to other legal restrictions recommended in the Donovan Report (Par. 42–50).

Moreover, the legal restrictions proposed in *In Place of Strife* were carefully limited. The White Paper suggested only two measures employing legal sanctions to restrict industrial action: a "conciliation pause" for strikes in breach of established collective-disputes procedure, which endangered the national interest, and "strike ballots" for official strikes where the proposed strike would involve a serious threat to the country or public interest and where there was some doubt whether it commanded the support of those concerned. In both instances, the legal sanctions included the use of penal sanctions against strikes. In both instances, the initiative would lie with the government, the Secretary of State for Employment, to invoke the legal sanctions.

The government had taken the point of the royal commission that employers could not be relied on to make use of legal sanctions. It had, however, greatly underestimated the extent of the political constraints upon a Labour government that attempted to impose restrictive legislation upon trade unions. The White Paper's proposals outraged both official and unofficial trade-union groups. The TUC made it plain that it was not prepared to accept the White Paper without the deletion of the penal clauses. Public demonstrations were arranged by trade councils, a large number of back-bench MPs either voted against the government or abstained in the debate on the White Paper in Parliament (3 March 1969), and several weeks later the National Executive of the Labour Party repudiated the White Paper, with the Home Secretary, James Callaghan, joining the vote against it. Only the CBI and Conservative opposition welcomed the proposals as a small step in the direction of stronger legal measures.

The government's reaction in the face of this opposition was distinctly odd. Instead of modifying its proposals in the White Paper, it chose to take the more contentious proposals in *In Place of Strife* and present them in a shorter bill. The decision was first announced by the Chancellor of the Exchequer in the course of presenting his budget. On 15 April 1967 Roy Jenkins included two statements about industrial relations in his budget speech. The government had no intention of renewing its powers to delay wage increases under the Prices and Incomes Act and proposed to enact a shorter version of *In Place of Strife*. The next day in Parliament, Barbara Castle informed the Commons that the short Industrial Relations Bill would include five measures:

1. It would establish a statutory right of every worker to belong to a trade union.
2. It would give the government power to order an employer to recognize a trade union when this had been recommended by the Commission on Industrial Relations.
3. It would give the government power to impose settlements in interunion

disputes under pain of fines, but only after the TUC or the CIR had failed to promote voluntary agreement.

4. It would give the government power to impose a 28-day conciliation pause in an unconstitutional dispute and to order that the status quo be restored and maintained. These powers would be backed by financial penalties.
5. It would remove the disqualifications from unemployment benefits from workers laid off in consequence of a dispute in which they were playing no direct part.

Finally, an assurance was given that "fines would not be permitted to lead to prison and if the trade unions did not like the government's suggestion, that this should be avoided by the automatic attachment of earnings, then alternative ways of recovering payment could be discussed."

The motivation for the timing of the introduction of legal restrictions upon industrial action appeared in part to be a need to fill the hole left by the absence of an incomes policy (Jenkins 1970; Thompson and Engleman 1975:20). Yet this may have been more a matter of presentation for the British public and the foreign exchange market rather than persuasion about the effectiveness of labor legislation as a substitute for incomes policy. The Labour government was certainly aware that the rather limited exercise in the use of legal sanctions to deal with the problem of unofficial and unconstitutional strikes with disproportionate effects could not serve as a substitute for a comprehensive limitation upon the growth of incomes (Jenkins 1970).

Nevertheless, the decision to introduce restrictive labor law, even in this limited form, was based on a profound miscalculation of the possibilities of winning the trade union's acceptance of penal measures. Despite the belief of the Secretary of State for Employment and the Prime Minister, neither the decision to abandon an incomes policy nor the inducements of positive legal rights to trade unions could be successfully traded off for legal penalties against unoffical strikers. The TUC had warned of this in its evidence to the Royal Commission. It had been careful to stress that favorable legislation would not be regarded as strengthening the argument for unfavorable legislation. This warning had been ignored.

The cabinet soon realized that the government did not have the necessary support to enact the penal clauses, and desperately sought a face-saving formula in the form of an acknowledgment by the TUC of some responsibility to intervene in unconstitutional and unofficial strikes. The trade unions were unwilling to consider a compromise in the form of action by trade unions to discipline strikers, backed by a firm guarantee that the TUC would discipline unions that would not take such action. The TUC argued that the trade unions had insufficient power over their members to attempt any such restrictive disciplinary measures and that the TUC had insufficient power over its own member unions. The most the TUC was prepared to do was to take on some responsibility in the form of a "solemn and binding" undertaking to place an obligation on trade unions "to take energetic steps to obtain an immediate resumption of work including action with the rules" in cases where the TUC deemed the strikers to be at fault. Where the TUC considered it unreasonable to order an unconditional return to work, the General Council would merely tender its considered opinion and advice. This formula was finally accepted by the cabinet and the proposed legislation was withdrawn.

In the end, the Labour government was able neither to incorporate the trade unions in legal machinery nor to obtain direct statutory powers of enforcement for the Secretary of State. As Thompson and Engleman (1975:21) commented:

> It is difficult to over-estimate the significance of this victory for the TUC and the defeat for the Labour leadership. While it was true that the TUC had been prodded into going further than ever before, it had retained complete autonomy of action . . . the magnitude of the victory for the unions on this occasion was a key to future Labour policy and to the opposition to subsequent Conservative legislation.

After *In Place of Strife,* the Labour government introduced the Industrial Relations Bill 1970, which contained all the positive recommendations of the White Paper, such as legal support for recognition and unfair dismissals protection, but with all legal restrictions on industrial action deleted. The 1970 Bill was never enacted,for in the general election of June 1970 the Conservatives were returned to office—in part with a mandate to attempt to deal with both the question of overall economic management and the regulation of trade-union organizations.

In its election campaign the Conservative Party had claimed it would enact legislation on the basis of the document *Fair Deal at Work*—its report introduced 3 weeks before the Donovan Commission Report. *Fair Deal at Work* clearly expressed an intention to move away from a voluntaristic approach to industrial relations. Legislation was to be used both to effect institutional reform and to restrict industrial action. The Consultative Document of the Conservative Government's Industrial Relations Bill, based on *Fair Deal at Work*, proclaimed:

> the Government believes that legislation has an essential role to play in the improvement of industrial relations; that a clear statement of what will be the first comprehensive Industrial Relations Act that this country has ever had will itself help to persuade managements and unions towards fairer and more constructive methods of conducting their relations and resolving their differences.

In the parliamentary debate, the Industrial Relations Act was presented as reformist legislation with an emphasis upon using law as a device to persuade social groups to reform. It could help to influence behavior by placing "on record the judgment of the community about what is fair and reasonable." Legal sanctions were stated to be only a background factor or a last resort. The possibility that civil sanctions in the form of labor injunction backed up by normal contempt powers might lead to "criminal-type" penalties was not fully admitted. Robert Carr, the Secretary of State for Employment stated: "We are convinced that legal sanctions should very rarely be brought into play. Above all they should on no account be criminal sanctions [*Hansard* 5th series 1970: Vol. 807, 646].'' Yet any close examination of the provisions of the Act revealed them to provide for the use of legal sanctions on a comprehensive scale to reduce industrial power.

There were two elements in the overall strategy of the Act against strikes. The first was to use law as a device to reform British trade unions into organizations with greater responsibility for curbing industrial action. The second was to provide legal sanctions directly against unofficial industrial action.[3]

The provisions of the Act that attempted to achieve the reform of collective bargaining were heavily influenced by the aim of making trade unions legally responsible for curbing industrial action. Thus the promotion of legally enforceable collective agreements was designed not merely to encourage the reform of collective bargaining institutions, as proclaimed, but also to ensure that, where such agreements were in force, trade unions would have to ''take all such steps as are reasonably practicable'' to prevent strikes in breach of procedure (S.36[2]). And though in most cases legally enforceable collective agreements required the consent of a trade union that was a party to the agreement, there was provision for an imposed procedure agreement where procedural arrangements were considered inadequate by the Secretary of State, the employer, or a relevant trade union (S.37). Similarly, the machinery provided to give legal support to the efforts of trade unions to achieve recognition for the purposes of collective bargaining was made available only to approved trade unions—that is, duly registered trade unions—and it was an unfair industrial practice for a trade union to authorize industrial action while an application for administrative or judicial decisions concerning the recognition dispute was pending (S.54).

The enactment also contained a web of provisions that were directly designed to encourage more ''responsible trade unions.'' In the first place, the legislative immunities from judicial liabilities for industrial action, which had existed since 1906, were withdrawn unless a trade union became a duly registered trade union. But even for duly registered trade unions the immunities were withdrawn for strikes in connection, first, with recognition disputes referred to the Commission of Industrial Relations (S.76); second, with secondary industrial pressure (S.77 and 78); and third, with emergency disputes involving a cooling-off period or strike ballot (S.138). Moreover, even for duly registered trade unions, the immunities were withdrawn for unofficial strike leaders (S.76). This was intended to be a major source of legal pressure directed against unofficial industrial action.

Further, to attain the status of a registered trade union, a status that was a prerequisite for almost all legal rights and immunities, a trade union was required to rewrite its constitution to bring it into conformity with certain

---

[3]The concerns of the Act to give protection to an individual caught in the collectivist pressures of the closed shop or injured by alleged unfair trade-union treatment are not discussed in this chapter but have been treated quite extensively elsewhere. See Wedderburn (1972) and Kahn-Freund (1977).

guiding rules laid down by the Act. The question of whether a trade union's constitutional rules were acceptable was left with an appointed official, the Registrar of Trade Unions. One noteworthy condition of registration was the requirement that a trade union must clarify who among its officials had authority to initiate industrial action and the circumstances in which they could exercise that authority.

A trade union that was not registered was not a trade union at all, according to the Act. It was an "organization of workers." It was debarred from access to most positive legal rights against employers. It was stripped of the traditional tax advantages that registered trade unions had enjoyed under the Trade Union Acts since 1913, or in some cases, 1871. Finally and most importantly, it was stripped of the legal immunities enjoyed by trade unions and trade-union officials under the Trade Disputes Acts of 1906 and 1965. Legally, the trade-union officials and funds of an unregistered union were reduced to the same degree of vulnerability as unofficial strike leaders (S.76).

The overall legislative design of the Industrial Relations Act proved to be fundamentally mistaken as a prescription for change in British industrial relations. The expectations that trade unions would assume legal responsibility for strikes in breach of procedure under legally enforceable collective disputes procedures were never realized. Almost all collective agreements were stamped with a clause stating "this agreement is not intended to be legally binding [Weekes, Mellish, Dickens, and Lloyd 1975]." Similarly, the expectation that trade unions would respond to the disincentives and incentives contained within the Act and reform their authority structures and rule books in order to register was not met. Instead, the great majority of trade unions deliberately remained unregistered as part of a campaign of noncooperation with the Act, which was promoted by the TUC (Weekes *et al.* 1975). The strategy of noncooperation had been devised by the TUC in a concerted effort to prevent the Act's enforcement after a major campaign against the enactment of the legislation had failed. This strategy proved remarkably effective. The nonregistration campaign by trade unions demonstrated clearly that the Act required the assistance and cooperation of trade unions in order to have any impact.

The immediate result of nonregistration, however, was to make trade unions vulnerable to a wide range of legal action by employers. This was clearly built into the Act but was equally clearly an unhoped-for consequence. The many unregistered trade unions, including almost all of the members of the TUC, were for the first time stripped of their legal immunity as organizations, for inducement of breach of contract since 1906. Thus, for the first time in 65 years, their funds were uncontrollably at risk to pay damages for torts committed in the course of industrial action.[4] The shop stewards and full-time trade-union officials who led strikes were also stripped of the immunities enjoyed since 1906 for in-

---

[4] Since 1906 trade unions have paid the damages incurred by trade-union officials in legal actions. But this expense has been voluntarily borne.

ducing breaches of contracts of employment (S.76). In either case an employer could now obtain an injunction against the leaders of even a "primary strike"—that is, a strike between employees and their own employer.

The inevitable confrontations between employers, tempted by the possibilities of legal sanctions to deal with industrial disputes, and the now legally vulnerable trade unions and strike leaders, occurred first on the docks. A "blacking" campaign by members of the Transport and General Workers Union, largely organized by joint shop-steward committees as part of a campaign against the impact of "containerization" upon the employment of dock workers, gave rise to a series of legal actions. In *Heatons* v. *TGWU* [1973], several "blacked" firms obtained an injunction against the trade union on the theory that the trade unions had "authorized" the unofficial activity. The TGWU did not appear in the National Industrial Relations Court, the court of first instance, in line with the TUC policy of noncooperation. It now, however, chose to pay the fine and appeal the case, first to the Court of Appeal and then to the House of Lords. In the meantime, cases directly against the unofficial leaders of the blacking were brought, first by a group of depot workers and then by a company called Midland Cold Storage Limited. Both were possibly influenced by statements made by the Court of Appeal in *Heatons* that the use of legal action against individuals leading strikes was the appropriate method of enforcing the Act. In the first case, the three individual defendants never appeared, and a sympathy strike of more than 310,000 workers in five different ports broke out on the docks, with a hint of a national stoppage. At this point their case was taken up unexpectedly by a court official, the Official Solicitor, who succeeded in convincing the Court of Appeal that there was insufficient evidence to prove that the individuals had violated the injunction. The Official Solicitor had not been asked for by the defendants but rather, it later appeared, had been requested to appear by the Court of Appeal on the instigation of counsel for the plaintiffs.

In *Midland Cold Storage* v. *Turner* [1972], however, five out of seven dockers were found by the NIRC to have violated the injunction and were ordered to be jailed. Their incarceration created a massive confrontation between the legal process and the trade-union movement: a nationwide strike on the docks, sympathy strikes elsewhere, and a vote by the TUC for a 1-day general strike. The deus ex machina this time was a decision by the House of Lords in the *Heatons* case, which found the trade unions vicariously liable for the actions of its shop stewards and allowed the NIRC to release the jailed dockers on the unusual ground that the primary means of enforcing the Act should be against the funds of organizations and not the liberty of individuals (*The Times* 1972). The application for the discharge of the dockers was made without their request; they neither apologized nor gave assurances they would abide by the Court's orders in the future (Anderman and Davies 1974:36).

The House of Lords' judgment in *Heatons* that trade unions might be vicariously liable for the actions of their shop stewards under a doctrine of implied authority at first glance appeared to have the virtue of providing a defendant susceptible to the enforcement processes of the law. In the last resort the funds of the union could be sequestered if fines for contempt were not paid. However, on closer examination the rather artificial legal bridge created between the trade union and unofficial industrial action by this new legal doctrine did not necessarily provide a defendant with the resources to end the industrial action. Given the relationship that existed between trade-union officials, shop stewards, and work groups, the net result of legal pressure on the trade unions was more likely to place trade-union officials in an impossible position than to produce a return to work (McCarthy and Ellis 1975:546). On the docks the ultimate return to work had been procured by an agreement to resolve the "containerization" issue, an agreement that had been negotiated by the General Secretary of the TGWU, Jack Jones, with a representative of the Port Employers, Lord Aldington. Throughout all stages of the legal proceedings the blacking had continued, the dockers remaining undeterred by the legal liabilities incurred by the trade unions or the shop stewards.

The failure of the Act to achieve its purpose of restricting industrial action by legal means was mirrored by its failure in other respects. As Thompson and Engleman (1975:126) describe it:

> It was clear long before the election of February 1974 that the Industrial Relations Act had failed in its major objective of bringing a viable new framework of law to British industrial relations. It had ceased to have any major impact on the leading industrial relations issues of the day and had virtually been placed in suspended animation because the potential repercussions of bringing cases were too risky for most possible litigants.

THE CONSEQUENCES OF THE FAILURE TO IMPOSE RESTRICTIVE LABOR LEGISLATION IN THE 1968–1974 PERIOD

The experience of 1968–1974 raised fundamental questions about the relationship in Britain between the trade-union movement and the state. Two sources of weakness of legislation when confronted by industrial power were clearly exposed. In the first place, the experience of the Industrial Relations Act led to a greater understanding that there were limits to the possibilities of implementing legal sanctions either to make trade unions artificially responsible for unofficial action or to provide legal restrictions aimed directly against rank-and-file unofficial leaders. Where groups of workers were determined to refuse to work, they could hold out regardless of the threat of enforcement of legal sanctions against their leaders. Given democratic assumptions, no government could afford to use legal compulsion to curb large-scale industrial action on any significant scale (Kahn-Freund and Hepple 1972:60).

Second, the attempts to impose restrictive labor legislation during the 1968–1974 period heightened awareness of the political difficulties of convincing trade unions in Britain as institutions to accept legislation containing legal sanctions against industrial action as part of a framework of law for industrial relations. Restrictive labor legislation was regarded by British trade unions as a threat to the tradition of autonomy, a tradition that had proved its worth to the trade unions (Flanders 1970:38). In other words, such legislation was viewed by the trade unions as a challenge to their very existence as institutions. In such cases, not only rank and file movements but also certain trade unions appeared to be willing to resist legislation even to the point of defying enacted legislation. Victor Feather, the General Secretary of the TUC, stated shortly after the jailing of the dockers that the unions had always respected the law but they did not accept the Industrial Relations Act as the law of the land. The second-largest trade union in Britain, the Amalgamated Union of Engineering Workers, would neither observe court orders nor voluntarily pay fines for contempt of court (Wedderburn 1972: Lewis 1976).

Yet if the power of trade unions to resist legislation was firmly established, it was less clear to what extent and under what circumstances the trade unions would use that power to insist on autonomy from legal regulation. On 22 July 1972 *The Times* argued: "the trade union claim is much more than to say that this is a bad Act. It is to say that their affairs, and their affairs alone, cannot be legislated for, and that they will not accept *any such* legislation." Only 2 years later, however, the TUC was prepared to countenance legislation on prices and incomes, which contained legal sanctions applicable against trade unions and others who organized strikes against an enforcement order of the Pay Board (Crouch 1977).

In the intervening period, the Conservative government had attempted to win the trade unions' consent to a policy of voluntary wage restraint along with a voluntary policy of price restraint by employers. Despite the simultaneous campaign against the Industrial Relations Act, TUC representatives participated fully in talks, treating them as a bargaining exercise. Wage restraint was considered in exchange for concessions on strict price controls, taxation policy, rent reductions, council-house building, social benefits and pensions, and the nonoperation or repeal of the Industrial Relations Act. In this exchange, which the TUC later claimed had included an offer by the government to "enter into a real relationship with both sides of industry in the management of the economy," some agreement had been reached on certain issues. However, the talks broke down because the government insisted that the issue of the Industrial Relations Act was not open to debate (TUC 1973b). When the Prime Minister announced a total pay freeze for 3 months, with some controls on prices (Hansard 5th series 1973:Vol. 848, 622ff.), following it with Stages 2 and 3 of a statutory incomes policy, the trade unions quite clearly took some effort to avoid confrontations and continued to participate in a tacit relationship with the state on incomes-policy issues. Motions calling for a total boycott of the Pay Board were rejected at the TUC Annual Congress (TUC 1973a).

This statutory prices and incomes policy ultimately did produce a confrontation between the government and the miners, which resulted in a decision by the government to use the confrontation as an election issue in an election that it lost. But the record prior to the 1974 election showed a pattern of tacit compliance by trade unions with the statutory pay policy that extended into the early months of the new Labour government (Crouch 1977:245). It is important to remember this point because the combination of the TUC's successful boycott of the NIRC and the Industrial Relations Act, taken together with the miners' strike of 1974 that allegedly "brought down the government," led to writings that suggested that Britain was ungovernable and that parliamentary democracy had broken down.

The Labour government that was elected in 1974 appeared to act upon the assumption that restrictive labor legislation was in large measure to be eschewed. It chose to engage in close consulation on the structure of labor legislation as well as the form of incomes policy as part of the "social contract" between the TUC and the government. Under the social contract the TUC was offered a high degree of influence in formulating labor legislation, apparently in part as a quid pro quo for cooperation with restraints on incomes. At least during the 1974–1978 period the social contract involved the exercise by the TUC of a high degree of influence in formulating labor legislation, initially in return for a high degree of responsibility by the TUC for the implementation of a jointly agreed policy on prices and incomes.

The immediate product of this cooperation was an Act to repeal the Industrial Relations Act[5] and new legislation on job security and trade union rights.[6] A commitment was also made to a law on industrial democracy—a legal entitlement for trade unionists to sit on the boards of companies—which was followed by a report of a committee of inquiry on this subject, the Bullock Committee (Report of the Committee of Inquiry on Industrial Democracy, Cmnd 6706 1977).

As a result, the structure of labor legislation in Britain today appears to be distinctly favorable to trade unions and trade unionists. A series of statutes provides a "floor of employment protections" for all employees in their contractual relationship with employers, whether those employees are members of trade unions or not.[7] The Employment Protection Act also provides a virtual charter of positive legal rights for trade union organizations and trade unionists against employers, including a legal right to recognition by employees for purposes of collective bargaining, a legal right to disclosure of information, and a legal right to consultation in advance of redundancies (Anderman 1976; Bercusson 1976). The rather unusual feature of this legal framework is that in almost all cases the

---

[5]Trade Union and Labour Relations Act 1974, later reinforced by the Trade Union and Labour Relations (Amendment) Act 1976.

[6]The Employment Protection Act 1975.

[7]Now consolidated into the Employment Protection (Consolidation) Act, 1978.

defendant is the employer: there are few liabilities placed on trade unions or trade-union officials.

In respect of collective disputes there is a return to a non-restrictionism on a scale that exceeds the legal framework of the 1906 and 1965 Trade Disputes Acts. The immunities for trade-union officials and unofficial leaders extend to economic pressure on secondary employers (Trade Union and Labour Relations Act, S.13). Trade-union funds are protected from almost all vicarious liability for the torts of its officials (S.14). Collective agreements can be legally enforceable only if trade unions agree to such an arrangement in writing. Finally, all positive legal rights have been given to the trade unions without a quid pro quo being exacted from them in the form of a peace obligation while using the legal machinery. The theory upon which the legal framework proceeds is that in all cases of collective conflict in pursuit of collective bargaining objectives, the method of resolution is to be negotiation, or conciliation or mediation by a voluntary government service, the Advisory, Conciliation and Arbitration Service. Legislation has therefore attempted, albeit not entirely successfully, to remove legal sanctions from the arena of economic industrial conflict.

This change in the legal framework reflects a wider social change. The Labour government has succeeded in incorporating trade-union leaders into the administrative machinery of government: the planning exercises of the National Economic Development Organization; the formulation of tripartite incomes and prices policies; and the Councils of the Advisory, Conciliation and Arbitration Service, the Manpower Services Commission, etc. These social developments have been viewed as a form of incipient "corporatism" between trade unions and the state, albeit a corporatism based on a bargaining process between the state and trade unions rather than forcible incorporation by the state (Panitch 1976:245–513; Crouch 1977).

One result of this bargaining process in constitutional terms is to give some trade unions a significant degree of influence directly with members of the cabinet and civil service departments. These direct consultations about legislation and policy may impinge upon the normal parliamentary processes. At the same time, the trade unions themselves have been demonstrably influenced by their participation in the processes of the formulation of economic and social policy. Thus in 1975 and 1976 negotiations produced fairly restrictive wages policies. And in 1977, when it was clear that a Stage 3 of incomes policy could not be jointly agreed upon, the trade unions tacitly adhered to an incomes norm set out unilaterally by the Chancellor of the Exchequer in his budget speech of April 1977.

This high degree of participation by trade unions in the formulation of economic and social policy, however, does not appear likely to result in a growing acceptance by trade unions of legislation that imposes legal sanctions on industrial action. The trade unions' reaction to restrictive labor legislation is influenced by their view of how such legislation affects their institutional interests. There seems to be something of a distinction drawn by the trade unions between general labor legislation and incomes-policy legislation in this respect. Thus, even though the favorable labor legislation of 1974 and 1975 has undermined the trade unions' argument that they have asked nothing more of the law than that it leave them alone, British trade unions are not likely to regard those legal rights as entitling a government to enact restrictive legislation imposing legal responsibility for industrial action where such legislation is regarded as a threat in institutional terms. On the other hand, the tacit acquiescence of trade unions in prices and incomes policies during certain periods suggests that the trade unions consider that in certain circumstances it may be regarded as institutionally useful to accept incomes restraint in return for a greater role in the formulation of social and economic policies.

One implication of this analysis is that a major constraint upon the exercise of political authority by the state in this sphere appears to be the trade unions' own perception of what threatens their institutional interests as much as the government's view of what should be the policy. As long as the trade-union movement is backed by extensive industrial power, this is undoubtedly the case, and it is one consequence of the 1968–1974 period that this is more clearly understood.

Yet it is also true that the trade unions, both by virtue of their functions and because of their experience of increased participation in the formulation of social and economic policy, may themselves have begun to identify those interests more closely with the preservation of economic stability, even at the cost of delaying social and economic reforms. Insofar as the trade unions take this view, however, they are constrained by their own members' views. The ability of trade unions to accept incomes policies depends in turn upon an acceptance by members of the leaders' views.

REFERENCES

CASES

Crofter Harris Tweed v. *Veitch* [1942] A.C. 435.
Heatons v. *TGWU* [1973] A.C. 15.
Midland Cold Storage v. *Turner* [1972] *I.C.R.* 230.
Rookes v. *Barnard* [1964] A.C. 1129.
Stratford Ltd. v. *Lindley* [1965] A.C. 269.

OTHER SOURCES

Anderman, S.
    1976   *Employment Protection: A New Legal Framework.* London: Butterworth.
Anderman, S., and P. L. Davies
    1974   "Injunction procedure in labour disputes II," *Industrial Law Journal 3* (1). (March):
Bercusson, B.
    1976   *The Employment Protection Act.* London: Sweet and Maxwell.

Conservative Political Centre
    1968   *Fair Deal at Work.* London: Conservative Political Centre.
Crouch, C.
    1977   *Class Conflict and the Industrial Relations Crisis.* London: Heinemann Educational Books.
Flanders, A.
    1970   *Management and Unions.* London: Faber.
Griffiths, J. A. C.
    1970   *The Politics of the Judiciary.* London: Fontana.
Hansard 5th Series
    1970   Vol. 807:676.
    1973   Vol 848:622ff.
Inns of Court Conservative & Unionist Society
    1958   *A Giant's Strength.* London: Inns of Court Conservative & Unionist Society.
Jenkins, P.
    1970   *The Battle of Downing Street.* London: Charles Kingsley.
Kahn-Freund, O.
    1977   *Labour and the Law.* (2nd Ed.) London: Stevens.
Kahn-Freund, O., and B. Hepple
    1972   *Laws Against Strikes.* Fabian Research Series 305. London.
Lewis, R.
    1976   "The historical development of labour law," *British Journal of Industrial Relations XIX* (1).
            (March)
McCarthy W. E. J., and N. Ellis
    1975   *Management by Agreement.* London: Hutchinson.
Panitch, L.
    1976   *Social Democracy and Industrial Militancy.* London: Cambridge University Press.
Pelling, H.
    1963   *History of British Trade Unions.* Harmondsworth: Penguin.
Robson, W. A.
    1973   "The constraints on British government." *The Political Quarterly* (April–June).
Royal Commission on Trade Unions and Employers Association, 1965–68
    1968   *Report,* Cmnd. 3623. London: HMSO.
Thompson A. W. S., and S. R. Engleman
    1975   *The Industrial Relations Act: A Review and Analysis.* London: Martin Robinson.
The Times
    1972   (London).
Trades Union Congress
    1968   *Evidence to RCTUEA. Selected Written Evidence.* London: HMSO.
    1973a   *Annual Report and Congress Proceedings.* London: Trades Union Congress.
    1973b   *The Chequers and Downing Street Talks.* London: Trades Union Congress.
Wedderburn, K. W.
    1971   *The Worker and the Law.* Harmondsworth: Penguin.
    1972   "Labour law and labour relations in Britain," *British Journal of Industrial Relations X* (2).
            (July).
Weekes, B., N. Mellish, L. Dickens, and J. Lloyd
    1975   *Industrial Relations and the Limits of the Law.* Oxford: Basil Blackwell.

14

WARTIME INDUSTRIAL RELATIONS LEGISLATION AND LEGAL INSTITUTIONS AND PROCEDURES: THE BRITISH MUNITIONS OF WAR ACTS, 1915–1917

G. R. RUBIN

This study is an examination of the impact on legal institutions and procedures of British legislation during World War I that was designed to promote
industrial discipline in the munitions factories. Against a pre-war background of
"voluntarist" industrial relations, characterized by the absence of a comprehensive code of labor regulation,[1] the novel provisions of this "emergency" legislation introduced a new dimension into the relations between capital and labor.
The effects of this controversial legislation on industrial relations throughout the
period of the war have been extensively covered in the literature, but less attention has been given to the effects on the tribunal machinery created to service the
enforcement of its provisions. It is this aspect that is the subject of the present
chapter. In particular, we shall consider some of the expedients devised by those
involved, principally munitions tribunal chairmen and government officials
themselves, to moderate the penal impact of the measure, actions taken plausibly
with a view to lessening hostility to an unpopular Act and to its wider objectives.

---

[1] For the most part, this state of affairs was a product of the powerful trade unions' conception of
their self-interests, and of their experiences with the nineteenth- and early twentieth-century judges
(Pelling 1968; McCarthy 1972).

257

The Imposition of Law

Copyright © 1979 by Academic Press, Inc.
All rights of reproduction in any form reserved.
ISBN 0-12-145450-9

The wartime background necessitating the statute has been described by numerous authors and thus requires only a brief outline here.[2] The essence of the matter was the failure of a number of voluntary agreements, involving at various times trade unions, employers, and government, designed in the main to relax trade-union restrictive practices. These restrictions prevented the "dilution" of skilled labor—that is, the replacement of craftsmen by less skilled and more plentiful workers—and was a necessary step if the output of munitions were to be significantly increased. It was this bottleneck, exacerbated by the War Office's widespread and reckless recruitment of skilled workers for military service, that led to near-catastrophic shell shortages at the front in the first half of 1915. As a compromise between voluntarism and industrial conscription under military rule, then, the first Munitions of War Act, that of July 1915, was conceived by its architect, Lloyd George, first Minister of Munitions, as a means of compelling trade unionists in general to reform their work norms and in the case of the skilled men in particular, to relax their opposition to dilution.

The provisions of the 1915 Act were fourfold. These were, first, to declare work stoppages illegal and to substitute compulsory arbitration; second, to enforce a system of factory discipline to punish minor infringements of work rules; third, to render unlawful any rules, customs, or practices of organized labor that hindered the output of munitions—that is, to forbid the maintenance of the craft unions' restrictive practices and to grant legitimacy to the dilution program; and, finally, to secure permanence of labor by requiring workmen to obtain a leaving certificate from their employers before undertaking alternative munitions employment, with a penalty of 6 weeks' unemployment imposed on the workman in the event that such certificate was lawfully withheld. All infringements were triable before specially constituted munitions tribunals, modeled on the existing national-insurance panels and comprising employers' and workmen's assessors as well as qualified chairmen.[3] How these tribunals reacted to their task of imposing controversial law is the central issue of this chapter.

The first question that arises is whether it could justifiably have been expected that such an alien legal framework would succeed in attaining its objectives, in view of the expectations of the period under review. Although the rank and file refused to accept large-scale dilution of labor and to refrain from engaging in strikes,[4] many of the trade-union leaders could see advantages for themselves in

---

[2] The most recent work is by Adams (1978). Other works are cited in the text.

[3] For a full discussion of the structure, organization, and jurisdiction of the munitions tribunals see Rubin (1977).

[4] It is not alleged that the men, for the most part, were unpatriotic. Patriotism and the spirit of sacrifice were considered proper attitudes, but different criteria were applied when a threat to one's economic livelihood was perceived. The fact that the skilled men were suspicious of the government's assurances that, after the war, the employers would agree to a return to the *status quo ante* did not help. Nor did the government's refusal to stamp out war profiteering by price controls promote mutual confidence.

supporting an agreed-upon measure of compulsion. Their credibility was being undermined by unofficial action, and they wished to regain firmer control over the membership. Moreover, being allowed a voice in government policy was a relatively novel and symbolically important experience for most of them. But in regard to the rank-and-file union members, could legal measures be used "effectively" in place of exhortation? Could the law be successfully invoked to render those on the shop floor submissive to government policy? Would it meet obstruction? If so, in what form?

There was no romantic faith placed in the symbolic appeal of the rule of law as the key to success. Indeed, as we shall see, there was no shortage of gratuitous advice as to the catastrophes that would befall such a policy when the blunt instrument of the law confronted deviant shop-floor norms. However, some believed that although confrontations might be the unavoidable accompaniment to the prosecution of a controversial policy, that policy was essential to national survival. The leading civil servants at the Ministry of Munitions and the Minister himself, Lloyd George, took this view. Once legislation was on the statute book, they believed, rigorous enforcement would have a salutary effect on the morale of the munitions workers. A policy of bold prosecutions undertaken by the ministry itself as well as by individual employers would sufficiently deter strikers and those committing breaches of works disciplinary rules (Harris 1977:212–213).

Other observers were not so sure. For example, two distinguished ministry advisers, Professors Adams and Geldart, after surveying the events of the previous few months, concluded that "an unsound Bill may pass the House of Commons but before long its application will give rise to serious trouble in the country [Wrigley 1976:121]."[5] G.D.H. Cole (1915:224), who became an adviser to the Amalgamated Society of Engineers (ASE), the union most affected by the Act's provisions, took the view that "the settlement reached with the passing of the Munitions Act is so unsatisfactory and shows so little appreciation of the real problems to be faced, that it will inevitably break down if the workers have a spark of life left in them." And Beatrice Webb's diary entry for 22 June confided, "if the Government persists [with the Munitions Bill] there will be considerable and perhaps dangerous reaction against the patriotism of some of the [trade-union] leaders [M.I. Cole 1952:41–42]."

Indeed, the ministry historians are said to have believed that the Act that eventually appeared was drafted "with a lack of understanding of the workman's mind." A recent historian has questioned whether there was indeed such a lack of understanding (Davidson 1971:334), but the evidence would seem to support the ministry historians. As those closest to the temper of the men on the shop floor, the full-time trade-union officials were in a favorable position to assess the

---

[5] W. G. S. Adams was Gladstone Professor of Political Theory and Institutions at Oxford. W. M. Geldart was Vinerian Professor of English Law at the same university, and a noted commentator on trade-union law.

potential impact of the Act. One of these officials, an ASE organizing district delegate, had no doubt that the government's legislative attempts would be a flop. "That the whole business is both fatuous and silly, time will tell," he reported to his members when the bill became law (ASE September 1915:21). Viewed against attempts at enforcement through the tribunals, his prediction was not wildly inaccurate.

THE LAW IN ACTION

With the Act on the statute book, the various parties—government, employers, and unions—had to decide individually on whether to utilize the tribunal provisions of the Act, and if so, how extensively. The first test was, in truth, no test at all. When on 15 July 200,000 South Wales miners struck in pursuit of a wage demand, noisy threats of prosecutions by the government could not be taken seriously. As the tribunal chairman wrote to Lloyd George:

> It is of course impossible to summon and try 200,000 men and only a few at first can be dealt with, and the length of time before there can be any real enforcement of the sentence will I fear only lead the men generally to regard the Act as ineffective. . . . The first prosecution will, I fear, prevent any settlement [Wrigley 1976:126].

And so no prosecution took place. Lloyd George, in effect, capitulated to the miners, and they obtained nearly everything they demanded. As the *Official History* of the Ministry of Munitions soberly observed, "The strike demonstrated the impotence of legal provisions for compulsory arbitration where a large body of obstinate men were determined to cease work rather than surrender their claims [Ministry of Munitions 1923:Vol. IV, ii, 9]." It was still a matter for speculation as to how the tribunals, when called upon to adjudicate, would respond to the challenge of enforcing unpopular laws.

Soon after this disaster, the initiative in prosecuting was taken by a number of employers, frequently the leading employers in the industry. On several such occasions, which have since become *causes célèbres* in the literature on the period, the result was to stiffen opposition to the Munitions Act and to set off a sustained and vociferous campaign against it, involving meetings, conferences, and other measures pressurizing the government to give way. These prosecutions naturally also reinforced the lesson drawn from the South Wales debacle—that in seeking to impose law in areas of extreme delicacy, traditionally hostile to compulsion, a policy of undifferentiated legal assault, injudiciously launched, was bound to meet with entrenched opposition to the use of legal measures. This defiance of, and contempt for, the law would in turn give rise to martyrs, the authority of the government would be further compromised, and its attempt to increase output would be further jeopardized.

The sequence of, and the sequel to, the well-documented prosecutions of shipyard workers employed by Fairfields of Glasgow between August and October 1915 shed further light on the above points (Ministry of Munitions 1923:Vol. IV, ii, 49-65). In the first Fairfields case—the prosecution of coppersmiths who went on strike when the firm altered working conditions without consulting the men—the fines imposed were eventually paid by the union because, as their branch secretary declared, the men "regarded the action of their members as quite legal." A dispute over the essence of legality, based on a competing logic, failed to impress the tribunal. The ministry historians explained that the men's actions could not be regarded simply as an "act of unreason." They were rather the result of the employers' professed determination to use the Munitions Act to enforce change. Thus, we probably have an example—predictable, one would have thought—of the Munitions Act's causing, and not preventing, a strike.

The next Fairfields prosecution arose out of the shipwrights' strike, caused by the sacking of two of their colleagues and the decision of the management to endorse the leaving certificates of the men with the reason for their dismissal—namely, "not attending to work." The work force, interpreting this as a collective slur on their character and as threatening their future employment prospects, demanded not only the removal of the obnoxious remarks, but complete reinstatement of the men—threatening, if their demands were not met, a total walkout. The latter duly took place. For its part, the ministry viewed these events as a test case—in retrospect a policy of crass foolishness, since the whole of the Clyde would be in danger of complete shutdown if prominent strikers were prosecuted. In trying to set an example by prosecuting carefully selected targets, the government allowed itself to be deluded.

Seventeen men were prosecuted for the strike. In giving judgment, the tribunal chairman, Sheriff Fyfe, declared that the court was not concerned whether the dismissal of the two men was reasonable or not: that was not relevant to the present complaint. He stressed that reasons for going on strike did not matter under the Act. Men might have a grievance or they might not. The tribunal had nothing to do with that. And so the 17 men were fined £5 each, a pointed contrast with the fines of 2/6d imposed on the Fairfields coppersmiths just one month earlier. The *Glasgow Herald* commented, "Yesterday's proceedings were intended to demonstrate that the Munitions of War Act is a weapon of powerful use and that it will be used, given just cause, with ruthless energy. . . . For the moment, the men seem to be disposed to think that further defiance of the Act is useless [4 September 1915]." Yet the realistic recognition that the mobilization of the Act would not necessarily result in the production of any additional warships or even a single shell haunted the editorial writer. In such an event, he thought, military discipline was the last weapon in the legal armory.

In fact, the imposition of fines did not dispose of the matter. Of the 17 prosecuted, 14 paid their fines (from money advanced by the union) some 3 weeks after the trial and after involved and fruitless negotiations as to their obligation, social as well as legal, to pay. Three others refused to pay and 2 weeks later were arrested and imprisoned. Local ministry officials reported on the increasingly hostile mood on the Clyde, and the position became critical when other grievances arose. A telegram was sent to the minister, threatening a stoppage unless the men were released, and Lloyd George agreed to an inquiry into the dispute and to the wider issues arising from the administration of the Act. In a sense, it was a remarkable concession to set up a committee of inquiry into a government measure barely 2 months in operation, and at the behest of organized workers of whom the unofficial movement was in the van and from whom the initiative had sprung. As to the immediate problem, Lloyd George insisted, in the face of a complete stoppage, that to release the men, which was the first demand addressed to the committee of inquiry, "would mean that the Munitions of War Act would become a dead letter. Yet it is my last resort short of conscription [Wilson 1970:150]." He managed to impress the national trade-union leaders that the only compromise acceptable would be if others paid the fines of the three men (apparently the Shipwrights' Union refused to do so). This was quickly agreed upon, and the dispute fizzled out, leaving the way clear for a thoroughgoing critique of the workings of the Act by the committee.

The episode had followed a predictable pattern. A narrow issue and a minor fracas became a constitutional crisis because of the heavy-handed use of inappropriate legal measures. If the original two shipwrights had been dismissed for neglect of work, given their certificates, and told to seek employment elsewhere, the subsequent convulsions might have been postponed. By insisting on the endorsements, and thus making gratuitous use of the penal provisions of the Act, the managment had introduced a new and more hostile element into the proceedings. Once this course had been taken, the issue moved to a higher plane, eventually requiring major ministerial concessions to reach a conclusion. As it was, the subsequent Amendment Act of 1916 removed only some of the grievances of the men, leaving more combustible material to ignite at any time.

CONFLICT IN COURT

Acute conflict was also experienced directly during the conduct of the tribunal hearings, presenting a different if somewhat less profound challenge to the authorities. Provision had to be made for the presence of police at tribunal hearings in order to deal with any disturbance (SRO:HH 31/22), and, indeed, disorder did erupt at a number of tribunals when unpopular prosecutions were taking place. At Liverpool, for instance, open resentment was shown of the litigiousness of the shipbuilding firm, Cammell Laird, toward its employees, and pointed comparisons between the firm and the Germans were voiced during the hearing. (PRO:MUN 5/353/344/1). After the second Fairfields prosecutions, the Shipbuilding Employers' Federation Secretary, Thomas Biggart, who was also a leading Glasgow solicitor, complained to Lloyd George that the Sheriff had "allowed the union's representatives to pop up and down. There were also

30 or 40 men sitting in the front seat of the court and he allowed at least half a dozen of them to begin to raise points and ask questions, and of course the matter got out of hand [PRO:MUN 5/48/300/9]." It is not recorded what Biggart made of the workman's claim, shouted to a company official addressing the court, that "It is *we* who are trying *you!* [PRO:MUN 5/48/300/9]." *The Times* (26 October 1915) later reported on "uproarious proceedings" with the chairman restoring order on one occasion only by threatening to commit the men responsible to prison. In another case it was reported that the clerk to the tribunal was obliged to seek the assistance of the police to maintain order (*The Times* 26 October 1915). On yet another occasion, when 40 men were prosecuted, the Chief Constable of Glasgow busied himself with working out the quickest way of obtaining military reinforcements for the tribunal if, in the event of findings of guilt, the army were required to "overcome the mob at once and completely get them in hand." The local ministry intelligence officer reported that "Gallacher, one of the biggest agitators from Paisley, was up at the trial making a great row [Hinton 1973:136]." This was a reference to William Gallacher, who became Communist member of parliament for West Fife during the 1930s and 1940s. In his autobiography he recalled:

> We were always able to get sufficient lads to pack the court when any worker was brought before it. McGill [another activist] was always there with the *Herald* [the leading Labour newspaper] and a selection of pamphlets, and used to go along the rows of seats selling his wares until the Sheriff came in. We were able to make such a farce of these courts that eventually the authorities had to abandon them and drop the practice of summoning workers on trivial charges [Gallacher 1966:71-72].

Indeed, the uproar became so widespread that the Treasury Solicitor was consulted on the applicability of the law of contempt and on the power of a tribunal chairman to keep order in his court. As regards contempt, he advised that no powers in fact existed, though the offender could be ordered out of the court and the police could assist in this. If the offender were sufficiently disorderly, he could be ordered to be taken in charge by a constable, and be brought before the magistrate to be bound over to be of good behavior (Ministry of Munitions 1923:Vol. IV, ii).

Yet a number of qualifications may be made. First, Gallacher was prone to exaggeration. Second, there were limits to what could be achieved by such public displays of contempt for the legal process. Note in particular how the Chief Constable credited the munitions workers with a sense of constitutional propriety—that they would riot only if found guilty! And even this assessment probably testified to overreaction on the part of a particularly nervous police official. But more important, the disorders, far from being a sign of powerful opposition, were rather the symptoms of frustration. True, the protest led to some minor reforms in procedure and certainly contributed to the decision to abolish imprisonment for practically all Munitions Acts offenses. But both the form and the content of the outbursts were dictated by a sense of impotence in the face of legal processes, which could not at this stage be significantly deflected from their natural course. Moreover, the rhetoric of defiance from the dock soon to be associated with John Maclean[6] (Broom 1973:Appendix II) could derive *its* impact from the colorful and majestic background of the High Court of Justiciary. With its bewigged and solemn Senator of the College of Justice on the bench and numerous counsel and flunkeys of every description, attired in black gowns and moving back and forth across the court, a lasting impression would be made. The atmosphere of the munitions tribunal, by contrast, would instantly deaden the impact of dramatic and defiant speechmaking, reducing it to the level of an embarrassing interjection. The tribunal was not the forum for inspired rhetoric. So the pattern took the limited and, at times, infantile form described above.

Crucially, there was a political element in the protests. For as long as the legal process characteristically individualizes politically inspired actions hostile to the establishment and treats them as mere technical breaches of the law—collectively opposing the dilution scheme, for example, is translated into failure to obey a lawful order—then the responses generated must be viewed as an attempt to reassert the *collective-political* in place of the *individual-legal* in order to counteract the internally consistent logic of the latter. Ineffective as such protests may have been (*pace* Gallacher), they nonetheless symbolized a deeper hostility to the political-legal order as seen by the participants and fellow travelers among the workers.

Despite this charged atmosphere, not all tribunal chairmen, as we shall see, reacted sternly to any display of contempt for the rule of law. But most of them, being middle-class and usually lawyers, naturally viewed the workers' predicament in a different light than did the workmen themselves. Their assumptions and values would frequently surface in the explicit manner in which they expressed their abhorrence of those appearing before them. They perceived such workers as unreasonable, and often unreasoning, particularly those found guilty of persistent loss of time or of refusal to work overtime, or who were absent from work without permission or who indulged in gambling and card playing during working hours. Implicit in the tribunals' condemnations of these very often petty breaches of rules was the belief that they arose from character defects and displayed a lack of responsibility, a condition that could be remedied only by a stiff dose of punishment washed down with an appropriate discourse on the superiority of middle-class values and patterns of behavior. In a case of individual misconduct, it was natural for the lawyer-chairman to treat it as an attack on the authority of the employer. Such behavior testified to the workman's lack of patriotism and thus provided an opportunity for a panegyric in praise of same, and also in favor of steadiness of work. This message, together with a round condemnation of the vices of slacking, drink, and gambling, constituted

[6] The educated and articulate Maclean was a socialist propagandist dismissed from his post as a schoolteacher because of his anti-war speeches. He was imprisoned several times during the war. His speech during his trial at the High Court in Edinburgh in May 1918 was later printed and sold as a pamphlet.

the stock fare delivered in the course of judgment to many a munitions worker; female as well as male.

Nor did the workmen's assessors succeed in mediating a sympathy for working-class conduct that formed the basis of a prosecution. Criticisms within the labor movement were additionally leveled against their own nominees because "these were chosen from obsolete panels constituted under the Insurance Act of 1911 and were often not *bona fide* Labour representatives. Consequently, all sections of workers joined in the demand . . . for the revision of the panels of assessors if the system was retained [G.D.H. Cole 1923:116]." Images of a despised "enemy within" constituted the one piece of common ground for patriotic chairmen and class-conscious craftsmen. Even more, however, it was the pettiness of many of the charges that added fuel to workers' criticisms of the Act, together with the failure on the part of the tribunals to take into consideration a complaint frequently voiced by the unions during such hearings—namely, the incompetent manner in which work schedules were arranged by the employers. It was this factor, so it was argued, which often left the men with ample spare time which they would naturally seek to fill by recourse to gambling—a recreation that those attuned to middle-class values considered culturally degenerate and a threat to survival in wartime.

THE CONTAINMENT OF CONFLICT

Many tribunal chairmen, however, were capable of appreciating the potential folly of bluntly enforcing a law that lacked consensual support. Indeed, in examining the origin of the tribunals it is clear that the final products of a two-tiered system that eventually emerged—the local munitions tribunal for most matters, particularly disciplinary and leaving certificate cases, and the general tribunal for the more serious offenses, such as striking—represented a compromise. The initial proposal had in fact assumed that the ordinary criminal courts would enforce the provisions of the Act. But under pressure from Henry Duke, Unionist Member of Parliament for Exeter (and later as Lord Merrivale, Lord Justice of Appeal and President of Probate, Divorce, and Admiralty), who suggested that unions should enforce the Act's disciplinary provisions before their own committees, the Home Secretary, Sir John Simon, assented to tribunals modeled on the then existing unemployment insurance panels. As he explained in the House, "Our object has been to secure . . . something in the nature of a domestic tribunal. You do not want to carry the workmen or the employer either, in a matter of this sort, before a Police Court in order to deal with it as if this was a criminal law matter [*Hansard,* 5th series 1915:Vol. LXXII,1548]." However, the *New Statesman,* among other journals favorably disposed to the labor movement, was not impressed by this assurance from high places. The Act *was* a criminal law measure, as the paper never tired of reminding its readers (13 November 1915:124).

The tribunals themselves, however, sought expedients to soften the impact of the provisions. Thus a leading civil servant, Humbert Wolfe, claimed that the touchstone of the tribunal system was its divorce from the traditional court system (Wolfe 1923:112). Formality could be dispensed with and the working class thereby put more at ease. Tribunals would often sit in more pleasant surroundings than austere town jails or imposing court buildings—Caxton Hall, for example, was selected for metropolitan hearings. It is perhaps symbolic of the tribunal's hopes that Caxton Hall was at that time best known for the marriage ceremonies conducted therein. Yet in actuality there were frequent complaints that the ''police court atmosphere'' often penetrated the hearings, forcing out the ''domesticity'' which the government sought (*Parl. Papers* 1917–1918). It would not be inaccurate to suggest that the existence of mistrust was endemic to the tribunal system.

But substantial efforts at accommodation were made. The exercise of discretionary justice and the adoption of conciliatory tones by tribunals were in evidence, if not on a grand scale. In the case of adults, this occurred on an *ad hoc* basis and it is difficult to assess its prevalence. Where ''boy labor'' was concerned, there was a more explicitly defined approach that sought, so it was claimed, to promote an atmosphere consistent with that of the juvenile courts. Admonitions were relied upon as a means of imposing a ''steadying'' influence. Yet the attitude of the tribunals to young workers depended, generally, on the nature of the offense. Thus gambling, considered more serious if engaged in by young people, attracted harsh punishment, as did insubordination, which shocked the sensibilities of a still paternalistic society.

Yet further expedients were devised by some tribunals to minimize the hostility engendered by vigorous enforcement. Many complaints were settled without a formal tribunal hearing. This allowed parties time to rethink the need of a prosecution, and to encourage workers to commit themselves to complying with the statutory requirements. Moreover, the tribunals possessed power to adjourn hearings: on occasion, the chairman would order an adjournment once a finding of guilt had been recorded and before a fine had been imposed. The case would not be revived, nor a fine extracted, if subsequent reports indicated that the man's conduct had improved since the hearing (anon. 1919:159). Statistics for both of these expedients do not appear to exist. If they did, the number of prosecutions would undoubtedly be larger, but it is suspected that these initiatives were only gradually introduced and may not have been prevalent before February 1916, the terminal date of the departmental survey mentioned in footnote 7.

The Ministry of Munitions itself was also prepared on occasion to waive the penalty imposed. It may have been activated by tactical considerations, as in the early case of the riveters of Caledon Shipyard in Dundee, who had refused overtime in the belief that the repair work they had been asked to do was private and not Admiralty work. They had claimed that they were genuinely unaware that by failing to comply with a domestic rule framed by the company directing them to such overtime duties, they had committed an offense under the Act. However, after they were found guilty, their suitably apologetic application for remission of fines was granted, probably because the ministry was embarrassed by the possible scope for future abuse that such a judgment could cause (SRO:HH 31/22). It hastened to insist that employers must frame domestic rules that conformed to the ministry's models if they wished to use these as a basis for successful prosecutions. Other remissions of fines, which were infrequent, were granted on an individual basis, but the reasons for these, being determined departmentally, remain obscure.[7]

Before concluding this account it is pertinent to refer to a number of extra-legal measures that must have moderated the impact of the Act. In the first place, the belief was fostered that "the friction engendered by complaints more than outweighed the advantages resulting from fines [Wolfe 1923:177]." Furthermore, following initial experience of the provision before the tribunals, there developed a "growing tendency to look to the Minister to bring complaints on the ground that the offense was rather against the State than the individual employer [Wolfe 1923:177]." Indeed, the ministry soon intimated to employers that it would be prepared in some instances to initiate prosecutions of offenders. Some employers welcomed this proposal since the relations between them and their men, and more especially between foremen and underforemen and the work force, would be particularly sour after a tribunal confrontation that at times produced angry outbursts between foreman and worker, with the tribunal chairman vainly trying to maintain order. Where the employer was also called upon subsequently to deduct the fine from the offender's wages, he would have had further reason to prefer a ministry prosecution instead (PRO:MUN 5/353/349/1).

Perhaps the most positive initiative taken was that by a number of employers who would have no truck with the tribunals at all, considering them a "nuisance," and preferring to join with unions in setting up joint disciplinary procedures. Thus the Ministry of Labour Report on Works Committees (Goodrich 1920), published in 1917, cited a number of experiments in joint regulation designed to circumvent the unwelcome tribunal jurisdiction. For example, the Whitehead Torpedo Works frankly conceded:

> There is a class of rules, offences against which are punishable by a fine of half a crown, dismissal, or a prosecution under the Munitions Act. None of these penalties is

---

[7] It should be stressed that the decisions summarized in the text are distilled from cases running into thousands. For example, in their first 12 months, the tribunals dealt with more than 5000 prosecutions and more than 21,000 cases in all during this period (*Labour Year Book 1919:* 106). No effort was made to examine the whole case load, a task as unproductive as it would be tedious. An internal departmental memorandum, drafted in August 1917, but surveying cases to February 1916, does not refer to any significantly different pattern emerging after the earlier date. If a divergence occurred, it presumably would have been mentioned. Other evidence is suggestive of a settled pattern, at least till the abolition of the leaving-certificate scheme in October 1917 (PRO:MUN 5/353/349/1).

a convenient one. Fines are as much disliked by the firm as by the men; dismissal entails the loss of services which may be badly needed; and prosecutions entail great
waste of time and may produce more evils than the original ones they are meant to
cure [Goodrich 1920:147].

Though employee members were naturally reluctant to impose discipline on
fellow workers, this was surely preferable to a system of employer or state
discipline. Indeed, in one instance the works tribunal responsible for adjudicating on complaints comprised a chairman and 12 jurymen elected by the
workers in the factory. To deal with a particularly widespread complaint, that of
bad timekeeping, the Ministry of Munitions suggested that special joint committees be set up in the ironworks of Cleveland and Durham. Though the Cleveland
committee had power to impose fines of up to 20 shillings, this could be reduced
or remitted altogether if the offender, over the following 4 weeks, showed im-
provement in his timekeeping (Goodrich 1920:148–149).

CONCLUSIONS

When the legislation is assessed from the perspective adopted in this chapter[8]
four issues in particular may be stressed. First, what is striking is the way in
which the legal authorities, both tribunal chairmen and judges of the appeal
courts established in 1916, would attempt to devise extra-legal mechanisms to

[8] A comprehensive evaluation of the Munitions Acts would require a consideration of two further
questions: first, whether the production objectives were attained; and second, whether the penal
provisions operated to minimize the level of industrial conflict. Both questions are exceedingly complex and the evidence difficult to interpret. On the first point, the output of munitions would also
depend on the scale and scope of other factors of production, including the number of factories,
technological development, availability of raw materials, capital, managerial skills, and so on. As
regards the second point, the history of the dilution struggle was eventful and complex. The removal
of trade restrictions was a lesser problem in more technologically advanced parts of British engineering. Unionists in these areas were less hostile to production changes required in wartime (though
other features of the legislation, such as strike laws, disciplinary rules, and the leaving-certificate
scheme, were just as fiercely opposed). Where the dilution problem was particularly acute, the
government "deported" militant shop stewards under military authority contained in the Defence
of the Realm Regulations. (Such a step was not a regular feature of the industrial scene. From 1916
the threat of compulsory military service could be just as effective in some cases of hostility.) Yet, as
the war progressed and changes in work practice took place in consequence of local negotiations,
widespread opposition was still experienced, even as late as September 1918. Indeed, the government's intention to introduce dilution on private engineering work was abandoned in 1917, as union
hostility was too entrenched (Hinton 1973:332–333; Kozak 1976:74–79). On the question of
workshop discipline, the *Official History* claimed that though the tribunals were, for the first few
months, effective on the whole, yet by their second year, they were facing considerable criticism of
their ability to enforce factory discipline. By the first half of 1917 there was an average of 2122 prosecutions a month for bad timekeeping (Ministry of Munitions: Vol. V,iii,143; Kozak 1976:
227–241). Finally, though the number of strikes fell in 1915 and 1916, the numbers climbed again
during the following 2 years. There were more strikes in 1918 than in any other year between 1910
and 1922 (Hinton 1973:37).

escape a strict application of the law, believing that such an application would be damaging to the wider society. The use of discretion, the waiving of fines, and the acceptance of payments of fines from other than the guilty parties were all widely employed to this effect.

Second, despite the hostility generated by the Act, the judiciary were not drawn into the political limelight following court decisions hostile to the unions and individual workers. For example, Lord Atkin, or Atkin, J. as he was at the time, was responsible for reversing a tribunal decision and holding that a worker who repudiated his contract of employment and never returned to work could nevertheless be in breach of a particular disciplinary rule by "not attending regularly and working diligently [*G. K. Stothert and Co. Ltd.* v. *Hooper (1916)*]." But the traditional view of judges as implacable class enemies of the trade unions, an image reinforced by the *Taff Vale* and *Osborne* decisions, in 1901 and 1911, respectively, failed to ignite the hatred of organized labor against the munitions appeal court judges. This may be largely due to the fact that the courts first sat in April 1916, after early hostility to the Act had diminished. Moreover, although they were frequently called upon to adjudicate, cases usually involved less emotive technical points, and judges therefore escaped much of the criticism leveled at tribunal chairmen, who also often acted in the localities where the cases arose. Thus, at least two chairmen were singled out for special mention. These were Sir William Clegg, known by the Sheffield shop stewards as the "Tsar of Sheffield" (Hinton 1973:207; *Hansard,* 5th series 1917:Vol. XCII, 398), and Sheriff Fyfe of Glasgow, whose moralizing tones during the Fairfields hearing were, as we have noted, a classic illustration of the inapplicability of an inflexibly legalistic and insensitive approach to industrial relations. (Ironically, these gentlemen were vilified because they came up to the workmen's expectations, whereas the workmen's assessors, mentioned by Cole (1923), were vilified because they did not.) It therefore appears that the ill feeling generated by the Act was generally directed against the tribunal chairmen and left no legacy of hatred for the judiciary after the war.

The third point of significance within the judicial domain—again illustrated in the second Fairfields case and its sequel—is the propensity of the law to magnify minor squabbles into massive confrontations. This was indeed frequently experienced at other times during the war.

Finally, it is not inappropriate to refer to the importance attached to the symbolic dimension of the law, in the sense that invoking "the law" is thought to guarantee compliance. The short-sightedness of this view was evident. The employers' proposal that the ministry undertake prosecutions was motivated in part by the related belief that compliance would automatically follow if policies backed by the authority of the state were enshrined in legislation. Moreover, the imposition of the law would be impersonal, it would not rebound on the employer, and the legal system's regard for procedural regularity would ensure that complaints of partiality would lack foundation. But these lofty ideals were not evidenced in practice, for they simply did not derive from shared expectations. Though ministry prosecutions were impersonal and not solely within the volition of the employers (who, however, had with the trade-union leaders originally given the measure guarded, and in some instances enthusiastic, support), the workers did not share the employers' expectations of impartiality. Given the historical tradition within which ministry prosecutions were implanted, the failure of their symbolic appeal was inevitable.

As an experiment in the legal control of industrial relations, then, the Act pointed up the difficulty, if not the impossibility, of securing the consent of those wedded to voluntarism, who were to be governed in their industrial behavior by the blunt instrument of the law. The search for more accommodating and conciliatory measures, particularly on the part of the government, which passed two amendment acts in as many years in response to the criticisms of organized labor, and on the part of some tribunal chairmen, exercising unauthorized discretion in the dispensation of the law, is adequate testimony to the challenge that faced the authorities.

REFERENCES

CASES

G. K. Stothert & Co. Ltd. v. Hooper (1916) 1 Mun. App. Rep. 233.

OTHER SOURCES

Adams, R.J.Q.
    1978   Arms and the Wizard. London: Cassell.
Amalgamated Society of Engineers
    1915   Monthly Journal and Report.
Anon.
    1919   "Munitions tribunals." Juridical Review 31:152-160.
Broom, J.
    1973   John Maclean. Loanhead: Manchester: Macdonald Publishers.
Cole, G.D.H.
    1915   Labour in Wartime. London: Bell.
    1923   Trades Unionism and Munitions. Oxford: Clarendon Press.
Cole, M.I. (ed.)
    1952   Beatrice Webb's Diary 1912-1924. London: Longmans.
Davidson, R.
    1971   "Sir Hubert Llewellyn Smith and Labour Policy 1886-1916," Doctoral dissertion,
            University of Cambridge.
Gallacher, W.
    1966   Last Memoirs. London: Lawrence and Wishart.
Glasgow Herald
    1915
Goodrich, C. L.
    1920   The Frontier of Control. London: Bell.
Hansard 5th series
    1915-1917 Vols. LXXII, XCII.

Harris, J.
    1977   *William Beveridge: A Biography*. Oxford: Clarendon Press.
Hinton, J.
    1973   *The First Shop Stewards' Movement*. London: Allen and Unwin.
Kozak, M.
    1976   "Women Munition Workers during the First World War with Special Reference to Engineering." Doctoral dissertation, University of Hull.
Labour Year Book 1919.
    1919   London: Labour Publications.
McCarthy, W. E. J.
    1972   "Principles and possibilities in British trade union law." Pp. 345-354 in W.E.J. McCarthy (ed.), *Trade Unions*. Harmondsworth: Penguin.
Ministry of Munitions
    1920-1924   Official History of the Ministry of Munitions (Vols. IV-V). London: His Majesty's Stationery Office.
New Statesman
    1915
Parliamentary Papers
    1917-1918   Commission of Inquiry into Industrial Unrest. Cd.8662-9; Cd. 8696. London: His Majesty's Stationery Office.
Pelling, H.
    1968   "Trade unions and the law." Pp. 62-81 in H. Pelling, *Popular Politics and Society in Late Victorian Britain*. London: Macmillan.
Public Record Office (MUN 5) London.
Rubin, G. R.
    1977   "The origins of industrial tribunals: Munitions tribunals during the First World War." *Industrial Law Journal* 5:149-164.
Scottish Record Office (HH31) Edinburgh.
The Times (London)
    1915
Wilson, T. (ed.)
    1970   *The Political Diaries of C. P. Scott 1911-1928*. London: Collins.
Wolfe, H.
    1923   *Labour Supply and Regulation*. Oxford: Clarendon Press.
Wrigley, C. J.
    1976   *David Lloyd George and the British Labour Movement*. Brighton: Harvester Press.

15

ECONOMIC CRIME AND CLASS LAW: POACHING AND THE GAME LAWS, 1840–1880

ALUN HOWKINS

And God said, let Us make man in Our image, after Our likeness: and let them have dominion over the fish of the sea, and over the fowl of the air, and over the cattle, and over all the earth, and over every creeping thing that creepeth on the earth [Genesis 1: 26].

A man hath not absolute property in anything which is *ferae naturae*. Property qualified and possessory a man may have in those which are *ferae naturae*; and such property a man may obtain by two ways, by industry, or by *ratione impotentia loci*. But when a man hath savage beast *ratione privilegii*, as by reason of a park warren &c . . . they do belong to him . . . for his game and pleasure as long as they remain in the privileged place [Lord Coke giving judgment in "The Case of Swans"].

In a society divided into classes, all law is, in some sense, the law of the ruling or controlling group. It may be possible in some cases to legitimize sections of a code of laws in such a way that the majority willingly accept them even where they go directly against the individual or class interest; on other occasions this may not be possible. This chapter will not consider arguments either about the nature of civil government and consensus or about the relationship between the notions of political theory and the concept of hegemony, which are central to any

273

The Imposition of Law

theoretical discussion of this kind. Suffice it to state that on occasion, for many different reasons, it is impossible to impose a law without resistance by a large section of those on whom it is imposed. This chapter is concerned with one such case. It will delineate public and governmental attitudes to game and the game laws and show how, because of poverty, these attitudes could not be shared by the majority of the laboring poor, who consistently, over a period of 70 or so years, defied the law.

To begin with, the game laws were (and still are) set within the realm of the law of property. To Locke, and to the legal theorists who accepted his views on property in the eighteenth and early nineteenth centuries, property became the "end" of civil society. "Government," he wrote, "has no other end but the preservation of property [Hay, Linebaugh, and Thompson 1975:18]." This doctrine continued through William Blackstone's *Commentaries*—"There is nothing which so generally strikes the imagination, and engages the affections of mankind, as the right of property [1793–1795: Vol. II, 2]"—to John Stuart Mill, who although he argued that since "no man made the land," none could truly own it (1970:384), also declared that the primary function of government was "the protection of person and property [1970:283]"; and to the Georgian House of Lords, where Lord Lansdowne said the principle of property was that "which was recognized by all, and which prompted a man to defend, not only that which was his own, but that which belonged to others [*Hansard* 6 May 1832]."

Game, though, was more of a problem. In Mosaic and Justinian law, wild animals were *ferae naturae*—in a state of nature—and were therefore common property. However, since the Norman settlement this principle had been modified in various ways along the lines of the Norman Forest Code, which essentially stated that all game belonged to the Crown. In 1671 the Forest Code was altered and the right to kill game was given to "qualified persons." Briefly, these were owners of land worth £100 per year, holders of 99-year leases of land worth more than £150 per year, the eldest sons of esquires, knights, and nobles, and their gamekeepers (Holdsworth 1938:543). No unqualified person could kill game, even on his own land, and no one, even if qualified, could sell game. This was aristocratic privilege of the most blatant kind and probably, like the tightening up of the forest laws in the same period, represents a backlash of the Whig aristocracy against the freedom of the revolutionary period (Thompson 1975:32, 40).

Nevertheless, this basic qualification to kill game—that one had to be a landowner and almost certainly a country landowner at that—survived intact until 1831. However, from the 1800s onwards it came increasingly under attack. The attack came in the first instance from the radicals. Cobbett wrote in *Two-Penny Trash* that any remedy for incendiarism must include the abolition of the game laws, and particularly "that act which punishes poaching with transportation, which act has filled the county jails with prisoners . . . which has thrown a burden on all the people in order to preserve the sports of the rich [1 February 1831:185]."

Opposition came from this group because, if the game laws were an "imposition" on the poor, they were equally so on the middle classes. The Act of 1671, as we have seen, restricted the right to kill game to the landed aristocracy. At the turn of the nineteenth century, all such privileges came increasingly under attack from the nouveau riche of the industrial revolution. All opposition trembled and fell before them—ultimately, even the right to political power. The game laws were no exception. As the middle classes grew richer they sought to ape their "betters," and the cult of the country villa and holidays in the Highlands developed. The right to shoot game was one symbol of recognition of gentlemanly status—and the cotton magnates demanded that recognition.

It was not that simple. The right to kill game was surrounded by a mystic aura (which persisted well into the 1840s even though the law had changed) which could not be attached to a rotten borough or even the Test and Corporation Acts or any of the other objects of major reform in the 1820s and 1830s (Hay *et al.* 1975:189–253). It epitomized the status of the country gentry in their prime and was a recognition of their fundamental importance in the structure of society. It was this right to kill game, according to the defenders of the unreformed laws in the 1820s, which kept country gentlemen in the counties. Reform that opened the right to all would, according to Lord Wharncliffe in 1828 (himself a "law reformer"), have the effect "of driving the country gentleman from the country to seek amusement in the town [*Hansard* 2 May 1832]." Similarly, the fact that game could not be sold (though, ironically, because of a loophole in the law it could be bought)[1] was elevated to symbolize a noncash relationship. In the debate on the Sale of Game Bill in 1827, the Earl of Malmesbury brought both these points together:

> Gentlemen now went out shooting, by sufferance on the property of small farmers, and gave them a brace or two of partridges, and both parties were satisfied . . . [If qualifications were abolished] . . . the whole thing would be reduced to a question of pounds, shillings and pence; every man would be anxious to make what he could by game . . . and there would be no more shooting on sufferance [*Hansard* 11 May 1827].

Malmesbury maintained that it was only by retaining these privileges that the country gentry would remain in the rural areas, and that the "character of our country gentlemen was of great importance," since they provided the army officers and the other leaders of civil society. If the privilege of killing game was taken away, then all would turn into "town fops."

In the Commons, even in its unreformed state, these arguments cut little ice. During the various debates on the sale of game and the reform of the game laws in the late 1820s no one could be found to defend the old principles even though no clear majority supported the different version of reform put forward. The basis of reform was clearly stated on a number of occasions, most notably by Peel (arguably Britain's first bourgeois Prime Minister) when he was Home Secretary in 1827:

[1] Although selling was a crime, the law did not provide for the prosecution of someone who had purchased game.

> He had long felt that a change had taken place in society which absolutely required
> that those laws should be revised and placed on a different foundation. . . . Such was
> the altered conditon of society, that those laws could not remain ten years without
> material modification [*Hansard* 11 May 1827].

Nor was it only Peel, the representative of the new social order, who perceived the change. The Marquess of Lansdowne lamented this in the Lords the following year: "The great fault of the present system was that there were but very few persons interested in upholding it, while the great bulk of the community was interested in opposing it [*Hansard* 6 May 1828]." The Earl of Malmesbury also complained that "nowadays" all classes spent their time "running down" country gentlemen. He singled out the City for special mention in this context (*Hansard* 11 May 1828).

The crucial problem as far as reform was concerned was the qualification for killing game that was based on the status of game as property. Stuart-Wortley, himself a country gentleman by his own definition, introduced a bill to reform the game laws in 1824. He said, "The principle of the bill was to make game property, and that being the case, it was but natural that an owner of the land should have the power of destroying the game on his own grounds [*Hansard* 12 April 1824]." Although Stuart-Worley's bill was rejected, his ideas continued to dominate debates on reform. The central points were that game should be salable and that the right to kill game rested in the ownership of land. Both these points were dealt with in the major reform of 1831.

The Act of 1831 (1 and 2, Wm. IV, c.32) repealed 18 statutes that had previously governed the killing of game by day and the sale of game. Only the Night Poaching Act of 1828 (9 Geo. IV, c.69) remained on the statutes. The 1831 Act laid down a closed season for most winged game, gave the right to all certified persons to kill game subject to the laws of trespass, established licensed game dealers, and allowed those with certificates to sell game. Crucially, however, it reserved the right of shooting game to the landlord and "his appointees." As Sir James Stephen, the great nineteenth-century writer on the Criminal Laws, put it in 1883, "the right to game became an incident of the ownership or right to possession of land [Vol.III, 281–282]." The penalties laid down by this Act were considerably less severe than those for night poaching as described under the Act of 1828: for a simple offense there was a maximum fine of £2 with confiscation of the "engine" used to destroy game, although any use of violence increased the penalty.

The disparity between the harshness of the sentence for night poaching and the comparative leniency shown to day poachers rested on the assumption that night poaching and also gang poaching were premeditated offenses, which increased the "criminality" of those involved. The night poacher was, to the nineteenth-century game preserver and policeman alike, a member of the criminal classes whose deviance was certain and proved and to whom poaching was simply one of many forms of crime. For instance, most of the senior police officers who gave evidence to the 1872 Select Committee on Game Laws drew this distinction. As Gold, the Chief Constable of Somerset said, "The man who poaches by night is a confirmed criminal [*Parl. Papers* 1872:35]." Similar evidence was given by the chief constables of Lincolnshire, Hertfordshire, Norfolk, and Derbyshire (*Parl. Papers* 1872:40,17,14,34). The same point was made in the Lords and Commons during the discussion preceding the passing of the legislation affecting night poaching. For instance, during the discussion of the 1828 legislation in the Lords, Lord Wharncliffe said, "such persons, when they went out at night, would not stop at committing other crimes [*Hansard* 6 May 1828]."

The Acts of 1828 and 1831 were amended at various times during the next 30 years, but remained the basis of legislation on game. In 1844 the 1828 Act was modified because "the provisions of the said Act have of late years been evaded and defeated by the Destruction, by armed persons at Night of Game or Rabbits . . . Upon Public Road and Highways [17 & 18 Vict., c.29]." The provisions were thus extended to cover public roads and highways. In 1862 both Acts were modified by the Poaching Prevention Act. This Act, one of the most unpopular of the century, which was described at its final reading in the Lords as "one of the most confused and bungling pieces of legislation that had ever passed through Parliament [*Hansard* 4 August 1862]," brought the new county police forces into direct enforcement of the game laws. It gave them the power to stop and search in any public place "any person whom [they] may have good cause to suspect of coming from any land where he shall have been unlawfully in search or pursuit of Game [25 & 26 Vict., c.114]."

These Acts together sought to bring together and make more efficient the ponderous and antiquated legislation of the pre-nineteenth-century period. The final Act we are concerned with here, the Ground Game Act of 1880, had a different purpose, at least on the surface, in that it was designed to rectify one of the least popular parts of the game laws, that part of the 1831 Act which vested the right to game in the owner of the land. The 1880 Act passed this right to the occupier: "Every occupier of the land shall have, as incident to and inseparable from his occupation of the land, the right to kill and take ground game thereon [43 & 44 Vict., c.47]." These reforms appeared to accomplish at least one of their purposes: the extension of the right of sport to the middle classes. Chester Kirby (1932) wrote of the 1831 Act: "As the motive power behind the reform had consisted chiefly of the jealousy of a game-eating and non-landed middle class their measures had met the principle demands of the time [p. 19]." Or, as Vernon Smith said in the Commons in 1845, the same Act "made the game laws more agreeable to the middle classes [*Hansard* 27 February 1845]." However, this extension does not seem to have been complete, nor did it solve the problems of poaching.

The end of the old qualifications was meant in theory to extend the right to kill game to those who could afford it. To quote Kirby again: "The Act of 1831 abolished this class discrimination, repealed the qualifications, and thus removed the element of social privilege from the game system [1932:19]." Would that had been true! Although it was possible for anybody with £3. 13s. 6d. to buy a game certificate (which automatically excluded most of the rural poor), it was still necessary to find land on which to shoot, and since the Act vested the right to game in the owner of the land, this restricted the right to the landlord or to the few wealthy people who could afford to rent a shoot. As one editorial in *The Times* put it on the day before the Act came into force:

> This, then is the new Game Bill, and an act more aristocractic in its principle, as it appears to us, never received the sanction of the legislature. The property of game is vested in the landlord; and the tenant, be his lease ever so long—even for life—cannot shoot or destroy the game on the land which he occupies [*The Times* 31 October 1831:3].

The only accurate figures we have for the numbers of game certificates issued as a result of this Act show that in the 1840s the number of people who legally killed game had not increased significantly. From the end of the eighteenth century, and if population growth is taken into account, the percentage of the population entitled to kill game had decreased from around .3% to .24% by 1840 (*Parl. Papers* 1844:40,35; 1850:333).

Thus, despite the optimistic forecast of its democratic supporters (and later a similar judgment by historians) even after the 1831 Act, the right to kill game remained the closely guarded privilege of a few. This situation might have persisted for many years if the majority of the population had not had very different ideas. The discussions of qualifications and the sale of game in the 1820s were clearly linked with poaching. Everyone agreed that it was on the increase and everyone agreed that the real problem lay in the fact that the rural poor did not regard game as property of the same type as farm animals or personal possessions. As Mr. Leycester said in the Commons in 1829:

> It had been said that the Bill would clothe game with something of the character of property. What was that to the poacher? Would he trouble his head to read the book of parliament? He read the book of nature. In that book he saw that the hand of nature made game wild, and "unclaimed of any" and he would act accordingly. [*Hansard* 6 April 1829].

Furthermore, the law itself, by making a distinction between poaching by day and poaching by night, reinforced this view: as we saw earlier, all the chief constables who appeared before the Select Committee of 1872 drew this distinction. After 1831 the tenant farmer had an interest in supporting the poacher, who at least killed some of the game that damaged his crops and that the farmer himself dared not touch. The problem of the farmer, though it assumed some importance in the mid-1840s, after which there seems to have been some reduction in game preserving (that is, breeding for sport), paled into insignificance when compared with the problem of the laborer.

From the 1790s onward, the huge increase in population in the rural areas and the process of enclosure, especially of waste and common land, pressed hard on the standard of living of the agricultural laborer. The same new social order for which Sir Robert Peel spoke in the Commons impoverished still further the countryside's poorest inhabitants. With the agricultural improvements of the late eighteenth century and the decline of "living in," the rural work force became increasingly casual (Morgan 1975) and faced most winters with the prospect of 2 or 3 months' unemployment before them. This was not wholly a new situation but it became more serious as a result of structural changes in the rural areas at the turn of the nineteenth century.

As a result, the game laws became the object of more intense hatred and consistent evasion. A substantial majority of the laboring population broke the law time and again because it did not, as Mr. Leycester's statement quoted earlier suggests, accord with their own morality, a morality justified by the harsh realities of extreme poverty. In this situation there could be no consensus; the law was seen as imposed and it was resisted. I want now to examine this resistance in some detail, to look at the people who poached and why they did so.

According to the testimony of those who grew up in the last years of the nineteenth century and the first years of the twentieth, poaching was a seasonal crime with a definite place in the cycle of village life and labor. Poaching reached its peak when work was short in winter and dropped away in summer when work was plentiful. When food was difficult or impossible to come by, the laborer depended for his livelihood on his own resourcefulness.

First, then, let us look at the evidence available. The highly seasonal nature of both the town and village laborers' work is graphically illustrated in both printed and manuscript sources from the last century. In 1820 Charles Richardson wrote a letter to a friend about conditions in Hanborough, near Woodstock, in February 1819. On entering the village he saw a large group of men of all ages gathered around a tree on the village green, asked what they were doing, and got the following reply: "We can get no work; the farmers will not employ us, and we and our families are starving . . . during the whole of the winter there was not any employment to be obtained for us [Bodleian MS]"; and so they waited under a tree for the parish officer to give out what little work there was. A hundred years later conditions seem to have changed very little. A letter in the *Oxford Times* in 1913 from an "Oxford Bursar" considers the general conditions of the farm laborer and includes the following telling quotation: "There are weeks and months during the winter season when his [sic] employer could easily dispense with nearly all his labourers [1 August 1913:6]."

By looking at the newspapers for Oxford in the year 1881, a particularly hard winter, we may see the sort of distress and hardship that occurred every year among working-class families. In an Oxford newspaper under the heading "Distress in South Oxford," "A Clergyman" writes of conditons among the poor: "There is a vast deal of distress amongst the poor in the South of Oxford at the present time . . . families living without fire and often going a whole day without food, in consequence of having no work; and in the summer there was so little work that it was quite impossible for the majority of the poor to save for the winter [*Oxford Chronicle* 22 January 1881:8].'' The following week all three Oxford newspapers printed a letter from Edward Elton, Vicar of Wheatley, a village on the outskirts of Oxford, about distress in that village, where the population was poor at the best of times:

> Destitution at Wheatley
> Sir, I would be obliged for a small space in your paper to make known the extreme destitution and poverty existing here in the present severe crisis. The experience of any one of the twenty-nine winters of my existence at Wheatley has left a *most painful impression* on my mind, but this exceeds them all.
> The causes of such exceptional suffering are not far to seek, one of them is that much of the labour in adjoining parishes is done by the casual employment of people living in this, and in consequence, as soon as the work is over (no tie subsisting between employer and employed), the latter are left to their own resources, so that when any severe weather occurs they are reduced to exceeding misery. It is no small trial to live among them and daily witness distress exceeding private efforts to relieve efficiently [*Oxford Chronicle* 29 January 1881:8].

Figure 15.1 examines the average number of convictions for poaching month by month for the years 1859–1880. It reveals just how closely poaching was connected with the seasonal nature of employment. Poaching offenses were most numerous in January and February, the months in which, as we have seen, economic distress was most keenly felt in the laborers' homes, and such offenses were lowest in the summer months, when employment was most available. The second peak of poaching activity that occurred (in October and November) may be similarly explained: these were the months when the availability of farm labor and building work declined, and when the laborer was likely to be left to his own devices. The game season seems to have been a further encouragement to poachers. October and November were the months when rabbits were at their

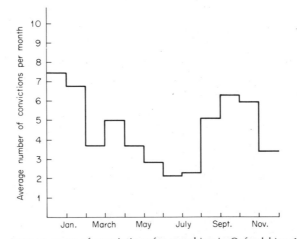

Figure 15.1 Average curve of convictions for poaching in Oxfordshire, 1859–1880.

best, and when the pheasants and partridges, preserved on the landowner's estate for the shooting season, were released from their protected roosts into the open fields and coverts: the poor followed in the wake of the fashionable shooting parties of the rich.

Thus, the periods of poaching activity significantly coincide with the shortage of both food and work. For the farm laborer—especially the man with no regular employer—the period from the end of harvest, in September, until early spring, when farm work started again, was a time when no regular work could be expected. Short-term jobs appeared—the potato harvest in October, threshing in November and December, sometimes hedging and ditching or drain laying—but there was very little in the way of regular work. Building workers, too, were likely to be unemployed during these months, and every other type of outside work was liable to suspension during frost. As winter progressed, the means of earning a livelihood, as well as the stores laid up by the provident from their harvest earnings, gradually disappeared and the laborer faced the winter with no resources to fall back on. It was then that the laborer turned to nature for his food and went out into the fields and hedgerows with his nets or snares, combed the fields for turnip tops, and defied the laws of property.

Table 15.1 analyzes the social class of those arrested for offenses under the game laws. Again, the economic nature of these offenses—that is, the recourse to

TABLE 15.1
Breakdown of Prosecutions under the Game Laws by Occupation,
Oxfordshire 1859-1880 [a]

Occupation	Number of convictions
Laborer	314
Boy or lad	19
Farmer	6
Chairmaker	5
Butcher	3
Sawyer	1
Publican	2
Hawker	1
Demobbed soldier	1
Woman	2
Dealer	2
Blacksmith	1
Ex-gamekeeper	1
Grocer	1
Mason	2
Clothes cleaner	1
Shoemaker	2
Tramp	1
Shepherd	2
Hurdlemaker	1
Unemployed	6

(continued)

TABLE 15.1 (cont.)

Occupation	Number of convictions
Carpenter	2
Spinner	1
Fisherman	2
Boatman	1
Carrier	1
Draper's assistant	2
Stone carter	1
Baker	1
Watercress grower	2

[a] Source: Petty Sessional Court Reports, 1859–1880.

crime as a result of proverty and hunger—is supported by the figures. The overwhelming majority of people arrested, almost 85%, are classed as laborers, and though there are reasons for questioning the adequacy of such a job description, there seems very little doubt that poaching was very much the activity of the laboring poor. In this context it should be emphasized that winter was likely to affect the unskilled worker much more severely than the skilled, and that most of the evidence quoted earlier refers to laborers.

An analysis of the poaching convictions, in terms of their poaching locations, supports this interpretation. Oxfordshire poaching seems to have been a very local affair, a matter of the laborer providing his family with a meal, rather than the enterprise of a professional gang, with its network of receivers and system of long-distance communications. The only case that can be put down to this latter type of poaching in Oxfordshire in this period is the case of the three men from Bristol who were arrested on Lord Abingdon's land at Wytham in 1860. These men were after pheasants, had traveled a long distance from home to carry out their raid, and were armed with guns rather than with long nets or wires, the usual equipment of the local poacher (*Jackson's Oxford Journal* 25 February 1860:8). The distances traveled by the local poacher—the man who supplemented his earnings by poaching—were comparatively small. The figures are easily summarized in Table 15.2.

TABLE 15.2
Breakdown of Distance Traveled to Catch Game [a]

	Distance in miles from place of residence				
	Same	Up to 2 miles	Up to 4 miles	Up to 10 miles	10 miles +
Number of cases	145	171	72	23	6

[a] Source: Petty Sessional Court Reports, 1859–1880.

The evidence is clear. Most poachers in mid-Victorian Oxfordshire did not travel away from their homes in order to poach. They stayed in the area they knew and understood, rarely venturing beyond its familiar bounds. If they lived in the immediate vicinity of a game preserve, they might hope to bring back a marketable haul of pheasants; but for the most part their poaching was limited to "conies": the rabbits that could be caught in the conveniently adjacent hedgerows and woods. Evidence taken by the Select Committee on the Game Laws, 1872, supports this point. In Norfolk, according to testimony of Colonel Black, Chief Constable of the County, only 61 of the 2156 arrested for poaching between 1865–1871 were strangers—that is, men who did not live in the county (*Parl. Papers* 1872:14). The Chief Constable of Somerset was even more emphatic: ". . . they [the poachers] were all Somerset people [*Parl. Papers* 1872:31]."

In nineteenth-century England, poaching was the most important type of "economic" crime to be found in the countryside, and it was the focus of a considerable amount of attention. Nevertheless, it ought to be seen as simply one of a range of devices and strategies by which the poor laborer attempted to support his family in the hard winter months. Evidence for this should be found by examining other forms of "economic" crime that display the same seasonal and social characteristics as poaching: that is, crimes that show a peak of activity during the winter months, occur within a few miles of the offender's home, and are committed by single individuals—or men going out in pairs—rather than by well-organized gangs.

There are certain difficulties in singling out "economic" crime from crime in general and subjecting it to such a statistical analysis. Obviously, in some sense all crime is economic and all theft involves some breach of property rights. For the purposes of this discussion, I distinguish two features of "economic" crime: (a) the type of thing stolen and (b) the use to which the stolen property is put. Thus, a crime is defined here as "economic" when to commit such an offense may be the only alternative a man has to letting his standard of living drop below the subsistence level.

Certain features are identifiable in this type of crime. First, the article stolen is generally one which is directly related to the standard of living—for example, wood, food, or animals obtained by poaching"—or is one taken "semi-legally" from the natural surroundings and sold: wood, nuts, wildflowers. Second, the person involved in the crime is not generally recognized as a criminal in that he or she has a normal occupation. Third, viewed over a period of years economic crime shows a fluctuation that correlates with regular patterns of employment and unemployment. Finally, the social class of the person committing the crime is at the lowest end of the scale.

As the figure and tables have shown, poaching falls clearly into this category. Most game killed by poachers was for the consumption of those who killed it. It was done casually and as a response to the hardships of winter and unemployment. Few, if any, poachers, as has been shown, were criminals in any subcultural sense; they were laborers and small tradesmen. Finally, there are quite distinct seasonal fluctuations, as Figure 15.1, showing convictions plotted over the year, indicates. When crime was as clearly related to both social class and poverty as poaching, and indeed most other economic crimes, were, the law not only was regarded as imposed but was difficult to enforce.

The line between legality and illegality is, in this context, often difficult to draw. Often, for instance, wooding was intimately bound up with a more general common-rights struggle, as in Headington Quarry from the 1860s to the 1880s. In this case certain legal wooding rights were conceded at various points in the struggle, whereas at other times people were prosecuted for taking wood. In some cases, the search for sustenance in winter did not always involve activities of questionable legality. The aged poor—or the lonely widow—often had neither the strength nor the courage to break the law in the manner of the able-bodied man who poached ''in the season of the year.'' The tragic death from starvation in St. Thomas's, Oxford, in 1868, may illustrate the pitiful character of some of the alternative expedients: ''She [the woman who died] used to work for Mr. Higgins at Binsey, as long as the weather would allow her. . . . She could not work after the cold weather set in, and used to go picking up things in the streets . . . the refuse of middens and dunghills [*Jackson's Oxford Journal* 4 January 1869:5].'' On the other hand, even the most modest forms of foraging might cross the border into ''crime''—stealing snowdrops, for example, for which convictions are recorded against a number of laborers from St. Thomas's in February and March 1893. One of them, Henry Johnson, said that ''he had taken snowdrops from the place for many years.'' The quantities of flowers they were taking plus the distance they traveled in order to get them in those quantities suggest that they were putting them into bunches and selling them in the streets of Oxford (*Johnson's Oxford Journal* 4 February 1893:7, 11 February 1893:8; 25 February 1893:7; 4 March 1893:7).

One of the most common of this type of ''scavenging'' crime was stealing vegetables from fields. Richard Hewlett, a laborer from Headington, in March 1863 told the Bench at Bullingdon that ''he'd not been in work since last November and had 6 children.'' In consideration of his plight the Bench fined him lightly (*Jackson's Oxford Journal* 10 March 1863:6).

In the eyes of the rural ruling class, those who poached, stole food from the fields, or gathered wood from the wastes were criminals. Poachers in particular were singled out because the rich felt that the other cases too easily aroused public sympathy for the ''criminal.'' As Mr. Walter, M. P., said in the debate in the Commons on the 1862 Act: ''The distinction drawn between game and other kinds of property was a very pernicious one. Poaching was neither more nor less than theft. Game was property of a qualified description—it was an attribute of land . . . Make poaching a simple larceny and its sentimental and romantic character would be destroyed [*Hansard* 23 July 1862].'' But distinctions were drawn in motivations for crime involving both property and non-property (game), at least in the case of the village poacher who poached primarily from poverty. Even the police, who after 1862 did most of the work connected with enforcement of the game laws, had sympathy with the poor poacher. The Chief Constable of Norfolk told the 1872 Committee that most poachers were otherwise "honest and industrious," and the Chief Constable of Derbyshire attributed the recent decline in poaching in his county to the fact that "the wages in the county are much better, and employment is very much better [*Parl. Papers* 1872:14,34]."

Whereas the police were sympathetic, the poor themselves produced a whole alternative morality based on the view that in a country rich with game, it was a fool who, if he had his health and strength, went hungry. Such pragmatism was illustrated by Fred Symonds, "a most flagitious poacher,' who came up before the County Magistrates at Abingdon (at least one of whom was a well-known game preserver) in 1859 and, when fined £2, laughed and said "it was 'their own money,' and that he would make it up before the week was over [*Jackson's Oxford Journal* 18 June 1859:6]"; or by the two men who appeared before the Bullingdon Sessions in 1870 and said: "Gentlemen engages us to catch rabbits, and when they doesn't we just catches [rabbits] [*Jackson's Oxford Journal 3* December 1870:7]."

But it could go deeper than that. Joseph Arch told the 1872 Committee that he believed that hares and rabbits "were the fair property of anybody who [could] take [them]; and that he would not blame a man who poached in the daytime [*Parl. Papers* 1872:274]." Arch was a Primitive Methodist and in all other respects law-abiding. One suspects he took his justification for breaking the law from the quotation from Genesis cited at the beginning of this chapter. Certainly others did, men like Anthony Liddell, whom Thomas Bewick remembered from his Northumberland boyhood:

> The whole cast of his character was formed by the Bible, which he had read with great attention thro' and through—Acts of Parliament which appeared to him to clash with the laws laid down in it, as the word of God, he treated with contempt—he maintained that the Fowls of the Air and the Fish of the Sea were free for all men—consequently Game Laws or Laws to protect the fisheries had no weight with him [Bewick 1975:25].

Thus the belief, which English law had sought to codify out of existence since the sixteenth century, that game was *ferae naturae,* continued as an underground law in eighteenth-century Northumberland. And it persisted into the nineteenth century. Crabbe in *Tales from the Hall* (1834:258) wrote:

> The poacher questions with perverted mind
> Were not the gifts of heaven for all designed.

Later still, in the early 1850s, an Oxfordshire magistrate said that there seemed to be a notion "among the peasantry" that "all the wild things under heaven were free for all [*Oxford Chronicle* 3 March 1852:6]." This view received its most articulate statement in a remarkable autobiography, *A Victorian Poacher,* written in the 1930s by James Hawker. Hawker was a lifelong radical and, as an elderly man, an early socialist, but he remained a poacher all his life. "All my life I have poached," he wrote. "If I am able I will poach till I Die [Hawker 1961:63]." Hawker had no illusions about the hypocrisy of the game laws: "If I had been born an idiot and unfit to carry a gun—Though with plenty of Cash—they would have called me a Grand Sportsman. Being Born Poor, I am called a Poacher [1961:47]." A voice like Hawker's is rare, and we seldom find more than an echo of it in the more prosaic records that form the basis of most history. However, it is very important because what Hawker said gives voice to the beliefs of many thousands of poor Englishmen (and a very few women) who poached every week of the winter throughout the nineteenth century. This systematic defiance of the law shows clearly that there was no consensus with the law and that this particular set of laws was imposed. It also points to a more important conclusion—that it was the economic interests of the laboring class that made acceptance of the law (in a moral sense) impossible. The rich could impose the law, but their legitimation of it was never accepted. Even the harsh sentences of the 1830s could not persuade a man that it was better to remain within the law and see his children starve.

Yet, in the end, poaching did decline. From the 1900s onward, the number of convictions dropped sharply. A number of reasons may be suggested for this. First, and most important, the standard of living among the rural poor was gradually rising. Taking 1871 as the base year equal to 100, by 1902 money wages had risen to 120. In 1850 they had been below 80 (Fox 1968:183). During the same period prices also fell, albeit marginally, in rural areas. The difference was crucial—it meant that for the first time in their lives many laborers had the chance to buy "butcher's meat." Second, and much more difficult to trace, is the influence of the "reformation of manners." Many writers have pointed to the increasing "rationality" and "order" of working-class leisure in the second half of the nineteenth century, and it may be that this had its effect on attitudes to crime. However, it is clearly very difficult to document such nebulous concepts. What did emerge in interviews carried out over the last few years with men born in rural areas after 1890 was that none would agree that poaching should be regarded as a crime. Finally, the increasing effectiveness of the police in the prevention and detection of crime must also be taken into account when attempting to explain changes in attitudes or behavior. Unfortunately, there are no comprehensive surveys of policing practice in rural areas. Only one thing is certain: by the 1940s, wholesale poaching on the scale of that in the previous century was over in rural England.

REFERENCES

Bewick, T.
    1975   *A Memoir of Thomas Bewick.* Oxford: Oxford University Press.

Blackstone, W.
    1793–1795   *Commentaries on the Laws of England,* 12th ed. 4 Vols. London: T. Cadell.
Bodleian Library MS Top. Oxon. d. 193.
Crabbe, G.
    1834   *The Life and Poems of the Reverend George Crabbe* (Vol. 8). London: John Murray.
Fox, A. W.
    1968   "Agricultural wages in England and Wales during the past half century." In W.E. Min-
        chinton, *Essay in Agrarian History* (Vol. 2). Newton Abbot: David and Charles.
Hansard
    British Parliamentary Debates (dates = date of debate).
Hawker, J.
    1961   *A Victorian Poacher.* Oxford: Oxford University Press.
Hay, D., P. Linebaugh, and E. P. Thompson
    1975   *Albion's Fatal Tree.* London: Allen Lane.
Holdsworth, Sir W.
    1938   *A History of the English Law.* London: Methuen.
Jackson's Oxford Journal.
    1859   18 June, p. 6
    1860   25 February, p. 8
    1863   10 March, p. 6
    1869   4 January, p. 5
    1870   3 December, p. 7
    1893   4 February, p. 7; 11 February, p. 8; 25 February, p. 7; 4 March, p. 7.
Kirby, C.
    1932   "The attack on the English game law system in the forties." *Journal of Modern History*
        *IV:*19.
Mill, J. S.
    1970   *Principles of Political Economy.* Harmondsworth: Penguin. (First published in 1848.)
Morgan, D.
    1975   "The place of harvesters in nineteenth century village life." Pp. 27–33 in R. Samuel
        (ed.), *Village Life and Labour.* London: Routledge & Kegan Paul.
Oxford Chronicle
    1852   3 March, p. 6; 6 March.
    1881   22 January, p. 8; 29 January, p. 8.
Oxford Times
    1913   1 August, p. 6.
Parliamentary Papers
    1844   Returns Vol. XLVI. London: Her Majesty's Stationery Office.
    1850   Returns Vol. XXXIII. London: Her Majesty's Stationery Office.
    1872   Select Committee of the House of Commons on Game Laws, Vol. X. London: Her Ma-
        jesty's Stationary Office.
Stephen, Sir J. F.
    1883   *A History of the Criminal Law of England:* London: Macmillan.
The Times (London)
    1831   31 October, p. 3.
Thompson, E. P.
    1975   *Whigs and Hunters.* London: Allen Lane.
Two Penny Trash
    1831   1 February, p. 185.

16

TOWARD AN INTEGRATED THEORY
OF IMPOSED LAW

ROBERT L. KIDDER

TRINITY **AND GREENLANE**

Imposed law. What is it? What other kinds of law are there, if any? Are its social consequences any different from those of other kinds of law? Judging by the chapters in this volume, these questions seem to arise persistently and evade conclusive answers stubbornly when a group of scholars treats imposed law as an object of study. The fact that it is treated as a distinct phenonomenon suggests that its characteristics can help us in the more general task of understanding law sociologically.

In this chapter I will present a critique of frequently used models of imposed law and propose an alternative analytic model which I believe provides a more comprehensive and less ambiguous set of concepts for guiding our research about legal imposition.

The prototype of imposed law as it seems most generally to be understood is the colonial situation, where legal systems are imported from dominant cultures and forced on indigenous populations. The novelist Leon Uris, using the freedom of fictional discourse, captures this view eloquently in the reflection of his Northern Irish Catholic narrator, who speaks of late nineteenth-century Catholic experience:

289

The Imposition of Law

> Law was something queer to us, as foreign as African tribal rites. Although we were
> under it, manipulated and maligned by it, it was ever kept as a grandiose and mystical
> force beyond our knowledge. All those connected to law—the Crown and the courts
> and the soldiers reading edicts—were bullies forcing us into a game played by their
> rules and spoken in a language only they understood. We knew little about our rights
> and nothing at all about the ability to use law. Law remained a bludgeon owned by
> Lord Hubble and the Protestants, and we'd no manner of defense against their judges
> all dressed up like princes and the documents all covered with seals [1976:30–31].

Uris's thesis throughout *Trinity* is that law was an important device by which
Britain subjugated Irish Catholics, protected the development of Irish estates by
British nobility, fractured Irish unity into warring religious camps, produced
disastrous land-use practices that resulted in the potato famines and mass
emigration, and facilitated the subsequent development of Northern Ireland as a
capitalist fiefdom.

Uris's unstated assumption, like that often made by social scientists using the
concept "imposed law," is that had the Irish been left to themselves, their own
legal practices would have been different. Evolving in harmony with agrarian,
communal, nurturant patterns of society that Ireland would have naturally
developed, the suppressed indigenous legal forms would supposedly have suited
everyone's needs and maintained tranquillity. Imposed law here is but one
aspect of invasion and domination. As such, it is treated, by Uris and similarly
inclined social scientists, as a one-way process of commands backed up by
superior force. Feeley (1976) identifies this as the "command model of law,"
citing Austin (1955) as one of its leading proponents.

Uris thus dramatizes the case of imposed law in its purest form—an all-
powerful colonial authority using law along with political trickery and economic
might to dominate a resentful, dispirited, debilitated native population. Doyle
(1978) and Okoth-Ogendo (Chapter 9 of this volume) both argue that legal imposition by definition involves alien origins of law. Doyle says that "[imposed
law] has the subterranean sense that the *source* of law is alien." Imposed law does
not originate from the governed. Okoth-Ogendo includes the lack of
"democratic consensus" as the third element in his definition of imposed law.

While clarity and simplicity surely characterize Uris's imagery, these
features eliminate other important subtleties of foreign rule. George Orwell,
reflecting on his experience as a police officer in colonial Burma, eloquently captures this feature in speaking of his own choice to shoot a rampaging elephant
rather than try to pacify it and risk being ridiculed by "the natives." As he says,
"when the white man turns tyrant, it is his own freedom he destroys. . . . For it
is the condition of his rule that he shall spend his life trying to impress the
'natives' and so in every crisis he has got to do what the 'natives' expect of him.
He wears a mask and his face grows to fit it [1950:8]."

Orwell had in mind, besides his own experience, people like poor Greenlane,
a British magistrate trying to apply British colonial law in the case of murder in
an Indian village:

> The relatives of the dead Karam called for justice; but it was not what Greenlane
> understood by justice. In the name of justice they were demanding the death of an in-

nocent man, and Greenlane knew that, so far as the law and legal evidence was concerned, they had every chance of obtaining it. . . . A week later Greenlane . . . committed Raja and Jahana to the Court of Sessions on a charge of murder. He could do
nothing else. Yet he was certain that Raja alone had murdered Karam and that
Jahana was innocent. But how could he prove it and who would believe him? His own
knowledge of the real facts was based on hearsay—on the reports of reliable men of the
locality. They in turn had got the true story from the timorous shopkeeper, who was
the solitary real witness of the occurrence. But this shopkeeper, a mild Hindu, unconnected with any of the factions and enmities of the turbulent Muslim peasants, was
never going to embroil himself with them by giving evidence in a case of this nature.
Greenlane . . . had once tried . . . to represent a similar matter privately . . . to a
higher official, and had been severely snubbed.

So Greenlane did nothing; and Jahana was hanged along with Raja [Moon
1945:34–36].

The case, as Greenlane knew, involved a complicated set of jealousies and
economic rivalries between factions of the village. He knew that the accusation
against Jahana was designed to get rid of a rival. And yet, with all the power of
that very same legal system shown by Uris as the oppressor of Ireland, he felt
helpless against an organized band of peasants. He could see his authority
transformed into putty in the hands of faction leaders who had figured out the
system.

Thus, the "judges all dressed up like princes" in *Trinity* seem transformed
into frustrated pawns like Greenlane in India. How can such a difference occur?
Are Irish and Indian peasants really so different from each other culturally, that
one group capitulates while the other co-opts? The striking feature of the
chapters collected in this volume, as well as of existing literature dealing with imposed law, is that many of them cast serious doubt on the universality and
perhaps even the accuracy of Uris's account of imposed law. Uris may have
written more fiction than he knew.

In this chapter, I shall argue that the command model of law is inadequate. It
oversimplifies the process known as law because it is static, treating imposition
as a fait accompli rather than an interactional process affected by power differentials. Furthermore, it misleads us into undue acceptance of cultural incompatibility as a feature of imposed law's effects. In place of the command model, I
will present a model of law that will be able to account for Greenlane's and
Orwell's experiences. It is an interactional model in which I treat law as an
arena for the promotion of interests. Seen in this light, imposition becomes more
clearly specified as a concept involving several not necessarily correlated
elements.

IMPOSITION: REAL OR ASSUMED?

The command model is apparent in several chapters in this volume. Forer's
description (Chapter 6) of the Potawatomi experience initially presents a picture
very similar to that in *Trinity:* a once proud society reduced, by deception and a
totally foreign process of thought enforced as law, to a small community riddled

by dissent, destitute from loss of wealth, and nearly powerless against the combined interests of government bureaucracy and high-finance capital. The technique of domination is to stimulate and maintain factionalism so that unified Indian action becomes impossible. Forer describes Potawatomi efforts at resistance, though he suggests that their effectiveness is doubtful.

According to Okoth-Ogendo (Chapter 9), the British did the same kinds of things in Kenya. Their persistent restructuring of land use and land tenure resulted in the demise of indigenous authority, breakup of solidarity, famine, and overcrowding. Pospisil (Chapter 8) describes a similar process of breakdown and change in New Guinea, as ill-informed administrators tried to bring modern services and practices to the fiercely independent tribes of the area. New Guinea's citizens also experienced a more subtle imposition in the form of licensing measures that froze them out of business ventures in favor of better-financed foreign entrepreneurs who could afford to conform with regulations (Fitzpatrick and Blaxter, Chapter 7).

Thus, the situation of Native Americans, Kenyan farmers, and New Guinean villagers appears similar to that of the Irish Catholics in Ulster: domination destroys native social patterns, cultural values, traditional trust, traditional authority, and economic self-sufficiency. Law imposers use the remnants of tribal solidarity as a device for further exploitation of the residual, passive, ineffectual population. Law plays a central role in this model of domination, and the flow of manipulation is all in one direction.

Other literature on imposed law, however, shows that we cannot assume subjugation and exploitation as inevitable consequences. The British, while dominating Ireland, were also developing an extensive legal system in support of colonial rule in India. A vast system of courts was created, an indigenous legal profession was developed leading gradually to an indigenous judiciary, and the courts were besieged by litigation from an essentially rural population. Yet none of the literature on this development suggests that the Indian population as a whole was rendered passive and demoralized by this process.[1] Instead, most literature suggests that Indians took to courts with great enthusiasm and that many became masters at manipulating them to their own ends. Much colonial correspondence concerning the courts dealt with the "despicable" native tendency to lie, scheme, and bribe their way to court victories. Administrators took umbrage at the fact that natives treated litigation as a form of speculation and entertainment. Throughout India, skilled native petitioners were able to deceive administrators and judges for the benefit of fellow villagers, caste-mates, relatives, or clients. Exploitation could occur through law, but it seemed frequently to be aiding one Indian against another. Using Doyle's terminology (1978) we would say the British–Indian law, though frequently oppressive and though having widespread effects, was not thoroughly imposed because of the complex response of a complex social system.

---

[1] See, for example, Cohn (1959, 1961), Galanter (1966, 1968), and Kidder (1977).

In this volume, we find descriptions of even more overt instances of resistance. Howkins (Chapter 15), for example, provides lively accounts of the resistance with which English working-class people met the changes contemplated in the anti-poaching laws. Anderman (Chapter 13) shows a case history of resistance to laws aimed at restricting labor-union autonomy in Great Britain. Rubin (Chapter 14), writing on restrictive legislation during the First World War in England, describes an earlier instance of more organized resistance.

In each of these cases, as in others we shall discuss later, the fact of imposition is itself in doubt. The sheer inventiveness of supposedly imposed-upon populations not only warms the hearts of those who cheer for underdogs; it suggests that the fact of imposition is itself questionable. At what point in the process of legal challenge and indigenous response do we conclude that law has been "imposed"? Should we become embroiled in the old debate summed up in Sumner's (1906) position that "lawways cannot change folkways," trying to determine whether laws can actually overcome the resistance of a society's customs? Or should we, as I suggest, step back and re-examine the whole process implied by the term *"imposed law"?* To illustrate the inadequacy of the static, or as I call it below, the "hypodermic" model of imposed law as dramatized in *Trinity,* I shall next discuss the problem of inferring *intent* and using it in a model of imposed law.

IMPOSITION: IS INTENT NECESSARY?

When a doctor or a drug addict injects a drug, we normally assume that the intent is to achieve foreseeable physiological effects. When Uris expounds on the rules imposed on Ulster, he clearly assumes that those rules were intended to solidify Catholic subjugation. Okoth–Ogendo is even more explicit. He insists that imposition "implies, first, an attempt to induce fundamental change [Chapter 9 of this volume]." Like the doctor with his needle, the legal imposer is assumed to have an objective that explains his use of the legal hypodermic. We face serious problems of proof and inference, however, when we try to apply this hypodermic model to legal processes.

We are confronted, for example, with evidence that the legislative process involves intricate maneuvering, compromising, and shifting of positions in order to achieve the necessary votes on a bill. Who can say with any certainty what the *intent* of a legislature was when much of its final product results from private conversations, unrecorded deals, and hidden agenda? [2]

Anderman, in Chapter 13, highlights another source of ambiguity. Even where the ruling party's purposes seem unified, external interests such as industrial investors manipulate the legislative process toward ends that are not obvious on the face of a piece of legislation. A bill apparently designed to

---

[2] See Feeley (1976) for a discussion of the difficulties in approaching sociolegal studies from the perspective of goals and questions of legal effectiveness.

"strengthen" labor unions is actually part of a plan to curb union power. Or is it both? We derive our knowledge of "actual intent" from historical analysis of speeches, debates, and related actions. But public stances often do not correlate with private purposes.

The problem of inference is even worse than this, however. Even if we could be confident of intent at the legislative level, we would still face endless corridors of cross-purposes at the level of legal administration and adjudication. Who can say, for example, what the single "intent" of the Bureau of Indian Affairs has been at any point in history toward Native Americans in general (Medcalf 1978) or toward the Potawatomi in particular (Forer, Chapter 6)? The Bureau of Indian Affairs' official policy has repeatedly shifted ground, whether in response to legislative action or simply to internal decision making. Even official policy is not the final answer because it does not fully account for the actions of regional BIA officials. Forer's answer to this dilemma is to assume destructive intent because the policies have come from a white society that stood to gain from Indian losses. Intent is inferred from class interests and consequences.

Intent, then, is an especially difficult variable to measure with any confidence. But even if we could measure it, what would it add to our understanding of legal processes? Would it help us to predict the consequences of imposed law?

If we compare available evidence on the intentions of British law in India and Soviet law in Muslim Central Asia, we find that a search for motives adds little of significance to our understanding of these events. Official British policy in India was to preserve local customs and culture by protecting its rules in court (Galanter 1966; Kidder 1977:157). *Pax Britannica* was supposed to rest on judicious use of local customs and religious law to determine the outcomes of legal cases. Britain, said its leaders, could ensure justice by guaranteeing that customs would be secure against disruptive, greedy opportunists.

The Bolsheviks, according to Massell (1968), took an entirely different approach in Central Asia. Their purpose was to obliterate "backward" Muslim culture so that the region's population could be drawn into the pursuit of revolutionary modernity. The legal system they imposed contained rules designed to demolish traditional polygamous family structure and liberate women. They redesigned the court system, introducing "modern" methods and rationalized procedures. But they also assigned these courts the task of hastening the demise of local culture by the invocation of modern Bolshevik rules. The Soviet intent could not have been more different from British intent in India.

Ironically, however, divergence of intent produced convergence of consequence. Both systems disrupted indigenous culture. British attempts to preserve Indian customs actually transformed them into supports for new patterns of social domination (Kidder 1977:162). Because customs and religious laws had never before been enforced by a "rationalized," "unified," record-keeping judiciary, they had operated as flexible guidelines for social control rather than as rigid laws (Galanter 1968:66). Using custom as grounds for adjudicated decisions, the British lent support to caste-determined patterns of social, economic, and political dominance. Seeking clear definitions of local custom and law, administrators and judges came to rely on interpretations given them by Brahmins whose literacy and familiarity with ancient scripture gave them an authoritative image in the eyes of the British. Whoever could master the routines of court could thus gain advantage over those who had less mastery. The populace reacted to this situation by developing schemes to fool judges, bribe court officials, falsify documents and testimony, and infiltrate court positions so that "the law" could be manipulated from within. The pursuit of privilege became a court-centered preoccupation for millions of villagers who could not (or would not) rely any longer on indigenous processes.

Thus the British, despite their stated intentions, actually altered the meanings of many customs, particularly those related to patterns of dominance. They reified customarily vague indigenous norms and tried to pin down the exact stratificational consequences of those norms. As Maine said over a century ago:

> The customs at once altered their character. They are generally collected from the testimony of the village elders; but when these elders are once called upon to give their evidence, they necessarily lose their old position. . . . That which they have affirmed to be custom is henceforward to be sought from the decision of the Courts of Justice, or from official documents which those courts received as evidence. . . . Usage, once recorded upon evidence given, immediately becomes written and fixed law [1871:72].

The Soviets also produced disruption in indigenous culture, though it was not the kind of disruption they had planned. Encouraged by new Soviet institutions, legal codes, and administrative policy, Muslim women began challenging traditional restraints. They began abandoning traditional conservative dress styles and proceeded through more serious changes to the point where thousands left their husbands in search of a more liberated existence. Once on their own, however, they typically found no economic alternatives open to them other than prostitution. Muslim men, including many who worked as officials and police for Soviet authorities, coalesced into a violent force resisting the move toward liberation. Uncloaked women were assaulted, raped, and murdered in the streets during a period of widespread disorder. To soften the harshness of Soviet disruption, Muslim men were drawn into Soviet administration and gradually transformed many "modern" rules and procedures into devices for restoring traditional order. Their subversion of Soviet plans drove many women back home begging for forgiveness and a return to custom.

Despite totally dissimilar intentions, then, Soviet and British plans produced similar patterns of disruption within both the legal systems and the indigenous social orders they were designed to control. Nor does it help to argue that their intentions were not what they seemed, that both powers expected and sought the disruption they caused. Such an argument becomes tautological because it uses consequences as a measure of a variable (intention) that is itself supposed to help explain those same consequences.

The point of this comparison is that intent makes no difference. We cannot conclude that imposed law had no effects. In both instances, fundamental disruption of established social patterns could be linked to legal action. But we cannot accurately estimate those changes from an analysis of the intentions of legal imposers. The conclusion I draw from this kind of comparison is that disruption of established indigenous social patterns, including their systems of authority and dominance, will result from any introduction of *external* law and that to predict the direction of those disruptions, we must measure factors other than intentions.

As Medcalf (1978) argues, our attention to law as an object of study has caused us to reify, and in some sense mystify, what is first and foremost a process of conflict, a set of relationships among people, groups, and institutions. Concerning motives, she has shown that even the most idealistic white attorneys who are trying to help Native American tribes regain lost land and resources end up forcing their clients to adopt modes of thought and action so alien to their traditions that even the most successful legal actions leave them permanently changed, unable to revert to the old ways. The sheer domineering presence of the American legal system and the society that has produced it makes it a force that must be reckoned with, even if it appears to be helping rather than oppressing.

When we treat law solely as an object, a thing to be manipulated or unilaterally imposed, a device for producing certain effects, we unnecessarily bind our attention to passing moments in a process, missing important elements in the process, and ignoring the interactive quality of it. Seeing law from the lofty position of controller, we accept those structural blinders that afflict anyone trying to look down from above—we take intentions and make false inferences about their correlation with results. Several errors ensue when we frame our questions around the definition of law as a manipulable device for producing social control and/or controlled social change. First, we ignore questions about the origins and susceptibility to modification, distortion, diversion, and co-optation of specific laws, general legal principles, or legal institutions. We take them as givens rather than as momentary residues of on-going struggles. Second, we tend to exaggerate the role of legal institutions in producing the changes we observe. We are less likely to consider the effects of changes in economic and political institutions that may be much more fundamentally linked to the changes. Finally, we chase the wild goose of distinguishing between imposed law and other kinds (indigenous, internal, organic, non-imposed). Is there such a thing as non-imposed law? The debate is endless and pointless—it addresses the wrong question.

EXTERNALITY AND POWER: AN ALTERNATIVE TO THE HYPODERMIC MODEL

In place of the static, hypodermic model of imposition, I believe we learn more by adopting an interactive model that distinguishes between external law[3] and assesses the role and sources of power at different levels of externality.

[3] Li (1971) makes a distinction between external and internal in his discussion of law in post-revolutionary China. My use of the terminology here represents a modification of his concepts.

If imposition means being forced to conform with a norm or order not compatible with one's interests or values, then it is easy to see that a university disciplinary committee, or a neighborhood court, or a council of village elders can be just as imposing as the U.S. Supreme Court or the British Raj. If they have the power to make a defendant leave the university, or leash a dog, or pay restitution, then their will is imposed.

The village elders differ, however, from the Supreme Court in terms of social distance and structural complexity. The elders are closer to the events and people involved in village conflict. They do not represent interests, institutions, or values extending beyond the community within which conflict is occurring. There are fewer layers of intervening organization complexity between lawmakers and the governed. The Supreme Court's decrees are external, compared to those of the elders, though they may be even less "imposed" (in the sense that people must actually respond to them) if they are not backed up by vigorous enforcement.[4] The Court is relatively external because its existence, and the processes by which it becomes involved in a conflict case, flow from the interactions of several layers of social organization and, therefore, of divergent meanings, interests, and political coalitions that are not centered in the community over which the elders preside.

By definition, the more external the legal system, the more any conflict introduced into it or induced by it will take on meanings not originally relevant to the conflicting parties. Externality means that "outsiders"—people with less direct involvement in the conflictual context—will find externally grounded reasons for becoming interested in the conflict's outcome. Lawyers, for example, may find a case interesting from an intellectual or an economic standpoint. Industrialists interested in extracting raw materials from a particular area may join in a local struggle over property rights.[5] Political figures may find a particular conflict useful for symbolizing or pursuing an issue they want to exploit for their own political ends.

External law offers alternatives to those whose interests conflict with indigenous norms. Anything that increases the power of external legal actors to offer alternatives thereby increases the vulnerability of the internal system. Similarly, the more external alternatives there are (in the sense of numbers of layers of organizational involvement), the more vulnerable the internal system. Participants in a conflict may be enticed with offers of assistance from allies with external objectives. But having allies means having to make compromises in order to satisfy the diverse purposes involved. It therefore means opening up the local unit, whether it be tribe, neighborhood, university, or village, to exploita-

---

[4] For example, see Muir (1968) for a description of the widespread pattern of nonconformity with the Supreme Court's school-prayer decision.

[5] As Forer says, for example, "the motivation for [termination bills] should leave little to the imagination. Western U.S. indian reservations currently hold between 25 and 40% of U.S. uranium reserves and about 5% of all oil and natural gas reserves. Those reservations also hold one-third of all western coal."

tion for external purposes. Furthermore, any change along this external–internal dimension means changes in those variables that affect the balance of power in the conflict.

This concept of externality is relative, and I do not mean to imply the existence of only two levels, as is often implied in the idea of imposition. Consider, for example, Erikson's study of the loss of community in the Buffalo Creek flood disaster (Erikson 1976). Before the flood, which was caused by the collapse of a negligently developed coal-mine dam, the community of miners was governed *internally* by its own informal codes and values. The owners constituted *external* law before the flood because they owned the land, granted most of the mortgages, and controlled all of the jobs. Company rules therefore prevailed when they clashed with community values. Law could be imposed by the company because it "held most of the cards," and its law was external because its operation was influenced by considerations of profit margins within a multi-national corporation whose directors set policy from their headquarters in New York.

But after the flood, the relationship between miners and company became the internal system relative to the law of torts and the principles of formal adjudication brought to bear by the flood victims' Washington-based attorneys. Their successful litigation against the negligent mining company mobilized the involvement of lawyers, judges, expert witnesses, national news media, state government officials, and national lobbying groups for both miners and mine owners. The flood and its legal aftermath thus ravaged the static, internal system of law which had determined relations between miners and the mine owner.

The flood also produced a third level of externality, because the drama of the flood triggered the involvement of federal flood-relief agencies. In this case, Washington became involved in providing damage clearance, National Guard protection of property, and temporary housing for survivors. Erikson criticizes the government's rigid rules and bureaucratic inertia, saying they contributed to the psychological trauma experienced by flood victims by intensifying the destruction of what he calls "community" among the survivors. In other words, *external* law (the bureaucracy of federal flood relief) contributed to the destruction of *internal* law (community solidarity among the survivors). The result, according to Erikson, was a drastic increase in incidents of social pathology, including skyrocketing divorce rates, increased rates of mental illness, the birth of the hitherto unknown phenomenon called juvenile delinquency, and the appearance of child- and wife-abuse.

The idea that we should be prepared to examine a multiplicity of layers of legal organization is one difference between my use of the external–internal distinction and the law–custom distinctions over which Bohannan and Diamond have argued (Bohannan 1965; Diamond 1971). Both of them assert, as I do, that law represents a transformation of custom into a new set of meanings through the development of legal institutions. Bohannan calls this "double institutionalization" and says that the precision of legal language and thinking combined with the existence of a specialized institution for the application of customary norms and values changes the way these norms and values affect social relationships. He thus sees law as an effort to use more effectively norms and values which come from custom, arguing that this step becomes necessary when customs by themselves can no longer meet the threat of conflict. Diamond views the same process as the "cannibalization of custom by law," saying that law is a deliberate device of a ruling elite to absorb customary practices of subordinate groups and dissolve these autonomous groups so that they may serve the interests of the elite. Clearly he disputes Bohannan's contention that law is born when custom proves inadequate. But they both treat the process as a dichotomy, and they both stake their positions on the intentions lying behind the development of law. In both cases, I contend, their analyses are weak.

My position is, however, more similar to Diamond's, in that I call for attention to the details of struggle between different levels of authority; I agree that we must look to the development of other centralized institutions—especially economic—in order to understand the sources of power that affect the development of external law, and I concur that the development of more centralized legal forms threatens parochial authority systems. But I contend that Diamond's dichotomy, like Bohannan's, is too simplified to account for the range of phenomena that suggests itself for study under the title "imposed law." Concerning intentions, it is worth noting that Diamond's model of "cannibalization" is more similar to the Soviet program in Central Asia, whereas Bohannan's benign "double-institutionalization" model is more similar to the British program in India. Yet, as we have already seen, the value of knowing intentions in these cases is nothing compared to the sheer fact of legal externality.

What does the notion of law contribute to this perspective? Am I not simply relegating law to a status of insignificance, equating it with any manifestation of conflict? My answer is twofold. First, because people generally endorse the ideal of law and assume its operation in many contexts, it must be analytically differentiated from other areas of conflict—though the difference must not be exaggerated. The very idea that "imposed law" could be the object of study, as though it differed from indigenous law, shows the strong influence of democratic assumptions about the way conflicts *should* be handled. For many, the ideology of democracy is synonymous with law. I consider it useful, therefore, to preserve the concept of law as a separate analytic category because people act as if it has a separate existence.

Second, law is a signal that can guide research, because many conflicts eventually engage legal institutions. Law creates one or more interest groups (lawyers, judges, prosecutors, police, legal scholars) whose purposes are not totally consistent with any other group or institution in society. Legal groups have specialized goals and special abilities to manipulate the symbolic and institutional artifacts of law. They respond *in part* to the need to maintain these special symbols and artifacts as justifications for their separate existence. Yet their actions are reactive, not proactive. That is, they are drawn into conflicts that originate elsewhere.

They enter as allies with a unique perspective, special skills, and a carefully nurtured aura of power in a mysterious realm.

Thus, to look at law and records of legal activity is to look at the tracks left by combatants and their allies. It is not, however, the only locus of conflict. Indeed, some kinds of conflict never leave a trace in law, and others leave only indirect evidence. So law is just one place to look for research into social process.

EXTERNALITY AND POWER: APPLYING THE MODEL

The chapters in this volume, as well as other studies already published, offer the opportunity to weigh the value of the model I am proposing. Taking the chapters by Anderman, Rubin, and Howkins, for example, we must ask, as we did in the case of British law in India: "who imposes law on whom?" In each case government initiatives were blunted or distorted. In Anderman's study, as in Rubin's, "the law" was as much in the hands of those upon whom government sought to impose controls as it was in the lawmakers' hands. The traditional autonomy of labor not only persisted, but led to changes in the law.

My position is further supported by Bedau's study of American attitudes toward capital punishment (Chapter 4). After demolishing the claim that a left–liberal coalition has imposed its "permissive" law on an unwilling populace, Bedau concludes by suggesting just the opposite: that Nixonian politics have imposed an artificial halt to the population's civilized drift away from physical retribution. I would argue that the notion of imposition simply obscures this analysis regardless of which side we call the imposers. Neither side has successfully imposed a final outcome. The battle rages on. The value of Chapter 4 rests not in Bedau's relocation of imposition, but rather in his longitudinal cataloguing of opposed views, strategies, interest coalitions, and specific political events. It is an unfinished debate with no clear winner. Law plays an occasional role in an enduring conflict that results from complex structures of incompatible interests.

Arthur's analysis (1978) of "indigenous" legal forums shows us another case of incomplete imposition. His point is well taken (and well documented) that alternatives to English common-law courts showed dogged persistence. But the persistence itself discredits the imposed–indigenous distinction. Where different courts proved useful to interests with the power to preserve them, they persisted. Where interests shifted, the courts lost their function and ceased to exist. Taking the perspective I propose, the best way to approach these data is to search for the persons and interests contributing to the expansion of common-law court jurisdiction and then show why those interests could not have been accommodated within indigenous legal structures. This, it seems to me, is the approach Rubin has used in Chapter 14 in showing instances where manufacturers tried to use the Munitions Act to alter basic features of their relations with labor.

Santos (1977) provides an even clearer example of the approach I am suggesting. There is considerable similarity between his analysis of legal ambiguities in Pasargarda law (law governing relationships among "illegal" squatters in Rio de Janeiro's slums) and Arthur's (1978) discussion of legal pluralism. Santos, however, provides longitudinal detail on the emergence of relationships between squatters and the state. He explains how patterns of interest conflict and converge at different points in Pasargarda history. Law is what sometimes happens among squatters themselves and what sometimes happens between them and agents of the state. Yet as squatters they are always somewhat vulnerable to the state's claim that their use of public land is illegal. The preservation of this legal ambiguity gives leverage to various state agents in controlling squatter residents and in using the squatters' situation to pursue diverse political ends. But the government would face crippling resistance to any attempt to "enforce the law" by clearing away all squatters.

Abel (Chapter 10) provides a detailed example of the kind of approach I am suggesting here, though he does not always apply it as consistently as I think he should. His longitudinal analysis shows how existing tribal structures, when confronted with modernizing court systems, decrease people's readiness to engage in litigation in rural Kenya. Although he occasionally sounds like an advocate for the cultural incompatibility school ("tribal social structures and modern courts are incompatible"), his analysis is in terms of those features of tribal social structures (for instance, multiplex relationships) which are "strengthened" by tribal litigation. The rise of modern courts produces a drop in litigation because modern procedures and rules cannot serve to strengthen tribal solidarity, and people in rural areas have not yet begun to seek alternatives to tribal solidarity in their pursuit of "modern" goals.

The main weakness at this stage of his analysis is that he treats tribal society as though it were egalitarian and as though intratribal litigation typically involves disputes among equals. By de-emphasizing the role of tribal-dominance strategies in litigation, Abel does not alert us to the weaknesses that can threaten tribal solidarity when modern courts become more accessible to rural people.

Abel nevertheless provides solid analysis of dominance issues in describing the emergence and use patterns of modern courts. The rise of external law can be most clearly seen in the growing use of criminal law by the government as a means of asserting its demands for compliance with administrative regulations. Modernization of the courts is not simply the inexorable result of inevitable, disinterested progress. It is, rather, the reflection of the coalescing interests of three new forms of domination: the multinational corporation, the bureaucratic bourgeoisie, and a comprador class of local business. Because rural tribal peoples perceive modern courts as an instrument of domination through their experience with criminal prosecutions, and because civil courts are relatively inaccessible to them, they become less inclined to use the court system. Abel's data thus suggest that the legal system, particularly the courts and bureaucracy, has played an integral role in the creation of a new system of domination in Kenya.

If we adopt the model I am suggesting here, we avoid two serious analytic errors often made in the debate over "imposition". The first error concerns boundaries and jurisdiction. It is the mistake of equating the external–internal distinction with a cultural dichotomy between exogenous and indigenous law. The existence of legal boundaries (national, state, municipal) has too often become a spurious distinction in discussions about imposition. For example, it is erroneous to assume that law is any more imposed (or oppressive, in Doyle's [1978] terminology) in a colonial situation than it is where a "free" nation such as Kenya, Gambia, Jamaica, or Czechoslovakia stands in economic subordination to international economic structures. Gambia receiving U.S. aid is in many important respects as dependent and controlled as the Potawatomi in Kansas. National boundaries and assumed cultural differences should not obscure that fact. On a scale of externality of law, both cases share important characteristics. When Kenya's "indigenous leaders" modify laws so that British sugar plantations in Kenya can become competitive on the world market, whose law is imposed? Is it indigenous law simply because Kenya is "independent"? How significantly different would it be if Kenya were still a colony and colonial administrators sought to encourage sugar production? How important is the difference between the law "imposed" on Japan by the United States after the Second World War and the federal law regulating the lives of welfare recipients and public-housing residents in American ghettos? Does a western-educated elite in New Delhi look any less imposing to an Indian peasant who has been ordered to report for mandatory sterilization than a colonial administrator who ordered his grandfather to stay out of Hindu temples reserved for the twice-born? Is a Korean businessman who tries to buy votes in the U.S. Congress significantly different from an American aircraft manufacturer doing the same thing? Legal boundaries tend to obscure the lines of conflict and dependence, cutting off vital connections by implying that there is unity within the boundaries. André Gunder Frank's (1969) theory of dependence warns us that many lines of dependence, and therefore of conflict, between metropolitan centers and their satellites cross political and cultural boundaries. The metropolitan–satellite distinction is a highly significant class of external versus internal law cases.

The second error we too often make is to attribute to imposed law all those effects which come from other social processes, especially political and economic subjugation, and from simple cultural contact. Whether the United States government had developed a BIA or not, the sheer presence of millions of non-Native Americans in the same area as Native Americans would have been disruptive to indigenous cultures. Even where two cultures exist side by side without exploitation, adjustment must be made to the presence of these "other people." No matter what kind of law the British introduced into India, there would have been measurable change in Indian society. Railroads and high-speed communications by themselves would have produced massive dislocations of "indigenous law" because of their impact on indigenous social structures. Pospisil (Chapter 8) describes the impact of the building of an airstrip. By giving native peasants their own separate income, the airstrip project stripped native elites of the economic basis of their authority (the unending indebtedness that guaranteed peasant loyalty). It is inaccurate to designate this as a consequence of "imposed law" just because it was a government project. Public or private, the project's results attract our attention because of the unforeseen consequence of economic action, not because of government involvement.

CONCLUSION AND RESEARCH SUGGESTIONS

The object of our research should be to identify variables related to the exercise of power in the pursuit of interests in conflict. Galanter (1974) shows the utility of this approach in his article "Why the 'Haves' Come Out Ahead." He shows how basic legal institutions, particularly in the area of litigation, can be used by those with the power to do so. And he shows how the charcteristics of the legal institution, along with those of potential users, combine to favor "repeat performers" (parties whose resources and activities support repeated use of legal forums) over "one-shotters." The special value of his analysis is that it shows how to make sense out of an otherwise bewildering array of evidence concerning patterns of use, success, and effects of specific legal institutions.

The diversity of data and analysis evident in this volume testifies to the need for a model like Galanter's. One group, such as the Potawatomi, shows signs of nearly total powerlessness in the face of law-backed interests seeking to exploit them. Other groups, such as unionized labor in Britain, or working-class poachers, seem richly endowed with strategies and characteristics which shield it (comparatively, at least), from legalized tyranny. One colonized population seems cowed and bewildered in the face of colonial law, as in Northern Ireland (Uris 1976) or in Kenya (Okoth-Ogendo, Chapter 9); another seems capable of cannibalizing colonial law and forging it to its own emerging needs, as in the case of India. These differences cry out for interpretation. Analysis of the parameters of power in the invocation of law, the manipulation of legal artifacts and institutions, and the reactions to legal initiatives can provide answers.

But power can be oversimplified, as I have tried to show by discussing the issue of intent and by presenting a model of legal externality. The effects of imposed law are discoverable, and differences in power affect the process. But a static command model of the exercise of power through law simply does not explain the variations I have discussed here. Each situation should be approached as a set of interacting interests that range on a continuum of externality and are affected by structural constraints and resource imbalances that determine strategies of interest assertion.

The studies contained in this book and issues raised at the conference where they were discussed suggest several promising lines of research that fit in with the model I have proposed. One set of questions concerns the effects of different indigenous social structures on patterns of reaction to attempted imposed law. Abel concludes that tribal units find legal modernization incompatible with the problems generated by tribal life; thus litigation declines. Okoth-Ogendo supports the view that Kenyan tribal society became a victim of legal modernization, unable to resist the exploitation inherent in it. Perhaps instead of focusing on incompatibility of beliefs and values or the incompatibility of modern institutions with multiplex, face-to-face relations, we should consider the possibility that patterns of dominance and subordination in tribal societies make them especially vulnerable to external manipulation through law.

Indian society and Muslim society in Soviet Central Asia certainly do not show the same degree of capitulation to external law. At least some elements of Indian society clearly adapted the ''alien'' system to their own purposes. Is this difference related to their nontribal social systems? India was primarily agrarian and Muslim Central Asia was semi-nomadic and agrarian. Both differed from tribal society in having more complex systems of functional and status differentiation. Both may have been just as steeped in multiplex, face-to-face everyday life as Abel's Kenyans. But agrarian patterns of kinship and land use may have created classes more prone to reliance on new legal arenas than any that might have existed in tribal society. Massell (1968:181) emphasizes that indigenous social structures (decentralization, mobility, and secretiveness) which Soviet authorities considered weaknesses to be used in breaking down Muslim resistance actually enabled the Muslims to deflect Soviet initiatives. Urban Muslim elites served as a buffer between rigid Soviet doctrine and equally rigid Muslim tradition. The point is that in these more complex differentiated societies, response to the imposed law was differentiated. The demarcation between elites and masses is less distinct than in tribal systems—supports for elite status are more varied. And the pattern of dominance is not total, as it appears to be in the tribal situation.

Another perhaps related way of categorizing social structures for this kind of analysis is by the degree of polarization of indigenous society. The Northern Irish model represents an extreme case of polarization. The society that Britain found in India was much more pluralistic. This comparison suggests that a polarized community is more vulnerable to legal manipulation because internal conflict can be used to gain a position of dominance. Many Indian nationalists made exactly this argument during debates over the British policy of partitioning India and Pakistan at the time of Independence.

I conclude by offering my opinion that the model I have presented here does not offer much support for the kind of program implied by Aubert in Chapter 3. Though he effectively exposes the limitations of a view of law that seems only to prohibit and constrain or to promote ''acceptable behavior,'' his alternative, to use law to encourage ''excellence,'' does not escape the problems of externality that I have discussed here. The idea that law as a distributor of state-controlled wealth somehow ''need not'' serve vested interests is a theoretical possibility that I believe rarely proves true in practice. But even the most disinterested collection of bureaucrats, if they become a conduit for government welfare distribution, will alter relationships and internal law among recipient populations just from the sheer magnitude of the consequences that flow from operational processes within the bureaucracy. And to alter law so that it promotes excellence would be to substitute one external standard for another.

REFERENCES

Arthurs, H.W.
  1978 "Imposing Law in a Pluralistic System: The Common Law and Its Rivals in Nineteenth-Century England." Paper presented at the International Symposium "The Social Consequences of Imposed Law," University of Warwick, Coventry, England, April 1978.
Austin, J.
  1955 *The Province of Jurisprudence Determined.* London: Weidenfeld and Nicholson. (First published in 1832.)
Bohannan, P.
  1965 "The differing realms of law." In *The Ethnography of Law* supplement to the *American Anthropologist 67,* Part 2:33.
Cohn, B. S.
  1959 "Some notes on law and change in North India." *Economic Development and Cultural Change 5*:79.
  1961 "From Indian status to British contract." *Journal of Economic History 21*:613.
Diamond, S.
  1971 "The rule of law versus the order of custom." *Social Research 38*:42.
Doyle, D.
  1978 "A Theory of Imposition and an Institutional Remedy: The Re-Constituted Jury." Paper presented at the International Symposium "The Social Consequences of Imposed Law," University of Warwick, Coventry, England, April 1978.
Erikson, K. T.
  1976 *Everything in Its Path.* New York: Simon & Schuster.
Feeley, M.
  1976 "The concept of laws in social science: A critique and notes on an expanded view." *Law & Society Review 10*(4):497.
Frank, A. G.
  1969 *Latin America: Underdevelopment or Revolution.* New York: Monthly Review Press.
Galanter, M.
  1966 "The modernization of law." Pp. 153–165 in M. Weiner (ed.), *Modernization.* New York: Basic Books.
  1968 "The displacement of traditional law in modern India." *Journal of Social Issues 24*:65.
  1974 "Why the 'haves' come out ahead: Speculations on the limits of legal change." *Law & Society Review 9* (1):95.
Kidder, R.
  1977 "Western law in India: External law and local response." *Sociological Inquiry 47* (3–4):155.
Li, V.
  1971 "The evolution and development of the Chinese legal system." Pp. 221–255 in J. Lindbeck (ed.), *China: Management of a Revolutionary Society.* Seattle: University of Washington Press.
Maine, H.
  1871 *Village Communities East and West.* London: John Murray.

Massell, G.
  1968   "Law as an instrument of revolutionary change in a traditional milieu: The case of Soviet Central Asia." *Law & Society Review* 2(2):179.
Medcalf, L.
  1978   *Law and Identity: Lawyers, Native Americans and Legal Practice*. Beverly Hills, California: Sage Publications.
Moon, P.
  1945   *Strangers in India*. New York: Reynal and Hitchcock.
Muir, W. K.
  1968   *Prayer in the Public Schools*. Chicago: University of Chicago Press.
Orwell, G.
  1950   "Shooting an elephant." In Walter Blair and John Gerber (eds.), *Repertory*. New York: Harcourt Brace Jovanovich.
Santos, B. de S.
  1977   "The law of the oppressed: The construction and reproduction of legality in Pasargada." *Law & Society Review* 12(1):5.
Sumner, W. G.
  1906   *Folkways*. Boston.
Uris, L.
  1976   *Trinity*. New York: Doubleday (Bantam Books).
Yngvesson, B. and P. Hennessey
  1975   "Small claims, complex disputes: A review of the small claims literature." *Law & Society Review* 9(2):219.

INDEX

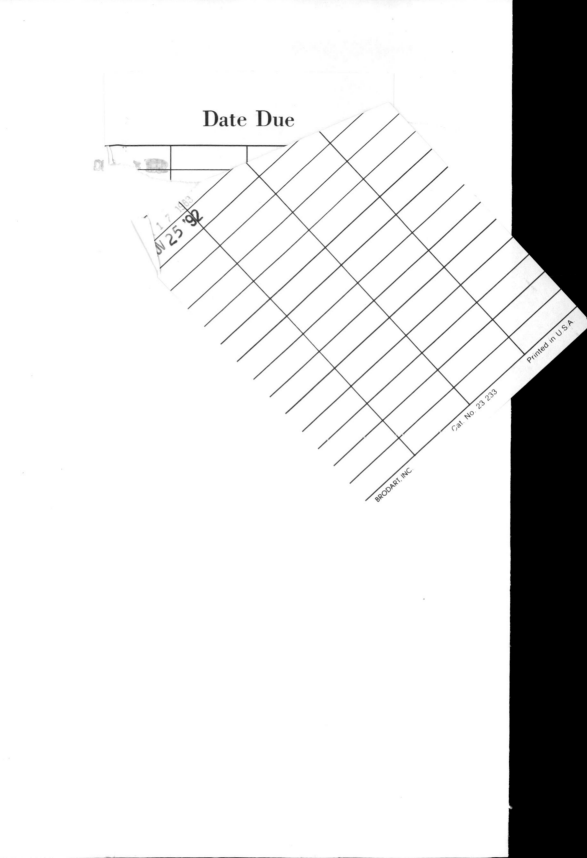

Date Due

JN 25 '92

BRODART, INC.   Cat. No. 23 233   Printed in U.S.A.